Stepfamily Relationships

Development, Dynamics, and Intervention

Stepfamily Relationships

Development, Dynamics, and Interventions

Lawrence H. Ganong

University of Missouri
Columbia, Missouri

and

Marilyn Coleman

University of Missouri
Columbia, Missouri

Kluwer Academic / Plenum Publishers
New York, Boston, Dordrecht, London, Moscow

Library of Congress Cataloging-in-Publication Data

Stepfamily relationships: development, dynamics, and interventions / edited by Lawrence
   H. Ganong, Marilyn Coleman.
      p.   cm.
   Includes bibliographical references and index.
   ISBN 0-306-47997-4
   1. Stepfamilies.   2. Stepfamilies–Phychological aspects.   3. Remarriage.
   I. Ganong, Lawrence H.   II. Coleman, Marilyn.

HQ759.92.S7294 2004
306.874'7—dc22   2003060446

ISBN 0-306-47997-4

© 2004 by Kluwer Academic/Plenum Publishers, New York
233 Spring Street, New York, New York 10013

http://www.kluweronline.com

10 9 8 7 6 5 4 3 2 1

A C.I.P. record for this book is available from the Library of Congress

Permissions for books published in Europe: permissions@wkap.nl
Permissions for books published in the United States of America: permissions@wkap.com

Printed in the United States of America

Preface

About a decade ago we wrote a book about stepfamily relationships (Ganong & Coleman, 1994). That volume was one of a series of books about various aspects and types of close relationships, and because it was part of a series there were page limits. Even with those limits, we believed we were able to adequately cover most of what was known about stepfamily relationships. Since then, there has been a phenomenal increase in the amount of research on stepfamily relationships; the total number of publications about stepfamilies has probably quadrupled. The quality of scholarship on stepfamily relationships has improved dramatically as well (Coleman, Ganong, & Fine, 2000). As both contributors to and consumers of this professional literature, we knew that the quantity and quality of scholarly work on remarriage and stepfamily relationships had changed profoundly (Coleman et al., 2000; Coleman & Ganong, 2000). The time seemed right for another comprehensive review of this literature. Thus the idea for the current book was born. Additional motivation for this new book was that our previous outdated volume was being translated in other countries. Translating our outdated volume when there is such an increased and improved corpus of literature seemed unfortunate to us.

As we started reviewing the literature on stepfamilies we expected to be able to simply update what we had summarized before—a straightforward task. However, once we began to systematically review the research, theory, and clinical writing about remarriage and stepfamily relationships, we were surprised to discover how profoundly the body of knowledge had changed in a short period of time. What we had expected to be an update has become, at least in some areas of step-relationships, an entirely new look at a substantially different body of knowledge.

Throughout our careers we have investigated stepfamilies using what we have called a *normative-adaptive perspective* (Ganong & Coleman, 1994). This perspective does not deny the possibility of problems in stepfamilies, nor does it preclude comparing stepfamilies with other family forms. However, the main focus is not on problems, nor is it on seeing how stepfamilies and stepfamily members fare against the standard of the first marriage family. Instead, the normative-adaptive perspective looks at both positive and negative dimensions of stepfamily life; stepfamilies are conceptualized as a legitimate family form with several variations, all of them worthy of examination and consideration. We have consistently raised research questions to explore the ways in which certain stepfamilies have been able to function well, meeting the individual needs of stepfamily members as well as the needs of the stepfamily as a whole. In short, our focus has not been on finding ways in which stepfamilies fail to function well—what we have labeled a deficit-comparison perspective. Instead, we have sought adaptive, well-functioning stepfamilies and tried to figure out how they differ from those who struggle to cope.

Other scholars also have employed this normative-adaptive perspective. Sometimes this has been labeled a risk and resiliency model (Hetherington et al., 1999), and sometimes researchers have eschewed labels, simply examining relationships in stepfamilies without taking a deficit-comparison perspective. In this book, we continue with the normative-adaptive perspective; we have made an effort to focus on a wide range of behaviors and outcomes in stepfamily relationships, both positive and negative.

We start this book with a brief history of stepfamily relationships as a field of study, reviewing the development of clinicians' and researchers' perspectives on remarriage and stepfamilies (Chapter 1). We then look at the cultural context in which stepfamilies live, and review what is known about how relationships are initiated, maintained, and generally influenced by cultural values (Chapter 2). Anyone familiar with our writing about cultural views, social stereotypes, and stigma will not be surprised at our attention to the cultural backdrop of stepfamily living.

We then look at precursors to stepfamily living (Chapter 3), with an eye toward how these various precursors affect stepfamily relationships over time. Continuing with this chronological orientation, we next examine courtship for stepfamily living (Chapter 4) and adult couple relationships (Chapter 5). After reviewing gay and lesbian stepfamily relationships in Chapter 6, in the next two chapters we present parenting and stepparenting processes, and the effects of stepfamily living on children. A range of siblings relationships are explored in Chapter 9, as we compare siblings, half-siblings, and stepsiblings. In Chapter 10 we review the growing body of knowledge about grandparents and stepgrand-parents. Throughout the book, we try to interweave researchers' and clinicians' contributions because, as applied researchers who have worked with stepfamilies (as educators, counselors, and mediators), we think this approach provides the reader with a more complete picture of the development and dynamics of step-family relationships. In Chapter 11 we deviate from this approach a bit by turning our attention almost exclusively on clinicians' contributions. Finally, we summarize briefly in the last chapter what we have learned about stepfamilies in the last decade. As part of this retrospective evaluation, we suggest future directions for researchers and clinicians.

As usual, we have many people to thank for making this book possible. Several colleagues read chapters and gave us valuable feedback—Larry Kurdek, Jean Giles-Sims, Kim Leon, Elizabeth Sharp, and Shannon Weaver went beyond the call of friendship and collegiality in their rapid and helpful suggestions. Connie Ahrons generously shared drafts of chapters from a book she is writing based on her longitudinal data set on post-divorce families. Jason Hans and Anne Gore provided us with great assistance in tracking down references. Tia Schultz and Tanja Rothrauff contributed greatly to creating the index. Other colleagues pointed us toward information that we would not have seen otherwise (Paul Amato). At Kluwer, Sharon Panulla was patient and supportive, and we thank her for giving us this opportunity.

Over the years, we have been privileged to have met and studied hundreds of stepfamily members. We clearly owe them a great debt for sharing their lives with us. Some of their stories appear in this book—in some ways, all of them are reflected in what we know and write about stepfamilies.

Finally, we are indebted to the members of our own stepfamily. We have learned the best lessons from them.

Contents

Chapter **1**

Studying Stepfamilies

In the 1950s, Betty Friedan revived the feminist movement writing about *the problem with no name*. In the 1970s, the rock group America sang about the "horse with no name." In the 1990s we wrote a book about relationships in "the families with no name"—or, to be more accurate, the families with no widely accepted name (Ganong & Coleman, 1994). It is our perception that the plethora of names and labels has lessened over the past decade with most social scientists using the term stepfamilies and a few using the term blended families. However, a review of professional literature yields many labels for stepfamilies: *Reconstituted, blended, reconstructed, reorganized, reformed, recycled, combined, semi-combined, rem, step-, synergistic, second-time around, merged, reconstructed*, and *remarried families*. None of these are satisfactory to us. Some seem awkward or even silly (e.g., *reconstituted* reminds people of orange juice, *blended* conjures images of whiskey), some are used inconsistently in the literature to describe different types of families (e.g., *blended* sometimes is used specifically to refer to families in which both adults are stepparents, and sometimes it is used broadly to identify all stepfamilies), some are inaccurate (e.g., not all stepfamilies are *second-time around families*; some are third- or fourth-time around, and a remarriage for one adult partner may be a first marriage for the other), some are too vague (e.g., *combined*), some carry negative connotations (e.g., *stepfamily*), and some suggest odd labels for individual family positions (e.g., a *reformed or reconstituted* father, a *merged or reorganized* mother). For the most part, these labels were attempts to avoid the centuries old stigma attached to stepfamilies and stepfamily members (e.g., wicked stepmothers, poor abused stepchild). We will use stepfamily, despite the negative connotations, because it is the most widely used term by researchers, and because it is congruent with labels for family positions (e.g., stepfather, stepmother, stepchild, stepsibling).

Several labels also have been applied to stepparents: *Non-parents, half-parents, acquired parents, added parents, social fathers, other mother, psychological parents*, and *second* or *third* parents have been used in the professional literature. We have heard stepparents call themselves *sociological parents*, and many stepfamily members refer to stepparents simply as parents. We will not use adjectives like *biological, genetic*, or *natural* to describe parents and children—all have drawbacks that we will discuss later. Instead, individual family positions in this book will be identified simply as *parent* (when referring to genetic or adoptive parents) or *stepparent* and *child* (when referring to the genetic or adopted child of a parent) or *stepchild*.

Given the historical as well as ongoing disagreements about how to label stepfamilies and stepfamily roles and positions, it is not surprising that there is some confusion about who and what stepfamilies are. Before we proceed, we will define and explain the types of relationships included under the rubric of *stepfamilies*.

DEFINING STEPFAMILIES

A stepfamily is one in which at least one of the adults has a child (or children) from a previous relationship. A stepparent is an adult whose partner has at least one child from a previous relationship. A stepchild is a person whose parent (or parents) is partnered with someone who is not the child's biological or adoptive parent. Notice that these definitions do not limit stepfamily status only to those who reside in the same household. A stepparent and stepchild do not have to live together all of the time, or even part of the time, to have a relationship together and to share family membership.

This definition of stepfamily is broad, because it is our intention to cover as much of the field as possible and to show areas in which more research and scholarly thought are needed. It will be obvious to the careful reader of this book, however, that most researchers and clinicians have assumed narrower definitions, and, in fact, the task of defining who is and is not in a stepfamily can be controversial. It should also be noted that the definitions above are not limited to marriages. Most stepfamily research has focused on legal remarriages, probably because the date a couple files the marriage license is an easily assessed indicator of when the stepfamily began. This is unnecessarily limiting, however, for two reasons. First, a large number of adults who live together and raise children, both from prior relationships and from their own union, do not legally marry. Such families are on the rise in the United States (Bumpass & Lu, 2000) and in Europe (Allan, Hawker, & Crow, in press). Second, most couples who remarry live together prior to remarriage (Brown & Booth, 1996). We argue that living together is a better psychological and social marker of the beginning of a stepfamily than is a definition based on legal remarriage. Researchers who measure the length of family life beginning with remarriage will miss cohabiting stepfamilies and may miscalculate the starting date by months and even years for a majority of stepfamilies in which the adults do legally marry. Also missed are people who have children but were not previously married. When they marry someone other than the child's parent, they form a stepfamily even though it is not a remarriage.

We want to also point out that the definitions we are using are not limited to heterosexual unions. Gay and lesbian couples in which one or both have children from previous relationships or from donor insemination match our definition. Such families have somewhat different dynamics than families headed by heterosexual couples, but many of the issues and dynamics are similar (Hequembourg, in press; Lynch, 2000).

DISCOVERING STEPFAMILIES

Just as *the problem with no name* was relatively unnoticed prior to Friedan's groundbreaking book, the families with too many names were relatively unnoticed until the 1980s. However, there have always been stepfamilies. Families formed as a result of marriages between adults who have children from previous relationships have existed in large numbers and in most cultures throughout history (Phillips, 1997; also, read Spanier and Furstenberg, 1987, or Ihinger-Tallman and Pasley, 1987a or 1987b, for concise and informative historical reviews of stepfamilies). In fact, rates of remarriage in Europe and the United States in the 18th century were similar to current remarriage rates (Phillips, 1997). The attention to stepfamilies generated in the 1980s was related to the precursors, which shifted from bereavement to divorce. In earlier times, it was primarily death of a partner that preceded remarriage and the societal assumption may have been that the new stepparent replaced the deceased parent and the family resumed. When divorce became the major precursor, stepfamilies became more observable, and to some people, more of a problem, because additional parents (stepparents in post-divorce families) create a more complex family structure than replacement parents did (stepparents in post-bereavement). Social scientists and clinicians continue to struggle with the phenomenon of "extra" parents.

Although stepfamilies are not more frequent than in the past, stepfamilies are more common in the United States than in other parts of the world. Nearly everyone in the United States marries, and often (U.S. Census Bureau, 2000). In fact, the United States has the highest remarriage rate in the world; about half of all marriages in the United States involve at least one previously married partner (U.S. Census Bureau, 2000, Table 145), and over 10% of remarriages in the U.S.

represent at least the third marriage for one or both partners (National Center for Health Statistics, 1993). Although the rates of remarriage in other industrialized countries are slightly lower than in the U.S. (Allen, Hawker, & Crow, in press; Kiernan, 1992; Wu, 1994; Wu & Penning, 1997), most people around the world who divorce or who have lost a partner through death eventually either cohabit or remarry.

In addition to remarrying at a high rate, people remarry quickly. The median interval between divorce and remarriage in the United States is less than 4 years (Wilson & Clarke, 1992), and 30% remarry within a year after the divorce. Keeping in mind that two-thirds of all couples cohabit before remarriage (Cherlin & Furstenberg, 1994), this means that the median interval from one relationship to another is indeed short.

People of all ages remarry. Although the median age of remarriage in the United States is 38.3 years for men and 35 years for women (Monthly Vital Statistics Report, 1995), an estimated half million people over the age of 65 in the United States remarry each year (U.S. Census Bureau, 1995). The existence of more divorced older adults, increased longevity of both widowed and divorced adults, and better health throughout the life course are factors related to increases in remarriage among older adults (Cornman & Kingson, 1996; Holden & Kuo, 1996).

Although remarriage rates remain high, they have been dropping in the United States and other countries except among older adults. However, this does not signal a reduction in re-coupling. Many people are choosing to cohabit as an alternative to remarriage (Allan et al., in press; Bumpass, Raley, & Sweet, 1995). In 2000, 4.9 million U.S. households were maintained by unmarried couples (Simmons & O'Neil, 2001), and cohabiting unions are more common among those who have been married than among those who have not (Seltzer, in press). Even older people in the United States cohabit; 4% live with a new unmarried partner (Chevan, 1996).

Stepfamilies

Just as marriage and parenthood have become disconnected in industrialized societies (Allan et al., in press; Nock, 2001), so have remarriage and stepparenthood gradually become relatively independent phenomena. That is, not all remarriages create stepfamilies—many individuals now remarry for reasons other than providing a replacement parent for their children. Likewise, not all stepfamilies are formed when a parent or parents remarry. For instance, some first marriages create stepfamilies and stepparent-stepchild relationships (e.g., when never married mothers marry a man who is not the child's father). Other stepfamily households are formed by cohabiting adults who bring with them children from earlier relationships. Although cohabiting couples are more likely to have children in their households than in the past (37% lived with one or both partners' children in 1998), it is somewhat difficult to determine whether or not the children were born to the cohabiting couple or if the couple live with children from prior relationships (Seltzer, in press). About 25% of cohabiting individuals bring children from prior relationships to their cohabiting unions (Bumpass, Sweet, & Cherlin, 1991). Cohabiting couples are more likely to enter the new union with children from previous relationships than are remarried couples (Wineberg & McCarthy, 1998).

For several reasons, Census Bureau data regarding the number of stepfamilies varies widely. However, in 1996, 17% of all children in the United States lived in a *household* with a stepparent, usually a stepfather (Fields, 2001). It is estimated that about one-third of U.S. children will live in a remarried or cohabiting stepfamily household before they reach adulthood (Bumpass et al., 1995; Seltzer, 1994). To this number must be added an unknown number of children who do not share a household with a stepparent and yet are members of a stepfamily. These are primarily children who live with their mother in a single-parent household and visit or stay occasionally with their remarried or cohabiting father.

About 40% of adult women will likely reside in a remarried or cohabiting stepfamily household as a parent or stepparent at some time during the life course (Bumpass et al., 1995). Complex marital and cohabiting histories over the life course result in complex family histories for children (O'Connor, Pickering, Dunn, Golding, & the ALSPAC Study Team, 1999; Wojtkiewicz, 1994) and for adults. In fact, children in stepfamilies may live in several types of families before they reach adulthood.

The numbers of multi-generational stepfamilies are likely to increase in the next few years as the "baby boom" generation ages. About half of this cohort's marriages will end in divorce, and about 75% of those who divorce will remarry at least once (Furstenberg & Cherlin, 1991). Many others will form *de facto* stepfamilies by cohabiting. The "boomers" and their children are the generations that have disconnected marriage and parenthood, and they also are likely to disconnect marriage and grandparenthood. Among this cohort will be unprecedented numbers of individuals who are stepparents (Cornman & Kingson, 1996), and it is likely that the number of families in the U.S. that include stepgrandparents will markedly increase from the current 40% when boomers reach retirement ages (Szinovacz, 1998).

In spite of the large numbers of stepfamily members in societies around the world, stepfamilies have been extensively studied only relatively recently, and many unanswered questions remain. Although we know a lot more now about stepfamily relationships than we did, much more needs to be known.

STUDYING RELATIONSHIPS IN STEPFAMILIES

Relationships in stepfamilies are among the most fascinating and most frustrating of family relationships to study. Stepfamily complexity presents challenges to researchers, clinicians, scholars, and students. One problem that has plagued remarriage and stepfamily researchers has been confusion over who is, and is not, being studied. Defining who is included in a study of stepfamilies is a more difficult task than one might think, and it certainly is more complicated than defining a sample of first-marriage families.

Unlike first-marriage, or nuclear, families, stepfamily members do not necessarily reside full-time in one household. In fact, the prevalence of joint legal and physical custody of children following divorce has made children's membership in two households much more common. Thus, children may link a stepfamily household to another stepfamily household or to a single-parent headed household (Doris Jacobson, 1995). These *binuclear families* (i.e., the households headed by two former spouses who share a child or children) may contain several combinations of full-and part-time step-relationships (Ahrons & Perlmutter, 1982). However, the fact that households and families are not the same is only part of the complexity of defining stepfamilies. Roles and relationships within and across these families and households are incredibly complicated and ever changing.

Bohannan (1984) identified eight roles and eight possible dyadic relationships in the nuclear family known by kinship terms recognized in English—husband-wife, father-son, father-daughter, mother-son, mother-daughter, brother-brother, sister-sister, and brother-sister. Death or divorce changes the family and household structure, resulting in vacant roles and absent dyadic relationships. For instance, a woman who divorces is no longer a wife and the family no longer has a husband-wife (marital) relationship. If she and her former spouse remarry new spouses who already have children, there will be a total of 22 possible dyadic relationships. The new stepfamily contains some of the original family relationships (e.g., mother-son), but it also contains relationships that do not exist in nuclear families (e.g., stepsister-stepbrother).

In addition, stepfamily households are different from first-marriage family households in that they contain *affinal kin*. Affinal kin are individuals related through the marriage of a family member, such as a mother-in-law. Stepchildren and stepparents are also affinal kin. They are in-laws in the same way as mothers-in-law and fathers-in-law.

STEPFAMILY TYPOLOGIES

In efforts to make the complexity of stepfamilies more manageable for scholars, a number of researchers have identified typologies for conceptualizing the structural variations of stepfamily life. (Four structural typologies are shown in Table 1.1). For example, Wald (1981) identified 15 types of stepfamily configurations based on the residence of children from the prior unions of both adults. The number of categories in Wald's typology doubles when children are born to the couple. Pasley and Ihinger-Tallman (1982) postulated a nine-category typology based on presence or absence of children from prior relationships or the present union, age of the children (i.e., adult or minor children), and custody (i.e., residence) of children from prior relationships. Clingempeel and colleagues developed a structural taxonomy based on two variables, the presence or absence of children from prior relationships and the physical custody (i.e., residence) of those children, resulting in nine types of stepfamilies (Clingempeel, Brand, & Segal, 1987). Finally, Doris Jacobson's typology contains six categories of *linked stepfamily systems* (1995) that are based on where the child resides most of the time. These typologies clearly illustrate the structural complexity of stepfamilies. Of course, all of these typologies implicitly ignore third and higher order parental relationships— some stepfamilies are linked to more than one or two other households through children from multiple prior unions.

These typologies aid us in understanding stepfamily structural complexity, but we should point out there is no single, uniform psychological definition of stepfamily membership. For example, Gross (1987) asked stepchildren to identify who was in their family. She categorized their responses into four groups—*retention, substitution, reduction*, and *augmentation.* In the retention group were children who psychologically retained both parents as family members and who were emotionally close to both their nonresidential and residential parent, but not to a stepparent with whom they lived. The children in the substitution group replaced their nonresidential parent with the stepparent they lived with, so that household members only, regardless of biological ties, were considered family. In the reduction group, children included only one parent (the one with whom they resided) as part of their family. The other parent and any stepparents were excluded. The final group, augmentation, contained those children who identified both parents and at least one stepparent as family. In an Australian study, stepchildren used a variety of criteria to decide who was in their family (Funder, 1991). Among the criteria were biological ties, sharing a household with the child, sharing a household with the child's nonresidential parent, and being important to the child. Gamache (1997) cautioned researchers and clinicians to consider children's perspectives on stepfamily membership rather than imposing definitions on them; she argued that adherence to a view of stepfamilies as re-created nuclear families impedes understanding of these families.

Adults also cognitively construct their families. An amusing, albeit idiosyncratic construction of family status was conveyed by Mary Catherine Bateson (1990), who shared in *Composing a Life* that her mother, anthropologist Margaret Mead, only counted her previous relationships as marriages if the union produced either a child or a book!

Table 1.1. Four Structural Typologies of Stepfamilies

Pasley & Ihinger-Tallman (1982)	Clingempeel, Brand, & Segal (1987)	Wald (1981) Children of prior unions		Jacobson (1995)	
		Husband	Wife	Home-based family	Visiting family
1. No children[a]	1. Remarried family[a] (if either were married before)	1. All[b]	None[c]	1. Mother	Father & Stepmother
2. Children of this marriage only[a]		2. All	Some/some elsewhere[d]	2. Mother & Stepfather	Father & Stepmother
3. Residential children from prior marriage only	2. Nonresidential stepmother family	3. All	All elsewhere[e]	3. Mother & Stepfather	Father
		4. All	All	4. Father	Mother & Stepfather
4. Nonresidential children from prior marriage only	3. Residential stepmother family	5. None	All	5. Father & Stepmother	Mother & Stepfather
5. Adult children only	4. Nonresidential stepfather family	6. Some/some elsewhere	All elsewhere	6. Father & Stepmother	Mother
6. Residential children from prior marriage and children from this marriage	5. Residential stepfather family	7. All elsewhere	All		
	6. Nonresidential stepparent family[f]	8. Some/some elsewhere	Some/some elsewhere		

#			
7.	Nonresidential children from prior marriage and children from this marriage	7. Residential stepparent family[g]	9. Some/some elsewhere	None
8.	Nonresidential and residential children from prior marriage	8. Mixed stepparent family (stepmother type)[h]	10. All elsewhere	Some/some elsewhere
9.	Nonresidential and residential children from prior marriage and children from this marriage	9. Mixed stepparent family (stepfather type)[h]	11. None	Some/some elsewhere
			12. Some/ some elsewhere	All elsewhere
			13. All	None elsewhere
			14. None	All elsewhere
			15. All elsewhere	All elsewhere

[a] A family type not covered in the definition of stepfamily used in this book.

[b] All = Marital partner has children from a prior marriage, all of whom live in the stepfamily household.

[c] None = Marital partner has no children from prior marriages.

[d] Some/some elsewhere = Marital partner has children of prior marriage, some of whom live in the stepfamily household and others who live elsewhere

[e] All elsewhere = Marital partner has children of prior marriages, none of whom live in the stepfamily household.

[f] Both adults are parents to children of prior unions; all children live outside of the stepfamily household.

[g] Both adults are parents to children of prior unions; all children live in the stepfamily household.

[h] Both adults are parents; only one set of children lives in the household.

Most psychological definitions of family membership are less unique than Mead's. For example, several researchers have created stepfamily typologies based on how family members think about and interact with each other. These typologies share common characteristics. Nearly every typology identifies a sizable proportion of stepfamilies that attempt to reconstitute themselves as first-marriage families (Berger, 1995; Braithwaite et al., 2001; Bray & Kelly, 1998; Burgoyne & Clark, 1984; Erera-Weatherly, 1996). We called these *Brady Bunch stepfamilies* because the Brady Bunch family in the popular television series embodied this type (Coleman, Ganong, & Fine, in press). Members of these stepfamilies think of themselves and interact as if they were a first-marriage family. Nonresidential or deceased parents of children are not mentioned, stepparents relate to stepchildren as if they were their parents, and role performances and relationships are expected to be identical to first-marriage families. In a second common type, what we called *stepfamilies with detached stepparents and engaged parents*, the stepparent, usually a stepfather, is far less involved with the stepchildren than is the parent (Berger, 1995; Bray & Kelly, 1998; Erera-Weatherly, 1996). Often the stepfather is added to a mother-child unit without fully integrating into that unit. Stepfathers are detached as stepparents but involved as partners, sometimes because they choose to be (Berger, 1995), sometimes because they have withdrawn after attempts to become closer were rebuffed by stepchildren (Hetherington & Clingempeel, 1992), and sometimes because parents serve as gatekeepers because they want to be the primary influences on their children (Bray & Kelly, 1998). Some stepfamilies are formed primarily to fulfill the adults' needs for a partner—what we called *couple-focused stepfamilies*. They are distinguished by a strong emphasis placed on the adult union (Bray & Kelly, 1998; Burgoyne & Clark, 1984). Usually the stepparent is relatively disengaged from parent-related activities on purpose, rather than in reaction to children's behavior toward them, and both of the adults focus energies on enhancing their relationship. Older stepfamilies, those in which the children were grown or nearly grown at the start of the stepfamily, might choose this pattern of interacting more often than stepfamilies with young children (Vinick, 1998). Also, nonresidential stepfamily households, those in which the children reside elsewhere all or most of the time, would seem to be more likely to be couple-focused, particularly if the couples do not reproduce. For a variety of reasons, most of which have not been investigated, some established stepfamilies develop communication and interaction patterns that are creatively adaptive to the structural and interpersonal complexity characteristic of many stepfamilies (Braithwaite et al., 2001; Bray & Kelly, 1998). For lack of a better label, we refer to them as *progressive stepfamilies*, a term used by Burgoyne and Clark (1984) in their in-depth study of British stepfamilies. In their study, progressive stepfamilies had resolved conflicts with former spouses and they approached stepfamily living with a sense of "the positive value of differentness" (p. 193). "Their imagery of family life is pluralistic; they are aware of a diversity of patterns in family and domestic life and depict themselves as making choices . . ." (p. 193). Although we are focusing on the definitional aspects of this typology, it seems clear that stepfamily members' cognitive constructions of their families have enormous pragmatic effects in the daily functioning of these families.

A BRIEF HISTORY OF THE STUDY OF STEPFAMILIES

In the remainder of this chapter we present a brief history of the study of stepfamilies. Examining the historical development of a field of scholarly inquiry can be instructive. For example, such an examination allows us to assess the relation among sociocultural and historical changes and transformations in how social scientists think about and conduct research about specific subjects (in this case, stepfamilies). Although researchers are often portrayed as impractical scientists working in an ivory tower apart from the cultural and historical forces that influence the rest of society, for those who study families, this is a myth (in Chapter 2 we discuss this at length). In practice, social and behavioral researchers are firmly entrenched in a cultural time and place and are reinforced by a variety of influences, such as funding agencies who are responding to social trends and concerns, colleagues who review journal manuscripts, editors, tenure committees, and the *invisible college* (i.e., scholars around the world who study the same topic; Crane, 1972).

THE GOLDEN AGE OF CLINICIANS: THE STUDY OF STEPFAMILIES PRIOR TO 1980

Early Research on Stepfamilies

Although stepfamilies have existed in many cultures for centuries, research on stepfamilies is a surprisingly recent phenomenon. Prior to the late 1970s, researchers showed little interest in stepfamilies. Why were researchers so slow in studying stepfamily relationships? It was not because they were unaware of them. Over 50 years ago Paul Landis (1950) described the state of American families as one of *sequential polygamy*, noting that multiple marriages were more common in U.S. society than in some polygamous societies, and over 30 years ago Margaret Mead (1970) predicted that *serial monogamy* (i.e., one partner after another, another term for sequential polygamy) would become the norm in American families. It was not lack of awareness, but rather researchers' values that contributed to the relatively slow development of stepfamily research until the 1980s (Furstenberg, 1979; Leslie, 1976). Researchers ignored stepfamilies, in part, because post-divorce stepfamilies were seen as violating accepted cultural practices that were part of the belief systems of most researchers. Family scholars, reluctant to accept divorce and remarriage as normative changes in the kinship system rather than as aberrations to accepted cultural practices, ignored them for as long as they could (Furstenberg). Similarly, Leslie attributed the paucity of research prior to the mid-1970s as a consequence of adherence to a family ideology that marriages should be permanent until one of the partners died. When most remarriages followed bereavement, researchers could assume that the family had been reconstituted, but as more remarriages followed divorce, stepfamilies became harder to ignore, even when researchers' values were affronted. From the perspective of these social scientists this was a social problem to be studied.

The first North American study on remarriage was published in the 1930s (Waller, 1930), a few studies appeared in the decade following World War II (e.g., Bernard, 1956; Landis, 1950; Smith, 1953), and a handful were published in the 1960s and 1970s (e.g., Bowerman & Irish, 1962; Duberman, 1975). As recently as 1979, a review of the literature yielded only 11 empirical studies on stepfamilies, including unpublished doctoral dissertations. These studies had sampled a total of only 550 stepfamilies in the United States (Espinoza & Newman, 1979).

Obviously, such a small body of research was limited in the dimensions of stepfamily life that were investigated. For the most part, the early studies focused either on the well-being of stepchildren or on stepparent-stepchild relationships. After reviewing the extant literature, Furstenberg (1979) identified 10 topics needing further study. Each item on the list represents dozens of potential research questions, most of which are still unanswered (see Table 1.2). Following the table through the years, it is easy to see that similar concerns have been raised for more than 20 years and Furstenberg's questions remain as relevant now as they were then.

The early research, as is true in most evolving fields of study, was methodologically and conceptually limited. There were no longitudinal investigations, few studies had large, representative samples of stepfamilies, and few used standardized measures (Price-Bonham & Balswick, 1980). Often stepparents were lumped together as a group regardless of whether they included stepmothers or stepfathers and regardless of whether they lived with stepchildren most of the time or not. Sometimes stepchildren were included in samples along with parents and stepparents, all categorized together as stepfamily members without efforts to distinguish the source of the data as coming from the perspectives of an adult or a child. Most of these studies were not guided by theory and basically were descriptive.

One major exception to the nontheoretical work in the 1970s was Andrew Cherlin's (1978) seminal article in which he described families formed after remarriage as *incomplete institutions*. Cherlin argued that stepfamilies following divorce have more difficulties than first-marriage families because they lack institutionalized guidelines and support to help them solve their family problems. This article has stimulated several studies designed to test aspects of the *incomplete institution hypothesis*, and it also has received attention from clinicians. We discuss Cherlin's influential article at length in the next chapter.

CLINICAL PERSPECTIVES

While the social scientific community slowly developed a body of research on the dynamics of stepfamilies, the applied community of clinicians, including clinical psychologists, social workers, and psychiatrists were more rapidly building a corpus of literature on the problems confronting remarried couples, stepparents, and stepchildren. In fact, it would be fair to say that the writing and thinking of clinicians dominated the early (pre-1980) literature. One consequence of this early domination of the stepfamily literature by clinicians may have been the reinforcement of beliefs that such families are inherently problematic. Clinicians, basing their views on individuals, couples, and families encountering intrapersonal and interpersonal difficulties, naturally focussed on the pathological elements of stepfamily life. This emphasis on family problems and pathology may have helped set the tone for later research efforts, although there was evidence that researchers did not generally consult clinical literature (Ganong & Coleman, 1986).

Several clinicians were influential in shaping this literature such as Lillian Messenger (Messenger, 1976; Messenger, Walker, & Freeman, 1978) and Clifford Sager (Sager et al., 1983), but it was the work of John and Emily Visher (1979) that had the greatest influence on how the dynamics of stepfamily life were concep-tualized. The Vishers, clinicians who were stepparents themselves, began writing extensively and lecturing nationwide to stepfamily members and clinicians during the 1970s. They also founded the Stepfamily Association of America, a national self-help and support group for stepfamily members. The Vishers' clearly articu-lated perspectives on remarriage and stepfamily functioning have had broad appeal to stepfamily members, clinicians, and researchers. Their beliefs that stepfamilies functioned differently than first-marriage families and should be conceptualized as having unique relationships and patterns of interactions have been extremely influential. They also were among the first to focus on strengths of stepfamily living as well as problems, serving as a counterbalance to the generally pervasive, problem-oriented views.

RESEARCHERS DISCOVER STEPFAMILIES: THE STUDY OF STEPFAMILIES IN THE 1980s

Research

The decade of the 1980s witnessed an explosion of scholarly interest in re-marriage, stepparenting, and stepfamilies. In a decade review, we located well

Table 1.2. Areas of Study Needed

Furstenberg (1979)	Ganong & Coleman (1984)
Consequences of prior marital experience on the remarriage transition	Longitudinal studies beginning prior to remarriage
Effects of divorce adjustment on remarriage	Effects of custody arrangements
Effects of remarriage on other life events and experiences	Comparing different structural configurations of stepfamilies
Changes in conjugal relations following remarriage	Relationship development
Remarriage effects on perceptions of social reality	Stepmother households and families
How childrearing functions are fulfilled	Studies of well-functioning stepfamilies
How ties with previous extended kin are maintained	Greater use of theory
How ties are initiated with new extended kin	Use of multiple methods of data collection
Effects of remarriage on self-image and self-identity	Studies of children of different ages
Former spouse relationships after remarriage of one or both	

Ganong & Coleman (1986)	Coleman & Ganong (1990)	Coleman, Ganong, & Fine (2000)
How boundaries are established within stepfamilies and between stepfamilies and other social systems	Interdependencies of stepfamilies and other social systems (e.g., schools, legal system)	Stepfamily processes over time
How coparental relationships affect stepchildren	Nonresidential stepparent-stepchild relationships	Factors that contribute to positive stepfamily functioning
Effects of myths and stereotypes on stepchildren	Effects of broader social environment on stepfamilies (e.g., mass media, public policy)	Ethnic and racial stepfamilies
Differences between complex and simple stepfamilies	Examination of race, sex, SES, cognitive, personality variables as possible mediators for individual & family well-being	Mothers in stepfamilies
Effects of stepparent's marital & parental experiences	Effects of multiple marital transitions	Cohabiting stepfamilies
How stepparent-stepchild relationships are developed	Developmental issues in children's adjustment	Gay and lesbian stepfamilies
		How children affect adults in stepfamilies

Effects of stepparents' role-taking behaviors on stepchildren
Effects of stepsiblings on each other
Effects of reproduction on half-sibling relationships
How stepparent adoptions are decided
Effects of stepparent adoption on stepchildren
How discipline decisions are made

How loyalty conflicts are resolved
Who disciplines stepchildren
Effects of custody changes
Effects of nonresidential parent's remarriage
How rules are developed and maintained in stepfamilies
Social support and stepparent gender
How rituals and celebrations are developed in stepfamilies
How children are involved in planning for stepfamily living
Personal flexibility and adjustment to stepfamilies
Effects of no legal ties on stepparent-stepchild relationships
How stepfamilies present themselves to outsiders
Effects of structural complexity and stressful reactions

Stepmother households and families
Effects stepsiblings have on each other
Finances in stepfamilies
Studies of well-functioning stepfamilies
How ties with extended kin are maintained
Effects of later-life remarriages on individuals and extended family relationships

Effects on nonresidential family members
How stepfamilies interface with social institutions
Experiences, perceptions, & reflections of stepfamily members
How stepfamily processes differ from first marriage families
Biological, psychological, interpersonal, cultural influences on stepfamilies

over 200 published studies from the 1980s (Coleman & Ganong, 1990) and Pasley and Ihinger-Tallman (1992) reviewed 284 studies done in the 1980s. Compared to the 11 studies prior to 1980, this was a phenomenal change.

The quality of the investigations improved as well as the quantity; although stepfamilies attracted more attention from researchers in the first half of the 1980s than in the previous 50 years combined, it was not until the mid 1980s that marked improvement in the quality of research began to be apparent. In the early 1980s, the research continued to be plagued with inconsistencies and methodological problems (see Table 1.3). This body of literature was criticized because most researchers assumed a *deficit-comparison approach* to the study of stepfamilies, which was an assumption that step-relationships would function at a deficit compared to relationships in first-marriage families (Ganong & Coleman, 1984). This assumption led to using first-marriage families as a comparison group even when it was not appropriate to do so, to interpreting differences as deficits, and to applying inappropriate norms to relationships in stepfamilies. This deficit-comparison perspective is not unique to research on stepfamilies; one can find similar trends in other bodies of family research, often employing what Smith (1993) called the Standard North American Family (SNAF) as the standard by which other types of families were compared, and usually found wanting. For example, an examination of the research on single-parent families, African-American families, and dual-career couples suggests that using the (white, middle class) first-marriage family as the standard for comparison is part of the early stages of the development of an area of inquiry.

In the early 1980s some of the research was characterized by *Whoozle Effects*, in which generalizations were drawn based on little evidence (Ganong & Coleman, 1986). According to Gelles (1980), a Whoozle Effect occurs when a particular finding that is reported in one study is subsequently cited by others without careful considerations of possible limitations to the study and without efforts to replicate the findings. Over time, frequent citations of a study result in the findings being treated as more solidly confirmed by data than is actually the case, and original caveats regarding study limitations are forgotten. Whoozle Effects are more likely when a body of literature is not comprehensive, and when there are few studies to cite. Such was the case of research on stepfamily relationships in the early 1980s.

One of the most notable *Whoozles* of this period persists to this day. Over the last 25 years, many clinicians and researcher have claimed that, at some year in the near future, *stepfamilies will outnumber other family forms* or, alternatively, that at some year in the near future, *stepfamilies will be the most common type of family structure*. This Whoozle began in the early 1980s as a calculation by a clinician that was based on *estimates* of the number of marriages and divorces filed every day in the United States and on demographers' predictions of the percentage of divorced

Table 1.3. Characteristics of Stepfamily Research

Ganong & Coleman (1984)	Coleman & Ganong (1990)	Coleman, Ganong, & Fine (2000)
Little use of theory	Little use of theory	Studies often grounded in theory
Limited assessment of stepfamily structural variables	Limited assessment of stepfamily structural variables	Structural variables often considered
Failure to account for stepfamily complexity	Failure to account for stepfamily complexity	Complexity often taken into account
Deficit-comparison approach	Deficit-comparison approach	Deficit-comparison approach continued
Overreliance on self-report questionnaires of unknown validity and reliability	Heavy use of self-report methods	Self-reports most popular data collection method, but other methods used as well
The use of data gathered from only one family member		More studies with multiple respondents from the same stepfamily
Small and nonrandom samples	Small and nonrandom samples	Many national data sets, some longitudinal
	Focus on problems applying norms from first-married families confusing stepfamilies with households	Focus on problems
		More in-depth qualitative studies
		Increasing attention given to nonresidential stepfamily members

people who *eventually* will remarry. From these estimated numbers, the clinician calculated that eventually there would be more stepfamilies than other types of families. Over time, as demographers reported the number of children living with a stepparent to be in the range of 10 to 17%, the rates of divorce declining, then leveling, and the rates of remarriages declining (Casper & Bianchi, 2002), the date in this Whoozle gets pushed back. When this Whoozle statement first appeared in the 1980s, the predicted year for stepfamilies to become the majority was 1990. Since then the target year has changed from 1995 to 2000. Recently, the target has become the year 2010—"It has been estimated that by the year 2010 there will be more stepfamilies than any other type of family in the United States" (Lutz, 1998, p. xxi) and even more recently the date has been projected even further into the future. This Whoozle Effect is our favorite because it illustrates how a "fact" that was never true in the first place can take on a life of its own and thrive in the face of contrary evidence.

In separate reviews of the research conducted prior to 1984 several critical needs for stepfamily research were identified (see Table 1.2). This extensive list echoed the earlier critical reviews (Furstenberg, 1979; Price-Bonham & Balswick, 1980), but a careful reading of the 1984 suggestions reveals that stepfamily scholars were becoming more sophisticated in their thinking, and perhaps, even more demanding of their colleagues. At least some researchers clearly were eager to abandon the well-trod ground of the oversimplified deficit-comparison designs in favor of exploring new territory with new maps.

The Rise of Theory: 1985–1989

Concerns about stepfamily research that were identified in the first half of this decade had begun to be addressed by researchers in the last half (Coleman & Ganong, 1990; Pasley & Ihinger-Tallman, 1992). A few longitudinal studies had been launched, more researchers were trying to account for the complexity of stepfamily structures, large national samples had been examined, some researchers were using multilevel-multivariable-multimeasure designs, there were indications that greater attention was being paid to theory, and, compared to the beginning of the decade, there was more information about previously understudied topics such as stepmother-stepchild relationships.

Although much of the research continued to be either atheoretical or based on the deficit-comparison assumption, near the end of the decade there were more attempts to test theoretical propositions, and there were some beginning efforts to build theory related to remarriage and stepfamilies. The range of theories represented in this work was broad, reflecting the diverse, multidisciplinary nature of the scholars who focused their energies on understanding relationships in stepfamilies.

CLINICAL PERSPECTIVES

Bold strides were also made in clinical scholarship during the 1980s. In fact, practitioners continued to publish more voluminously than researchers and theorists (Ganong & Coleman, 1986). New strategies for working with stepfamilies were developed while established techniques were elaborated (cf. Sager et al., 1983; Visher & Visher, 1988). There were advances in how clinicians conceptualized stepfamilies as well (cf. Mills, 1984; Papernow, 1984, 1987). Unlike the research literature, the body of clinical writing from this decade is not easily divided into periods.

Unfortunately, clinicians and researchers tended not to consult each other's works. In a comparison of the clinical and empirical literature on stepchildren, we found little congruence between the two literatures, concluding, "There is much evidence to indicate that researchers and clinicians interested in stepchildren are professionally segregated and little evidence demonstrating communication between the groups" (Ganong & Coleman, 1986, p. 315). We thought then that both clinical practice and research would be enhanced if there were greater communication between the two groups of professionals, a perspective that we continue to hold (see Chapter 11 for further discussion of this point).

THE DEVELOPMENT OF AN AREA OF STUDY

Several events occurred during the decade of the 1980s that helped spur further development of research in this area of study. In 1982, an interdisciplinary group of scholars formed a Focus Group on Remarriage and Stepparenting within the National Council on Family Relations. In 1983, the Society for Research in Child Development funded an interdisciplinary study group of scholars interested in the effects of remarriage on children, a project that resulted in an edited book of theory and research (Pasley & Ihinger-Tallman, 1987). In 1987, another interdisciplinary group was convened, the Wingspread Conference on Remarried Families, sponsored by the Stepfamily Association of America (SAA), the American Family Therapy Association (AFTA), the National Council on Family Relations (NCFR), and the American Association of Marriage and Family Therapy (AAMFT). The Wingspread conference was to be a one-time meeting, but it evolved into an informal network of researchers, clinicians, and policymakers who met annually at either NCFR or AAMFT conferences for several years. One notable outcome of the Wingspread group was to convince the editor and publisher of the *Journal of Divorce* to rename it the *Journal of Divorce and Remarriage*, a name change that took place in 1990.

The growing recognition of stepfamily life as an area worthy of more focus by researchers was seen not only in the increased number of publications in the 1980s, but in the special issues of journals devoted to remarriage and stepparenting (*Journal of Family Issues*, 1980 and 1992; *Family Relations*, 1984 and 1989). It is fair to suggest that in the 1980s stepfamily research emerged as a clearly identified area of investigation, partly because researchers and clinicians made a strong case for the uniqueness of the dynamics of stepfamilies.

Although only a few of the questions raised by Furstenberg in 1979 had been answered by 1990, the 1980s clearly was a time of exciting methodological, conceptual, and empirical progress in the study of stepfamilies (see Table 1.2). Pasley and Ihinger-Tallman (1992) concluded, after comparing the research literature to the recommendations made in earlier reviews, that researchers had "given serious attention to the many recommendations" but still "have a long way to go in effectively addressing the theoretical and methodological limitations noted" (p. 166).

THE ERA OF EXPANSION: THE 1990s

The outpouring of research, clinical, and theoretical writing about stepfamilies that began in the 1980s became a thunderous torrent in the final decade of the 20th century. In preparing a decade review article that appeared in the *Journal of Marriage and Family*, we and colleague Mark Fine located over 850 professional publications (Coleman, Ganong, & Fine, 2000).

Research

Great strides were made in understanding stepfamilies and stepfamily relationships in the 1990s. Researchers from many disciplines and countries made contributions, and investigations were more often theoretically grounded and methodologically sophisticated than was true in the 1980s. Several large-scale studies were initiated that focused primarily on stepfamilies—many of these were longitudinal projects that allowed researchers to look at changes in stepfamilies and in stepfamily members over time. In addition, there were many small-scale, in-depth studies of whole households or stepfamilies, often with data from multiple family members. There were more observational studies, multiple methods of data collection were used more frequently than before, and there was an increase in qualitative studies. The existence of large national data sets allowed researchers to examine more variables and to think complexly about stepfamilies. The research also was characterized by increased frequent use of grand and mid-range theories to explain phenomena and to test propositions.

What Was Studied?

More than 200 studies focused on the effects on children of living in a step-family household. This was the most frequently investigated area of research in the 1990s, reflecting not only the importance of the topic, but also the availability of large data sets and the ease with which family structure and a variety of child outcomes could be measured. Researchers tended to study child outcomes using between-group designs that compared stepchildren to children in other family structures. A typical approach was to examine the distribution of selected outcome variables by family structure, control for various demographic characteristics, and family process variables, and then see if the relations between family structure and the outcome variables persisted. This design, although useful in determining why one group of children differs from another based on certain predictor variables, all too often leaves researchers trying to infer causal relations from correlational data.

Perhaps not surprisingly, given the emphasis on stepfamily effects on children, stepparent-stepchild relationships were frequently examined. Thanks mostly to in-depth investigations, many of which employed qualitative methods or mixed methods, progress also was made in understanding stepfamily processes. There was also growing interest in the legal aspects of remarriage and stepfamily living. Additionally, researchers in the 1990s often tested ideas proposed initially by clinicians in the 1980s—as a result, this decade saw significant movement towards integration of applied and scholarly professional work.

CLINICAL PERSPECTIVES

During the 1990s, researchers' contributions increased, while the volume of writing by clinicians decreased. Perhaps clinicians thought that the Vishers' (1996) clinical work had said it all, and there was little to be added. The influence of the Vishers' work certainly prevailed throughout the decade, and there was evidence that a few therapists were considering stepfamily issues with greater sophistication (e.g., Browning, 1994; Papernow, 1993). New prevention and educational programs for stepfamilies were developed.

STEPFAMILY SCHOLARSHIP AT THE END OF THE 20TH CENTURY AND BEYOND

The increase in the volume of studies from 1979 until the present was phenomenal and the quality steadily increased as well, and yet much remains to be learned about stepfamilies. In contrast to earlier work, more researchers are attempting to reflect the complexity of stepfamilies, but it is prohibitively expensive to recruit as many stepfamilies as are needed to examine or control for all relevant structural variables. Certain types of stepfamilies are hard to identify (e.g., members of father-stepmother households may share a last name; some stepfamilies are reluctant to identify themselves to researchers), so they end up being under-investigated.

In our view, the emphasis of too many researchers has continued to be on identifying problems. Researchers seem to focus more on negative findings (e.g., stepchildren were more likely than children living with both parents to be depressed), while barely mentioning others (e.g., three-fourths of stepchildren were *not* clinically depressed). Advancements in understanding stepfamily dynamics are hampered when small, but statistically significant effects are treated as if they were large and generalizable to all stepfamily members (see Amato, 1994, for a succinct, but clear discussion of this issue applied to research on stepchildren). Progress is also stymied when extremist positions are taken (Cherlin, 1999), such as when Rutgers sociologist David Popenoe (1994) argued that remarriage was a form of child abuse. Polarized discourse based on extreme positions makes it harder for other scholars and the general public to sort through the hyperbole to find the subtle, conditional, and less publicized "truths." The extremist position that stepfamily relationships are inherently harmful to children and to adults had the loudest voice, and still does.

DEMOGRAPHIC CHANGES AND THE DEVELOPMENT OF THE FIELD

The increased interest in stepfamilies among members of the scientific community came approximately 10 years after the rapid acceleration of the divorce rate. The increase in the divorce rate meant that many more American families than ever before experienced transitions from nuclear to single-parent or binuclear families. A majority of those individuals eventually made additional transitions into stepfamilies.

It became harder to ignore the stepfamilies resulting from the accelerated divorce rate in the 1960s and 1970s, because, unlike in the case of post bereavement, the stepparents in these post-divorce stepfamilies were additional rather than substitute parent figures. Remarriage post-divorce no longer closed the family circle and reconstituted the nuclear family; adding a stepparent post-divorce created new levels of kin and new interaction patterns. It also created issues that could not be ignored, stimulating new research and clinical practice.

However, when scholars began to explore the terrain of post-divorce stepfamily life, it was predominately with a nuclear family map. Because this map did not allow for children to have more than two parents in one role (i.e., mom, stepmom, dad, stepdad) at a time, researchers, practitioners, and stepfamily members were forced to become pioneers in navigating this family terrain. In recent years the mapmakers have worked hard to fill in the topographical features, but much of it remains uncharted. In this book, we attempt to traverse the territory of stepfamily relationships.

In this book we will examine stepfamily relationships from both research and applied perspectives. First, we examine the cultural context in which stepfamilies, researchers, clinicians, and policymakers reside. After considering what is known and what still needs to be known regarding stepfamily relationships, we end this volume with directions for future research and practice with remarriages and stepfamilies.

Chapter 2

The Cultural Context of Stepfamilies

Stepfamilies do not live in a cultural vacuum. Neither do researchers, educators, practitioners, or policymakers. As we noted briefly in the first chapter, prevailing cultural values and belief systems about remarriages and stepfamilies affect the perspectives of individuals who study and work with stepfamilies. More importantly, cultural beliefs and values wield strong influences on the ways in which stepfamily members think about their relationships, interact together, and feel about each other (Bray, 1999; Berger, 2000). In short, stepfamily relationships and the dynamics of stepfamilies are determined, at least in part, by the prevailing ideologies in their cultural contexts. For this reason, we present a brief overview of the cultural milieu in which stepfamilies live before we explore stepfamily functioning in depth in later chapters. We think it is important to understand the social and psychological environments in which individuals create stepfamilies (e.g., remarrying adults), find themselves conscripted into stepfamilies (e.g., stepchildren), or interact with stepfamily members (e.g., teachers, clergy).

What are the prevailing ideologies in the cultural context in which stepfamilies live? Over the last 2 decades researchers from around the world have examined how people perceive stepfamilies and stepfamily positions (e.g., stepmother, stepfather, stepchild). Ideologies about stepfamilies are remarkably similar in Western cultures—studies from Australia (Webber, 1991), Canada (Claxton-Oldfield, Goodyear, Parsons, & Claxton-Oldfield, 2002), Norway (Levin, 1997), the United Kingdom (Collins, 1995), the United States (Ganong & Coleman, 1997a, 1997b), and other countries reveal comparable images and ideologies about stepfamilies.

These studies also indicate that the ideal model for *all* families within Western societies is the middle-class, first-marriage family, often called the nuclear family, consisting of a mother and father and their genetic or adopted children residing together in a household (Coontz, 1997; Scanzoni, 2004). What this means is that a particular type of family serves as the standard by which all families are evaluated, even though a wide diversity of family structures and family practices are present in all Western societies. In the idealized nuclear family, the husband/father is employed for wages and is generally considered to be the primary wage earner, even if the wife/mother also works for wages and even if she earns more income than the husband/father. Her primary responsibilities are to provide care for the husband, household, and children. In the idealized version of this family form, children are loved and socialized by both parents to be obedient, mentally and physically healthy, and socially skilled. Spouses love each other and fulfill each other's emotional, social, and physical needs. In North America, this cultural ideal of the private nuclear family residing in one household is based on white families of European descent—it ignores cultural and historical family patterns of African Americans, Native Americans, Asian Americans, Latinos, and other groups of families from collectivist cultural orientations.

How does this *nuclear family ideology* influence the cultural context of step-families? We think there are three broad societal views of stepfamilies, all of them rooted in the nuclear family ideology—the stepfamily as an *incomplete institution* (Cherlin, 1978), the stepfamily as a *deviant or deficit family* form (Coleman & Ganong, 1997c), and the stepfamily as a *re-formed or reconstituted nuclear family* (Levin, 1997).

STEPFAMILIES AS INCOMPLETE INSTITUTIONS

Andrew Cherlin (1978), in perhaps the most frequently cited stepfamily article ever published, argued that remarried families were incompletely institutionalized in U.S. society. He posited that the absence of guidelines and norms for role performance, the dearth of culturally established, socially acceptable methods of resolving problems, and the relative absence of institutionalized social support for remarried adults contributed to greater stress, inappropriate solutions to problems, and higher divorce rates for stepfamilies. Cherlin pointed to the paucity of language and legal regulations as illustrations of how remarriages are incompletely institutionalized.

Cherlin's (1978) *incomplete institution hypothesis* has been extremely influential for researchers and clinicians, and it has engendered several studies, despite being difficult to operationalize (cf. Booth & Edwards, 1992; Clingempeel, 1981; Fine, Coleman, & Ganong, 1998; Ganong, Coleman, & Cable, 1997; Giles-Sims, 1984; Grizzle, 1999; Hequembourg, in press). Although this hypothesis has been criticized (Grizzle, 1996; Jacobson, 1995), for the most part the results of studies have lent support to Cherlin's ideas.

Absence of Appropriate Terms

Cherlin (1978) wrote that, "Where no adequate terms exist for an important social role, the institutional support for this role is deficient, and general acceptance of the role as a legitimate pattern of activity is questionable" (p. 643). In Chapter 1 we mentioned some of the many labels for stepfamilies and positions within stepfamilies; Cherlin argued that this confusion of labels was a consequence of the incomplete institutionalization of stepfamilies.

In addition to the lack of consensus about what to call stepfamilies and step-family positions and a plethora of options, some relationships in stepfamilies remain nameless. For example, there is no word in English for the relationships between a father and a stepfather or between a mother and a stepmother. The absence of terms is indicative of cultural expectations that such relationships do not and should not exist. There are other relationships in stepfamilies that have no labels, but are identifiable by simply adding a *step-* prefix (e.g., step-aunt, step-cousins).

The absence of appropriate terms for specific relationships makes it hard to think about, much less communicate about, them. Although such *quasi-kin* relationships do not exist in nuclear families, they are common in stepfamilies, particularly in an era in which many children are in the legal and physical custody of both of their divorced parents. In shared custody stepfamilies, stepparents as well as parents become involved in planning the logistics of transporting children from household to household, in helping children with school, scouts, and 4-H projects, and in supporting children's activities through attendance at sporting, theatrical, and musical events. In these stepfamilies, a father and a stepfather may indeed communicate and interact about the child/stepchild, as do mothers and stepmothers. From the perspective of the incomplete institution hypothesis, these stepfamilies must create relationships for the good of their households in spite of the absence of normative assistance and the implicit expectation that such relationships should not exist. In our experience in interviewing stepfamily members, when they talk about the mother and stepmother (or father and stepfather) who talk to each other about the children, they preface their comments with, "I know it sounds odd, but . . . ," or "We are probably the only people who do this, but. . . ." These comments indicate that stepfamilies often operate in ways that they perceive to be at odds with cultural expectations.

Little Institutional Social Support

Stepfamilies receive less social support than first marriage families from the social institutions and organizations with which they interact. For example, step-parents who are involved in their stepchildren's schooling frequently find that the customs and procedures of school systems make little allowance for the presence of stepparents. Although there has been considerable improvement, enrollment forms may still have places for parents' names only, graduating seniors are given only two tickets for their parents to attend graduation ceremonies, and teachers are ill-prepared for a child to have three or more step/parents show up for parent-teacher meetings (Coleman, Ganong, & Henry, 1984; Crosbie-Burnett, 1994). Other social organizations, such as youth groups, religious groups, and health care systems also are based on policies and procedures designed primarily for first marriage families (Ganong, 1993). Members of stepfamilies and other family forms are usually welcome to participate in these organizations, but there are few attempts, if any, to accommodate organizational practices to facilitate their participation. A clinical nurse specialist who worked in a hospital intensive care unit (ICU) once told us that whether step-kin were allowed into the unit to see patients or not depended on who was working in the ICU at the time. The hospital policy was that only immediate family members were allowed into the ICU—some nurses considered step-kin to be immediate family, and some did not. This nurse, who was a stepmother, advised step-kin to omit the prefix *step* when describing their relationship to the patient. This subtle social coercion of stepfamilies to act like or present themselves as first-marriage families puts pressure on stepfamily members to imitate as closely as possible the normatively expected behaviors of members of first-marriage families.

Nonexistent or Ambiguous Laws and Social Policies

Family laws also are seen as failing to provide support to stepfamilies. Stepparents have been generally overlooked in federal and state laws in the United States; they have few legal responsibilities toward their stepchildren, and few rights as well (Fine, 1997; Mason, 1998; Mason, Fine, & Carnochan, 2004). Mahoney (1994) noted, "The preference for nuclear family finds expression in the legal system through laws that create distinct protections, entitlements, and responsibilities for spouses, parent, and children" (p. 1). Although there have been changes in family law in recent years that indirectly affect the legal relation between stepparents and stepchildren (e.g., more states are allowing third parties to have post-divorce custody), there is still little consensus on what legal changes are needed, and little political pressure on legislatures to alter existing policies and laws (Mason et al., 2004).

The prevalence of the nuclear family ideology in Western societies is one reason why stepfamilies are incompletely institutionalized. There is little motivation for societies to support stepfamilies via social policies, partly because from the perspective of the idealized nuclear family, stepfamily structures are deficient in a variety of ways. According to historian A. T. Miller (1993), the nuclear family ideology has "had a stultifying impact at policy levels where programmatic and social assumptions are often designed with only that model in mind . . . It therefore remains as a burden and stands as . . . a singular model in a culture of diversity" (p. 13).

Relative Absence of Norms

"The day-to-day life of remarried adults and their children also includes many problems for which there are no institutionalized solutions" (Cherlin, 1978, p. 646). We can think of many issues that affect day-to-day stepfamily life for which there are no institutionalized solutions. For instance, how should children be told about their parent's marriage? When should they be told? What do stepchildren call their stepparent? How do stepfamily members introduce each other (i.e., these are my parents? My mom and my stepdad?)? How involved should stepparents be in child discipline? Who should make household rules for children to follow? Do children who are part-time household residents follow the same rules and have the same chores as full-time residents? Should stepparents be financially responsible for their stepchildren? How should stepchildren and stepparents feel toward each other—like parent and child, like friends, like what?

Clinicians have filled volumes over the last 30 years with example after example of similar daily dilemmas that stepfamilies face. Given their exposure to stepfamilies struggling to develop rules for functioning as a family together, and because their stepfamily clients often attempt to solve these dilemmas by using institutionalized solutions designed for first marriage families, clinicians generally attribute substantial validity to the incomplete institution hypothesis (Mills, 1984; Papernow, 1993; Visher & Visher, 1988). Finally, in our studies of normative beliefs about stepparents and stepchildren's roles and responsibilities (e.g., Coleman & Ganong, 1998a, 1998b; Ganong & Coleman, 1998, 1999), we have found, in general, that there is more consensus about nuclear family roles and responsibilities than about stepfamily roles and responsibilities.

STEPFAMILIES AS DEVIANT OR DEFICIT FAMILY FORMS

Nuclear Family Ideology and Stigma

The nuclear family model is associated with a moral, natural imperative—other family forms are considered to be immoral, or less moral, than the private nuclear family (Coontz, 1997). Part of the ideology is based on the belief that the nuclear family exists as a universal, necessary entity in nature (Scanzoni, 2004). The nuclear family ideology therefore contributes to stepfamilies being seen as deviant or operating at a deficit.

No doubt some of the social stigma related to divorce has been reduced in recent years, but there is still an undercurrent of moral outrage directed toward individuals who divorce (Coleman & Ganong, 1995). Remarriages and stepfamilies are generally seen as extensions of divorce, the consequences of *failed marriages* and *broken homes*. Although there now is less tolerance for the overt expression of such ill will, deep-seated feelings persist against those in non-nuclear families (Hackstaff, 1999; Mandell, 2002). At the social level, the veneer of civility hides the righteous nature of traditional mores that suggest those who do not conform to the family ideal should be punished (Scanzoni, 2004). The nuclear family ideology thus serves as a deterrent for stepfamilies to be open with outsiders and with themselves.

Although impression management (hiding their stepfamily status) may be an effective strategy to avoid unpleasant reactions from others (Dainton, 1993; Ganong, Coleman, & Kennedy, 1990), hiding one's status excludes others from providing assistance, encouragement, and moral support when needed. In hiding their step status to avoid stigma, members of stepfamilies may be unintentionally contributing to their social isolation. Overall, stepfamilies are stigmatized via language, cultural stereotypes and myths, and media images.

Language

The noted family sociologist Jessie Bernard wrote nearly 50 years ago that, "Because of the emotional connotations of the terms stepchild, stepmother, and stepfather, they are avoided . . . for they are, in effect, smear words" (1956, p. 14). The prefix *step* still triggers negative reactions in people and may be considered to be a pejorative (Claxton-Oldfield & Voyer, 2001; Ganong et al., 1990). Hardly a week goes by that we do not see the term *stepchild* in a newspaper or magazine article being used metaphorically to refer to someone or something that is abused, neglected, or unwanted. In fact, this use of the term is not only metaphoric, it is one of the standard definitions of stepchild in most English dictionaries! People associate the term *stepmother* with the adjectives *mean* and *wicked* (Ganong & Coleman, 1995), and the *stepfather* label frequently conjures images of an abuser or a sexual predator (Claxton-Oldfield, Goodyear, Parsons, & Claxton-Oldfield, 2002). In fact, the proliferation of labels for stepfamilies (see Chapter 1) may be less a matter of social scientists being unable to agree on a suitable term, than a consequence of the cultural ambivalence toward step-relationships and remarriage and attempts to re-label stepfamilies and stepfamily positions in order to reduce negative reactions (Ganong et al., 1990).

Other language usage, such as describing biological parents as *real* or *natural* parents, implicitly conveys the message that stepparents (and adoptive parents, foster parents, and others) are unreal, or unnatural. Identifying first-marriage families as *normal*, *real*, *regular*, or *traditional* similarly signifies that other families are abnormal, unreal, irregular, and nontraditional. The use of language can serve to legitimize certain family forms and place others on the fringe of acceptability. Language helps shape thinking, and the lack of language about relationships in stepfamilies may make it more difficult for family members to develop positive identities and satisfying relationships (Coleman & Ganong, 1995).

Stereotypes

As a test of your ability to recognize cultural views of stepfamilies, put a check next to the following descriptors that you think were written about stepfamilies, and an X in front of those that were given as descriptors of nuclear families.

❑ 1. Secure, stable, happy, moral, normal
❑ 2. Complex negotiations, sacrifice, understanding, extra opportunity, options
❑ 3. Stability, lifelong relationships, strong sense of belonging, well-defined roles
❑ 4. Conflicts, anger, confusion, children acting out, insecurities, compromising
❑ 5. Happy, legitimate, a real family, normal, functional, structured, closely knit
❑ 6. Dysfunctional, wicked, complex, tumultuous, rocky/shaky, childrearing problems
❑ 7. Correct, happy, well functioning, father as leader, mother as helpmate
❑ 8. Together but not unified, complex, confusion or chaotic interaction, many children
❑ 9. Happy, several children, conscrvative/religious
❑ 10. Lots of arguing, somewhat happy, lots of children, liberal, less educated
❑ 11. Intimate, help each other, support each other, democracy
❑ 12. Confusion, dysfunction, complex
❑ 13. Togetherness, loving, normative, correct, compromising, good communication
❑ 14. Misunderstandings about feelings, power issues, disagreement over possessions
❑ 15. Tied by blood, normal, close, loving, whole, unblemished
❑ 16. Confusion, jealousy, feeling of intrusion
❑ 17. Security, consistent discipline, caring parents, working together, stability
❑ 18. Openness to ambiguity, insecurity, more accepting of differences in others
❑ 19. Together, cohesive, communication, loving, caring
❑ 20. Chaos, confused children, conflicts in all areas, divided, stressful

We asked some college students to generate descriptors that they believed to be characteristic of either stepfamilies or first marriage families. According to these midwestern U.S. college students, the odd-numbered statements above described first-marriage families and the even-numbered statements described stepfamilies. We are not suggesting that descriptions from students from one university represent cultural stereotypes about stepfamilies. Obviously, we would need to collect data from multiple and diverse samples before conclusions could be drawn, but the list above illustrates that there are some clear differences in the stereotyped characteristics of nuclear families and stepfamilies.

We have consistently found in our studies and studies with our colleagues that stepmothers and stepfathers are perceived more negatively than are mothers and fathers, respectively, and stepchildren are stereotyped more negatively than are children living with both of their parents (e.g., Bryan, Ganong, Coleman, & Bryan, 1985; Bryan, Coleman, Ganong, & Bryan, 1986; Ganong, Coleman, & Cable, 1997; Ganong, Coleman, & Mapes, 1990). However, not all studies have found that stepparents and stepchildren are stereotyped negatively (e.g., Claxton-Oldfield & Kavanaugh, 1999), and some have found that individuals rely on cultural stereotypes of stepparents in some situations, but not others (Claxton-Oldfield et al., 2002).

Most investigations of cultural stereotypes of stepfamilies and stepfamily members have assessed perceptions only, which led us to conduct two studies designed to assess behaviors as well as perceptions (Ganong & Coleman, 1999a, 1997b). In these studies, trained actresses, one portraying a patient and one portraying a nurse practitioner giving a physical examination were video taped. Study participants, all female registered nurses, were given information about the patient's marital and parental status (e.g., married mother, married childless, unmarried mother, stepmother). All of the information given to study participants, except for the patient's marital status, was identical. In both studies using this design, but with different presenting problems of the patient, we found that nurses evaluated and perceived the patients in similar ways, regardless of family structure. However, we also asked the participants to pretend they were the nurse examining this patient, and to answer questions that the videotaped patient asked (we stopped the tape after each question to allow for nurse participants to write their responses). The nurses supplied appropriate factual information to patients regardless of family structure, but differences in affective tone toward the patient and in providing opportunities to give them more information indicated that the nuclear family ideology subtly affected the behaviors of even well-trained and experienced nurses. Nurses' responses to women who they thought were in first-marriage families were warmer and more elaborate than were responses to women in stepfamilies and single-mother families.

Myths

Myths are beliefs that reflect cultural standards and ideals. They often contain kernels of truth, although they are seldom accurate as generalized truths. The main function of myths is to communicate cultural values. Stepfamily myths include: (a) stepchildren resent and dislike their stepparents, (b) stepchildren have more problems than other children, (c) stepfamilies are just like other families, (d) stepparents and stepchildren never can learn to love each other, (e) adoption transforms stepfamilies into normal families, (f) children should be loyal to one mother and one father only, (g) stepparents should love their children easily and immediately, and (h) stepmothers are mean and evil (Coale Lewis, 1985; Coleman & Ganong, 1987; Leslie & Epstein, 1988; Visher & Visher, 1985). As this list attests, myths can be directionally oppositional. For instance, in contrast to the myth that stepparents and stepchildren can *never* learn to love each other, the myth of instant love says that stepparents should *immediately* love their stepchildren. The underlying assumption of this myth is that remarriage reconstitutes a nuclear family, and the stepparent functionally and emotionally replaces the nonresidential parent. This myth is clearly based on nuclear family ideology, complete with the expectation that love is both an automatic experience and a requisite emotion. Clinicians argue that the myth of instant love puts stepfamilies under great strain; stepparents feel pressured to feel love even when they hardly know their stepchild. On the other hand, the myth that stepparents and stepchildren can never learn to love each other is unduly pessimistic and may hamper efforts to even try to relate positively to each other.

Every culture has myths and stereotypes that are idiosyncratic, but the evil stepmother myth is apparently common in many cultures (Wald, 1981). The Cinderella tale, or one of the 345 variations of it, has been traced to 9th century China (Smith, 1953). We have observed that stepmothers are disturbed by this myth, and the myth influences their behavior and how they think about themselves.

Media Images

From fairy tales to motion pictures, stepparents and stepchildren have been portrayed in ways that stigmatize them (Claxton-Oldfield, 2000). In fairy tales, children's stories, and movies stepmothers are portrayed as mean, uncaring, and interested in their husbands' money and little else (Ganong & Coleman, 1997c). Stepfathers escape negative images in fairy tales but make up for it by being portrayed as evil, predatory, and abusive in books and movies (Claxton-Oldfield, 2000). In a review of 55 movie plot summations that mentioned stepparents, Claxton-Oldfield reported that over half depicted stepparents negatively and none presented them in a positive manner. According to Oldfield, "unless the plot summary information about the stepparent was neutral, there was almost bound to be an element of step-parental wickedness—a bullying or sexually harassing stepfather or a murderous or destructive stepmother" (p. 55). Of course, not all cinematic stepparents and stepchildren are so depicted, but for every benign stepfather (e.g., *Tender Mercies*) or stepmother (e.g., *Stepmom*) there are dozens of horrible, mean stepparents with neglected and unloved stepchildren. As if there were not already enough hostile terms for stepparents, the movie *St. Elmo's Fire* gave us *stepmonster* as a way to refer to stepmothers.

The medium of television has occasionally depicted stepfamilies over the years, the most famous being *The Brady Bunch*, a popular U.S. sitcom of the 1980s. Although television programs have not been systematically studied for stepfamily content as have other media, it seems to us that stepfamily depictions on the small screen have stigmatized stepfamilies less than other media (e.g., *Eight is Enough, Something so Right, Once and Again, Step by Step, NYPD Blue*). However, most movies appear on television eventually, and some made-for-TV movies and special programs seem designed to exaggerate stepfamily relationship problems.

Researchers who have examined popular publications like magazines find that authors focus on stepfamily problems more than on positive dimensions of stepfamily living (Coleman, Ganong, & Gingrich, 1985; Pasley & Ihinger-Tallman, 1985). Stepfamilies in novels written for children and adolescents have fared slightly better than in visual media (Coleman & Ganong, 1988), but it has not been empirically determined how authors of adult fiction depict step-relationships.

Textbooks for college students should present information that focuses on positive, neutral, and negative aspect of stepfamilies. However, reviews of family textbooks in the past have reported that stepfamilies, tended to be marginalized as a topic (Coleman, Ganong, & Goodwin, 1994). It is our general impression that these textbooks for the most part now provide more coverage and more balanced coverage of diverse families, including stepfamilies, than they have in the past. It should be noted, however, that this increased coverage has raised the ire of conservative scholars. Glenn (1997) castigates most current textbook authors because "No book draws the obvious conclusion that the increase in single parent families and stepfamilies has very likely tended to increase child abuse or says anything about reversing trends in family structure in discussing how to reduce the abuse" (p. 201). To be fair, Glenn's primary complaint is that family textbooks are anti-marriage, but it is not clear where he aligns remarriage and whether or not he would have textbook authors offset negative conclusions about stepfamilies with more positive findings (see Chapter 7 for more discussion of stepparent-stepchild relationships). It is hard to know which would be more disheartening to a college student—to find no mention of the family type they grew up in or to have it presented only in negative ways.

STEPFAMILIES AS RECONSTITUTED NUCLEAR FAMILIES

The final way in which stepfamilies are viewed in Western culture is as re-created or re-formed nuclear families. Given the choices of struggling to find solutions to problems without being supported in their efforts to do so or being stigmatized as deviant, it is not terribly surprising that many stepfamilies choose to present themselves as if they were a first-marriage nuclear family and to model their family interactions after nuclear families. By doing this, they can enjoy the normative support provided for nuclear families, they avoid stigma and social disapproval, and they become or feel they become "normal" again. They can go from being *unclear families* to *nuclear families* (Simpson, 1994), which from the perspective of many newly remarried adults is a welcome thing.

There is some cultural support for stepfamilies to make this transition. Obviously, adoption legally transforms a family and relationships within it from step to nuclear. Friends, extended kin of the newly remarried couple, and others with whom they interact (neighbors, teachers, store clerks) generally will treat the step-family as if it were a first-marriage family. It is almost as if the nuclear family is the cultural default, so when an adult male and female and children live together, outsiders react to them as if they were a first-marriage family, until they find out differently. Often adults in stepfamilies find it easier to go along with this than to explain their family structure (e.g., "Susan is my wife's daughter"), and sometimes even a little family history (e.g., "Susan and Tim are not brother and sister. Susan is my wife's daughter from a previous marriage and Tim is my son. That is why they don't look like each other"), to people they encounter. In general, as the preceding pages must surely have implied, it is easier to pass as a first-marriage family, at least if everyone in the stepfamily agrees.

IMPLICATIONS OF THE CULTURAL CONTEXT OF STEPFAMILIES

Implications for Stepfamily Members

Throughout the rest of this book we identify and explain the implications of cultural values and beliefs for stepfamilies and for the well-being of individual members of stepfamilies. For now, it is sufficient to repeat the point made at the beginning of this chapter—cultural values indirectly and directly affect how stepfamily members think, feel, and interact with each other. People have beliefs about stepfamilies before they ever consider becoming part of one, and the cultural values to which they have been exposed help to shape their expectations for what stepfamily living will be like. These expectations can be profound forces on the subsequent relationships that develop.

Nearly everyone who stepfamily members encounter is affected by cultural values and beliefs about stepfamilies. Despite the fact that everyone who we have ever met has a remarriage and step-relationship somewhere in their family histories, a lot of what people know about stepfamilies comes from media images and fairy tales. Many people think they don't know anyone who lives in a stepfamily. When we have asked graduate students to think about the step-relationships in their family trees, many claim that they do not have any, because nobody in their family has ever divorced. We point out to them that when life spans were about 40 years, and when many women died in childbirth, most people remarried if they could. Most students can find a step-relationship in their extended families without a lot of effort, sometimes going back only a generation. More than one student has discovered past divorces that nobody in the family talks about, and there are always post-bereavement remarriages in family histories. Some have mentioned not finding out until they were young adults that one of their parents (usually a father) had been previously married and that they had half-siblings they had never met. We mention this because this illustrates to us how strongly we mold our experiences, and those of our ancestors, to fit the ideal. Consequently, we fail to recognize remarried people or stepchildren or stepparents, because everyone we know is "normal."

Implications for Clinicians

Cultural values also shape clinicians' behaviors. Cultural beliefs about how families should function, combined with beliefs based on the idealized family model, influence clinicians' assessment and treatment of all kinds of families, including stepfamilies. Clinicians who followed interventions and preventions that ignored societal and cultural influences probably found that there was much they did not comprehend when working with stepfamilies. As we note in Chapter 11, some practitioners were slow to abandon therapeutic and educational models that were based on middle-class first-marriage families. This hindered practitioners as much as it did stepfamilies. Gradually, clinicians have come to recognize the limiting influences of the prevailing ideology on stepfamilies. Clinicians who specialize in working with stepfamilies have created alternative models for thinking about family relationships and family functioning that account for the unique dynamics of stepfamilies. We want to end this chapter by examining how cultural values and beliefs have affected researchers.

Implications for Researchers

It would be naive to assume that social science researchers are not influenced by cultural ideologies and belief systems about family life (Gamache, 1997; Ganong & Coleman, 2000). Researchers' values, opinions, and beliefs about stepfamilies likely have influenced every aspect of the research endeavor, including the types of issues addressed, the way hypotheses and research questions are worded, the selection of samples and measurement instruments, and interpretations of the meaning of data (see Cherlin, 1999, and Amato, 2004, for excellent discussions of the roles played by values in family research in general). In spite of social science researchers' attempts to limit biases in their research designs, their personal values and beliefs about families may introduce subtle biases into their investigations.

Epistemic and Nonepistemic Values

Clingempeel, Flescher, and Brand (1987), in a review of the research on stepfamilies from a constructivist perspective, identified what they termed *paradigmatic constraints* on the development of this body of knowledge. The constructivist perspective holds that all knowledge is invented, rather than discovered, and is based on the beliefs and cognitions of researchers, rather than on a single set of objective facts (Gergen, 1985). The belief systems of researchers are based partly on the values and beliefs they have been taught as scientists regarding how research should be conducted (*epistemic beliefs* and values), and partly on personal values and beliefs (*nonepistemic beliefs*). Applied to family research, Clingempeel and his colleagues defined nonepistemic values as attitudes about what is good or bad for families, and epistemic values as the best methods for conducting research on families. Both epistemic and nonepistemic values of social scientists are influenced by sociocultural and historical factors.

Clingempeel and colleagues argued that nonepistemic beliefs that comprise the *nuclear family ideology* are responsible for several of the research limitations noted in Chapter 1: (a) minimal attention given to the structural complexity and heterogeneity of stepfamily forms, (b) emphasis on the problems and weaknesses of stepfamilies rather than on potential strengths and advantages, and (c) generally ignoring the possibility that relationships within stepfamilies may differ in fundamental ways from relationships within nuclear families, yet still be functional. There are undoubtedly other nonepistemic values that have impacted research on stepfamily relationships.

According to Clingempeel and his colleagues, epistemic constraints that have influenced the shape of stepfamily literature include a bias toward between-group comparisons (i.e., comparing stepfamilies to other family structures), a disciplinary ethnocentric bias (i.e., ignoring the methods, perspectives, and theories of disciplines other than the one in which the researcher was trained), and the *rational objectivity bias* (Clingempeel et al., 1987). This last bias is a result of the belief that scientists should be objective and emotionally removed from their subjects; study participants are seen as passive objects to be examined, rather than active co-participants in the research endeavor (Thompson, 1992), which slows the process of understanding. The net effect of these epistemic constraints has been to limit the breadth, depth, and speed at which the body of knowledge on stepfamilies has been developed.

Since Clingempeel and colleagues made their insightful argument there has been noteworthy movement, at least by some scholars, away from these research biases. If nothing else, researchers more often are aware of their epistemic biases, which makes it harder for them to conduct business as usual. One result has been an increase in qualitative or interpretive methods of gaining knowledge about stepfamilies. We find much to be optimistic about when considering the changes over time in the approaches to studying stepfamily relationships.

However, the nuclear family ideology is still a major influence on scholars, and the functionalist framework is not dead. There are many examples—a well-known sociologist recommends that policymakers should discourage remarriage because stepchildren are at risk, researchers continue to compare stepfamilies to "intact" families, evolutionary researchers devote an issue of a major journal on studies of why stepfathers invest less in their stepchildren and harm them more than do fathers (interestingly, adoptive fathers escape such scrutiny, despite also lacking genetic connections to children), and clinicians continue to refer to first-marriage families as "natural," "intact," or "real" families which juxtaposes stepfamilies as being "unnatural," "broken," or "unreal."

On a personal note, we have had many opportunities to encounter examples of what the prevailing truths are about stepfamilies. Over the past few years, other scholars have called us *ideologues* because we encouraged researchers to consider factors that may contribute to well-functioning stepfamilies, *naïve* because we examined and wrote about stepfamily strengths, and *well-intentioned but misguided* because we investigated cultural beliefs about stepfamilies and stepfamily positions. Because we think that much of stepfamily life is socially constructed, we have been accused of engaging in a "flight from reality." In response, we argue that none of us—stepfamily members, researchers, clinicians, policymakers—are immune from cultural beliefs. In both our research and our applied work with stepfamilies we have observed that the nuclear family ideology is a powerful influence. Even when researchers, clinicians, and stepfamily members attempt to use other models of family life to guide their thinking, the idealized nuclear family functions as the implicit comparison (e.g., Gamache, 1997; Levin, 1997; Smith, 1993). It is nearly impossible to think about stepfamilies, to study them as a researcher or to work with them as a practitioner, without implicitly or explicitly holding them to an idealization of first-marriage families. However, we attempt in this book to use a normative adaptive approach, one that begins with the premise that stepfamilies can function well and can be effective environments for children and adults.

Chapter 3

Paths to Stepfamily Life

Stepfamilies do not begin as *tabula rasa*. Members of stepfamilies are well into the process of writing their life stories when step-relationships begin. Although remarriage or cohabiting may start a new chapter in those life stories, the plot lines from earlier chapters continue. Characters and events that were important in the development of earlier stories generally continue to influence the directions the stories take. In fact, forming a stepfamily has been likened to beginning a novel in the middle of the book. Family members are trying to combine and understand multiple, and often diverse, story lines from prior families; these story lines may include comedies, tragedies, mysteries, romances, science fiction, and even post-modern narratives that are hard to follow.

Clinicians have long recognized that the paths by which individuals find themselves in stepfamilies have important implications for stepfamily dynamics (Visher & Visher, 1979). More recently researchers also have started to examine precursors to stepfamily living. There are three general pathways an individual could take to remarriage and stepfamily living (see Figure 3.1), but there are at least 18 possible partner combinations, each of which could influence remarriage and stepfamily dynamics.

DIFFERENT PATHS

Stepfamilies are formed in many ways. The pathway written about most often by family researchers and clinicians is illustrated in the following scenario:

> Bob and Sue met when they were in their 20s and dated a couple of years before they married. In the first few years of marriage they had two children, Bobby and Susie. Gradually, Bob and Sue drifted apart, and when Bobby was 10 and Susie 7, Bob and Sue separated. Bob moved out of the family

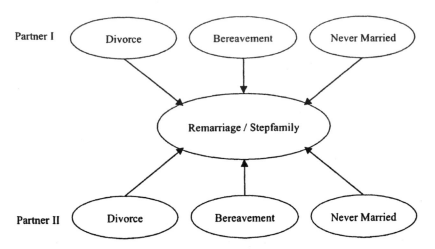

Partner I

Partner II

Figure 3.1. Pathways to Stepfamily Life. One of both partners must have a child from a previous relationship. A divorced Partner I could form a relationship with a Partner II who was also divorced or who was bereaved or had never married. Partners I and II can be opposite or same sex.

home, while Bobby and Susie remained with Sue. Following hostile divorce proceedings, Sue retained physical and legal custody of the children, and Bob was required to pay child support. Two years later, Bob remarried Linda, a divorced woman with a 6-year-old son. A year later, Sue remarried Alan, a childless man who had never been married.

This scenario describes a first marriage that is ended by divorce as the precursor to two remarriages, one forming what is often called a *complex stepfamily*, because both adults bring children to the stepfamily (Bob and Linda), and the other creating a *simple stepfamily*, in which only one adult is a parent when the marriage begins (Sue and Alan). There are obviously other pathways to becoming a stepfamily:

- a couple *remarries* after their first marriages end by the death of their spouses;
- a single woman bears children, raises them alone for awhile, then *marries* a man who is not the father of the children;
- a single mother *cohabits* with, but does not marry, a man who is not the father of her children;
- a gay or lesbian person forms a *committed partnership*, in which one or both have children from prior relationships.

Note that only one of these pathways includes a remarriage, but all contain step-relationships, or de facto step-relationships. Note also that these examples focus on second marriages or second relationships only; well over 10% of remarriages represent at least the third marriage for one or both of the partners (National Center for Health Statistics, 1993). Because of the increase in cohabiting relationships of adults with children from earlier unions, marital and cohabiting histories over the life course are becoming more complex. For example, a study from the first two waves of the National Study of Families and Households found that 24% of 6,913 adults had experienced a relationship transition (marriage, divorce, or cohabitation) in a 5-year period and 3% had experienced two transitions during this relatively short time frame (Kim & McKenry, 2000). These increasingly complicated partnership histories result in greater numbers of children having complex family histories (O'Connor et al., 1999; Wojtkiewicz, 1994). An estimated 10% of children will experience at least two divorces of their custodial parent before they turn 16 (Furstenberg, 1988), and according to Bumpass (1984), 15% will experience a second divorce of their parent's remarriage within 2 years, and nearly 50% will experience one within 10 years. A sizable number of these children experience living in a second or third stepfamily (Furstenberg, 1988).

The family histories of *serial marriers* or *serial cohabitors* and their children are likely to be substantially different from those of stepfamily members who have experienced only one marriage/committed relationship prior to the formation of the stepfamily (Brody, Neubaum, & Forehand, 1988; Capaldi & Patterson, 1991; Kurdek & Fine, 1993a). The number of family transitions is obviously greater for families in which adults have experienced a series of marriages and/or cohabiting relationships than it is for those in first-time stepfamilies. These transitions represent many potential changes for both adults and children, such as changing residences, the addition and loss of new household members, economic changes, and alterations in family identity. Unfortunately, relatively few researchers have examined the differences between those in their first remarriage and those who have had multiple marriages. Often they all are categorized together as remarried.

We focus primarily on second unions, mostly first remarriages, in the rest of this chapter because doing so simplifies the discussion of potential influences of individuals' prior histories on stepfamily life and stepfamily relationships. Recognizing that we are oversimplifying the discussion further by focussing on the prior experiences of only one of the adult partners, we briefly discuss potential differences in three pathways to stepfamilies—post-divorce, post-bereavement, and never-married (see Figure 3.1 for an illustration).

POST-DIVORCE STEPFAMILIES

Family transitions are ongoing processes, occasionally marked by a discrete legal event, such as divorce. Courtship may transition to cohabiting, followed by legal remarriage. Marriage may move to separation followed by legal divorce. The process may then begin anew—courtship, cohabiting, legal marriage, etc. In this section we discuss stepfamilies formed after divorce.

Divorce is a verb as well as a noun, a process that occurs over time as well as a legal event. Many people think only of the event, but the divorce process is what is most significant in shaping subsequent family dynamics and individual adjustment. The divorce process begins when one or both spouses begin to consider the possibility of ending the marriage. For some people, this occurs months and even years before they initiate a separation. Others may act quickly to terminate the marriage once they decide to do so.

The divorce process is almost always a substantial disruption in people's lives, and most people experience and describe it as predominately a negative experience. Fear, sadness, and anger are common feelings of both children and adults during and following separation and divorce (Hetherington & Kelly, 2002).

However, divorce does not have uniform psychological and emotional effects on either children or adults. For most adults who divorce there is an array of responses, including relief and regret, sadness and hope, despair and anger, ambivalence and anticipation. Children often are sad and miss the nonresidential parent, but other children and adults welcome separation and divorce because they offer relief from family conflicts, physical or psychological abuse, and the psychopathological behaviors of certain family members (Clingempeel & Brand-Clingempeel, 2004). Rather than assume that divorce has uniform outcomes, it is more accurate to consider that the divorce process has multiple, diverse effects on individuals, that the effects of divorce vary for different family members, and that the influence of divorce changes over time (Hetherington & Kelly, 2002).

CONNECTIONS BETWEEN MARRIAGE, DIVORCE, AND REMARRIAGE

We hypothesize that how individuals evaluate and cope with divorce is related to how they adjust to post-divorce family life, which, in turn, is related to the functioning of post-divorce stepfamilies. Adults and children who welcome divorce, or who define it as basically a good transition for them, may be more likely to view remarriage and stepfamily life as a chance for a new start, than are those who define divorce as a crisis. On the other hand, those who welcome divorce and define it as good for themselves may be quite reluctant to reenter marriage and risk the pain of starting over, especially if children are involved. However, the relation between the meaning of the divorce experience and subsequent relationships in stepfamilies has not been empirically examined.

How the divorcing partners evaluate the divorce is probably related to their perceptions of the marriage prior to separation. It is not hard to imagine marriages in which one partner may be eager to end the marriage—a physically abused spouse, those in high-conflict marriages who tire of the hostility, spouses who feel demeaned and unloved by their partners, and those whose spouses have had a history of extramarital affairs. It is also not hard to imagine partners who are reluctant to end the marriage and are shocked when their spouse seeks divorce. Such persons are likely in marriages in which the partners have drifted apart emotionally, in which only one spouse's needs are being met, and in which one partner but not the other is generally satisfied with the marital relationship. Some people may even surprise themselves with a decision to end a marriage—individuals in *passive congenial marriages* (Cuber & Harroff, 1965), stable relationships that are characterized by little mutual involvement and low levels of emotional investment, may unexpectedly find themselves involved in a passionate romantic relationship with a new partner and decide to divorce.

Research by Mavis Hetherington and her colleagues sheds some light on the relation between adjustment to divorce and remarriage and stepfamily living. Based on three panel studies of divorced adults and their children, Hetherington proposed six patterns of responses to divorce—*Enhanced, Competent Loners, Good Enoughs, Seekers, Libertines*, and *The Defeated* (Hetherington & Kelly, 2002). About 20% of the divorced adults in her studies found that their lives were Enhanced *because* of the divorce, not in spite of it. Although their marriages and the reasons for ending them differed, all of these individuals were able to increase the quality of their lives professionally, socially, and personally, and their subsequent romantic relationships, including remarriage, were better than their marriages had been. The Competent Loners comprised a smaller, but similarly capable group of divorced adults who found greater success professionally and personally after their marriages ended, but differed from the Enhanced in their desire to remarry. Hetherington did not address why these two groups differed in their remarriage behaviors, although it may be surmised that the marital experiences of the Competent Loners had soured them on the notion of marriage. The other pattern of remarriage avoidance was the Defeated. Devastated by the divorce, depressed, passive interpersonally, and barely able to function, these individuals probably lack the energy and motivation to pursue new partners and would not be especially attractive as potential partners. Many seemed to be stuck in a backward-looking pose, embittered by the divorce.

In sharp contrast, Seekers remarried quickly after divorce. As if frightened by being single, nearly 4 out of 10 divorced adults sought eagerly to find a new spouse, and many of them remarried within a year. The perceived security and regularity of married life appealed to these individuals, although from Hetherington's description it seems that they were less concerned with choosing a *good* partner for themselves than choosing *any* partner. The Libertines also pursued relationships after divorce, but these were often only sexual encounters and did not necessarily lead to remarriage. The enthusiastic pursuit of sensual experiences was relatively short-lived, however—more than 6 years after divorce many of the Libertines were in conservative and faithful remarriages. Finally, the large group of Good Enoughs consisted of people who coped fairly well, adjusted adequately to the challenges of divorce, and did their best to move on with their lives. They neither noticeably succeeded nor conspicuously failed at childrearing, jobs, and interpersonal relationships. They had problems, most of which they could solve or resolve, but not all. When they remarried, and they frequently did, their new relationships often were no better than their prior marriages, with some of the same problems.

These typologies of divorced adults are interesting to consider, and they provide an opportunity to speculate about post-divorce remarriages. However, much more needs to be known about the connections between marital dynamics, divorce, and remarital dynamics.

Initiators and Non-initiators

The divorce process may extend over months or even years, and it is not unusual for one marital partner to have begun the psychological and emotional process of divorce well in advance of the other (Price & McKenry, 1988). Few scholars have explored how divorce initiation affects subsequent relationships, although we might speculate that initiators of divorce remarry more rapidly than do spouses who do not want a divorce. Initiators adapt to divorce slightly better than non-initiators do (e.g., Price & McKenry, 1988), at least for the first few years after separation (Spanier & Thompson, 1987), and initiators more positively evaluate the benefits of divorce and alternatives to a current marriage than non-initiators do (Black, Eastwood, Sprenkle, & Smith, 1991). It is likely that unhappily married individuals are more apt to initiate divorce when they perceive that their chances to remarry are greater (White & Booth, 1991); in fact, exposure to a large number of single adults of the other sex is a predictor of marital dissolution (South & Lloyd, 1995). Some divorce initiators may already have a new partner whom they are eager to marry, which would contribute to their positive evaluation of the effects of divorce.

Using the first two waves of the National Study of Families and Households interviews, Sweeney (2002) found that initiators of divorce entered new relationships much more quickly than did non-initiators. In general, a stronger association existed between wanting a divorce and re-partnering for older women (older than 35) than for younger women, but there was no association for men's ages and re-partnering. Sweeney speculated that older women in unsatisfying marriages were more likely than younger women to delay initiating separations until they had determined that their prospects for another relationship were good. Age was less of a factor for men in re-partnering because social norms about men, women, and marriage (i.e., men marry younger partners, women marry older) tend to increase the potential pool of eligible partners for men as they age, while diminishing the pool for women.

Given the paucity of research, we can only speculate on the reasons why initiators are more likely to remarry than non-initiators. Compared to non-initiators, divorce initiators may:

- be less happy in current marriages, and thus more motivated to develop fulfilling relationships with a new partner.
- be further along in psychologically adjusting to divorce than the other partner, and consequently they may be psychologically ready to enter another relationship earlier than their former spouse (Vaughn, 1986).
- have more psychological strengths and personal resources (e.g., confidence, high self-esteem), and thus are more capable of attracting new partners.
- have personalities that draw them to change and stimulation.
- be idealistic about marriage and have unrealistically high expectations, thus becoming disenchanted and dissatisfied when their expectations are not met. Such individuals may be prone to projecting idealized qualities onto a potential new partner.
- have found a new partner before they initiate the divorce process.

Researchers have not yet investigated how initiating a prior divorce affects husbands' and wives' behavior in remarriage unions. However, it seems reasonable to propose that remarriage and stepfamily dynamics may be affected in some ways based on whether the dissolution of a previous marriage was sought or not.

CONNECTIONS BETWEEN CO-PARENTING AFTER DIVORCE AND STEPFAMILY LIVING

Over the last 15 years or so, researchers, practitioners, and policymakers have become more interested in co-parental relationships after divorce. We define co-parenting as both parents being involved in making decisions about their child's education, health care, religious training, and social activities (clubs, social organizations, sports). Co-parenting involves taking care of a child's physical, emotional, social, mental, and spiritual needs when the parent and child are together. Co-parenting does not mean that divorced parents must interact with each other in raising their child, but it does involve some level of communication between parents and some level of interaction with the child by each parent.

The increased interest by researchers is due in part to the movement within judicial systems to award parents joint or shared legal and physical custody (Mason,

Fine, & Carnochan, 2004). This judicial movement was stimulated both by judges' interpretations of social science research findings (see Bauserman, 2002, for a review of research on joint versus sole custody arrangements) and by the activism of fathers' rights groups (also known as children's rights organizations) that pushed for laws and policies that granted divorced fathers more access to their children (Mason et al., in press). Although research findings on the benefits of joint custody are equivocal and the scholarship on co-parental relationships after divorce is in its' infancy, there seems to be general agreement that co-parenting has important implications for children's and adults' well-being.

Later in this book we examine former spouse relationships more closely. In this section, we consider how co-parenting dynamics after divorce affect subsequent experiences on the pathways to remarriage and stepfamily living. The issue of co-parenting is more relevant to post-divorce stepfamilies than to stepfamilies formed by never-married parents (and, obviously, to bereaved parents) because post-divorce stepfamilies are more likely to have both biological (or adoptive) parents involved in childrearing. Never-married parents may have their own parents actively involved with helping them raise their children. Co-parenting also adds to the complexities of stepfamilies formed post-divorce, because stepparents in these situations become the third, or perhaps the fourth, adult (when both parents remarry or cohabit) involved in helping to raise children.

Little or No Co-parenting

Not every divorced couple engages in co-parenting, because some nonresidential parents, usually fathers, gradually reduce their contact with their children over time (Furstenberg & Harris, 1992; King, 1994; Seltzer, 1991), sometimes to the degree that there is no contact at all. For example, Furstenberg and Nord (1985), in a nationally representative sample, found that less than half of children aged 11 to 17 years with divorced parents had seen their fathers the previous year, and almost 40% had had no contact with their fathers in 5 years. Nonresidential fathers with low socioeconomic statuses and levels of education tend to be less involved than noncustodial fathers with higher socioeconomic statuses and education (Arditti & Bickley, 1996; Arditti & Keith, 1993; Cooksey & Craig, 1998; Furstenburg, Nord, Peterson, & Zill, 1983; Gersick, 1979; Seltzer, 1991; Seltzer & Brandreth, 1994). Black fathers are more likely to continue involvement post-divorce than other fathers (Furstenburg et al., 1983). The relation between children's ages and father involvement after divorce is not clear (Cooksey & Craig, 1998; Dudley, 1991; Seltzer, 1991).

There are many reasons why nonresidential fathers lose contact with their children after divorce. One set of reasons is rooted in fathers' pre-divorce relationships with children. Fathers who had close relationships with their children when they were living together are more likely to maintain contact with them than are fathers whose relationships were more distant (Arditti & Keith, 1993). Men who do not see fatherhood as central to their self-identity are less likely to have been active co-parents when married, and are even less likely to continue to be involved with their children after divorce (Stone & McKenry, 1998). The more that fathers feel competent as parents, the more involved they are with their children after divorce (Cooksey & Craig, 1998; Minton & Pasley, 1996). Perhaps not surprisingly, divorced fathers with substance abuse problems have less involvement with their children than do other fathers (Dudley, 1991).

Other reasons for reduced co-parenting are related to the divorcing process. Fathers are more likely to continue to be involved with their children when they feel they have more control over legal decisions (Braver & Griffin, 2000), are satisfied with the legal process (Arendell, 1995; Ihinger-Tallman, Pasley & Buehler, 1993), and when legal custody arrangements allow them to have contact (Arditti, 1992; Braver & Griffin, 2000). Dissatisfaction with the legal system and with custody arrangements are related to the quality of the co-parental relationship, specifically to the amount of conflict between mothers and fathers, which in turn is related to the amount of fathers' involvement with children (Ahrons, 1983; Dudley, 1991).

When mothers and fathers do not get along, mothers who have physical custody of children can interfere with fathers' involvement with the children by making it hard for them to get together (Arditti & Allen, 1993; Dudley, 1996; Kruk, 1992). For example, in one study about a third of the nonresidential fathers reported having been denied visitation privileges at least once by the custodial mother (Braver & Griffin, 2000). Although children generally miss their nonresidential parents, and parent-child relationships are negatively affected, mothers often report being satisfied with sole-parenting arrangements (King & Heard, 1999). It is not difficult for parents with physical custody of children to place barriers in the way of their co-parents. For example, activities can be planned when the other parent is supposed to be with the child, the residential parent can arrange to make the child difficult to locate ("I don't know where Bobby is today"), or they can make communicating with the child so much of a hassle that the nonresidential parent gets discouraged and gives up. One of the most common barriers is physical distance. Mothers often move after divorce for many reasons, such as finances and to be nearer kin—but among the reasons to move is to get farther away from hostile or abusive former spouses and to punish the ex-spouses for marital transgressions by making access to the children more difficult. Consequently, one of the best predictors of parental involvement is physical distance from the children (Arditti & Bickley, 1996; Arditti & Keith, 1993; Cooksey & Craig, 1998).

Continued conflict with former spouses can negatively influence the father-child relationship in other ways. For example, some nonresidential fathers limit their contacts with their children to avoid more conflict with their ex-wives (Arendell, 1992). For these men, losing time with their children is preferable to enduring hostile interactions with their former wives.

Others either limit or end their involvement with their children because saying goodbye to their children and dealing with the hassles of living apart from each other is too emotionally painful for themselves and, they believe, for their children (Arendell, 1992, 1995; Hetherington, Cox, & Cox, 1982; Kruk, 1992). We have talked to nonresidential fathers who have trouble figuring out how to be a "part-time father." Most of the men we have spoken with continue to remain actively a part of their children's lives, but it took some of them months or even years to develop a comfortable routine for handling the reality of children moving in and out of their homes and, from their perspectives, their lives. Some also had difficulty partitioning the animosity they felt for their ex-wife from the love they felt for their children. Those who were unable to do so dissolved their relationship with their children as well as their ex-wife.

The stepfamilies formed after co-parental relationships have dissolved, the divorced couples that Ahrons (1981) called *Dissolved Duos*, are perhaps the most likely to live as if they were reconstituted nuclear families, especially when children are young at the time of remarriage. Given the absence of a parent, it becomes easier for the stepparents in these families to adopt their stepchildren (at least compared to other post-divorce stepfamilies) and consequently, for the family to legally join the ranks of nuclear families. Role definition problems are less salient in these families because the nonresidential parent is no longer in a functioning parenting role. The stepparent in these families often tries to serve as a replacement or substitute parent, and this effort is often welcomed by stepchildren who feel abandoned by their nonresidential parent. In fact, in many states, after adoption, the birth certificate is altered; the stepparent's name is substituted for the parent's name on the child's birth certificate. It is likely that relatives of the stepparent also substitute for the extended kin of the parent with whom there is no contact.

One motivation to remarry for divorced residential mothers and fathers who do not co-parent is to have help raising the children. This may entail help with finances as well as discipline and child rearing. As we will see in later chapters, these motivations have profound implications for parent-child as well as stepparent-stepchild bonds.

Some fathers who have maintained little contact with their nonresidential children have even less contact with their children, or sever ties altogether, after their own remarriage or their ex-wife's remarriage (Arendell, 1992; Cooksey & Craig, 1998; Furstenburg et al., 1983; Hetherington & Camara, 1984; Seltzer, 1991). When nonresidential fathers remarry, it has been speculated that they withdraw from co-parenting children from prior relationships because their emotional needs are met by their new spouse and stepchildren (Stephens, 1996). There is evidence that some fathers are able to transfer/substitute their paternal feelings and behaviors (e.g., financial support) from children from prior relationships to stepchildren or to children born in new unions (Smock & Manning, 2000).

Some fathers reportedly withdraw from their children when their former wives remarry because they do not want to confuse their children (Dudley, 1991). These men believe that children cannot handle having a stepfather and a father, so they bow out, expecting the stepfather to replace them. Presumably, some of the men who think this way expect to replace their stepchildren's father if they remarry a woman with children. There are many reasons that men refuse to engage in co-parenting or withdraw from involvement over time, but these reasons and speculations about them are beyond the scope of this book.

Conflictual Co-parenting

The cultural stereotype is that divorced couples are so angry with each other that they cannot effectively co-parent, and will not do so willingly (Whiteside, 1998). In a review of 15 research reports on post-divorce co-parenting, Whiteside estimated that only a small percentage (2–5%; Johnston, 1995) truly cannot work together at all, although 20–30% of divorcing couples' interactions can be classified as reflecting high conflict. However, most divorcing couples have some conflict about raising their children; two studies reported that between 53% and 71% of parents reported differences of opinion about child rearing issues (Bowman & Ahrons, 1985; Goldsmith, 1981). Longitudinal studies suggest that disagreements between parents are highest in the first 2 years following separation but that these gradually decrease (e.g., Hetherington, Cox, & Cox, 1982) because parents figure out how to cooperate better and because, in some families, they interact less often.

Conflict between co-parents is related to negative child outcomes (i.e., Amato & Booth, 1996; Amato & Keith, 1991). This is one of the most robust findings we have about co-parenting, and in fact, some researchers attribute most of the harmful consequences of divorce on children to co-parental conflicts (Clingempeel & Brand-Clingempeel, 2004). Children with divorced parents who continue to fight with each other, particularly when the fighting is about the children, tend to experience the most difficulties emotionally, behaviorally, interpersonally, and academically (Cummings & Davies, 1994). Stepfamilies formed by adults who are engaged in angry interactions with their ex-partners over co-parenting are more likely to have children who are having problems in school, with peer groups, or intra-personally. These behaviors are often attributed to the remarriage.

It is not unusual for divorced parents to continue their bitter, resentful feelings about the past marriage as well as the divorce process. For some couples, their anger with each other is an integral part of their divorced relationship. Typically the mother has control of the children and the father has control of the money. The mother often "punishes" the father by not allowing him access to the children, and the father retaliates by withholding child support (Visher & Visher,

1996). The children get caught in the middle and tend to express ongoing loyalty conflicts. Remarriage by either ex-spouse is likely to exacerbate the other's hostility.

Loyalty conflicts on the part of the children and poor parenting communication between the ex-spouses often spill over into the stepfamily household dynamics, creating difficulty. Planning for holidays and vacations is frequently traumatic. Stepparents may feel as if individuals whom they don't like or may not even know (i.e., the ex-partner of their spouse) are controlling their lives. These difficult dynamics may contribute to the higher divorce rate among stepfamilies with children (Tzeng & Mare, 1995). Sometimes stepparents can help by serving as a neutral go-between for the children, but they also may team up with their spouse in the continuing battle with the ex-partner. Jealousies among the adults make it difficult for children to establish positive relationships with all parents (Crosbie-Burnett, 1984), and parents and stepparents vying for their children's loyalty can be very stressful for children. Their response may be to become manipulative (e.g., "If I have to be home by 10 on school nights, I'll go live with Dad." "If you don't get me a new bike, I'll bet my stepfather will.")

The most intensely hostile co-parents lose sight of their real task of raising their children and instead escalate their war with each other. These couples have almost no ability to effectively co-parent. Their anger is so intense they cannot accept each other's parenting rights. The other parent is the enemy! One or both parents may remarry to gain an ally in their war with the other parent. Every attempt is made to remove the ex-spouse from the lives of the children. These couples are still attached to each other, although they would deny it. The children are caught in the middle and often take sides with one parent or the other. Among these couples, one parent, usually the father, sees the children less and less frequently over the years. Both parents blame each other for this, and the children become pawns in the continuing battle.

It is difficult for a stepparent to enter such a volatile situation. The noncustodial parent may say damaging things to the children about the stepparent as a means of upsetting their ex-spouse. These efforts, in turn, may make it difficult for the stepparent-stepchild relationship to positively evolve. The stepparent may also come to resent the amount of emotional energy their spouse spends on maintaining the battles with the ex-spouse. In some cases, the children are told that the stepparent was the cause of the divorce—an attempt to sabotage any chance for positive stepparent-stepchild relationships.

Hostile relationships between former spouses demand a lot of time and energy and often present problems for the stepfamily (Giles-Sims, 1987). In one small-scale study, stepfamilies formed when there were ongoing hostile former spouse relationships had less cohesion, less expressiveness, and more conflict than other stepfamilies did (Giles-Sims, 1987). Although the direction of effects could not be determined from this study (i.e., did the hostile relationships with former spouses affect stepfamily interactions, or did better stepfamily functioning lead to better former spouse ties?) it is probable that stepfamily interactions were influenced more by the nature of the former spouse bonds than vice versa, since the patterns of former spouse interactions were established prior to the formation of the stepfamily. It is also possible that people who have a hard time getting along with former spouses have a hard time getting along with stepfamily members because of their personalities or interpersonal skills.

Midrange or Parallel Co-parenting

Some divorced couples evolve into a pattern of interaction in which they are *parallel parents* rather than interacting co-parents (Whiteside, 1998). These parallel co-parents avoid contact when they can, are businesslike when they do interact, and tend to have brief discussions limited to information that must be shared. These are couples who gradually reduce their conflict over time, and as anger between the former spouses diminishes they are able to interact more civilly with each other, at least most of the time. Whiteside estimated that researchers have found that about 24% of couples fell into this midrange category.

Cooperative Co-parenting

Despite cultural stereotypes to the contrary, the largest single group of divorced co-parents can be described as cooperative (Ahrons, 1994). In Whiteside's review, between 19.5% and 67% of the respondents were described by the researchers as cooperative. A small number of divorced parents continue to have mutual respect for each other as people and as parents, and they remain good friends. Often, there was a sense of mutuality about the divorce. Open, flexible, but clear boundaries are kept between the two households, and the shared parenting arrangements are of high quality. These couples often continue the rituals of the married family such as sharing holidays and birthdays together with their children and maintaining relationships with each other's extended families. They are likely to sit together at their children's ball games and school events and co-parent essentially as they did prior to the divorce. These high functioning, cooperative co-parenting relationships result in the most positive outcomes for children. (However, in an interesting twist, Amato and Booth (1996) found that children of married parents who divorced after exhibiting little or no conflict adjusted to the divorce more poorly than did children whose parents ended high-conflict marriages.) These findings suggest that children fare better after divorce if high-conflict couples learn to work together on child rearing issues after they separate.

From many perspectives, these cooperative co-parents have the best post-divorce relationships. The children do not have to contend with warring parents, and custody and child support issues are settled fairly with minimal conflict. In

Ahrons' (1980) study, post-divorce couples whom she labeled *Perfect Pals* had remained single; it was difficult for each individual to develop an independent lifestyle. In a study from the NSFH data set, divorced parents who had high contact with their children but low conflict between the parents also were less likely to be remarried than other groups of divorced parents (King & Heard, 1999).

If co-parents get along too well, then we hypothesize that a stepparent entering remarriage might feel quite threatened by the continued intimacy maintained by the divorced couple. Finding roles within the new stepfamily could be extremely difficult. The open, flexible boundaries maintained by the divorced couple that worked well when they were single, might feel like an invasion of privacy to the new spouse. The new spouse also may be less than enthusiastic about spending holidays with their spouse's previous partner and the stepchildren! Additionally, the children may resent any changes in routines and family rituals such as holiday celebrations brought about by the remarriage. Conflicts and jealousy are likely to occur between the biological parent and the stepparent (i.e., between father and stepfather or between mother and stepmother), and loyalty conflicts for the children may be quite common as well.

However, cooperative co-parent relationships may provide the most functional post-divorce path to remarriage. Cooperative co-parents who do not necessarily describe themselves as good friends, but who are able to cooperate well as parents and respect each other's parenting skills, are the most likely to make compromises for the sake of the children and not let conflicts escalate into huge power struggles (Ahrons, 1994). Giles-Sims (1988) found that positive contact between ex-spouses was associated with cohesion, expressiveness, and lack of conflict in stepfamilies. Children had frequent and regular contact with their nonresidential parent and mutual parenting was basically cooperative. In these families, the children's needs are met because the parents are able to put their differences aside for the sake of the children, yet there are clear boundaries drawn between the parent's role as co-parent and their role as ex-spouse. The ex-spousal relationship of what Ahrons called *Cooperative Colleagues* is likely not to be intrusive in subsequent remarriages. It may be, however, that some children have a more difficult time determining unique roles for stepparents when parents are so cooperative with each other. Clinicians have argued that children fantasize about their divorced parents re-uniting (Sager et al., 1983; Visher & Visher, 1988; Wald, 1981); this may be especially true when children see parents who cooperatively share resources and had satisfying co-parental relationships that are characterized by positive affect.

Regardless of the level of co-parental conflict or cooperation, it appears that divorced parents generally do not do an adequate job of communicating to their children what is happening—many children feel that family changes and transitions are not explained, which confuses them (Dunn, Davies, O'Connor, & Sturgess, 2001). "There is often a gulf between what an adult thinks has been communicated to a child and a child's need to process the information in repeated conversations through time" (p. 283). Therefore, when the children's parents divorce and enter into new relationships, and they inadequately communicate about these changes, they may find that their children are resentful. This can play out as a refusal to talk to the parent's new romantic partner or it can lead to hostile communication.

POST-BEREAVEMENT STEPFAMILIES

Older Post-bereavement Stepfamilies

Post-bereavement stepfamilies have quite different experiences from those formed after divorce. In general, post-bereavement stepfamilies formed after the death of a spouse are formed later in life. Widowed grooms in 1988 averaged 60.9 years, and widowed brides had a mean age of 53.1 (Wilson & Clarke, 1992). As widowed people get older, the likelihood they will remarry decreases; widows' chances diminish more than widowers.

Because the adults forming post-bereavement partnerships are older than the partners of post-divorce stepfamilies, their children are often adults. This reduces, but does not eliminate, the likelihood of children living with their parent and step-parent, even though the children are adults, often with partners and children of their own. They may move back in with parents after divorcing, often accompanied by their children. Older post-bereavement stepfamilies would appear to be simpler than post-divorce stepfamilies. For instance, they would be less likely to face discipline issues, problems in sharing space and possessions, disputes over household rules, and other common challenges faced by younger stepfamilies. However clinicians assert that post-bereavement stepfamilies, even if formed later in life, still encounter issues such as loyalty conflicts, feelings of loss and anger in children, and resentment of time lost with a parent (Visher & Visher, 1988). Financial issues, often related to inheritance of family wealth and treasured family heirlooms, may be even bigger issues for these stepfamilies. As longevity increases, the odds of more post-bereavement stepfamilies being formed in the future increases.

Post-bereavement Stepfamilies with Younger Children

Children serve as a deterrent for remarriage for middle-aged widowed men and women (Smith, Goslen, Byrd, & Reece, 1991). Presumably, no one has looked at this question for older widowed persons, perhaps because the assumption is that children of the elderly widowed are middle-aged adults themselves and are less likely to play a role in decisions to remarry.

For post-bereavement stepfamilies with minor-aged children, co-parental hostility does not exist, but neither are there the opportunities for sharing and the divisions of labor with the children's other parent. Custody issues, a major source of contention for some post-divorce stepfamilies, also are unlikely to be a problem for post-bereavement stepfamilies. The feelings of children torn between divorced parents who have legal custody rights and who interact with the child regularly are likely to be different from the torn loyalties children feel when one parent is deceased. For one thing, in stepfamilies formed following parental divorce children may be torn between feelings for both parents or between feelings for a nonresidential parent and the residential stepparent. Following the death of a parent, loyalty conflicts may be more likely to be experienced by a child wondering if she can be close to a stepparent and still honor the memory of a deceased parent. Clinicians advise that it is important for children to be allowed to mourn their deceased parent and to be given the freedom to define the role of their stepparent as something other than their parent's replacement (Visher & Visher, 1988). We have talked to many middle-aged adults who remain bitterly resentful of being forced as a child to refer to their stepparent as Mom or Dad. Others remained upset because the surviving parent would not allow them to talk about their deceased parent in the stepfamily household. In attempting to re-create a nuclear family, all memories of the deceased parent were essentially banned.

The levels of social support provided the head of a single-parent household may differ considerably depending on their gender and the circumstances that led to their single-parent status (Furstenberg & Cherlin, 1991; McKenry & Price, 1991). Widowed single parents are likely to receive a great deal of social support from their own kin as well as the kin of the deceased spouse (Lopata, 1979). However, divorced parents receive less support from their kin and very little, if any, support from their former in-laws.

Empirical studies provide little guidance for members of stepfamilies formed post-bereavement, and guidance from clinical and self-help literature is limited as well. Ironically, works of fiction may provide the most insight into the issues facing the members of post-bereavement stepfamilies (see Chapter 11 for a discussion of the use of fiction in bibliotherapy; Coleman & Ganong, 1988).

STEPFAMILIES FORMED BY NEVER-MARRIED PARENTS

Although they are increasingly common, little is known about stepfamilies formed when a previously unmarried parent (usually the mother) brings a child to the new relationship (Bernhardt & Goldscheider, 2001). Childbearing outside of marriage increased dramatically in the second half of the 20th century. In the past 30 years the birth rate for single women increased by 70% from 26.4 to 45.0 per 1,000 (Martin et al., 2002). Most unmarried women who bear a child are without a partner (Raley, 2001); however, the nature of nonmarital childbearing has changed over time so that increasing percentages of children born outside of marriage are born to cohabiting parents. In fact, most of the recent increase in childbearing outside of marriage is due to the increase in births to cohabitors (Bumpass & Lu, 2000).

By the mid 1990s over half of all first unions (marriages and cohabitations combined) were cohabiting unions (Bumpass & Lu, 2000). About 25% of cohabitors bring children from prior relationships to their cohabiting unions (Bumpass, Sweet & Cherlin, 1991). Although some of these were from former marriages, an unknown percentage of these children were born to unmarried mothers.

Filinson (1986) labeled stepfamilies in which a never-married parent brings a child into their new union *de facto stepfamilies*. Due to the increase in cohabitation and childbearing outside of marriage, it is no longer justified to confine the study of stepfamilies to only those constituted legally through remarriage (Bumpass & Raley, 1995; Filinson, 1986).

One of the two basic types of de facto stepfamilies is formed when an unmarried parent marries. Because these families contain a first marriage and stepparent-stepchild relationships, they fall somewhere between a first marriage family and a stepfamily. We hypothesize that most choose to emulate first marriage nuclear families and to assume that identity, particularly if the nonresidential father is not involved with the child. In fact, Filinson (1986), using data from a study of the family lives of children born outside of legal marriage in Great Britain, found that more than half of the children living in these stepfamilies were unaware that the adult male in the family was their stepfather (although the men were aware that the children were their stepchildren). Children in these families think of the stepparents as their parents and they address them as such. These families probably do not identify themselves to researchers as stepfamilies; partly because of this invisibility, information about these stepfamilies is limited.

The other category of de facto stepfamilies contains cohabitors who never marry, at least one of whom has a child from an earlier relationship. These families may or may not be categorized as stepfamilies by demographers and other researchers, depending on how questions about marital status, parental status, household membership, and family membership are asked (Bumpass & Raley, 1995). They definitely do not get included when (legal) remarriages are used to define stepfamilies.

The adults who form these de facto stepfamilies are probably less conventional than remarried stepfamilies. This is especially so for gay and lesbian cohabiting couples. Cohabiting stepfamilies likely receive less formal and informal social support and they are stigmatized more than remarried stepfamilies (Smock & Gupta, 2002). Consequently, they tend to be less stable than other types of stepfamilies (Manning, 2002). Consequently, children in these families will experience more family transitions than most other children (Manning, 2002), a point we return to later in this book.

SUMMARY

There is not a single pathway to stepfamily living. However, a number of factors have been identified that tend to push people along the stepfamily pathway. It is important to keep in mind that positive and negative life events are not randomly distributed between these pathways. For instance, the life experiences of widows and divorcées who remarry are likely to differ. Perhaps the key thing to keep in mind is that one cannot understand stepfamilies without properly considering the precursors to stepfamily living.

Unfortunately, for most of the last 25 years, few researchers have considered the importance of knowing about stepfamily members' histories. Some researchers may have ignored stepfamily members' previous family experiences because the complexity of studying stepfamilies is greatly magnified when pre-stepfamily life is considered. However, the major hindrance to considering precursors to stepfamily living has been the absence of longitudinal secondary data sets and the difficulty for individual researchers of doing their own panel studies of family transitions. There are now several longitudinal secondary data sets—these data sets have allowed researchers to assess some precursor characteristics (e.g., number of marital transitions, years single) as potential predictors of stepfamily outcomes (such as stepparent-stepchild closeness). Sometimes these precursor characteristics are statistically controlled when other variables of interest to the researchers are examined. For example, if a researcher was interested in the relation between marital conflict in remarriage and stepchildren's well-being, the researcher might statistically control for the effect of "pathway" variables such as the number of previous marriages and the number of children from prior marriages for each adult.

Even when researchers want to examine how various aspects of individuals' lives prior to the creation of the stepfamily are related to stepfamily relationships, they are hindered because many of the data sets that are available for secondary analyses do not contain adequate information for them to do so. Consequently, some researchers, recognizing the potential influence of previous family life experiences on stepfamily functioning, but lacking data sets that contain such information, try to control these unmeasured influences by limiting the types of stepfamilies in their samples (e.g., post-divorce stepfather households only). The problem with this approach is the implicit assumption that previous life experiences, such as divorce, are discrete events with uniform effects on children and adults, an assumption that has been discredited by a growing body of research (Amato, 2000; Amato & Booth, 1997; Emery, 1999). Moreover, attempts to control for previous family experiences through sampling criteria generally result in samples that are often limited to post-divorce stepfather households because they are more prevalent.

Researchers increasingly are aware of the importance of understanding pathways, and they are employing methods that allow them to assess stepfamily precursors. Although there are still many studies being done that are cross-sectional comparisons of stepfamilies to other family forms, greater awareness and the availability of longitudinal data sets have contributed to increased empirical attention to the various pathways to stepfamily life. As a result, we know more than ever before about stepfamily development, although many questions remain.

Chapter 4

Courtship in Stepfamilies

We live in an era when the term *dating* is considered old fashioned, and in fact, the concept of dating may be passé as well. However, dating, or whatever term is currently used, is a relevant concept when considering the processes by which individuals find and choose romantic partners. We use the term *courtship* to describe the general methods used by adults when seeking and selecting a mate. This chapter focuses mostly on courtship for remarriage because there is far more information about remarried couples than cohabiting couples who have children from prior relationships. When there is relevant information on cohabiting couples, either gay or heterosexual, we include it.

In Chapter 3 we looked at various precursors to stepfamily living. In this chapter, we begin by examining the demographics of who remarries and cohabits in stepfamilies. Then we examine how the courtship process in remarriage differs from that of first marriages. In order to understand couple relationships in stepfamilies, it is important to understand how courtship processes set the foundation for later couple and family dynamics.

REMARRIAGE COURTSHIP IN STEPFAMILIES

Samuel Johnson, the 18th-century English author, philosopher, and social critic, once wrote that remarriage is the triumph of hope over experience. Apparently his sage observation is still true, and hopeful people are in abundance. In the United States the majority of those who divorce remarry (Bumpass, Sweet, & Castro Martin, 1990; U.S. Bureau of the Census, 1999), some more than once, an indication that even though people may reject specific partners, they are still attracted to the cultural institution of marriage or to the *idea* of marriage. They may feel social pressure to marry as well because married people typically receive more social support and status than cohabiting individuals do.

According to a nationally representative sample of U.S. women in 1995, 75% of divorced women will remarry within 10 years (Bramlett & Mosher, 2001); 79% of white non-Hispanics, 49% of black non-Hispanics, and 68% of Hispanics. The number of remarriages following bereavement has dropped to a fraction of the number of post-divorce remarriages (Wilson & Clarke, 1992).

Another trend has been the remarkable increase in cohabitation as an alternative to remarriage. The growing interest in cohabitation may be partly due to previously married individuals' attempts to avoid legal complications associated with marriage. In particular, some divorced people may be reluctant to enter another marriage contract because of unpleasant experiences related to the dissolution of their marriages. Many people only realize that they and their partner have entered into a legal contract in which the state has a vested interest when they attempt to dissolve the contract through divorce. Because the legal process of divorce can be emotionally and financially wrenching, some persons would rather not repeat it. Widowed individuals may have had fewer unpleasant legal complications related to the ending of their marriages than divorced people, but nonetheless, legal concerns, such as children's inheritance, may lead them to cohabit as well. Finances also probably play a role in cohabitation decisions for some widows and widowers because insurance or public benefits may be lost if they remarry.

DEMOGRAPHICS OF REMARRIAGE

There is a large and growing body of demographic studies describing who remarries and who does not. Demographers generally have focused on a few predictors of remarriage—income, age, education, race, gender, and the presence of children (Ozawa & Hong, 2002; Sweeney, 1997).

Income

Women and children generally lose economically following divorce (Hackstaff, 1999). Consequently, the financial motivation to remarry is greater for women than men; per capita income of females goes down substantially after divorce and increases after remarriage, but for men the opposite pattern ensues (Day & Bahr, 1986). The remarriage rate for women who are financially secure, securely employed, and well-educated is lower than for women who are financially insecure (Oh, 1986). This suggests that economic survival may be an impetus for many women to remarry. In fact, for divorced women the most common way to escape poverty is to remarry (Folk, Graham, & Beller, 1992).

Widowhood lowers economic well-being, and remarriage substantially improves economic well-being for both men and women, although women benefit more (Zick & Smith, 1988). This would lead one to think that the widowed would seek new partners for economic stability. However, widowed people who remarry are better off financially *before* they remarry than the widowed who do not remarry (Zick & Smith, 1988). Higher levels of financial security have an insignificant effect on the likelihood of remarriage for widows and widowers (Smith et al., 1991). For widows over the age of 60, education and remarriage rates are inversely related (Smith, Zick, & Duncan, 1991), but for widowers over 60, the more education they have the greater the likelihood they will remarry.

Racial Differences

Whites are more likely to remarry than other racial groups, and blacks are the least likely to remarry (Bumpass, Sweet & Castro Martin, 1990; Bramlett & Mosher, 2001; Smock, 1990; Wilson & Clarke, 1992). Non-Hispanic black women are less likely than other women to stay in a first marriage, more likely to separate without divorcing, less likely to remarry, and less likely to remain in a remarriage (Bramlett & Mosher, 2001). In the first 10 years of remarriage, 48% of black women will have divorced, compared to 39% of white non-Hispanics, and 29% of Hispanic women (Bramlett & Mosher, 2001). The effects of other variables on remarriage probability, such as the number of children and education level, sometimes vary substantially for blacks and whites (Koo, Suchindran, & Griffith, 1984; Smock, 1990).

Blacks are less likely than whites to remarry after widowhood (Smith et al., 1991). Blacks also have longer intervals between marriages than whites, even though African-American widowed persons are younger on average than whites. It has long been believed that differences were mostly due to greater cohabitation by blacks than whites, but Bumpass and Sweet (1989) found no evidence to support higher cohabitation rates for nonwhites. This could be explained by the differences in partner availability for African-American women—it may take them longer to find a partner, if one is available.

New Partner's Marital Status

The majority (61%) of divorced men and women remarry other divorced people, 35% marry single men and women, and 4% marry widowed individuals (Wilson & Clarke, 1992). The previous marital status of the new partners of divorced persons is related to age: those under 30 are more likely to remarry single persons, those 30 to 64 are more likely to marry divorced partners, and after age 45 the proportion marrying previously divorced persons decreases and marriages to widows and widowers increase.

Gender

There are gender differences in who remarries following divorce. Men remarry more quickly and at a higher rate than women. This is true for every age group except those between the ages of 20 and 24 (Wilson & Clarke, 1992). For both middle aged and older widowed persons, men, who are less likely to outlive a spouse than women, are far more likely to remarry than women if they do (Smith et al., 1991). In general, divorced women who are older (Wilson & Clarke, 1992), who are highly educated, and who are occupationally and financially independent are less likely to remarry (Bumpass, Sweet, & Castro Martin, 1990; Oh, 1986). For men, the opposite pattern is generally true.

These gender differences in remarriage are not surprising. Jessie Bernard (1972) reported decades ago that men with little education and low incomes and well-educated women with high incomes were the least likely to marry, a phenomenon she attributed in part to the *marriage gradient norm*—men are expected to be older, taller, better educated, and more financially successful than their female partners. Although there is evidence that relationships are becoming more egalitarian, the marriage gradient norm may still be relevant in explaining gender differences in remarriage mate selection. Gender differences in remarriage rates suggest that the opportunities to remarry are not the same for women as they are for men. They also suggest that men and women have different economic, emotional, and familial motivations to remarry. Bernard (1972) pointed out that every marriage is really two marriages, his and hers, and his marriage is a lot better emotionally, physically, socially, and financially than hers. Therefore, previously married women, whether they wanted their marriage to end or not, may be less enthusiastic than men about contracting a remarriage. Women may be reluctant to give up the autonomy and personal freedom they enjoy as single adults to enter another union, particularly if they are financially secure.

Ambert (1983), in a qualitative, longitudinal study of divorced families and stepfamilies, found that the courtship behaviors of financially secure women differed from those of financially insecure women. Women with financial means exercised a higher degree of choice in the men they dated, had more opportunities for dates, met more men, and had more steady relationships than women with limited finances. Yet they were more selective about whom they dated, and they rejected relationships more often. Financially secure women also were less often exploited, manipulated, or abused by the men they dated. In general, women who had economic resources less often planned to be married in the future.

COURTSHIP DIFFERENCES BETWEEN FIRST MARRIAGES AND REMARRIAGES

Most research on courtship and mate selection has focused on young people who have never been married and do not have children (Cate & Lloyd, 1992). Although some findings about mate selection for first marriages can be generalized to remarital courtship, there are substantial differences between the two, given distinctions between adults who have been married before and those who have not. There are probably even larger differences between first-marriage courtship processes and courtship for repartnering relationships that result in cohabitation but not remarriage.

There are three primary differences between never-married adults and previously-married adults who are in the *marriage market*—age, past marital experience, and children. Of course, not every adult in a stepfamily has been married before or has children (see Chapter 3), but these are general characteristics that distinguish most remarriage courtship processes from first-marriage courtship. In addition, there are gender and racial differences in who remarries.

Age

Individuals who remarry are older, on average, than those who marry for the first time. In the United States, the mean age of divorced individuals who remarry is about 10 years older than the mean age of people who marry for the first time, and widowed individuals who remarry are, on average, more than 3 decades older than individuals in their first marriages (Clarke, 1995).

Age is a proxy variable representing several other characteristics of individuals, such as life experience, expectations for marriage and for oneself, and lifestyle choices. As people get older they bring more to courtship than do younger people; in general, they have done more, known more people, and have had a broader range of experiences. As people age their expectations for what they want in a partner may change, they have established a lifestyle, and they have clear preferences about leisure time activities, religion, and careers. In short, as adults age they generally develop a more complete sense of themselves than is true of younger adults. Consequently, they are more likely than younger, never-married people to have made some choices about their lives that should affect who they choose and perhaps even *how* they choose a mate. Some of these lifestyle choices may be helpful and some may be detrimental in making sound, compatible mate choices.

A consequence of the older age of formerly married persons seeking mates is that as people get older there are fewer eligible (i.e., single) partners. Remarriage rates decline with age for both men and women. This demographic squeeze is generally harder on women than on men, however. The male-to-female ratio increasingly favors men with each older age group because men tend to choose younger and women tend to choose older partners. Consequently, as individuals get older the pool of eligible partners for women is reduced far more than is the case for men.

Aging, and the smaller collection of eligible partners that is a consequence of aging for both genders, probably has a number of effects on remarriage courtship behavior. If adults perceive that the pool of eligible mates is small and growing smaller with each passing year, they may make hasty choices once a potential partner is found, fearful that they may not have many more chances to find a suitable marriage partner. Middle-aged and older women in particular might be susceptible to the belief that "a bird in the hand is worth two in the bush." In some ways the psychological advantages of aging, such as knowing oneself better, may be offset by the restricted choice of partners.

Marital Experience

An obvious difference between remarriage courtship and first-marriage courtship is that those who are seeking a remarital partner have been through the courtship process at least once and have had the experience of establishing a household with someone else. This firsthand knowledge and marital experience may very well have an impact on how they look for future partners and/or what partner characteristics they seek.

The *training ground perspective* of remarriage holds that first marriages serve as a learning experience that influences the type of person chosen for subsequent marriages. Previously married individuals potentially have learned through experience what they want and do not want from marriage. Presumably some people seek a partner who is quite different from their previous mate, particularly if they believed characteristics of the former partner contributed to marital problems. Other individuals may believe that they understand themselves better as a result of the previous marriage and thus seek mates who are compatible with their true selves. Individuals who were satisfied with their prior relationships and did not want them to end might seek someone as much like their prior partners as they can find. Regardless of the lessons learned from prior marriages, the courtship of previously married persons is likely to be different from the courtship of those without prior marriage experience.

Children

A substantial difference between remarriage courtship and the courtship of most young, never-married persons may be the presence of children from prior relationships. Parents, particularly those whose children reside with them, probably have less time to spend in courtship-related activities, such as dating. This may be one reason why divorced men, who usually do not have physical custody of their children, remarry more quickly and at a higher rate than divorced women with children (Wilson & Clarke, 1992). They may be so busy earning a living and raising children that courtship behaviors are low priorities for them. Parents also may have different criteria for future partners than childless persons do. For example, they may be seeking someone who they believe would be a good co-parent as well as a romantic partner. Mothers may seek someone who can help provide financial stability and economic advantages for their children.

The presence of children from prior relationships as a predictor of lower remarriage probability, especially for women, has been a robust finding over several decades (e.g., Becker, Landis, & Michael, 1977; Buckle, Gallup, & Rodd, 1996; Bumpass, Sweet, & Castro Martin, 1990; Furstenberg & Spanier, 1984; Wu, 1994). Several researchers have explained these findings using a *social exchange* model of mate selection (e.g., Becker et al., 1977; Wu, 1994). Social exchange theory postulates that children represent costs to prospective partners that may make them decide not to marry a person with children. (It should be noted that exchange models of remarriage probability include other costs and barriers besides children, as well as benefits and rewards.) Another way of looking at the costs of children in courtship comes from evolutionary social scientists. They view marriages as reproductive contracts, in that men and women seek mates who will produce healthy children with them (Buckle et al., 1996). From this perspective, children from earlier relationships decrease the likelihood of remarriage for women because, although the children demonstrate women's fertility, men would be reluctant to invest their resources in someone else's child (we discuss this issue further in Chapter 7). From an evolutionary perspective, men's parental status should not be as important to their likelihood of remarriage because their reproductive lifespan is longer than women's, men tend to choose younger women as spouses, and men are more likely to acquire more resources as they age, increasing their *reproductive fitness*.

Another reason why mothers remarry less frequently than childless women is because some children actively discourage their mothers from remarrying, at least until they are out of the home. For example, we once interviewed an extremely large young man, a university football player, who told us that he made a point when he was in high school of greeting his mother's dates at the door in a manner carefully calculated to physically intimidate the men and scare them away. Another young woman recounted to us how, at age 7, she told her mother's suitor that "Nobody sleeps with my Mama except me!" Both of these young adults were successful in keeping their single mothers to themselves.

Although it is clear that children generally lower the likelihood of remarriage, the fact that many parents find new spouses or cohabiting partners means that children are not always a deterrent to finding a new partner (Koo & Suchindran, 1980). It could be that the benefits to remarriage or repartnering with a parent outweigh the costs of stepchildren, but it is also possible that children represent benefits to some prospective partners; gaining an instant family is appealing to some childfree men and women. Having children also may increase some individuals' motivations to find a partner, thus accelerating their search behaviors (Schmiege, Richards, & Zvonkovic, 2001). Motivated parents may get help from their children—some children welcome replacements for an absent parent (i.e., a divorced father who no longer keeps in touch). Other than demographic studies, researchers have seldom examined how children fit into the courtship process. Clinicians generally suggest that single parents include their children in the later stages of the courtship process, after parents and prospective partners have become serious about their relationship (Visher & Visher, 1996). The assumption is that this facilitates bonding between children and their future stepparent, but group dates that include a single parent and his or her children with a prospective stepparent do not automatically lead to close emotional bonds between stepparents and stepchildren (Ganong, Coleman, Fine, & Martin, 1999). However, there is more theorizing and speculation about courtship behaviors of people with children than there is information about them. Much of what we know about including or not including children in courtship is anecdotal.

REMARRIAGE COURTSHIP BEHAVIORS

We know several things about remarriage courtship—previously married individuals court for brief periods of time, they do little to prepare for remarriage, they tend to live together before marriage, and their reasons for marriage are apt to be pragmatic (Ganong & Coleman, 1989). We also know that there are gender differences in remarriage courtship behaviors, and we know that remarriers are more likely than individuals in first marriages to wed someone who is not similar to them (e.g., different religions, age discrepancies, racial differences). What follows is a brief overview of what is known, and not yet known, about remarriage courtship behavior.

Length of Courtship

Most studies indicate that the time between marriages is generally short. On average, both men and women remarry within 4 years of their divorce; as people get older the interval between marriages increases (Wilson & Clarke, 1992). The likelihood and time between marriages for divorced women varies by race—for divorced women in general the probability of remarriage within 5 years was 54%–58% for white women, 44% for Hispanic women, and 32% for black women (NCHS, 2001). About three-fourths of women remarry within 10 years of divorce—79% of white women, 44% of Hispanic women, and 32% of black women (Bramlett & Mosher, 2001).

Research data on the length of time between relationships should only be considered as estimates, particularly for individuals who remarry following divorce. Most calculations are based on the period between the legal divorce decree and legal remarriage. However, many people begin dating and cohabiting before they are legally divorced, and a majority of couples live together prior to remarriage (Montgomery, Anderson, Hetherington, & Clingempeel, 1992), so the time between residing with romantic partners is less than most studies indicate.

The evidence suggests that courtship for subsequent relationships (including remarriages) is generally quite short (Kim & McKenry, 2000). For example, O'Flaherty and Eells (1988) found that a sample of remarried Catholics courted a median of 9 months, which is nearly half the time they spent courting in their first marriages. In the Virginia Longitudinal Study of Divorce and Remarriage, 80% of the remarried women dated their future spouse for one year or less before cohabiting, and for over a third of the women the period of courting was 3 months or less (Montgomery et al., 1992).

For older people (over 60) the interval between remarriage and divorce or bereavement is longer than for younger people, but their interval between courtship and remarriage is generally brief. Vinick (1978) found that more than half of the 24 older remarried couples she interviewed married within a year of starting their relationships. The mean interval between marriages for widowed men is similar to divorced men, except after age 35, when widowers actually remarry more rapidly than divorced men. Widowed women wait a longer period of time between marriages than widowed men or divorced men and women (Wilson & Clarke, 1992). In general, if those who are relatively older at divorce are going to remarry or cohabit at all, they do it sooner rather than later (Lampard & Peggs, 1996). Women who do not feel they have completed their childbearing histories are more likely to remarry than those who do not desire more children or are past the age (Lampard & Peggs, 1996).

Does the length of courtship have an effect on subsequent family relationships? Rodgers and Conrad (1986) hypothesized that shorter time periods between divorce and remarriage would enhance stepfamily relationships. They reasoned that remarriages are less disruptive if post-divorce families do not have time to develop new patterns of interaction and new family rituals. Once parents and children have adapted to new patterns of interaction following divorce, they argued that remarriage becomes another disruption to which children and adults must adjust. Of course, it is equally plausible to hypothesize the opposite—that multiple family transitions (divorce-remarriage) occurring rapidly would be detrimental to family relationships. This hypothesis could be based on the notion that because there suddenly are new people and many changes in routines with multiple transitions that there would be a pileup of stressors that could overwhelm the coping capacities of adults and their children (Crosbie-Burnett, 1984). However, in the only study in which this relation was examined the length of courtship had no connection to stepfamily relationships (Montgomery et al., 1992). Future researchers who examine the relation between length of courtship and subsequent stepfamily relationships should also include information about children's ages, the type of stepfamily household (i.e., stepmother, stepfather, complex), and the quality of relationships that parents and children have with nonresidential parents/former spouses.

Previously married individuals appear to make relatively quick decisions about future partners. It's unknown whether this is because they have a clear idea of what they want in a relationship and when they find a person with the qualities they seek they move with haste or whether, because opportunities are few, they settle quickly when *any* potential partner appears. Ambert (1989), in a longitudinal study, found that multiply-divorced persons remarried much more quickly, and after a shorter acquaintance, than once-divorced individuals. She concluded that getting married *per se* was important to the multiply-divorced, whereas getting married to the *right* partner was the goal of the once-divorced. Although hasty remarriages have more often than not been viewed as problematic, data from the British General Household Survey showed that longer rather than shorter duration between divorce and remarriage was linked to redivorce (Lampard & Peggs, 1996).

Preparation for Remarriage

Given the relatively short courting periods, it is not surprising that remarried couples do little to prepare for remarriage (Ganong & Coleman, 1989). Less than 25% of the 105 stepfamilies in one of our studies, sought remarriage counseling, attended support groups or educational offerings designed to prepare people for life in stepfamilies, or discussed their pending remarriage with friends. Less than half read self-help books and magazine articles about remarriage and stepparenting (Ganong & Coleman, 1989). Other researchers have found a similar lack of preparation in remarried couples (Hanna & Knaub, 1984), and clinicians have reported the difficulty of getting stepparents and their spouses to attend workshops and educational programs, both before and after remarriage (Hughes & Schroeder, 1997).

The lack of purposeful planning for remarriage is puzzling, particularly in light of the generally pessimistic cultural images held regarding stepfamily relationships. It would seem that adults entering a remarriage would make extra efforts to prepare themselves. Why do they not? There probably are several reasons.

1. The Avoidance Hypothesis

The beliefs, *if it ain't broken, don't fix it*, and *leave well enough alone*, are pervasive perspectives that discourage couples from working to prevent problems or to resolve small problems before they become crises. Individuals who have been married before may not think they need to prepare, particularly if there are no obvious difficulties on the horizon and/or if they attribute problems in previous marriages to the former partner. We think this hypothesis may be the best explanation for the lack of preparation for remarriage. Most remarrying adults are divorced, and they often feel odd about this status. For some white middle-class Americans in particular, being divorced is their first experience of being in a stigmatized group. They are often sad at the loss of their dream family life, and they may feel like they have failed at one of life's most important tasks, but, even for those who sought the ending of an unhappy marriage, they long to be married again and to feel "normal." Remarriage is a solution to some or most of their problems, they believe. Consequently, they do not want to borrow trouble by looking too carefully at their decision to remarry nor do they want to dig too deeply into stepfamily problems that, from their perspectives, do not exist and may not ever exist. We have known clergy, counselors, educators, and lawyers who regularly work with troubled divorced and remarried individuals who have, nonetheless, swiftly moved into remarriages and stepfamilies in their own lives allowing minimal time for preparation. One attorney of our acquaintance, a noted expert on family law, sheepishly admitted to us that he did not have a prenuptial agreement when he remarried even though he advises all of his remarrying clients to do so!

2. The Naiveté Hypothesis

Too often couples planning to form stepfamilies simply are naive about what to expect and so they feel that there is little need, or at least they do not recognize the need for preparation. In our study, the majority of adults had unrealistically positive expectations for remarriage and step-relationships, suggesting that they viewed formal preparation as unnecessary.

3. Various Myths

Emily and John Visher (1988) and other stepfamily clinicians (Browning, 1994; McGoldrick & Carter, 1999) have long discussed the myths that newly remarried individuals hold when they begin stepfamily lives together. For instance, belief in the myth of *instant love* between stepparents and stepchildren encourages remarrying adults to ignore the necessity of preparing children for a new stepparent. In general, myths encourage people to ignore the need to carefully prepare for remarriage and stepfamily living.

For instance, Janine Bernard (1981) identified what she called *Marriage and Divorce Myths*. We later elaborated on them by adding *Remarriage Myths* (Coleman & Ganong, 1985). These myths are shown in Table 4.1. Not all of the remarriage myths affect preparation for remarriage, but several do. For instance, "Things must work out" and "Keep criticism to oneself and focus on the positive" are beliefs that foster pseudomutuality, which is the tendency to deny history, felt ambivalence, and conflict (Sager et al., 1983). Couples whose goal is to avoid another marital failure at all costs adhere to the first myth tenaciously. Few would fault a couple hoping that their marriage will work, but when intense fear of failure interferes with direct, open communication and a willingness to discuss problems, then problems that might have been resolved prior to remarriage are left to fester and cause more trouble later (Visher & Visher, 1996).

The remarriage myth that "Marriage makes people significantly happier" is a product of a phenomenon that might be called *romantic blindness*. In Western cultures marriages are thought to be inherently able to make people happier and healthier than they were as single persons (Holland & Eisenhart, 1990). Couples who believe that remarriage will cause them to live happily ever after are blind to the need to discuss potential problems and to plan for a future that may fall short of a fairy tale. Couples planning to remarry, caught up in the bliss of a romantic love relationship, may be oblivious to anything but their own joy and excitement, a form of tunnel vision that prevents them from seeing potential problems that could be avoided by pre-remarriage planning (Kaslow, 2000).

The myths that "What is best for us is best for the children" and "Having a real family again is best for everyone" deny that children will have to make difficult adjustments and may experience stress when a parent remarries. These myths encourage adults to confuse their own joy and pleasant anticipation regarding the addition of a new partner with the children's reactions to the acquisition of a new stepparent. There are probably other remarriage myths as well; the relevant point here is that unrealistic expectations often lead to a lack of remarriage preparation.

4. Lack of Available Resources

Another reason why people do not prepare is because there may be an absence of well-qualified assistance for remarriage and stepfamily preparation. Stepfamily self-help groups may not be available, couples may not have access to counselors and clergy who are trained in understanding the dynamics of stepfamily life, and helpful reading materials may not be accessible. In a graduate course that we teach, students are assigned to locate resources in our community for a hypothetical couple that is planning to remarry. Considering that we live in a university town with a highly educated population and that our graduate students are far more adept than most adults are at finding information on the Web and in libraries, we are always surprised, as are the students, at how difficult it is for them to locate reading

Table 4.1. Marriage, Divorce, and Remarriage Myths

Marriage Myths	Divorce Myths	Remarriage Myths
Things will work out if we love each other.	Because we don't love each other anymore, nothing will work out.	Things must work out.
Always consider the other person first.	Always consider oneself first.	Always consider everybody first.
Keep criticism to oneself and focus on the positive.	Criticize everything; focus on the negative.	Keep criticism to oneself and focus on the positive.
If things aren't going well, focus on the future.	If things aren't going well, focus on the past.	If things aren't going well, focus on what went wrong in the past and make sure it doesn't happen again.
See oneself as part of a couple first, as an individual second.	See yourself as an individual first, as part of a couple second.	See yourself as part of a couple first, as an individual second./See yourself as an individual first, as part of a couple second.
What is mine is yours. What is yours is mine.	What is mine is mine.	What is yours is yours.
Marriage makes people significantly happier. What is best for the children will be best for us.	Divorce makes people significantly unhappy. What is best for us must be devastating for the children.	Remarriage makes people happier. What is best for us is best for the children./Having a "real" family again is best for everyone.

materials and Web sites of known validity and therapists who profess expertise in stepfamilies. Even though there are an increasing number of remarriage preparation programs that are offered by religious organizations and public agencies (Hughes & Schroeder, 1997), we suspect that even when adults want to educate and prepare themselves before they get remarried, they find it difficult to do so.

Whatever the reason for this, the lack of preparation for remarriage is unfortunate because clinicians assert that the majority of problems confronting stepfamilies, apart from individual problems such as alcoholism and personality disorders, are preventable (Browning, 1994; Visher & Visher, 1988). For some couples at least, these preventable problems are hard to avoid on their own. Obviously, couples planning to remarry communicate with each other as part of their courtship, but their conversations may not cover pertinent issues. For example, in our study only about half of the adults discussed issues related to raising children from prior relationships, less than 25% discussed finances, and no other topic was discussed by more than 15% of the couples (Ganong & Coleman, 1989).

5. Cohabiting

Apparently, the primary way that people prepare for remarriage is to live together prior to legally remarrying. Although this preparation method may have intuitive appeal as a good way to assess compatibility, there is little evidence that it is effective. In a study that we conducted, couples who had cohabited did not discuss stepfamily issues any more frequently than those who had not cohabited. Cohabitation is related to marital instability (Brown & Booth, 1996; Seltzer, 2004), so cohabiting before remarriage does not necessarily seem to be an effective preparation strategy.

Cohabitation, in addition to serving as a way of assessing compatibility and getting to know one another via daily interaction, also could be more comfortable than dating for previously married adults. Their social scripts for dating may be outdated, and they may feel foolish, nervous, or uncertain about what to do. For many, their previous dating experiences preceded concerns about STDs and AIDS, and their sexual experiences may have been quite limited, especially if they married at a young age. The social norms for dating are generally aimed at young, never-married childless individuals. Although a number of self-help organizations and entrepreneurial dating services have attempted to make dating easier for middle aged and older adults, formerly married persons, especially those who had been married for many years, may be more comfortable setting up housekeeping with a partner than dating. Combining two households is seldom easy, but for some it may be a more familiar and simpler alternative to contending with the ambiguities of dating.

What is the process of cohabiting? Montgomery and colleagues (1992) reported that some remarried mothers in their study *partially cohabited* for a period of weeks or months before fully merging households. This meant that the prospective male partner spent a few days and nights per week in the mother's household for a time before he moved in and resided with his future wife and stepchildren on a full-time basis. Aside from this study, little is known about the process of cohabitation prior to remarriage. Given the pervasiveness of cohabiting as a prelude to legal remarriage, it is surprising that so little is known about the process by which couples decide to live together, how children are informed, and what effects there are on the entire stepfamily system.

Reasons to Remarry

Previously-married individuals often have more pragmatic than romantic motivations to marry than do people who have never been married before (Ganong & Coleman, 1989; Schmiege et al., 2001; Vinick, 1978). Among the pragmatic reasons for remarriage are: Financial security, help in raising children, response to social pressure, response to legal threats regarding the custody of children, relief from loneliness, the need for a regular sexual partner, pregnancy, the need to have someone to take care of them, and convenience. These practical reasons help explain the short courtships of some remarried couples, as well as the tendency for them to cohabit prior to remarriage. Certainly, remarried individuals do not choose a partner solely for practical reasons—love, a desire for companionship, shared interests, and liking the partner are also common reasons why people remarry.

Courtship for Stepfamily Cohabitation and Courtship by Gays and Lesbians in Stepfamilies

We intended to have sections in this chapter on the courtship processes of cohabiting couples with children from prior unions and courtship among gays and lesbians forming stepfamilies. However, we could not find research about this topic for either group.

SUMMARY

Most clinicians argue that the early stages of stepfamily relationships are critical periods for the development of stable and satisfying stepfamilies (see Chapter 11). In short, according to leading clinicians, a good start to the creation of a stepfamily can pay enormous long-term dividends for stepfamily members and their relationships (e.g., Burt & Burt, 1996; Visher & Visher, 1996). Unfortunately, most researchers start studying stepfamily dynamics after a household has been created, which means that courtship processes have been relatively neglected by researchers.

We do know, however, that children are key figures in courtship for remarriage, either hindering or helping their parents' opportunities for developing new romantic relationships. We also know that courtship periods are quite short for most remarrying individuals and we know that people do little to prepare for remarriage once a partner has been found, except to live together.

The catalog of what we would like to know about courtship dynamics would include many phenomena, including how children are introduced to new potential partners, how children are involved in courtship, what couples discuss as they make decisions about their relationships, and the influences that former spouses/partners may have on courtship dynamics. We also would like to know more about the courtship processes of under-investigated groups, such as gay and lesbian parents, couples who cohabit and who have no intention to marry, older adults, African American and Hispanic parents, and single parents in rural areas. Gender differences in courtship dynamics are also of interest. Finally, we would like to see research done on children's perceptions of their parents' courtship. The beginning of stepfamily life starts with courtship—more attention must be paid to the foundation of stepfamily relationships.

Chapter **5**

Couple Dynamics in Stepfamilies

The adult couple relationship, whether it is a remarriage or a cohabiting relationship between heterosexual or homosexual partners, is an important one in stepfamilies. After all, most stepfamilies are created because two adults decide to live together or to get married, so it is logical to expect that the couple will be a critical element of most stepfamilies.

In this chapter we examine the relationship dynamics between the adult partners in stepfamilies. We begin by examining what is known about establishing a strong couple bond in remarriage. We then examine various dimensions of couple dynamics (e.g., communication and conflict, decision-making power, division of labor, financial management, childbearing) and the effects of remarrying and re-partnering on the well-being of adults. Various explanations for the quality and stability of remarriages are then reviewed, followed by an assessment of the challenges of remarriages and re-partnering in later life. Finally, we examine studies that compare cohabiting re-partnerships with remarriages.

BUILDING A COUPLE BOND

Clinicians often identify a strong couple bond as one of the primary requisites for having a successful stepfamily, the rationale being that a strong bond between adult partners is helpful in facilitating the development of positive stepparent-stepchild relationships, and having a solid, unified couple relationship serves as a buffer when other family relationships are stressful (Burt & Burt, 1996; Papernow, 1993; Visher & Visher, 1996). In traditional family systems theory, which is still popular with many marriage and family therapists, the married couple is considered to be the foundation upon which any family is built (Browning, 1994). Although this position has been challenged by stepfamily researchers (Bray, Berger, Silverblatt, & Hollier, 1987; Clingempeel & Segal, 1986) and clinicians (Browning, 1994; Crosbie-Burnett, 1984; Mills, 1984) who think that the pivotal relationship in stepfamilies is the stepparent-stepchild relationship, there is consensus that adult couple relationships in stepfamilies are extremely important for the well-being of everyone in the family and the stepfamily as a whole (Papernow, 1993; Visher & Visher, 1988).

Couple bonding in stepfamilies is different than in first marriage families because remarrying couples must concurrently develop relationships with new stepchildren and new extended kin as well as maintain ties with their children's other parent and perhaps nonresidential children. Multiple relationships are difficult for some people to handle. The couple relationship may be neglected because other relationships demand more attention. Moreover, the presence of children means that adult couples have an audience of interested and powerful third parties all or most of the time. Consequently, couple relationships are developed and maintained in the presence of third parties who may be interested in dissolving those bonds.

For example, in some stepfamilies, it may be hard for couples to establish boundaries around the remarriage relationship in a way that excludes children (Coleman & Ganong, 1995; Pasley, 1987), particularly if children had been involved in activities prior to the arrival of the parent's new partner that generally are considered to be within the purview of the marital dyad.

For example, clinicians (Visher & Visher, 1996) and researchers (Weaver & Coleman, in review) observe that in single-parent households sometimes a child becomes the parent's confidant. Children enjoy their elevated status as mom's best friend (Visher & Visher, 1996). Older children in a single-parent household are sometimes allowed or even encouraged to discipline and supervise younger children. In essence, single parents sometimes promote a child or children to fulfill some of the functions of the nonresidential or absent parent. When this is the case, children may see a new stepparent as a competitor who has caused them to be demoted back to the status of child. Children may resent this demotion, even when they feel relief from the burdens of overseeing younger children and being responsible for mom or dad's emotional stability, making it difficult for the adult couple to establish the legitimacy of the new partner in the minds of the children (Visher & Visher 1996). When children are jealous of the new stepparent, they may attempt to sabotage the new marriage in their efforts to restore themselves to their previous status.

Former partners can also be intrusive and disruptive to couples' relationship maintenance efforts, and when they are actively co-parenting they can also make it difficult to establish boundaries around the remarriage (Roberts & Price, 1991; Weston & Macklin, 1990). Remarried persons who share parenting tasks with former partners have to figure out how to maintain a working relationship as co-parents, yet not let the former spouse intrude on the remarriage (Crosbie-Burnett, 1989). This may be difficult for some individuals because in first-marriage families, the married couple usually fulfills both parental tasks and marital tasks. In remarriages, the couple fulfills marital tasks but parental tasks may continue to be split between the children's parents (i.e., the residential parent and the children's nonresidential parent), or shared between the children's parents and the stepparent(s). Over time, especially when children are young, stepparents eventually do a large share of the childrearing in many stepfamilies, so there is not a clear-cut boundary between the marital and parental subsystems in all stepfamilies, but initially there usually is.

Unfortunately, few researchers have examined the processes by which adults in stepfamilies build a strong couple bond. In a qualitative study of the dialectics of remarriages, Cissna, Cox, and Bochner (1990) reported that remarried adults saw themselves as engaging in two interactive, simultaneously occurring tasks associated with relationship development in newly formed stepfamilies. The first task was for the remarried couple to establish the solidarity of the marriage in the minds of the stepchildren. The couple tried to do this in two ways: (1) by telling the children that the marriage was the most important relationship to them, and (2) by spending time together as a couple planning how to present a unified front to the children. The second task these adults saw was to establish the credibility of the stepparent as a parental authority. The adults felt that in order to achieve this both the parent and the child had to develop trust in the stepparent's ability to act like a parent, to discipline wisely and fairly, and to establish a warm emotional bond with the child. In a study by Kvanli and Jennings (1986), 10 remarried couples reported that learning to trust the new partner, accepting differences, and learning how to resolve conflicts were among the most important marital tasks they had encountered. Part of the difficulty in achieving these tasks may be due to issues of boundary ambiguity.

In family systems theory, part of the task of building a couple bond is conceptualized as establishing a *boundary* around the marital dyad (Browning, 1994). The concept of boundaries refers to system or subsystem *rules* that define who is in a specific relationship and that specify the tasks and functions that will be performed within that relationship. Ambiguous and unclear boundaries are thought to be related to increased stress for family members and to problems in relationship functioning in first-marriage families (Boss, 1980). It is likely that former partners continue to have a psychological presence in the stepfamily household, which can affect couple dynamics. In addition, internal family boundaries between subsystems may be ambiguous as well, particularly if single parents have elevated a child to a higher status position as their confidant and close friend. It may be stressful and challenging for the adult couple to discern where the new couple boundaries are; it may even be challenging to establish new boundaries in the face of what might be ambiguity and ambivalence (Weaver & Coleman, in review).

Clearly, more studies are needed of the process of building satisfying remarriages. In particular, the effectiveness of couples' strategies to build close relational bonds need to be assessed. Given the theoretical and pragmatic importance of the adult couple relationship in stepfamilies, the lack of attention by researchers on bonding processes represents a major gap in understanding stepfamily development.

MAINTAINING A COUPLE BOND

In this section we review what is known about what couples do to maintain their remarriages. By maintenance we mean what remarried partners do to achieve a more satisfying marriage, to maintain its stability, or to improve the remarriage after it has deteriorated (Ganong, Coleman, & Weaver, 2001). Generally, researchers have tended to look at specific aspects of remarriage relationships, rather than focusing on general maintenance behaviors.

COMMUNICATION AND CONFLICT MANAGEMENT IN REMARRIAGES

Clinicians have long identified communication problems as an area of concern in remarriages (e.g., Visher & Visher, 1996). However, their focus has been on communicating during the early months and years of remarriage. Few researchers have studied marital communication in remarriages at all, although in recent years researchers have shown more interest in studying stepfamily communication as a whole (Braithwaite et al., 2001; Golish, 2000; Golish & Caughlin, 2002). Several of the studies in which marital communication in stepfamilies was examined focused less on the communication dynamics between partners and more on how remarital conflict affected children (Coleman & Ganong, 1987; Hanson, McLanahan, & Thomson, 1996; MacDonald & DeMaris, 1995).

Some family scholars have argued that remarried individuals have poorer communication skills than do individuals in first marriages (Farrell & Markman, 1986). For example, remarried couples have been found to possess poorer conflict resolution and problem-solving skills and to be more coercive toward each other than couples in first marriages (Bray et al., 1987; Larson & Allgood, 1987). Remarried couples also were found to agree less often about marital issues and were less accurate in perceptions of each other's values and beliefs about marital issues than first-marriage couples (Farrell & Markman, 1986). Farrell and Markman speculated that remarried individuals lack communication skills because they have low self-esteem, fear conflict and avoid it, and because they choose partners to fulfill immediate needs (i.e., financial needs for women, loneliness for men) without regard for the partners' communication skills. They also speculated that remarried partners are more interested in the direct, instrumental rewards they receive from marriage (i.e., tangible things the spouse does for them) than in indirect, expressive rewards (i.e., feeling loved and valued by the spouse). It is hard to know whether or not these arguments are true, but developing effective patterns of negotiating disagreements and expressing one's needs, likes, and dislikes is probably easier for first married couples who do not have interested parties witnessing these efforts (such as children from prior relationships) than for stepfamily couples.

However, not all researchers have found remarried couples to be more deficient communicators than first-marriage couples. Anderson and White (1986), using a revealed differences technique, found that functional stepfamilies were more able to reach agreement than were dysfunctional stepfamilies, functional nuclear families, or dysfunctional nuclear families. In another study, remarried couples, whether in therapy for a child-focused problem or not, reported better communication and problem-solving skills than the normative sample on ENRICH, a measure of marital dynamics (Brown, Green, & Druckman, 1990).

Although clinicians have expressed concern that remarried individuals are prone to avoid conflict unnecessarily, there is not much empirical evidence to support this. If anything, the evidence points to greater marital conflict in remarriages than in first marriages (Hobart, 1991), and as much willingness to confront marital problems by remarried individuals as by first married individuals (Allen, Baucom, Burnett, Epstein, & Rankin-Esquer, 2001). Of course, it may be that remarried couples do try to avoid and deny disagreements that might lead to conflicts, as clinicians have suggested, but then "blow up" when problems do not get resolved or when strategies for avoiding and denying problems fail.

The primary topics that remarried couples argue about are issues related to children from prior relationships (e.g., rules for children's behavior, discipline techniques; Stanley, Markman, & Whitton, 2002) and financial issues (Coleman, Ganong, & Weaver, 2001; Hobart, 1991). Other sources of conflicts for remarried couples include strife over resources, loyalty conflicts, and disputes with (and about) extended family members and former spouses (Coleman et al., 2001). Most disagreements are manifestations of the underlying issues regarding negotiating boundaries around and within stepfamilies (Coleman et al., 2001).

Some stepfamily researchers assume that disharmony is inevitable in remarriages and that it is destructive to individuals and to relationships. In contrast to this view, although conflict theorists agree that disputes and competition are inevitable, they see conflict as natural, normal, functional, and necessary to the survival of social systems (Farrington & Chertok, 1993). Contemporary conflict theorists view disharmony as arising from a range of sources. Common sources of conflict in all social systems are inequality and access to resources (Sprey, 1979). Conflict theorists generally see power as based on control of resources; scarce resources in families include time, attention, affection, money, and space (Winton,

1995). We believe that conflict theory has promise in furthering our understanding of stepfamily disharmony because it focuses on the normative nature of conflict and directs attention to the ways in which conflict is resolved. Although some stepfamilies may have high levels of conflict (Visher & Visher, 1982), there are many ways in which this conflict, if resolved, can be functional. One area has to do with remarried couples' negotiations and communications surrounding marital power and control of resources.

POWER AND EQUITY IN REMARRIAGE RELATIONSHIPS

Decision-making

Although not all researchers comparing individuals from first marriages and remarriages have reported differences between them in marital decision-making (Allen et al., 2001; Kurdek, 1990), several have found that remarried individuals perceived that decision-making was now shared more equally than in their first marriage (e.g., Coleman & Ganong, 1989; Crosbie-Burnett & Giles-Sims, 1991; Furstenberg & Spanier, 1984; Pyke, 1994). It should be mentioned that shared power and decision-making is a characteristic that likely holds for homosexual stepfamily couples as well (Koepke, Hare, & Moran, 1992), considering that homosexual couples in general, and lesbian couples in particular, value egalitarian relationships (Kurdek, 2004). However, one area of family life that often is not equitably shared is decision-making about children from prior relationships (see Chapters 6 and 7 for further discussion of this point).

A number of possible reasons have been offered to explain why the distribution of power in remarriage may be more equitable than in individuals' first marriages. The leading argument is that personal experiences in prior unions and as divorced single persons cause some women to seek more power and some men to relinquish power in remarriages (Burgoyne & Morison, 1997; Coleman & Ganong, 1989; Furstenberg & Spanier, 1984; Hobart, 1991; Pyke & Coltrane, 1996; Pyke, 1994). In other words, previously married men and women think differently about marital roles as a result of earlier experiences, which seems to lead them to interact with new partners in more egalitarian ways (Burgoyne & Morison, 1997; Ishii-Kuntz & Coltrane, 1992), or at least they perceive that they are more egalitarian. Some women sought greater involvement in decision-making in their remarriages than they had experienced in their first marriages because they had learned to make decisions as single mothers and were unwilling to give up decision-making roles when they remarried (Furstenberg & Spanier, 1984). Mothers may be especially unwilling to relinquish decision-making over their children because they enjoy child rearing, consider themselves to be good parents, and they neither need nor want parenting help from their partners (Bray & Kelly, 1998).

Women's reluctance to relinquish child rearing decision-making could be due to the *ideology of motherhood* (Williams, 2000). According to the motherhood ideology (see Chapter 6), women feel they should be responsible for decision-making regarding their child as well as the child's care—if this is not the case a woman judges herself, and others judge her, to be a bad mother.

Other women sought egalitarian relationships because they believed their lack of decision-making power was a major problem in their first marriages and they did not want to repeat it (cf. Burgoyne & Morison, 1997; Coleman & Ganong, 1989; Pyke, 1994). Men similarly sought more egalitarian remarriages if they thought marital power imbalances contributed to problems in their first marriages (Pyke & Coltrane, 1996).

Another popular perspective is that women have more bargaining and decision- making power in remarriages because they bring greater resources (such as money, skills, a household) to their remarriages (Giles-Sims & Crosbie-Burnett, 1989). Giles-Sims (1987), using normative-resource theory, a corollary of exchange theory, speculated that ideology and resources are factors that help determine post-remarriage marital power relations. Remarried couples may hold less traditional views about how marital roles should be performed. Resources, joined with the couple's desire to share power or, at least, to share more power than they did in first marriages, lead to marital processes that include implicit and explicit negotiations around issues of power and control.

However, all women do not have resources to bring to a remarriage, but seek remarriage as the solution to providing for their children. Unfortunately, women who need resources the most (poor women) are the least likely to remarry (Oh, 1986). This may be an indication that men as well as women are searching for more financial stability via remarriage. In North American societies, it is increasingly difficult for one family wage earner to support a middle-class standard of living. Therefore, women may feel especially obligated to earn income to help support their children from a previous relationship, and men may be unwilling to take full financial responsibility for their stepchildren. This could be forcing couples into more equity or shared power in their relationships. Remarried couples may actually portend the wave of the future—both partners earn income and share power in relation to their earnings.

Remarried or repartnered individuals use their previous marriage(s) or relationship(s) as a kind of baseline by which to compare their current relationship, and they make great efforts to distinguish their current marriage from previous unhappy ones (Coleman & Ganong, 1985; Furstenberg, 1982). How much of this is due to rationalization and cognitive dissonance (i.e., "I'm much better off with this partner than my previous one; otherwise, I would have been stupid to marry him/her, and I'm not a stupid person"), and how much of this reflects purposeful changes in couple dynamics as a result of lessons learned is open to speculation. Two reasons why remarriages might be perceived differently from prior marriages are related to life course differences (Spanier & Furstenberg, 1987). For one thing, first marriages and remarriages begin at different points in an individual's life span. Older ages at remarriage often mean that remarriages begin under quite different conditions (e.g., wiser, more desperate) than first marriages, which may influence perceptions of subsequent marital events. Second, individuals whose first marriages were lengthy have been exposed to different cultural expectations about how relationships should function. For instance, a person who married first in 1957 and then remarried in 1977 was exposed over time to dramatically disparate views of how men and women should relate to each other in marriage. These different expectations may lead to thinking anew about marital dynamics and evaluating marital interactions using quite different standards.

Division of Labor in Stepfamily Couples

Sullivan (1997), in a British national sample, found some support for the resource/marital power perspective in that women in second and higher order relationships (both remarried and cohabiting) did relatively less household work than women in first relationships and contributed relatively more to household incomes. Ishii-Kuntz and Coltrane (1992) also found support for the resource perspective; remarried wives were more likely than other wives to be employed outside of the home, to hold less traditional views, and to earn a greater proportion of the family income. They also found less segregation of labor based on gender in stepfamilies than in first-married families.

Other researchers have *not* found this same correspondence between decision-making power and involvement in task sharing in remarriages, however. In a study of remarried fathers and their new wives, Guisinger, Cowan, and Schuldberg (1989) found that couples described their decision-making as egalitarian, but their division of household labor tended to be split along traditional gendered lines. This means that the women were doing the vast majority of the household work, including most of the care of their stepchildren. Demo and Acock (1993), in a nationally drawn sample, found that couples in stepfather-mother households also adhered to a traditional, gender-based division of household tasks. Mothers in stepfamilies did not differ from mothers in first marriages in the amount of household work they did, and both groups of women did far more work than did their husbands. Despite the discrepancy in the amount of domestic work being done by husbands and wives, remarried mothers described the division of household tasks as generally fair to both partners.

In contrast, many of the stepmothers in the Guisinger et al. (1989) study did not think the amount of work their husbands did was enough. Their dissatisfaction grew over the first 3 years of remarriage, and they were particularly displeased with the division of labor related to care of their stepchildren. Marital satisfaction of both husbands and wives was related to how satisfied they were with the degree to which childcare, household tasks, and decision-making were shared. Marital satisfaction also was related to the *perception* that household chores, childcare, and decision-making were divided equitably. Other studies find that division of labor is more evenly distributed in stepfather households than in first-marriage families (Deal, Stanley Hagen, & Anderson, 1992), although women do more of the work than men do in either type of household.

How can these diverse findings be reconciled? Resource theory can explain most, but not all of these findings. Using insights from gender theory, Pyke and Coltrane (1996) proposed that in order to understand the complex relations of power and the division of labor in remarriage, it is necessary to consider the *economy of gratitude* as well as feelings of *obligation* and *entitlement* that are rooted in societal beliefs about gender and power. The economy of gratitude refers to the meanings that partners attach to behaviors—what is a gift or resource to one spouse may be a burden or cost to another (Hochschild & Machung, 1989). The perceptions of resources and costs are made in the context of gendered power relations and gender inequality in society—judgments about household labor fairness and relational expectations do not occur in a vacuum (Pyke, 1994). In addition, for remarried individuals, judgments of gender-based entitlements and obligations to a spouse are made within the context of prior marital experiences. Consequently, remarried women may seek a more equitable power-sharing marriage and *move into* greater involvement in the labor force, if what they and their spouses want is this type of arrangement. Other women may seek more shared power in remarriage than they had in their first marriage but *move out* of the labor force. Although this is inconsistent with resource models, Pyke and Coltrane found that about 20% of the women in their study did this. These women had been employed in low-skill jobs in their first marriages and had felt forced to work outside of the home by their dominant husbands. After divorce, these women purposefully sought less dominant men who would appreciate their unpaid family work and who made enough money to support that choice (Pyke, 1994). Women who were reluctant to remarry gained bargaining power in these remarriages, which helped them assert more decision-making power. The men in these marriages wanted a stay-at-home wife and were willing to share power in exchange. Regardless of what couples chose to do, both men and women implicitly and explicitly compared their current spouses' participation in household labor and decision-making to that of their former spouses (Pyke & Coltrane, 1996). Consequently, it is important to know the meanings that people attach to gender, to marital roles, and to family work (Rogers, 1996, 1999), and to keep in mind that these studies primarily measure perceptions of household labor distribution, often from only one household member's view. Observational studies of unpaid family work in stepfamilies have yet to be conducted.

Clinicians have asserted that stepfamilies fare better when the adults do not adhere to gendered stereotypes to guide their beliefs and behaviors (Carter, 1988).

Exploring the links between decision-making, equity, and the distribution of power in remarriage holds considerable potential for future research on couple relation-ships. Moreover, knowing the meanings that people have regarding work roles and family roles should yield a clearer understanding of the dynamics of remarried couples.

Handling Finances

Studies of financial decision-making and money management in stepfamilies have not fully captured the complexity of the issues involved. Although there is evidence that women have more say, or at least perceive that they do, in the financial matters in their remarriages than they had in their prior marriages (Burgoyne & Morison, 1997; Coleman & Ganong, 1989; Crosbie-Burnett & Giles-Sims, 1991; Pasley, Sandras, & Edmondson, 1994), the variety of ways in which finances are organized and managed by remarried couples in stepfamilies is so diverse and complex (Burgoyne & Morison, 1997; Jacobson, 1993; Lown & Dolan, 1988) that it is difficult to determine how equitable financial decision-making actually is.

Greater sharing of power between remarried husbands and wives does not necessarily mean that financial decision-making is shared equitably. Partly because of financial commitments to support children from present and prior unions who may or may not reside in the stepfamily household, and partly because of remarried individuals' desires to retain some degree of financial independence, remarried couples are more likely than those in first marriages to maintain at least part of their economic resources under the individual control of each partner (Burgoyne & Morison, 1997).

In an ethnographic study of 16 stepfamily couples, Fishman (1983) found that half pooled their incomes and half did not. She proposed that pooling wealth (the *common pot* model) could result in closer stepfamily relationships, presumably because economic futures were intertwined and thus communication and coopera-tion would be enhanced out of necessity to cooperate. Retaining separate accounts (the *two-pot* model) divided money along biological ties, and, Fishman observed, may have fostered greater independence between the adults. We examined these ideas (Coleman & Ganong, 1989), and found that most remarried couples (76%) in our sample managed income in a common pot, and most were satisfied with that method. However, two-pot couples also were satisfied. Pasley and her col-leagues (1994) reported a third method of handling finances, the *mixed method*, in which some wealth was pooled in a common pot and other resources were retained under the individual control of one of the adults. These researchers also found no connection between how finances were managed and satisfaction with remarriage and stepfamily life. British researchers Burgoyne and Morison (1997) added yet another type of financial management system—an *allowance system*, in which one partner, usually the husband, gave the other spouse a fixed amount to manage the household and kept the rest. In their ethnographic study, Burgoyne and Morison found that most remarried couples maintained an *independent management system*, in which both adults had their own sources of income and neither had access to all household funds. A few couples used a *pooling system* in which all or nearly all of the household income was shared and both had access to it. Although women in this study reported that they had considerably more say about finances in their remarriages than they had in their first marriages, the couples for the most part operated under a traditional male-dominated economic system, although this was often quite subtle. Similar to other studies, Burgoyne and Morison did not find that financial management arrangements were related to relationship satisfaction as a whole.

The absence of a relation between marital satisfaction and financial management may be due to the complex nature of finances in stepfamilies—and to the fact that different individuals have different concepts of fairness, that various family members have different needs and claims to resources, and that situational factors sometimes dictate what must be done with finances, even if that violates personal norms of distributive justice (Jacobson, 1993). To date no researchers have examined the range of financial decision-making with large enough samples to adequately assess how financial management practices relate to relationship processes and satisfaction in remarriage. Given the importance of finances to the well-being of individuals and families in general, this is an important area for researchers to explore further.

Certainly many couples in stepfamilies face economic hardships because they lack sufficient resources to meet family members' needs. However, lack of funds is probably not the only source of financial problems for stepfamily couples. In fact, it may not be the primary source of economic difficulties—deciding how resources will be distributed has been found to be a major source of conflicts in remarriage (Coleman et al., 2001; Hobart, 1991; Pasley, Koch, & Ihinger-Tallman, 1993). For example, Burgoyne and Morison (1997) found that how decisions actually were made could not easily be discerned from asking couples only about how finances were managed. For instance, a couple may pool resources, yet the husband wields the most influence when spending decisions are made. Goetting (1982) argued that issues defined as financial problems in remarriage centered more on resource distribution issues and the instability of finances as a result of the unpredictable nature of child support payments than on issues related to not having adequate resources. In many stepfamilies, remarried couples' decisions about finances are connected to, and sometimes dependent on, the economic decisions and behaviors of former partners (e.g., paying or not paying child support, asking for more financial aid for children's expenses). For example, a remarried couple may have to postpone financial investments, such as buying a home, because a former spouse has decided to send a child from that union to an expensive private college instead of a cheaper public institution. It is easy to imagine the frustration that remarried partners experience when faced with the dilemma of having "outsiders" (e.g., former spouses, children from earlier unions) making decisions about how their household income or how a partner's income will be spent. It is also easy to imagine how a couple might be satisfied with the manner in which they have negotiated decisions about distributing their household finances and yet be stressed and angry because child support payments they expect to receive are not paid or they are paid late.

CHILDBEARING

Half of all remarried women bear children in their new union (Griffith, Koo, & Suchindran, 1984; Wineberg, 1990). This underestimates fertility in stepfamilies, however because these statistics do not include individuals who have children from prior unmarried unions but who are in their first marriages. Reproduction in cohabiting stepfamilies is also an unknown (Bumpass et al., 1995). Obviously, a lot of stepfamily couples have children together, and probably an even greater number consider reproducing but decide not to do so.

Stewart (2002) found that adults in stepfamilies in which both brought children to the union were less likely to want more children than when only one of the adults was a parent. Although there were sex differences in intentions to have children, when only one adult was a parent intentions to reproduce remained high until each partner had a genetic child. Women's fertility intentions were reduced if either she *or* her partner already had children. In contrast, men's intentions to have a child were reduced by having stepchildren but were not related to having biological children. Agreement between partners on intentions to have a child together was highly predictive of bearing more children, leading Stewart to conclude that stepchildren indirectly affect fertility by mediating parents' and stepparents' intentions to reproduce.

The decision to reproduce in stepfamilies is a complex one, involving considerations regarding children from adults' prior unions, finances, ages of both parents, and partners' expectations regarding the costs or benefits of adding a child to the stepfamily (Ganong & Coleman, 1988). A few years ago we became intrigued with the advice from self-help authors and clinicians about whether or not remarried couples in stepfamilies should have a child together, and so we decided to investigate what we came to think of as the *concrete baby* effect. This odd label occurred to us because self-help authors repeatedly asserted, with little empirical evidence, that mutual children (those born to the stepfamily union) had the effect of *cementing* stepfamily bonds. The rationale was that because a child born to the stepfamily couple would be genetically related to everyone else in the stepfamily, this shared connection would facilitate integration as a family unit and would draw the couple and step-relationships (e.g., stepparent-stepchild, stepsiblings) closer (Ganong & Coleman, 1988). Although this assertion was not supported in responses on standardized measures of marital closeness and quality, parents in our study who had reproduced in the remarriage perceived some benefits of having a child together. However, it is hard to imagine, if only for reasons of social desirability, that parents would admit to researchers that having a mutual child had been a mistake. Cognitive dissonance also could once again have been an operating factor—"we are reasonable, rational people, and we decided to have this baby so it must have been a good thing to do." Some of the women in our study felt that they owed their husband a child because the husband had financially supported the stepchildren. Remarried parents in Bernstein's (1989) study generally perceived that having a baby strengthened their marriage, and they felt that the baby provided "a reason to ride out the rough times" (p. 89). However, there also were indications that mutual children were sources of stress. One way to determine the effects of a mutual child on stepfamily processes would be to compare over time matched samples of stepfamilies with and without mutual children. The practicality of doing such a thing, however, is questionable. Stepfamilies are so complex that matching on all of the potentially critical variables would be nearly impossible. Qualitative designs may be better suited to explore this question.

Clinicians have long pointed out that the effects of a child born in a stepfamily can be positive, negative, or mixed, depending on such factors as the motivations to reproduce (To save a marriage in trouble? As an expression of love?), the quality of step-relationships prior to the baby's birth, and the age of stepchildren. Unfortunately, few researchers have examined the effects of concrete babies on stepfamilies, and, given the frequency at which women in stepfamilies bear children, this is worth further study. In Chapter 9, we look at the relationships between concrete babies and their half-siblings.

RELATIONSHIP QUALITY AND STABILITY IN REMARRIAGES

A Seeming Paradox

There is a relatively large body of literature on remarriage satisfaction, remarriage adjustment, and remarriage quality. A lot of these studies are comparisons of the marital quality of individuals in remarriages and first marriages. In general, researchers find that individuals in first marriages have higher marital quality than those in remarriages (e.g., Rogers, 1996), or that there are no differences between individuals in first marriages and remarriages (e.g., Anderson et al., 1992). With two colleagues we conducted a meta-analysis of over 100 such studies and generally found that the difference in marital quality of remarriages and first marriages was minimal (Vemer, Coleman, Ganong, & Cooper, 1989). Although this study was done over a decade ago, it is doubtful that the overall conclusion has changed.

However, the divorce rate for remarriages is higher than for first marriages (Amato & Rogers, 1997; Bumpass et al., 1990), which seems to present a paradox. If remarriages are as satisfying as first marriages, why do they end more often in divorce? Booth and Edwards (1992) suggested that when there are marital problems, individuals who have divorced previously turn to divorce more rapidly than individuals in first marriages do. It apparently takes a smaller decrease in marital satisfaction for remarried persons to end their marriage than it does for people in first marriages. Booth and Edwards' speculation can only be assessed with longitudinal designs, and findings from longitudinal studies have been mixed in support for their assertion (e.g., Kurdek, 1991, 1999).

Remarital Instability: Selection Factors

A number of reasons for remarriage instability have been proposed that share the assumption that individuals who remarry, particularly after divorce, are different in fundamental ways (e.g., personalities, attitudes, values) from individuals who stay married until they or their spouses die. These proposed differences are often called *selection factors* because individuals are differentially selected into remarriage. For example, it has been hypothesized that remarriages contain an overrepresentation of individuals who are poor marriage material because of personality characteristics such as low frustration tolerance, impulsivity, and risk-taking (McCranie & Kahan, 1986). Similarly, alcoholism, drug abuse, and antisocial behaviors also have been proposed as the kinds of factors that negatively affect marital quality and stability and are more characteristic of remarried individuals, particularly among individuals who marry three or more times (Brody et al., 1988). The notion that some people are not suited for marriage because of personality or temperamental predisposition has support from studies that find a genetic component to the risk of divorce (McGue & Lykken, 1992), and there is a sizeable body of research relating personality traits and marital satisfaction in first marriages. Moreover, studies of the effects of family structure transitions on children indicate that parental antisocial personality characteristics and poor problem-solving skills are better predictors of children's outcomes than are the number of parental marital transitions (Capaldi & Patterson, 1991; Degarmo & Forgatch, 1999)—findings that suggest adults in stepfamilies with difficult personalities or poor interpersonal skills may have a harder time managing relationships, including their marriages.

Support for the contribution of personality problems on remarital stability has been limited (Kurdek, 1990), and the effects are generally small (Johnson & Booth, 1998). However, given the widespread search for genetic factors that contribute to interpersonal behaviors, it is likely that researchers will continue to investigate the potential effects of extreme or deviant personality traits on remarital stability and satisfaction. In addition, researchers have started to examine the effects of personality traits that may predispose individuals to cope poorly with the demands of stepfamily living, such as attachment style (Ceglian & Gardner, 1999). Researchers might find the assessment of personality and behavioral variables in remarriage more productive if they assess the characteristics of both spouses because it is likely that the effects of one partner's personality characteristics on remarriage can only fully be understood in the context of how such characteristics intermesh with those of the other partner (Johnson & Booth, 1998).

Other selection factors include attitudes and expectations. For example, attitudes and values about divorce differ between individuals in first marriages and remarriages (Booth & Edwards, 1992). Among the pool of remarried individuals are people who view divorce or separation as acceptable ways for handling unhappy relationships. In contrast, the pool of individuals in first marriages contains a larger number of people for whom divorce is not an option under any conditions. They stay in unsatisfying marriages because of religious beliefs or for other reasons. These individuals are committed to the *institution of marriage*. A larger proportion of remarried individuals are people who see themselves as committed to a particular partner than to the institution of marriage; when they become disenchanted with the partner, they are more likely to leave the marriage (Schmiege et al., 2001). The unwillingness of remarried individuals to stay in an unsatisfying relationship has been labeled *conditional commitment* (Furstenberg & Spanier, 1984). Remarried people may be fearful of marital dissolution, but they nonetheless may prefer a(nother) divorce to living in a conflictual, unsatisfying relationship. Furstenberg and Spanier found that remarried individuals held more favorable attitudes toward divorce as a solution to marital problems than they had held in their first marriages, and we found that nearly one third of our sample had discussed the possibility of their remarriage ending in divorce prior to remarriage (Ganong & Coleman, 1989). However, Booth and Edwards found that a willingness to divorce was weakly related to re-divorce.

Economic status is another selection factor related to re-divorce. Persons of lower socioeconomic status more often divorce than persons of higher socioeconomic status. Thus the pool of potential remarriers contains a greater proportion of individuals with low incomes, jobs that require little training and provide little employment security, and low levels of education. These persons are under greater economic stress, they have fewer financial and personal resources to withstand threats to their well-being, and it is harder for them to access community support systems. Accordingly, the greater incidence of divorce in remarriage is at least partially due to the greater risk for divorce of those with lower socioeconomic status (Voydanoff, 1990). In fact, Castro Martin and Bumpass (1989) reported that two variables associated with lower socioeconomic attainment—lower educational achievement and being married the first time as teenagers—statistically accounted for remarriages being less stable than first marriages. This finding lends indirect support for the socioeconomic explanation.

In addition to the selection factors argument for remarriage instability, another explanation is that prior life experiences and other contextual factors such as parental divorces and one's own divorce function differently for remarriages than for first marriages (for a discussion of various micro- and macro-contexts that affect marriages see Bradbury, Fincham, & Beach, 2000). Prado and Markman (1999), in a longitudinal observation study of couples in first marriages and remarriages, found that the levels of positive communication were higher in the remarriages, which could be a sign that the individuals had learned from earlier marital experiences how to interact with spouses in more positive ways. However, the level of negative communication did not change from first marriage to remarriage. Remarried individuals tend to report that, as a result of what they learned from prior marital experiences, they remarry for different reasons than they married the first time (Byrd & Smith, 1988; Smith et al., 1991), and they think their prior marriage experiences helped them adjust to remarriage and contribute to making their remarriages more satisfying than their first marriages had been. Indeed, if "remarried men and women were more oriented to a balance between self-interests and the other's interest in the remarriage decision than in the first marriage decision" (Smith et al., 1991, p. 3), then it is likely that lessons had been learned that would help them adapt to a new marriage. Unfortunately, we cannot determine from these studies if there really was a causal link between experiences that occurred within the first marriage and new behaviors in remarriages. There are a number of competing explanations (e.g., faulty memories, age-related developmental changes, cognitive dissonance, social desirability).

Remarriage Instability: Evolutionary Explanations

According to evolutionary scholars, marriage and remarriage instability is programmed into our genetic makeup. Humans are genetically motivated to seek new partners with whom to reproduce (Fisher, 1989). Serial pair bonding is a reproductive strategy that "evolved in response to an increased female reproductive burden . . . and functioned to ensure survival of the hominid infant through the period of lactation" (p. 332). The advantages of this reproductive strategy compared to lifelong monogamy are that females in unsatisfactory unions can find new male partners to provide them with better protection and subsistence for themselves and future offspring. For males, serial pair bonding allows them to select younger females who are more likely to bear healthy babies. For both males and females, this reproductive strategy means that offspring have a larger array of genetic backgrounds, which produces more variety in their lineages, an advantage in increasing the odds of surviving. Fisher found support for this perspective from a cross-cultural study of patterns of marriage, divorce, and remarriage. Other researchers have also found some support for serial pair bonding as a reproductive strategy, at least for men (e.g., Buckle et al., 1996; Kaar, Jokela, Merila, Helle, & Kojola, 1998). From an evolutionary perspective, stepparenting also can be seen as a reproductive strategy for men who have been unsuccessful in reproducing (Anderson, 2000). By taking care of female partners' children, men can convince the women of their abilities to protect and provide, leading them to bear children for these men; Anderson (2000) and Stewart (2002) found that men with one or two stepchildren were as likely to have children of their own as men with no stepchildren, suggesting that stepparenting provides a fertility benefit for some men, or at least stepchildren are not a fertility barrier.

Remarriage Instability: Interpersonal Causes

The presence of stepchildren has been examined as a potential predictor of both marital quality and marital stability. Some researchers have found that stepchildren destabilize remarriages and reduce marital quality (Becker et al., 1977; Booth & Edwards, 1992; Rogers, 1999; Tzeng & Mare, 1995; White & Booth, 1985), but others have found no connection between having stepchildren and marital quality (Kurdek, 1999) and stability (Castro Martin & Bumpass, 1989; Furstenberg & Spanier, 1984). The relation between couple functioning and the presence of children from prior relationships is unclear; some researchers have found that children affect couple functioning negatively (Clingempeel, 1981; Clingempeel & Brand, 1985; Pasley & Ihinger-Tallman, 1982), while others have not (Kalmuss & Seltzer, 1986; Koepke et al., 1992; Schultz et al., 1991).

Custody arrangements of stepchildren may affect marital quality. Shared or joint legal and/or physical custody means that contact with former spouse(s) is likely to be greater than if either physical or legal custody were solely in the hands of one parent. It has been hypothesized that joint custody frees stepparents of functioning in the parental role, thus allowing them time to focus on the remarriage and on more pleasant interactions with stepchildren (Crosbie-Burnett, 1989). An alternative hypothesis is that joint custody diminishes remarriage quality because the former spouse must be interacted with more regularly, thus introducing more complexity and stress into the remarriage household. Crosbie-Burnett (1989) found that joint physical custody affected marital satisfaction negatively only for stepfather households in which the stepchildren were adolescent girls. Clearly, household and couple dynamics are different when stepchildren are present, compared to when they are not. The question is whether the presence of children from prior unions destabilizes adult couple relationships and/or lowers their quality. The influence of children as interested third parties to their parents' remarriages and other romantic unions is not likely to be insignificant, depending on such factors as the emotional closeness of parents and children, the amount of contact that children have with parents and their partners, the ages and genders of children and the romantically involved parent and stepparent, and the nature of the stepparent-stepchild relationship.

Bohannan (1970) coined the term *quasi-kin* to refer to former spouses, the new partners of former spouses, and the kin of former spouses. Contact with stepkin and quasi-kin are often considered to be indicators of stepfamily complexity and role ambiguity and, when studied at all, they often have been examined as predictors of remarriage quality. Clinicians have pointed out that former spouse relationships are important for predicting overall family functioning (Ahrons, 1980). However, the relation between contact with quasi-kin and marital functioning has received limited support (Clingempeel, 1981; Clingempeel & Brand, 1985).

This is not to suggest that former spouse relationships do not alter remarriages. In fact, the influence of remarriages on former spouse relationships is reciprocal, but research on the influence of former spouses on remarriage has yielded mixed results. For example, Clingempeel (1981) found a curvilinear relationship between the frequency of contacts with former spouses and remarital quality; those with moderate amounts of contact with former spouses reported higher remarital quality than those with low or high amounts of contact. However, in a partial replication of this study, Clingempeel and Brand (1985) found no relationship between former spouses' contact and remarriage satisfaction. Simply measuring the frequency of contact between former spouses may not be sufficient to assess the impact of former spouses on remarriage functioning. Weston and Macklin (1990) found that the relation between contact with a former spouse and remarriage functioning was moderated by other factors, such as the degree to which former spouses cooperate on parenting and the congruence between the kind of former spouse relationship that exists and ideal expectations for such a relationship. It might also be that partners' expectations for how much contact and communication there will be with former spouses and partners are relevant as well—issues such as current partner jealousy and related issues should be explored further. The amount of contact between former spouses may actually reveal little about the nature of those relationships or about the effects of former spouses on remarriages; couples who communicate and compromise with each other may have a great deal of contact, as might couples who hate each other but interact frequently in order to fight more about the children. In this first situation, the former spouse may functionally serve as a source of social support for the remarried couple, and in the second situation, the former spouse may be a source of great stress on the remarried couple's relationship (Weston & Macklin, 1990). In a study of remarried fathers and their new wives, the men's former spouses were a greater source of stress on the remarried couples than the stepchildren were, and negative perceptions of the husband's former spouse were related to lower remarital satisfaction for both husbands and wives (Guisinger et al., 1989).

Remarriage Market

With the exception of those who are widowed or divorced at very young ages, most of the people in the remarriage market face a smaller selection of available mates who have similar interests, beliefs, and lifestyles. This can lead to remarriage with persons from different backgrounds (Booth & Edwards, 1992) and suggests that individuals in the remarriage pool have less control over mate selection than those in first marriages, because they have fewer good choices.

Remarriage and Social Support

Social support is an important resource for married couples (Bradbury et al., 2000). Satisfaction with the amount of social support received has been found to be related to lower distress in remarried couples (Kurdek, 1991), and support from extended kin may be a particularly good predictor of remarriage adjustment (Roberts & Price, 1991). Unfortunately, remarried couples tend to be somewhat isolated from extended kin (Booth & Edwards, 1992), particularly in marriages in which both spouses were married before (Ihinger-Tallman & Pasley, 1986; Kurdek, 1989). However, remarried couples may compensate by seeking support from friends and coworkers; the remarried couples in Kurdek's sample had support networks that were similar in size to other couples.

Kurdek (1991) speculated that the parents of remarried couples may offer less family support for two reasons: (1) they are generally older, and so may have less energy, and (2) they may be reluctant to get involved in their offspring's marital conflicts, although they may have offered support in their child's previous marriage. Clingempeel, Colyar, Brand, and Hetherington (1992) identified what they called a *norm of noninterference*, a norm that indicates that older family members should not cross household boundaries when the younger household is headed by a couple—this norm would tend to reduce social support for remarried couples. For instance, when a daughter divorces, her parents may feel comfortable offering her advice, money, lodging, and other resources while she adapts to her changing family situation. If that daughter remarries, the norm of noninterference would suggest that her parents continued efforts to help would be considered by both generations to be too intrusive, and generally unwelcome.

Which Model Explains Remarriage Stability and Quality the Best?

Booth and Edwards (1992) concluded that no single explanation of remarriage stability and quality is sufficient. They noted that many remarried couples who have one or two risk factors for divorce obviously find ways to stay happily married (Booth & Edwards, 1992). This point deserves further comment. Researchers have made many attempts to document the differences in marital stability and marital quality between first marriages and remarriages. Earlier in this chapter we presented models that have been proposed to explain these differences, and we mentioned several studies designed to assess the validity of these models. We feel compelled to point out, however, that the magnitude of the differences in marital quality and marital stability between remarriages and first marriages (what researchers call *effect sizes*) is generally quite small. To paraphrase Shakespeare, this work may be characterized as "Much ado about next to nothing." In fact, some researchers have suggested that there is no need for explanatory models of marital quality differences because, for all practical purposes, the differences are miniscule (Furstenberg & Spanier, 1984).

What is proving to be a more fruitful line of research is the study of processes within remarital relationships. Qualitative research and longitudinal studies that examine couple dynamics in depth and from the perspectives of both partners as well as that of outsiders to the relationships are rapidly expanding what is known about remarried couples. There is still a need for more investigations that ask such questions as, "What factors contribute to satisfaction in remarriages?" "What do happily remarried couples do that is different from what unhappily remarried couples do?" "What are the processes by which couples build strong relationships?" "How do remarried couples maintain satisfying relationships over time?" Researchers generally have chosen to focus on stressors and risk factors even when explanatory models include benefits, buffers, and factors fostering marital commitment and satisfaction (e.g., social exchange theory). We discussed some of the trends in research on stepfamilies at length in Chapter 1, but it is worth noting again that researchers are influenced by their own beliefs, by cultural influences, and by disciplinary biases. In this case, there appears to be a bias towards focusing on differences between groups that are more similar than they are different, what Hare-Mustin and Marecek (1988) have termed the *alpha bias*.

OLDER ADULTS AND REMARRIAGES

Compared to earlier studies of the incidence of remarriage among older adults (Cleveland & Gianturco, 1976; Treas & VanHilst, 1976), more recent investigations indicate that remarriages among older Americans are on the rise, and the marital histories of older Americans are becoming increasingly complex (Cornman & Kingson, 1996; Holden & Kuo, 1996; Wilmoth & Koso, 2002). Compared to previous cohorts, there are now more older adults who have been divorced, some more than once. Moreover, the numbers of later-life cohabiting relationships, remarriages, and stepfamilies are likely to increase in the next few years as the baby boom generation reaches retirement age. About half of the marriages of this cohort will have ended in divorce, and about 75% of those who divorced will have remarried at least once (Furstenberg & Cherlin, 1991). Among this group will be unprecedented numbers of individuals who are stepparents (Cornman & Kingson, 1996).

Some older remarriages are long-term, established relationships that began when the couple was much younger (Wu & Penning, 1997). However, a growing number of remarriages will have begun in later life due to increased longevity and better health throughout the life course (Holden & Kuo, 1996).

Remarriages Begun in Later Life

Little is known about the dynamics of later life remarriage or cohabiting. A few older studies of widows and widowers reported that later life courtships were brief (often less than a year) and were shorter for men than for women (McKain, 1972; Vinick, 1978). In these early studies, even though the period of time between bereavement and remarriage was relatively short, the remarried individuals typically had known each other for several years, and a few were even distantly related to each other. Motivations to remarry included companionship, sexual intimacy, financial resources, to relieve loneliness, and to have someone to help with household chores (McKain, 1972; Moss & Moss, 1980; Talbot, 1998; Vinick, 1978).

Later life remarriages generally are satisfying (Bograd & Spilka, 1996), although Chipperfield and Havens (2001) found increased life satisfaction only for men that remarried in later life. In general, later life remarriages appear to bestow benefits to older men and women—compared to widowed individuals who did not remarry, remarried individuals reported lower stress, higher self-esteem, greater life satisfaction, better feelings about friendships, and more resolution of grief related to bereavement of former spouses (Burks, Lund, Gregg, & Bluhm, 1988; Gentry & Schulman, 1988). People with partners were less lonely than single older adults but were lonelier than those in first marriages (Peters & Liefbroer, 1997). Later life remarriages were also related to health, satisfaction, and happiness for men (Bulcroft, Bulcroft, Hatch, & Borgatta, 1989). Although some of this may be due to selection factors, in that physically and mentally healthier persons are more likely to remarry than those in poor health (Bulcroft & Bulcroft, 1991), results from longitudinal studies mirror those from cross-sectional studies. Despite these benefits, most widows are not interested in remarrying because of negative attitudes toward men, low expectations for finding marital satisfaction, unhappy experiences in prior unions (Talbot, 1998), and a desire for independence (Tucker, Taylor, & Mitchell-Kernan, 1993). Talbot saw a dilemma for older widows who liked men and wanted companionship from them, but did not necessarily want to remarry; norms and expectations about dating designed for younger people do not work well for older women and men.

Remarriage in later life may be an attempt to resolve some of the problems facing widows and widowers, but the new unions also bring concerns regarding new family relationships (Gentry & Schulman, 1988). Women are more affected by later life remarriages than men are, but the family satisfaction of both men and women is related to their communication and conflict resolution strategies (Bograd & Spilka, 1996; Pasley & Ihinger-Tallman, 1990). Bograd and Spilka compared people who had remarried at mid-life (ages 30–45) and late-life (ages 60–75), and although they found that marital satisfaction was greatest in late life remarriages, primarily due to the high level of male satisfaction in that group, there was a positive association between marital satisfaction and self-disclosure in both groups. However, rather than the amount of self-disclosure, it was the intentionality, positiveness, depth, and honesty of disclosure that were communicated that correlated with marital satisfaction. Pasley and Ihinger-Tallman also found communication, in the form of conflict resolution strategies, to be important among the relatively recently remarried men and women aged 55 and older whom they surveyed. The use of neutral conflict resolution strategies such as silence, ignoring or dropping an issue, and few disruptive interchanges (high consensus on issues) were more likely to result in greater family satisfaction.

As with younger remarriages, later life remarriages develop under the close observation of children and other interested third parties (e.g., friends) who may not be reluctant to share their opinions about the new union. In many cases, adult children do not welcome their parents' remarriage, although according to older adults' self-reports, their adult children eventually support them when they see how happy they are as a result of the remarriage (McKain, 1972; Vinick, 1978). This may be true, but clinicians point out that adult children are often concerned about inheritance, and they may be upset at parents who they believe are not honoring the memories of the deceased parent (Visher & Visher, 1996). Researchers have not yet examined these claims, but clinicians argue that later life remarriages trigger many of the same reactions among adult children as is true of minor-aged children (i.e., loyalty issues, jealousy). Given the expected increases in healthy single older adults, this seems like a critical area to investigate.

Long-Term Remarriages

Relatively few researchers have investigated long-term remarriages of older adults, those that started when stepchildren were quite young or adolescents. Instead, the focus of the few studies that have been done on older remarried people have been of remarriages contracted later in life. It is doubtful that these two groups of older remarried people have a great deal in common, but this is speculation and not based on empirical evidence. However, most remarriages contracted in later life are formed after bereavement and are second marriages that follow lengthy first marriages, while long-term remarriages of older adults are more likely to follow divorce, and more of these remarried individuals may have been involved in several unions, both marriages and cohabitation. Long-term remarriages of older adults also may resemble long-term first marriages more than they do later-life remarriages formed by individuals at or near retirement ages. The study of remarried couples in older stepfamilies, whether they are long-term stepfamilies or stepfamilies formed by older adults marrying, is exceptionally complex.

SUMMARY

There are a number of moderating and mediating variables that potentially influence the couple dynamics in remarriages. Among them are: ages of partners; children (i.e., where they live, how many there are, how old they are, gender, legal custody, whether they are shared by the couple or not); frequency of contact and the nature of relationships with former spouses; contact and support from extended kin; marital expectations; belief systems and ideologies (i.e., about marriage, parenting); socioeconomic status; education; the prior marital histories of both partners; partner personalities, both individually and collectively; finances; communication and conflict resolution skills, power imbalances, and interpersonal skills brought by each partner into the relationship. This lengthy list is nonetheless a partial one; there likely are many other variables that impact the functioning of remarriages. Unfortunately, this list also represents a considerable amount of conjecture; some of these variables have rarely or never been studied.

Clearly, much more examination of remarriage relationships is needed. The existing literature on remarriages illustrates some of the problems mentioned in Chapter 1; for example, stepfamily complexity is often not adequately addressed, and too many researchers try to explain small differences between first marriages and remarriages, often ignoring similarities. The literature on remarriage is noteworthy for two reasons, however. First, research on the remarried couple has been guided by theory to a greater extent than research on other stepfamily relationships. Second, a relatively large number of remarriage researchers have taken a developmental view, looking at changes in remarriage dynamics over time, or examining the effects of antecedent conditions on subsequent remarriage dynamics.

Chapter 6

Gay and Lesbian Cohabiting Couples in Stepfamilies

Estimates of the number of gay and lesbian couples are likely to be lower than the actual number because identifying oneself publicly as part of a gay or lesbian couple may be riskier than coming out of the closet as an individual (Bryant & Demian, 1994; Kaiser Family Foundation, 2001). Based on data from the latest U.S. Census (2002), 301,026 households were headed by a male householder and a male partner and 293,365 households were headed by a female householder and a female partner. Some of these are long-term relationships—between 8% and 21% of lesbian couples and between 18% and 28% of gay couples have lived together 10 or more years (Blumstein & Schwartz, 1983; Bryant & Demian, 1994; Falkner & Garber, 2002; Kurdek, 2004; *The Advocate* sex poll, 2002).

There are no reliable data on the number of gay and lesbian parents nor are there data on the number of children living part-time or full-time with gay and lesbian couples, so there are no sound estimates of gay and lesbian stepfamily households (Kurdek, 2004). In one study, 21% of the lesbians and 9% of the gay men reported caring for children, although it was not clear how many of these children lived with the couple (Bryant & Demian, 1994). Blumstein and Schwartz (1983) reported that 7% of the lesbian couples in their sample had children living with them more than half of the year, and 11% of the gay and lesbian respondents from another study reported having children under age 18 living with them (Kaiser Family Foundation, 2001). Given that mothers most often have physical custody of children, it is likely that there are more lesbian stepfamily households than there are stepfamily households headed by gay couples. Gay fathers and their partners are more likely to be nonresidential step-households, having children with them periodically rather than most or all of the time.

Gay and lesbian couples create stepfamilies primarily in three ways. The most prevalent precursor to gay and lesbian stepfamily formation is for one or both adults to have reproduced or adopted children in earlier heterosexual relationships—in one study approximately three-fourths of the children of both lesbians and gay men were offspring from a previous marriage (Bryant & Demian, 1994). These families are structurally most similar to heterosexual stepfamilies in that the children's parents no longer reside together and, in the step-household, children are emotionally connected more to one adult than to the other. Because of their prevalence, most research on gay and lesbian couples in stepfamilies has been of this type of stepfamily.

The second way in which (mostly) lesbian couples form stepfamilies is via donor insemination (DI). In Bryant and Demian's study (1994) 13% of the lesbians were impregnated through DI. Although gay men could conceivably have children via DI with surrogate mothers, the incidence of this is probably extremely rare. Among lesbians, however, motherhood via DI has grown in popularity and will likely continue to represent a substantial number of lesbian couples with children (Nelson, 1996).

Adoption of a child by a gay or lesbian individual, whether currently in a committed relationship or not, is a third way of forming a gay and lesbian stepfamily, although this appears to be relatively uncommon. There are two types of adoptions, second-parent adoptions and stranger adoptions (Hequembourg, in press). Second-parent adoption is when there is a parent in the household and a second adult in the household, the stepparent, adopts the child. These adoptions are fairly common among heterosexual stepfamilies (Ganong, Coleman, Fine, & McDaniel, 1998), but relatively uncommon for gay and lesbian stepfamilies. In the United States adoption laws require that the child's nonresidential genetic parent must legally relinquish his or her parenthood before the stepparent can adopt, because children in the United States cannot have more than two legal parents. Nonresidential parents are reluctant to do this in many cases, and attempts to terminate parental rights can result in angry interactions and hostile legal fights between the parents. Adding the stigma against gays and lesbians to this scenario discourages many gay and lesbian stepparents from attempting second-parent adoptions (Hequembourg, in press). *Stranger adoptions* are when a child has no recognized parent and a legal stranger wants to adopt the child. These adoptions are limited in the United States to one adult in a cohabiting relationship or to a married couple, and because some states prohibit gay and lesbian individuals from adopting, it is not a viable option for many gay and lesbian couples (Hequembourg, in press).

In general, gay and lesbian stepfamilies formed after either or both partners were in heterosexual unions that produced children function differently than when children were born after the formation of the homosexual couple. For example, couples in which one adult adopts a child or has a child via donor insemination usually regard themselves as forming a nuclear family rather than a stepfamily (Hare & Richards, 1993; Hequembourg, in press). Structurally, they may have more in common with nuclear (first marriage) families than stepfamilies in that usually the couple relationships exist prior to the addition of the children, and children do not recall a time when both adults were not present. There also usually are not issues regarding shared time and control with a nonresidential parent (Hare & Richards, 1993; Hequembourg, in press), which are major concerns of gay and lesbian couples in stepfamilies formed after heterosexual unions (Berger, 1998; Lynch, 2000). Only a few studies (e.g., Hare & Richards, 1993; Hequembourg, in press; Lynch, 2000; Nelson, 1996) have compared children in different forms of gay and lesbian stepfamilies.

It should be noted that few members of gay and lesbian stepfamilies think of themselves as being part of a stepfamily. "Because the whole notion of stepfamily implies remarriage, I think many gay and lesbian individuals involved in functional stepfamily situations don't regard themselves in this way" (L. Kurdek, personal communication, June 18, 2003). In other words, even though individuals in gay and lesbian families may serve in the functional roles of stepparent and stepchild, it is likely that the individuals in those roles think of themselves and each other as something other than stepfamily members (e.g., "Jake is my dad's partner and my good friend"; "Danielle is my partner's daughter").

GAY AND LESBIAN COUPLES IN STEPFAMILIES

Most research on gay and lesbian couples has been of childless men and women (see Kurdek, 2000, 2001, for studies of similarities and differences between gay couples, lesbian couples, and heterosexual childfree couples, and Kurdck, 2004, for a review of research on gay and lesbian couples). Just as there are differences between heterosexual couples with and without children (Bulcroft & Teachman, 2004), the relationship dynamics of gay and lesbian couples who have children differ from those who do not have children. However, there have been few studies comparing gay and lesbian couples with and without children— Koepke, Hare and Moran (1992) found that lesbians with children reported more relationship satisfaction and sexual satisfaction than those without children, but in most other ways there were few differences in how lesbian partners responded to questions about their relationships.

In general, researchers have been more interested in how children of gay and lesbian individuals fare (see reviews by Patterson, 2000, and Stacey & Biblarz, 2001) than they have been in the dynamics of gay and lesbian couples and their families. Nearly all of these studies have been about the children of lesbians, and comparisons are usually made to children of heterosexual mothers (Kurdek, 2004). The functional co-parental role of partners has been largely ignored in these studies; if partners are included researchers appear to assume that the most important predictor of children's outcome is their mothers' sexual orientation rather than family structure.

Most of the research on gay and lesbian stepfamilies has been descriptive—researchers are trying to figure out how gay and lesbian stepfamilies are similar to and different from heterosexual stepfamilies and from each other (see Erera & Fredriksen, 1999, and Hall & Kitson, 2000, for reviews of research on lesbian stepfamilies). Samples are small and methods are usually interpretive or qualitative. Scholars appear to be at the initial stages of developing research programs on gay and lesbian stepfamilies.

CHALLENGES FOR GAY AND LESBIAN STEPFAMILIES

Stigma

Not surprisingly, gay and lesbian individuals are highly aware of the social stigmas and homophobia associated with being a homosexual (Kurdek, 2004). When a gay or lesbian person is part of a couple, and even more so when there are children involved, then concerns about the effects of stigma increase (Bryant & Demian, 1994; Kaiser Family Foundation, 2001). Many of the prejudicial attitudes about homosexuals concern children—gays and lesbians are thought by some people to recruit children to be homosexuals, some people confuse homosexuality with pedophilia, believing that gays and lesbians (especially gay men) want to have sexual relations with children, and many heterosexual adults think that gays and lesbians are damaging role models for children (Bennett, 2003). Given the level of hatred and violence still directed towards gays and lesbians, homosexual parents are legitimately concerned for the safety of family members.

Stigma against gays and lesbians contributes to their fears about losing custody or visitation rights of children from prior relationships if nonresidential parents seek legal changes in custody (Erera & Fredriksen, 1999; Hall & Kitson, 2000). Researchers have reported that lesbian mothers in stepfamilies get along better with nonresidential fathers of their children than heterosexual mothers do (Hare & Richards, 1993). This may be because lesbian mothers recognize the importance of male role models for their children (Hare & Richards, 1993), but it may also be due to their fears that if co-parenting relationships turn contentious, fathers have homophobic and stigmatic attitudes on their side if they seek physical custody of the children (Lynch, 2000).

Gay and lesbian stepfamilies may also experience stigma as a stepfamily (Berger, 1998). This appears to be particularly true for stepfamilies formed after heterosexual unions (Lynch & Murray, 2000) because of their structural similarities to heterosexual stepfamilies. Gay and lesbian stepfamilies in which one adult is the genetic parent and the adult couple existed prior to the child's birth generally avoid stigma associated with stepfamilies by not referring to the non-genetic parent as a stepparent but rather as a second parent, using language that suggests equal or equivalent status for the two adults (e.g., co-mother), and, in general, acting as if they only differed from first-marriage families in the sexual identities of the adults. Many of the strategies employed by these gay and lesbian stepfamilies are framed as ways of building a sense of family, such as giving children born from DI the last name of the non-genetic parent (Oswald, 2002), but these strategies also function to hide or deny their stepfamily status. As we noted earlier, not all gay and lesbian couples with children think of themselves as stepfamilies, and, just as many heterosexual stepfamilies rely on the first-marriage family as a model, gay and lesbian stepfamilies with children in their households may do the same.

Berger (1998) argued that gay and lesbian couples in stepfamilies experienced *triple stigmatization*—stigma as homosexuals, stigma as stepfamily members, and from the gay community, stigma as homosexuals who have children. Other gay and lesbian individuals may see raising children as inconsistent with gay and lesbian lifestyles (Bozett, 1987). This latter stigma may actually be hardest on gay and lesbian parents and their partners, because it creates distance between themselves and the gay and lesbian community, which potentially could be a major source of social support.

Coming Out

Letting others know that they are homosexual, or *coming out of the closet*, is an incredibly difficult and important process for gay and lesbian individuals (Bozett, 1987). For the most part, concerns about coming out of the closet for gay and lesbian couples with children center mostly on the children and how peers and community members will treat them if it is known they have a homosexual parent (Lynch & Murray, 2000). Consequently, some previously married gay and lesbian parents are reluctant to come out to their children and to the community, not just because they fear rejection, but because they want to protect children from having to deal with ridicule and retaliation by peers and others in the community (Lynch & Murray, 2000). Although there is empirical evidence that young children, and even adolescents, generally are accepting of their gay parents' sexual orientation (Bozett, 1987; Clunis & Green, 1988; Hare, 1994), the coming out process for gay and lesbian parents is primarily influenced by their perceptions of the needs of their children rather than their own needs (Lynch & Murray, 2000). Lesbians who have children via DI tend to be out to their children when children are younger than is true for lesbians with children from earlier heterosexual unions. Lesbians who have children before coming out are older, on average, than lesbians who have children after they come out and than lesbians who do not have children (Morris, Balsam, & Rothblum, 2002).

A task for children is related to their parent's coming out. When a parent comes out, children must ultimately figure out what this means for them and for their families. Depending on the children's ages when this occurs, they reach some degree of understanding about what the differentness of their family situation means to them in terms of public attitudes about their parent's homosexuality, issues related to disclosing to friends and other people, and their personal identities. If parents come out when children are young, the children may have to re-think personal identity issues when they reach adolescence and are more able to think abstractly. Not only must the children of gay and lesbian parents negotiate these personal identity issues, but they must work out how to come out as a child of a gay or lesbian parent. This may be especially stressful for adolescents for whom peer opinion and avoiding ridicule can be so important.

Stepfamily Issues

Tasks and problems that gay and lesbian stepfamilies face in common with heterosexual stepfamilies include: Negotiating with nonresidential parents and managing issues related to the fact that children belong to two households, developing satisfying stepparent-stepchild relationships, coping with children's felt loyalties to both genetic parents, helping stepparents and nonresidential stepchildren feel that they belong, and developing a comfortable identity as a stepparent or stepchild (Berger, 1998; Crosbie-Burnett & Helmbrecht, 1993; Erera & Fredriksen, 1999; Hall & Kitson, 2000; Hare & Richards, 1993; Hequembourg, in press). These challenges are not limited to gays and lesbians with children from prior unions. However, when children are born after the formation of the homosexual union, although there is a genetic parent and a non-parent in the household, nonresidential genetic parents are rarely involved in children's lives (e.g., they may be anonymous sperm donors), the non-parent rarely identifies himself or herself as a stepparent, and children consider both adults to be their parents (Hare & Richards, 1993; Lynch & Murray, 2000; Nelson, 1996).

No or Few Legal Obligations and Rights

Although some European nations and a handful of legal jurisdictions in the United States recognize homosexual unions as domestic partnerships or *civil unions*, marriage, and the legal rights and responsibilities attendant to marriage, are not available to gay and lesbian couples (Mason, Fine, & Carnochan, in press). Just as with heterosexual relationships, this lack of legal ties creates even more problems when children are involved. When an adult and a child or children are not legally related, as is the case with stepparent-stepchild relationships, then the dissolution of the adult couple, from death or separation, can and often does sever the stepparent-stepchild relationship. Heterosexual stepparents are slowly gaining legal rights to maintain contact and to be involved with stepchildren after the dissolution of their marriage (Mason et al., in press) by filing for third party visitation in states where this is available or by filing civil suits to gain access to stepchildren. These are not likely to be successful strategies for homosexual stepparents, however (Dalton & Bielby, 2000).

Lack of Support

Given the double or triple social stigma faced by gay and lesbian couples and the challenges they face in establishing individual and family identities that are acceptable to themselves and to the society as a whole, it is not surprising that several scholars have applied Cherlin's (1978) notion of incomplete institutionalization to gay and lesbian stepfamilies (Hall & Kitson, 2000; Hequembourg, in press). These stepfamilies certainly fit what Cherlin described as incompletely institutionalized systems—we do not have language to adequately describe relationships (some authors point out that terms such as *gay fathers* and *lesbian mothers* are oxymoronic to some individuals, who think that parents must be heterosexual), they are not supported by laws and social policies, and they lack normative guidelines to follow for prescribed roles and rules for conduct. If heterosexual stepfamilies are incomplete social institutions, then gay and lesbian stepfamilies are doubly incomplete. How do they manage?

RESILIENCE STRATEGIES AMONG GAY AND LESBIAN STEPFAMILIES

Given that there are a number of longstanding gay and lesbian stepfamilies (e.g., Hequembourg, in press; Koepke et al., 1992; Nelson, 1996), some of them must have figured out ways to survive and even thrive despite severe challenges. Although resilience researchers have seldom examined gay and lesbian stepfamilies, a review of research on the family networks of gays and lesbians sheds light on two general resilience processes they employ—intentionality and redefinition (Oswald, 2002).

Intentionality

Intentionality has been defined as strategies used by gay and lesbian individuals and their loved ones to create and to sustain a sense of family (Oswald, 2002). This strategy includes choosing a kin network from among friends and family of origin members, managing disclosure of sexual identity and relationships, building community with supportive resources both within and outside of kin networks, engaging in rituals that affirm identities and create supportive environments, and making efforts to legalize relationships. Many of these strategies are used by gay and lesbian stepfamilies.

For instance, gays and lesbians often choose other-sex friends, including former spouses, as part of their kin networks so that children are exposed to various role models (Gartrell, Hamilton, Banks, Mosbacher, Reed, & Sparks, 1996). Family rituals such as bedtime routines are used to solidify bonds between children and co-mothers in lesbian stepfamilies (Reimann, 1997), and commitment ceremonies that involve children may be engaged in to connect the entire family as a unit. One of the primary motivations for stepparents to adopt is to protect the continuity of the step-relationship (Ganong et al., 1998), which is as true for gay and lesbian stepparents as for heterosexual stepparents (Reimann, 2001). Legalizing step-relationships is believed also to validate and legitimize the relationship to extended kin and other community members (Hequembourg & Farrell, 2001).

Redefinition

The second general strategy in resilience processes is to engage in redefinition processes by which gay and lesbian individuals and their families can be affirmed (Oswald, 2002). Redefining includes political action, naming individuals and relationships in ways that recognize their familial connections and importance, integrating homosexual identity with other aspects of identity, and conceptualizing and envisioning family in more inclusive ways than just biolegal relationships. In gay and lesbian stepfamilies, names are used to connect people in ways that enhance solidarity—stepparents may change their names to match that of the genetic parent, and the child or children reproduced via DI may be given the last name of the "co-parent" (Reimann, 1997). In addition, using inclusive definitions of who is in the family, definitions that include non-genetic and non-legal kin, is also a strategy that gay and lesbian stepfamilies can employ to facilitate feelings of integration as a unit.

SUMMARY

Clinicians and researchers who have written about gay and lesbian stepfamilies in recent years have decried the lack of attention to them by the scholarly community. The problems we have in discussing gay and lesbian stepfamilies mirror the problems in writing succinctly and cogently about all stepfamilies—we lack an accurate assessment of their prevalence, the demographic characteristics of such families are not clear, the diversity of gay and lesbian stepfamilies makes generalizing about them difficult, and there have been few studies of their family dynamics and relationships. From what has been written, we can conclude that the experiences of gay men and lesbians are likely to differ significantly, because gay fathers and their partners are far less likely than lesbian couples to have children as full-time residents in their homes. Moreover, the precursors to gay and lesbian stepfamily formation influence how family members think about themselves and how they relate to each other and to outsiders. Some gay and lesbian parents bring children from previous relationships into their homosexual unions, and these families resemble heterosexual stepfamilies in many ways. However, when children are born after the gay and lesbian couple has been formed, these families function quite differently from heterosexual stepfamilies. One point of interest is that many of the intentionality and redefinition strategies that Oswald (2002) identified as resilience processes of gays and lesbians and their families are also strategies engaged in by heterosexual stepfamilies. It may be that marginalized families of all kinds develop similar methods of making a go of it in a society that predominately supports only one family form, the first marriage heterosexual, nuclear family.

Chapter 7

The Dynamics of Parenting and Stepparenting

In this chapter we examine the *dynamics* of parent-child and stepparent-child relationships. Our primary interests center on *relational processes*—the *development* of step-relationships during stepfamily formation, the *maintenance* of ongoing genetic or adoptive parent-child relationships throughout the stepfamily's existence, and the maintenance of stepparent-stepchild relationships in established stepfamilies (Coleman & Ganong, 1995). In addition, we are interested in *changes* in relationships that occur over time and how those changes are brought about.

Most of our attention will be on the dynamics of residential mothers and stepfathers with young children and adolescents because stepfather-mother households have been studied more often than other stepfamilies (Coleman & Ganong, 2000). This is primarily because they are the most frequent type of stepfamily household (Fields, 1996), and, therefore, the easiest for researchers to sample. However, we also review what is known about relational processes of residential father and stepmother relationships. Finally, we inspect the small but growing literature on adult children and stepchildren and their family relationships. In this chapter we primarily examine research—in Chapter 11 we present clinicians' perspectives on parent-child and stepparent-stepchild relationships.

MOTHERS IN STEPFAMILY HOUSEHOLDS

Women are the "... unsung heroines of social integration. As child bearers, caregivers, and kin keepers, women provide the glue that holds families and lineage together" (Rossi, 1995, p. 275). Women, specifically mothers, are certainly the glue that holds stepfamilies together. The mother is the fulcrum in stepfather family households, a family that would not exist if it were not for her. Clearly, mothers in stepfamilies are important figures, and it is likely that one cannot understand the dynamics of stepfamilies without understanding how mothers function in them.

In fact, mothers are important in all family structures. Because they are so critical to family functioning, mothers have been studied much more than fathers in almost every area of family research (Coltrane, 2004). (It should be noted that there also may be practical reasons for mothers having been studied more—they volunteer for research more than fathers.) Given this heavy emphasis on mothers in family research in general and the fact that most stepfamilies would not exist if not for mothers, it might be expected that mothers in stepfamilies would have been so extensively studied that more is known about them than about other stepfamily members. This is not the case, however.

Although it is true that mothers are included in many stepfamily studies, there remains much to be learned about the dynamics of mothers' relationships with their children in stepfamilies (Solomon, 1995). This gap in the literature may be due to the perceived importance of step-relationships to family stability (Crosbie-Burnett, 1984), which leads researchers to focus their attention on step-relationships, rather than on parent-child relationships in stepfamilies.

Findings from the stepfamily research on mothers seem to support the assumption that good mothering in stepfamilies is similar to good mothering in nuclear families. That is, children perform better in school and have fewer internalizing and externalizing behavior problems when mothers engage in *authoritative parenting* (Bogenscheider, 1997; Pong, 1997). Authoritative parenting is engaging in supportive and warm behaviors along with providing structure and assertive control of children's behaviors. Greater warmth and involvement, better communication, and more maternal assertiveness are related to better parent-child relationships, regardless of family structure (Bray, 1992). In stepfather families, when mothers do fewer things with their children, such as talking with them, working on projects, and helping them with homework, the children misbehave more in school and exhibit more internalizing and externalizing behavior problems (Thomson, Hanson, & McLanahan, 1994).

Research findings on mothers' monitoring of children (i.e., enforcing rules, keeping track of where children are, who they are with, what they are doing, and assuring that they are supervised) have been inconsistent. Although some researchers have reported that monitoring is less well done by remarried mothers than by mothers in first marriage families (Kim, Hetherington & Reiss, 1999), other researchers have found no differences in monitoring of children by adults in stepmother, stepfather, and nuclear families (Bulcroft, Carmody & Bulcroft, 1998; Fisher, Leve, O'Leary, & Leve, 2003). It is difficult to interpret differences in findings regarding mother-child relationship processes in stepfamilies because of limitations in the studies of mothers' parenting styles (mostly defined as warmth and control) (Bulcroft et al., 1998). First, variations between studies may be a consequence of who provided the information—although respondents vary, adolescents and mothers are the most frequent reporters in these studies, and they are likely to have different perceptions about mothers' styles of parenting (Sweeting, 2001). Second, although the few researchers who have separately analyzed cohabiting and remarried mothers have reported differences in parental and family processes, most studies have grouped cohabiting mothers with remarried mothers (sometimes cohabiting and single mothers are grouped together) for analysis (Bulcroft et al., 1998). It is likely that important distinctions and variability in mothers' interactions with their children in stepfamilies are lost when disparate types of families are categorized and analyzed together. Third, researchers do not always distinguish between parents and stepparents when examining the effects of parental styles on children in diverse family structures. Fourth, although researchers have found that mother-child interactions change over time in stepfamilies, most studies of mothers' parenting in stepfamilies have not assessed and controlled for the length of time the stepfamily has been together. Finally, few of the researchers investigating mothers' parenting behaviors have examined the potential for interactions between race, child's age, child's gender, and family structure, variables that some researchers have found to be related to parental behaviors.

From the few studies in which mothering processes in stepfamilies have been examined over time, we can conclude that mothers in stepfather households experience difficulties in parenting shortly after remarriage, but after a period of adjustment their parenting styles resemble those of mothers in first marriages (Bray & Berger, 1993; Henderson & Taylor, 1999; Hetherington & Jodl, 1994). Bray found that newly remarried mothers of 6 to 8-year-old children engaged in authoritarian parenting more often than a comparison group of first marriage mothers, who were more authoritative. That is, remarried mothers were more likely to use stern, dogmatic control without explaining the reasons for their discipline to children, whereas mothers in first marriage families were more likely to control their children's behavior using warmth and logical explanations for their rules. In contrast to Bray's findings, Hetherington and her colleagues reported nearly the opposite—that rather than being authoritarian, mothers exhibited greater permissiveness and lack of control of children during the remarriage transition. However, mothers in established stepfamilies (average length of remarriage was 9 years) generally resembled mothers in first marriages in how they interacted with their children (Henderson & Taylor, 1999; O'Connor & Insabella, 1999). Using data from two waves of the National Survey of Families and Households to investigate changes in parenting associated with the remarriage of single mothers, Thomson, Mosley, Hanson, and McLanahan (2001) found that remarried mothers less often yelled, spanked, or hit children than did single mothers. However, mothers in single parent households provided more child supervision than remarried mothers did. Additionally, children, but not mothers, indicated that mother-child relationships were better after remarriage. Although the findings from these studies are not entirely consistent regarding mothering behavior, there is agreement that re-marriage transitions change what mothers do and how they interact with children, at least for a while. Once they have adjusted to the changes in their households, mothers appear to relate to their children much as they had before the marital transition.

Although the data on monitoring and parenting style are interesting, what is missing from the research on mothers in stepfamilies is a clear sense of how changes in mothers' behaviors are brought about, and why. Erickson (1993) opined that being the family caretaker is something women *are* rather than something women *do*, and therefore, it is not necessary to study them. We propose, however, that because mothers are so critical to stepfamily functioning, researchers must try to determine what roles mothers play, how they feel about those roles, and how these roles affect stepfamily functioning and the mothers' own well-being. An understanding of the cultural values related to mothering is helpful in exploring motherhood in stepfamilies.

The Motherhood Mandate and Mothers in Stepfamilies

Women's family behavior appears to evolve from what Lois Braverman (1989) called *the myth of motherhood*. This myth dictates that motherhood is instinctual, that having a child fulfills a woman in ways that no other experience can, and that mothers are the best care providers for their children. The myth of motherhood is reflected in cultural belief systems, patterns of family interaction, and societal values regarding what is best for children—how they should be raised, who should raise them, and who should be held accountable for their physical and mental health. Russo (1976) referred to this as the *motherhood mandate*.

More recently, Hays (1996) defined motherhood as a historically constructed ideology that influences all women's behavior, whether they have children or not. The social construction of motherhood assumes that women will care for others both within and outside families, and that they will define themselves within the context of relationships. In Western culture, the myth of motherhood places full responsibility on women for family relationships regardless of the context. If children have significant problems, it must be the mother's fault.

According to Braverman (1989), the socially constructed myth of mother-hood organizes the thoughts, feelings, and behaviors of women, their families, and the society in which they live; women organize their lives around being a good mother. She says that women do this because they receive satisfaction from fulfilling the myth, and they feel guilty when they do not. Kranichfeld (1987) has a slightly different view of why women organize their lives around being a good mother. She asserts that it is through motherhood that women gain family power, which she defines as "the ability of individual members to change the be-havior (including thought and affect) of other family members . . . " (p. 43). Given that "family power exists because of one's relationship within the family system" (p. 43), mothers gain power with their ability to fulfill the motherhood mandate. Kranichfeld believes that researchers have incorrectly assumed that family power is generated by acquiring status outside the family (i.e., skills, money, jobs) rather than being generated by acquiring relationship skills within the family. "Women's power may have low visibility from a nonfamily perspective, but women are the lynchpins of family cohesion and socialization, and this is certainly a position of power" (p. 48). More specifically, it is the power within the mother-child relationship rather than within the marriage and marital decision making process that is most significant and enduring.

These views—(1) motherhood as the means by which women gain family power, and (2) failing to fulfill the motherhood myth leading to feelings of guilt—have received little attention by stepfamily researchers. However, clinicians have long posited that some mothers feel guilty about the potential effects of divorce on their children, which may lead them to remarry rapidly (Visher & Visher, 1979). Remarriage may be seen by these mothers both as a way to restore financial stability (Hill, 1992) and to re-create a nuclear family for the children. Mothers usually gain financially for their children by remarrying (Hill, 1992), but the problems related to re-creating the nuclear family in a stepfamily household are expressed throughout this book (see Chapter 11 for clinicians' views). The effects of the motherhood mandate on stepfamily functioning may be dependent on how the mother interprets her identity within the new stepfamily.

In order to explore mothers' views about their roles and relationships in stepfamilies, Weaver and Coleman (in review) conducted in-depth interviews with 24 remarried women. Being a mother was extremely important to these women; even to one who described herself as resentful of her maternal responsibilities. In general, particularly during the early stages of stepfamily formation, these women perceived their mother and wife roles as quite distinct. This is not surprising since they had been performing the mother function much longer than the role of spouse, at least with their current husbands. In first marriage families, the spousal role is typically performed first and mothering comes later. Even considering the strength of the motherhood mandate, a married woman has time to integrate the two roles of mother and wife into one overarching family role. When remarriages begin, being a mother is typically much more salient to the woman's identity than her relatively new spousal role. In this sample of remarried women, if the demands of these two roles were incompatible, there was little doubt which one these mothers would choose to fulfill. One mother said, "When you're asked to choose between your child and your spouse. . . I think you would probably have to choose the child, because they are your child, and they are your responsibility."

In general, the remarried mothers whom Weaver and Coleman interviewed saw their responsibility in the stepfamily primarily as the *protector* of their children. They did this through four role functions—*gatekeeper, defender, mediator,* and *interpreter*. For example, as gatekeepers, mothers controlled stepfathers' access to their children both before and after the marriage. Mothers in all families perform the gatekeeper role function to some extent. For example, in first marriage families, a father's involvement with children is often contingent on the mother's attitudes toward, expectations of, and support for him (DeLuccie, 1995), and single mothers (and grandmothers) control the access of unmarried or divorced fathers to their children (Doherty, Kouneski, & Erickson, 1998). The interviewed mothers began gatekeeping with their children's stepfathers from the start of their relationship—most did not introduce their children to the men who became their husbands until they perceived the relationship would lead to remarriage (Weaver & Coleman, in review). They continued to gatekeep their husbands' interactions with their children to some degree for years after remarrying, which may partially explain stepfathers' disengagement from their stepchildren as discussed later in this chapter. Considering the combination of a strong cultural motherhood mandate and the social stigma of stepfathers as predators, it is little wonder that mothers in stepfamilies are reluctant to share parenting tasks and childrearing responsibilities. It is important to note here that none of these mothers indicated that their husbands had ever abused their children in any way. The mothers were protecting their children from perceived slights, lack of insight regarding the child, and unrealistic expectations for the child's behavior.

A second role function common among the remarried mothers was that of *defender* (Weaver & Coleman, in review). Mothers defended their children against any perceived threat to their safety or well-being (one mother described herself as being like a grizzly bear with her cubs). The myth of motherhood establishes that women are responsible for the health and safety of their children; a good mother should diligently defend her child, even against members of her own household (i.e., stepfather, stepsiblings). There were some indications that this defending behavior started when the mothers were single. Many conveyed a sense of "us against the world" mentality that developed as they struggled to provide financially and emotionally for their children during the single parent family period.

Remarried mothers also serve as *mediators* (Weaver & Coleman, in review). The myth of motherhood implies that women are not only responsible for the health and safety of their children, they are also responsible for the interpersonal relationships within their family. To control interpersonal relationships, mothers reported mediating conflicts that arose between their husband and children, mediating behind the scenes to avoid conflicts from arising, and mediating after disputes occurred to smooth things over. This was an important function during the early part of stepfamily formation and perhaps especially during their children's adolescence. Although the women saw themselves as successful mediators, they found the process stressful, and some of them eventually abdicated this role function. Those who abdicated the role perceived that conflicts between their husbands and children increased, but over time the conflicts diminished in both intensity and frequency.

The final role function was *interpreter*. As interpreters the mothers attempted to educate their husbands about the children and vice versa with a goal of shared understanding. Interpreting sometimes, but not always, was practiced in conjunction with mediating; a mother might step in to mediate a conflict and then follow up with interpreting. For example, if a stepfather and adolescent stepson got into an argument about how loud the adolescent's music is, the mother might intervene by telling the child to turn the music down and by shutting her son's bedroom door and her husband's office door. Later, she might explain to her son when they are alone that the stepfather is not used to being around teenagers and so he is unsettled by the loud music when he is working at home. She would remind her husband later that adolescents like loud music, that teenagers do not always think before they act, and that the stepson was not trying to be disruptive on purpose. The mothers often described these interpreting examples as "parent education" or "teaching."

These maternal role functions had varying effects on stepfamilies. Gatekeeping served to regulate the amount of stepfather involvement in childrearing. Although mothers' gatekeeping typically lessened over time in stepfamilies, few abandoned the practice completely, and in some stepfamilies, mothers' gate keeping was fairly constant over the course of the family history. In general, stepfathers had less involvement with stepchildren than fathers do in first marriage families (Bray & Berger, 1993; Henderson & Taylor, 1999); which may have been a result of mothers' gatekeeping behaviors. Whether or not this is harmful to stepfamily functioning may depend on the stepfathers' expectations for his role in the family. For instance, some mothers may enter remarriage with clearly articulated expectations that they will be the primary parent for their children, and the stepfather is to be their husband (Bray & Kelly, 1998) and not a parent. Bray called these households *matriarchal stepfamilies*, because the mothers are strong, effective parents who ask for little help and want little involvement by their new or former partners. Some stepfamilies are formed for the *adult couple relationship* (see chapter 1), and in these stepfamilies mothers are content to be responsible for raising their children while they and their partners focus most of their energies on the couple relationship (Berger, 1995; Bray & Kelly, 1998; Burgoyne & Clark, 1984). Gatekeeping would be normative and acceptable to individuals in these two kinds of stepfamilies. However, if stepfathers expect to be involved with parenting the children and make an effort to do so, then continued gatekeeping may be detrimental to stepfamily integration and individuals' well-being.

The effect of the defender role on stepfamily integration is less ambiguous. Mothers who defend clearly value their role as mother over their spousal role (Weaver & Coleman, in review), and although defending lessened as the children got older and the mothers determined the children could look after their own interests, the constant triangulation of mother and child against the stepfather places a strain on marriages (Browning, 1994). Defending suggests a lack of trust in the stepfather's abilities to raise children or an unwillingness to allow stepfathers and stepchildren to work out disagreements without the mother as a referee or child advocate. Defending also creates coalitions that inhibit the growth of a family identity (Browning) and leaves stepfathers uncertain about their role in the stepfamily. Studies have reported that stepfathers who are uncertain about how to relate to their stepchildren are less satisfied with their stepfamilies (Erera-Weatherly, 1996). Stepfathers' uncertainty may be a consequence of mothers' defending behaviors, but it also may be a result of mothers and stepfathers not clearly communicating about desired childrearing roles. For example, stepfathers may be asked to do some parenting duties (e.g., pay for school lunches, enforce curfews), but defended against when they overstep the mothers' preferences for stepfather involvement (Visher & Visher, 1996). Although the women Weaver and Coleman interviewed were remarried, we hypothesize that mothers who continue to take a strong defending posture against the stepfather will not stay married.

Although mothers' mediator role was one that was appreciated by stepchildren, the mothers found it stressful and a source of internal conflict and few continued it. On the other hand, mothers perceived that the interpreter function worked well, and they believed that it continued to serve a valuable purpose over time. It is likely that mothers do not engage in mediating or interpreting unless they are invested in the remarriage and are committed to a long-term relationship with the stepfather. We hypothesize that cohabiting mothers would be less likely than remarried mothers to engage in either mediating or interpreting because of less commitment to their partners than remarried mothers have to their spouses (Bumpass & Lu, 2000). The added efforts demanded by mediating and interpreting are unlikely to occur in the context of low partner commitment.

Role Conflicts

In general, the women in the Weaver and Coleman study were quite gendered in their expectations for the stepfamily. According to clinicians, conventional gender issues such as the mother being in charge of the household and the children are not challenged unless either the mother or the stepfather believes that she is not managing the children well (Carter, 1988). However, the belief that she is not managing the children well is quite common, at least early in the stepfamily formation. In our experience with dozens of stepfamilies, it has become a given that when interviewed separately, parents complain that stepparents are too hard on the children and do not understand them, and stepparents complain that parents are far too lenient and require too little of the children. Although these disparate perceptions do not necessarily mean that mothers and stepfathers will disagree about her ability to control children's behaviors, it hints that there is the possibility of conflicts surrounding mothers' management of children. Mothers may feel caught between their children and their spouses and overwhelmed by mother/spouse role conflict. The following mother expressed a poignant example of role conflict:

> I kept having to choose between my son and my husband, my son, my husband . . . I was just this divided person, you know. I would think, I love my husband I want to be with him. I want to make this marriage work. But then, I'd think, but I love my son and I don't want my husband to be disrespectful to him. It was just like, I wasn't able to love both of them or something.

In remarriage the continued conflict between mother and spousal role functions is unlikely to lead to either stepfamily integration or to the well-being of the mothers. Mothers who suffer severe role conflicts are likely to leave the marriage. Her spouse is also likely to leave the marriage if it becomes obvious that his wife would always choose her child over him. Mothers may need assistance from clinicians in gradually integrating the two role functions (mother, spouse). This is not an easy task in light of the strong motherhood mandate in our society. In-depth longitudinal studies of mothers in stepfamilies could provide insight regarding how roles change over time and how women's perceptions of themselves as mothers change.

NONRESIDENTIAL MOTHERS

There are very few studies in which nonresidential mothers in stepfamilies have been included. Clinicians also have had little to say about nonresidential mothers. These mothers are truly forgotten stepfamily members. Nonresidential mothers have to deal with more stigma, given the motherhood mandate and gendered expectations regarding mothering. A relatively recent study by Stewart (1999) found that nonresidential mothers (not all of whom were in stepfamilies) were similar to nonresidential fathers in that nearly half had not seen their children in a year; however, mothers maintained more regular, frequent contacts with nonresidential children via phone calls and letters than did fathers. The involvement of nonresidential mothers with their children living in stepfamily households may be a mixed blessing. Clingempeel and colleagues found that the stepfamily dynamics were negatively affected when nonresidential mothers maintained involvement with their children after their ex-spouse had remarried. More needs to be known about this phenomenon.

FATHERS IN STEPFAMILY HOUSEHOLDS

Fathers who live with their children in stepfamilies may live in simple stepmother households where all of the children are his, or he may be raising stepchildren in addition to his own genetic or adopted children (see Table 1.1). Of this latter group, some fathers are in complex step-households in which both the mother and father have brought children from prior relationships into the household, and some are fathers to children born in the remarriage union.

Residential fathers who are also stepfathers exhibit more father-like role identities toward stepchildren than do men who are stepfathers only (Marsiglio, 1992). Living with children of their own appears to help fathers be better stepfathers to their stepchildren than they would be otherwise (Marsiglio, 1992; Palisi, Orleans, Caddell, & Korn, 1991). Children may serve to enhance their fathers' relationships with their stepsiblings in several ways. For example, stepfathers may be drawn closer to their stepchildren, and they may have fewer negative attitudes toward them because of the strategies they adopt in striving to treat both sets of children in an equitable manner. The presence of their children in the household, in effect, may force men to parent to a greater extent than if they had merely been absorbed into a pre-existing family. It is also possible that fathers who have joint or sole physical custody of their children are selectively those who are more committed to the parental role. It can be argued that these men might be psychologically predisposed toward a positive perception of the parental role and a greater commitment to parenting (Palisi et al., 1991). Crosbie-Burnett (1989) found less competition between the men in complex stepfamilies (i.e., the father and stepfather) and concluded that stepfathers who are actively participating in raising their own children are either not attempting to function in the father role with their stepchildren or can co-father better. Because both men in these complex stepfamily situations frequently are non-residential fathers at least part of the time, they may have more empathy for each other.

NONRESIDENTIAL FATHERS IN STEPFAMILIES

In Chapter 3 we discussed post-divorce co-parenting. We examined some of the rapidly growing research on nonresidential fathers and the effects of remarriage on co-parenting between nonresidential fathers and mothers.

Most nonresidential parents (90%) are men (McKenry, McKelvey, Leigh, & Wark, 1996). Relationships between nonresidential fathers and their children are often not maintained after remarriage of either parent; as many as 50% of children lose contact with their fathers (Stephens, 1996). However, a substantial minority of children (25%) see their fathers at least once a week (Seltzer & Brandreth, 1994). It has been hypothesized that the new responsibilities and constraints on time and resources that come with remarriage reduce contact between nonresidential fathers and children (Stephens, 1996), but findings from empirical investigations are mixed (McKenry et al., 1996; Seltzer & Bianchi, 1988; Veum, 1993).

However, frequency of contact may not be the most important factor in maintaining and enhancing the relationship or the well-being of those involved. Duration of visits is an aspect of the relationship that also should be assessed (Stephen, Freedman, & Hess, 1993). Some relationship maintenance strategies may be met in shorter visits while others require longer periods of time.

The quality of the contact may be even more important in maintaining nonresidential parent-child relationships than either the frequency or duration of contact (Buchanan, Maccoby, & Dornbusch, 1996). Emotionally supportive fathers who set, explain, and uphold guidelines for behavior positively influence their children. Implementing such behaviors takes time, however, and requires a certain degree of contact. The nature of the nonresidential relationship may make this a challenging task if fathers want to make the most of the limited time with their children and perceive that disciplining them would negatively interfere. Therefore, it is not surprising that activities commonly engaged in by nonresidential fathers and children revolve around leisure activities (Stewart, 1999).

How nonresidential fathers feel about maintaining their parental role may change after remarriage. Remarried and cohabiting nonresidential fathers have lower perceptions of the manageability of the parent role than first-marriage fathers do (Seltzer & Brandreth, 1994) and the influence they have on their children's lives (McKenry et al., 1996). When the nonresidential father acquires a new partner, relations with his children may still be enjoyable and involvement in important activities continued, but the combination of old responsibilities with new ones from the remarriage may create stress. How these potentially competing responsibilities are handled may have important implications for enhancement and maintenance of the parent-child relationship. Braver, Wolchik, Sandler, and Sheets (1993) hypothesized that greater rewards and fewer costs result in greater nonresidential fathers' involvement with their children. Therefore, ways to manage possible costs are important considerations for relationship maintenance.

On the other hand, boundaries and guidelines for the involvement of the nonresidential father are also important for the functioning of the stepfamily. Family members must figure out a way to incorporate the nonresidential father but at the same time maintain and develop relationships within the residential family household. Clear communication of expectations is one way to facilitate understanding and agreement and to maintain the role nonresidential parents play in the lives of their children.

The ways in which individuals maintain nonresidential parent-child relationships are largely unclear. There are few norms for relationships between nonresidential parents and children (Greif & Kristall, 1993), and this ambiguity may be one reason why nonresidential father involvement greatly varies and contact is erratic (Seltzer, 1991). Furthermore, although there have been many investigations of factors that influence the frequency of contact between nonresidential parents and children and the implications this may have for children's well-being, research on the maintenance and enhancement of nonresidential parent-child relationships after remarriage or repartnering of one or both parents is lacking.

THE DYNAMICS OF STEPPARENTING

Individuals who need immediate gratification may not enjoy being a stepparent. Stepchildren seldom express gratitude to stepparents for the financial assistance, guidance, and other support provided them during childhood. If they do show gratitude it is usually after they become adults, sometimes with children or stepchildren of their own. As we have noted earlier in this book, fairy tales, movies, and other media tend to show stepparents in an extremely negative light—abusive, exploitive, neglectful, even murderous. Some social scientists present a similarly bleak picture (Daly & Wilson, 2001; Popenoe, 1994), while other social scientists, such as Mavis Hetherington (2002), and we include ourselves in this category, are much more positive about stepparent-stepchild relationships in stepfamilies. Who is right? Who is wrong?

One point of agreement is that being a stepparent is challenging, and individuals are poorly socialized in Western cultures to become stepparents. In addition, the process of developing a mutually satisfying stepparent-stepchild relationship is challenging because stepparents are trying to build these relationships within the context of ongoing parent-child relationships, the ongoing co-parental ties between stepchildren's mothers and fathers, and the multiple and possibly conflicting expectations of parents, children, and the stepparent.

Stepparents have been referred to as *intimate outsiders* (Beer, 1991) and as *relative strangers* (Beer, 1988). These oxymoronic terms convey the ambiguity of these relationships. Such labels evoke the image of stepparents as being members of the family as well as intruders who are not privy to the secrets and knowledge shared by family insiders. The status of being both an insider and an outsider can be unsettling and uncomfortable. Becoming a stepparent also has been likened to setting up housekeeping on an ice floe (Peterson, 1985). The tasks of integrating into the family are indeed slippery ones, difficult to firmly grip, especially in what may be an inclement environment. None of these images brings to mind the giddily happy *Brady Bunch*. Instead, they are rather sad and poignant. Perhaps these descriptions emerge because it is difficult to raise other people's children, especially when performance expectations are often high, unrealistic, or ambiguous.

When people remarry, they expect stepparenting to work out (Ganong & Coleman, 1989). Stepparents who have always liked children look forward to the opportunity to take a parenting role. Some make it clear that they do not want to be involved in childrearing from the start. Others give little thought to their role as a stepparent, perhaps assuming things will naturally fall into place or that their spouse will guide their interactions with the stepchild. Some nonresidential stepparents, and older stepparents whose spouse's children are adults, may not expect much involvement with the stepchildren, assuming that periodic visits by them will be the extent of their limited interactions. It is likely that most nonresidential stepparents do not anticipate that there might be changes in physical custody.

The terms *nonresidential* and *residential stepparent* suggest discrete types of experiences. However, these categorical terms often misrepresent the dynamic experiences of stepparents whose stepchildren split their time as residents in both parents' households. To add to the complexity, stepparents may also be parents, both to children born before they became stepparents and to children born to the stepfamily couple. Stepparents may or may not be legally married to the parents of their stepchildren. Stepparents may be in gay or lesbian relationships as well (see Chapter 9). Although there are commonalities experienced by stepparents in all types of stepfamilies, generalizations should be made with extreme caution.

Here are some examples of stepparenting diversity:

Jose lives with his second wife Rita and her children from a prior marriage. This is Jose's first marriage, and he has no children. Researchers might label this a *simple stepfather household* (only one adult brings children to the relationship).

Tom lives with his girlfriend Deborah and they are visited on weekends occasionally by her children from earlier relationships. Tom has no children. Some people would consider Tom a *nonresidential stepfather* in a *cohabiting stepfamily*. Other people would *not* consider Tom to be a stepfather at all, and they would not see him as part of a stepfamily.

Mary recently married Bill. Bill has had no contact with his two school-aged children since he divorced their mother over 8 years ago. Although Mary would be considered a *nonresidential stepmother* to Bill's two children, she has had no contact with them whatsoever. There is *no relationship*.

Thelma lives with Louise. Louise is the mother of two school-aged children who visit every other weekend and during the summer. The rest of the time they live with their father, who was married to Louise before she came out as a lesbian. Some individuals would consider Thelma to be a *nonresidential stepmother* to Louise's children, but Thelma sees herself as their friend.

Maria recently married Hernando. He has joint physical custody of his two school-aged children. They spend half the week with Maria and Hernando and half the week with their mother. Maria is a stepmother, but there is no clear adjective for the type of stepmother she is. Is she a semi-residential stepmother, a part-time residential stepmother, or should some new term be applied in this case?

LaDonna is married to Malik, who has sole legal and physical custody of his two children. They live with him most of the time and stay with their mother occasionally. LaDonna, in this case, is a *residential* stepmother.

Andre and Willetta have each been previously married three times; they live with his son from his first marriage, her son from her second marriage, and a daughter born to them. Every other weekend, their two boys leave to stay with their other parents, and Andre's daughter from his second marriage and Willetta's son from her first marriage come to spend a weekend with them. This family is a *complex stepfamily household* that contains his, hers, and their children. Andre is a father as well as a stepfather to both residential and nonresidential children and stepchildren.

William has three daughters who live with their mother all of the time. He is remarried to Elizabeth, and her daughter from a prior marriage lives with them. Elizabeth's son lives with his father, although he sees Elizabeth and William regularly. This is a *complex stepfamily*, but the household is a *simple stepfather household*. William is a *nonresidential father*, a *residential stepfather*, and a *nonresidential stepfather*.

Both of the last two families described would fit what Visher and Visher (1996) called *accordion stepfamily households* because the household membership expands and contracts similarly to the bellows on an accordion.

The stepparents described above have very different family situations. You could easily imagine several more variations to these vignettes by changing children's ages, gender, residence, and contact patterns with stepparents. We mention this complexity issue to alert you to our concerns about generalizing too broadly from any study.

The complexity issue is important. For instance, where a stepchild lives is not a trivial matter in making sense of the stepparent-stepchild relationship. Sharing a residence creates more opportunities to interact and to develop a close relationship than is the case if stepparents and stepchildren spend time together only a few days or weeks per year. Expectations for role enactment differ depending on whether stepparents are in contact with the stepchild daily, rarely, or never. The effects of stepparent-stepchild relationships on other close relationships in the stepfamily also are likely to be dependent on the amount of contact between them. The importance of defining the specific relationship and distinguishing between family and household is critical when interpreting the data on stepparenting in a meaningful way.

In considering the dynamics of stepparent-stepchild relationships, two processes are of interest—relationship development and maintenance. A third process, the *dissolution* of step-relationships, is also of interest, but few researchers (or clinicians) have examined this phenomenon. Perhaps the most fundamental issue to address is the development of the stepparent-stepchild relationship. Arguably, many of the difficulties faced by stepparents, stepchildren, and stepfamilies are related to confusion and uncertainty about the roles that stepparents should play in their stepchildren's lives, and how they should relate to each other. Among the problems identified most often by clinicians and researchers are role ambiguity (i.e., lack of clarity regarding expectations for the stepparent role), role confusion (i.e., choice of roles), and conflict between multiple roles (Whitsett & Land, 1992). Problems associated with role change, role captivity (being stuck in one role while wanting to perform another), and self-image role incongruence have also been identified as potential difficulties for stepparents.

RESIDENTIAL STEPFATHERS AND STEPCHILDREN

"The empirical literature generally has concluded that stepfathers have little or no effect on child outcome" (White & Gilbreath, 2001, p. 156). This remarkable statement is based on the fact that researchers often find that stepchildren in stepfather households do not differ significantly on outcome measures from children in single-mother headed families. White and Gilbreath cite McLanahan and Sandefur's (1994) conclusion that "in terms of substantive outcomes, children from stepfamilies have only one parent" (p. 156). Although they note that this conclusion is based on a "simple family structure variable rather than on family process measures" (p. 156), they point out that some researchers indicate that the most common parenting style among stepfathers is to be disengaged from stepchildren (Hetherington, 1988), which lends support to the *no effect hypothesis*.

We do not dispute the general findings regarding research on stepchildren's outcomes, but we question the conclusion that stepfathers have no or minimal effects on stepchildren, and we doubt that there are many members of stepfather households who would agree with it. Such a conclusion is as much a consequence of researchers' epistemic values as it is anything—secondary data sets provide great opportunities for researchers who want to compare large representative groups of individuals on various outcomes. However, such data sets are more limited when researchers try to extract information about relational processes to help them explain the outcomes. Process explanations can be examined with secondary data sets, but even when longitudinal data sets in which individuals are contacted multiple times are used, the external validity of the findings is limited in capturing relational processes. It can be likened to watching a series of still photographs of stepfamily relationships instead of an action movie.

Stepfathers have been variously portrayed as: (a) *competitors* to nonresidential fathers; (b) *heroes* who have come to rescue the family from poverty, chaos, or worse; (c) *intruders* who disrupt established patterns of family life; (d) *friends* to children; (e) *resources*; (f) *abusers*; (g) *quasi-kin*; (h) *father replacements*; and (i) *nonparents* (Ganong & Coleman, 1994). In the absence of societal guidelines and consensual agreements about the nature of stepfather-stepchild relationships stepfathers are challenged to figure out appropriate roles and relationships with their stepchildren (Whitsett & Land, 1992).

Developing Step-relationships

How do stepfathers develop relationships with their stepchildren? Perhaps surprisingly, the development of stepparent-stepchild relationships has seldom been studied. This may be a consequence of the data that are available to researchers— as noted earlier, assessing processes with large secondary data sets is difficult. Consequently, we must rely on a handful of in-depth longitudinal studies and a few small scale qualitative or mixed-method investigations to get a picture of how step-relationships develop.

Perhaps the most widely cited studies of stepfather-stepchild relationship development are those of Mavis Hetherington and her colleagues (e.g., Hetherington & Clingempeel, 1992; Hetherington, Henderson, & Reiss, 1999). In their multi-method, multi-informant longitudinal studies of newly formed stepfather households with young adolescents, they found considerable family turmoil in the early stages of stepfamily life, with little improvement over the first few years in the quality of stepfather-stepchild relationships. Hetherington and Clingempeel reported that stepfathers initially interacted like *polite strangers* with stepchildren. In general, stepfather-stepchild relationships became more distant and stepfathers became less skilled at controlling and monitoring the stepchildren's behavior. This same pattern was found among fathers and children in a nondivorced comparison group, which was attributed to developmental changes in the adolescents, but stepfathers disengaged more than fathers, perhaps because their relationships with the stepchildren were more tenuous.

Bray and Kelly (1998) also found that the first 2 years of stepfamily life were particularly stressful and tense, a phenomenon that they attributed to unrealistic expectations held by stepfamily members. In Bray's (1999) longitudinal study stepfathers also became less involved with stepchildren over the first 2 years, in part because children rebuffed their attempts to engage in "effective parenting skills" (p. 263). However, Bray found, as did Hetherington (1993; Hetherington, Cox & Cox, 1982) in two separate studies, that stepfathers who developed the closest relationships with stepchildren had focused on developing warm relationships that were characterized by a high degree of communication with the stepchildren.

We had similar findings when we studied the process of how stepparents, mostly stepfathers, attempted to elicit liking (affinity) from their stepchildren in a small sample of stepfamilies (Ganong et al., 1999). The families in our study were generally not in the early years of stepfamily life (the average length of remarriage was about 5 years), but stepfamily members reported retrospectively on their perceptions of the early years of their stepfamily and, indeed, even before the remarriage. We identified three patterns of stepparent affinity-seeking. In the first pattern, *continuous affinity-seekers* regularly tried to become friends and build affinity with stepchildren, both before and after the remarriage. The *early affinity-seekers* initially tried to elicit liking from their stepchildren, but stopped doing so after the remarriage. The early affinity-seekers discontinued such efforts after they moved in with their stepchildren, assuming the role of parent, which they apparently saw as incompatible with getting their stepchildren to like them. Finally, there was a group of stepparents who made relatively few attempts at any time to generate affinity from their stepchildren, and we labeled this pattern, *nonseekers*. Not surprisingly, the continuous affinity-seekers had the most cohesive relationships with their stepchildren, which was reported independently by both the stepparents and stepchildren. These stepparents were far more likely than other stepparents to engage in activities in which the child wanted to participate, as opposed to activities of interest to the stepparent only. Moreover, they reported engaging in dyadic interactions alone with the stepchildren, which were more effective at developing affinity than activities that involved everyone in the household, probably because they allow stepparents and stepchildren to get to know each other without being distracted by the presence and reactions of third persons. Dyadic activities provide opportunities for stepparents and stepchildren to spend more time directly interacting, which is an important factor in affinity development (Daly & Bell, 1996). These stepparents were more likely to communicate empathy and an understanding of the children's needs and interests than were the other stepparents. Certainly, the stepparents who continued to seek affinity either asked their stepchildren what they liked to do, or they observed their stepchildren carefully enough to know what activities to suggest. These stepparents communicated warmth and an interest in becoming friends with their stepchildren. Non-affinity-seeking stepparents either seldom communicated with stepchildren or they conveyed little of the interest and affection normally associated with making friends.

These findings echoed those of earlier studies (Kelley, 1996; Stern, 1982), and shed light on why some of the stepfathers in Hetherington's studies and in Bray's study were more successful than others were in developing close step-relationships. The results of these studies indicate that step-relationships more often are characterized by liking and affection when stepparents focus on developing friendships with stepchildren before they attempt to discipline and set rules for them (Bray & Berger, 1993; Crosbie-Burnett & Giles-Sims, 1994; Hetherington & Clingempeel, 1992). (See Chapter 11 for a full discussion of clinicians' views.) Obviously, research is needed that employs larger, more representative samples of stepfamilies than these studies, but we think it is safe to conclude that affinity-seeking strategies used by stepparents result in greater liking of them by their stepchildren. Further, the findings suggest that affinity-seeking efforts need to be *maintained* for them to be most effective. Disciplining appears to get in the way of affinity seeking, so it may be helpful for stepparents to focus on affinity developing and delay assuming a role as disciplinarian for as long as possible (Kelley, 1996).

Relationship Development as a Bi-directional Process

What stepfathers (and stepmothers) do to build a good relationship with stepchildren is only part of the story. Relational development is clearly a bi-directional process. If stepchildren do not respond to affinity building efforts (Ganong et al., 1999) or if they rebuff stepfathers' attempts to get close to them (Bray, 1999; Hetherington & Clingempeel, 1992), then all but the most self-assured stepparent is likely to reduce or completely stop their efforts.

Why would a stepchild not respond to friendly overtures? First, they may not recognize the stepfather's behavior as affinity building. In our study, the closest step-relationships occurred when the stepchildren recognized their stepparent's attempts to become friends and responded in kind. For this reason, we speculated that engaging in activities that are chosen by the stepchild are more effective at affinity building because they are activities that the stepchild values, making it more likely that they will appreciate the stepparents' efforts. A second reason that stepchildren may not respond is because they have little in common with the step-parent, other than their mutual love for the child's parent. Finally, stepchildren may not respond positively to stepparents' warm overtures because they feel pressure not to respond from other people. The success of relationship building efforts cannot be understood without also understanding the interpersonal contexts in which they occur.

Relationship Development in Interpersonal Context

Among the host of interrelated factors that affect stepparents' affinity seeking are the behaviors of residential and nonresidential parents and the presence and influence of other children in the family. The social context of relationship development is significant in that other people either negatively or positively affect the frequency and efficacy of stepparents' affinity seeking. Parents, both residential and nonresidential, and other children in the family are more than casual observers of the stepparent-stepchild relationship, they do things that either facilitate liking and affinity or they try to discourage the affectionate step-relationships from developing.

Third parties appear more likely to hinder affinity efforts than to facilitate them. For example, residential mothers can ignore stepfathers' affinity-seeking efforts, or worse, they can interfere by not allowing the stepfather chances to spend time with the stepchild having fun together one-on-one. Further, mothers can be aligned so closely with their children that there are few opportunities for stepfathers to build close relationships with the children, or mothers can push stepfathers prematurely into disciplinarian roles. Nonresidential fathers can criticize stepfathers and put children into loyalty binds. Additionally, other children in the stepfamily may compete for the stepfathers' time and attention, making it difficult for stepfathers to engage in affinity-seeking strategies, particularly one-on-one activities. Unfortunately, nobody has investigated why some stepchildren respond positively to stepfathers (and stepmothers) and others do not, nor is it known why some stepchildren are negatively affected by nonresidential fathers' comments about the stepfathers and others are not. However, we do know that children's frequency of contact with their nonresidential father and a competitive relationship between the father and stepfather is not sufficient to explain the efficacy of affinity seeking by stepparents. Stepchildren who had affectionate ties as well as those with distant relationships with stepfathers had frequent contact with nonresidential fathers who disliked the stepfather (Ganong et al., 1999). Other researchers also have found little or no relation between stepchildren's feelings for a stepfather and for a nonresidential father, suggesting that stepchildren can handle two "father-like" relationships and treat them as separate (Buchanan, Maccoby, & Dornbusch, 1996; White & Gilbreath, 2001).

A key to understanding how stepchildren affect relationship-building efforts by stepfathers (and stepmothers) may be to know how they define their relationships with nonresidential fathers (and mothers) and stepfathers (or stepmothers). For example, White and Gilbreath (2001) examined three perspectives on the importance of residential stepfathers and nonresidential fathers on stepchildren—an *accumulation model* that implies that both men play important roles in children's lives, a *loss model* that suggests that children only lose fathers, they don't gain stepfathers, and a *substitution model* that proposes that stepfathers functionally replace nonresidential fathers. They found support for the accumulation model, and recommended that researchers pay attention to how stepchildren feel about all of their parents, not just the ones in the household in which they live. Moreover, they argued from their findings that how children *feel about* their parents and stepparents predicts outcomes like internalizing and externalizing behaviors better than does contact or involvement with stepfathers and fathers.

The concept of *boundary ambiguity* is relevant to understanding the role of nonresidential parents. Boundary ambiguity in stepfamilies has received some attention by clinicians (Boss, 1999), but almost no attention by researchers. Boundary ambiguity refers to a situation in which family members are uncertain about who belongs to the family and who does not and what roles family members have in the system. According to Boss, divorce provides a context for confusion about the presence or absence of the nonresidential parent (this would hold as well for separated, but never married cohabiting parents). For children, a nonresidential parent may be *psychologically present* even when they are *physically absent*, but the residential parent and their new partner may not consider the nonresidential parent to be part of their new family, and, as such, the nonresidential parent may be *psychologically absent* as well as physically absent to them. When there is disagreement about who is and who is not a viable member of the family, and such disagreements are likely in stepfamilies (see Chapter 11), then boundaries are unclear and there is more stress and conflict in households as a result (Boss, 1999). Although no relation between boundary ambiguity and re-marital adjustment has been found (Pasley & Ihinger-Tallman, 1989), measurement of the concept of boundary ambiguity has been crude (e.g., "list who is in your family"). It is clear, however, that when a stepchild tells a stepparent they cannot tell them what to do because they are not the "real" parent, the nonresidential parent has a strong psychological presence in the stepfamily household. Additionally, when a new stepparent is ignored by a stepchild, the stepparent, although physically present, may have little, if any, psychological presence for the stepchild. In a Finnish study, researchers found that when household boundaries were unclear, and particularly when nonresidential parents were physically close but psychologically distant, there were more child behavior problems in single parent and stepfamily households (Taanila, Laitinen, Moilanen, & Jarvelin, 2002). With the steadily increasing incidence of joint physical custody of children after divorce, boundary issues in stepfamilies will be more critical to investigate than was true when children spent the majority of their time in one household and only occasionally visited the other.

We speculate that stepchildren who define their relationships with the nonresidential parent and the residential stepparent in different ways will be more likely to welcome stepparents' affinity seeking than stepchildren who are not able to demarcate their roles. By thinking of the nonresidential parent and the residential stepparent as fulfilling unique functions in their lives, stepchildren could then be freer to develop close relationships with both. This hypothesis obviously needs to be examined. Future research should explore the contexts within which affinity-seeking efforts are effective. Probably a better question than 'Which strategy works best?' is 'Which affinity strategies are effective under what conditions?'

What Type of Relationship?

A fundamental question is, What kind of relationship is being developed? Almost 4 decades ago, Fast and Cain (1966) identified three roles for stepparents—parent, stepparent, and nonparent, all of which they saw as problematic, probably because they drew their conclusions from a clinical sample. More recent research indicates that some stepfathers try to function like fathers, some try to act as friends to their stepchildren, some struggle to define a role, and others give up trying to develop an active role and relationship (Berger, 1995; Bray & Kelly, 1998; Erera-Weatherly, 1996; Fine, Coleman, & Ganong, 1999; Giles-Sims, 1984; Marsiglio, 1992). Many residential mothers and stepfathers expect the stepfathers to relate to stepchildren as fathers, although often they are expected to be less actively involved in child rearing than the mothers are (Fine & Kurdek, 1994; Fine, Coleman, & Ganong, 1997; Giles-Sims, 1984; Marsiglio, 1992).

The type of residential stepfather-stepchild relationship that develops appears to be the result of several processes. For some stepfathers and stepchildren, a process of trial and error learning is followed until the relationship is acceptable to stepchildren, mothers, and stepfathers (Erera-Weatherly, 1996). Other studies imply that children's reactions to the stepfathers' efforts to develop a relationship are the most critical determinants of the types of relationships that ensue (Erera-Weatherly, 1996; Hetherington & Clingempeel, 1992; Hetherington et al., 1999). As we have noted before in this chapter, for some stepfamilies specific types of stepfather-stepchild bonds are created as a result of purposeful planning and decision making by mothers and stepfathers (Berger, 1995; Bray, 1999). Unfortunately, there needs to be much more research about these various processes before we can either describe or recommend them.

Stepfathers as Fathers

Clinicians assert that most stepfathers attempt to fill the role of father (Visher & Visher, 1988). Some stepfathers simply assume they will function as fathers to their stepchildren and they work towards that goal with little discussion or planning (Berger, 1998; Bray, 1999; Erera-Weatherly, 1996). In some cases, these stepfathers give little thought to how their roles might differ from that of fathers because they do not expect to be involved with the stepchildren very much (Berger, 1998; Bray, 1999). For instance, if stepfathers perceive the father role as secondary to that of the mother and one that is relatively uninvolved, then they can take a somewhat passive role in child discipline and will be unlikely to run into conflicts with the stepchild (Hetherington & Henderson, 1997). Of course, some men see the father role to be the primary disciplinarian, so they become highly involved in discipline because they see this as an important family responsibility. By laying down a strict set of rules and enforcing them, these stepfathers see themselves as teaching their values to their stepchildren. The reaction of wives and children in many of these stepfamilies ranges from active support and acceptance to passive resistance and resentment to outright rebellion.

Another aspect of the traditional role for fathers is that of breadwinner. There is evidence that many people believe that stepfathers should assume financial responsibility for those stepchildren living with them (Ganong & Coleman, 1995; Ganong, Coleman, & Mistina, 1995). Stepfathers assume that role to varying degrees (Manning & Smock, 2000), although they are more likely to financially support genetic children than stepchildren.

Stepfathers who really are serious about becoming their stepchildren's father can do so by adopting the stepchildren (Ganong, Coleman, Fine, & McDaniel, 1998). Adoption is seen as a way to solidify and strengthen relationships, or to recognize strong feelings between step-kin. For some of the stepfamily members we interviewed, adoption was seen as a way to legitimize the use of family labels (i.e., dad) and the assumption of mother and father roles for stepparents. For others, adoption was perceived to be a way to remove some of the daily hassles of being in a stepfamily, such as having different last names. Still others saw it as a means to legally remove an undesirable parent from the child's life.

Of course, not all stepfathers who function as fathers adopt their stepchildren. In many stepfamilies, stepfathers function as if they were their stepchildren's new fathers and stepchildren are expected to think of them in that way. Stepparents who function as substitute parents for stepchildren are likely to perceive that they maintain and enhance their relationships with stepchildren by fulfilling parental responsibilities. From the stepparents' perspective they have voluntarily taken on the difficult and expensive tasks of raising children to whom they have few legal obligations (Fine, Coleman, & Ganong, 1999; Mahoney, 1997), and they expect stepchildren to recognize and appreciate their efforts.

Stepparents who try to replace parents, however, are not always successful. Clinicians argue that this exacerbates loyalty conflicts for children who may feel torn between their nonresidential parent and the new stepparent (Visher & Visher, 1996), and researchers report that it is easier for stepchildren to accept stepparents whom they do not perceive as trying to replace their nonresidential parent (Erera-Weatherly, 1996).

There is some research evidence that stepfathers in general do function like fathers, at least in daily family situations. Although expectations for fathers are changing, it is still possible to fulfill fatherly activities and let the mothers do most of the parenting. For instance, in several investigations stepparents and their partners were similar to parents in first-marriage families in support and monitoring of children (Bulcroft, Carmody, & Bulcroft, 1998; Shucksmith, Hendry, & Glendinning, 1995) and in permissiveness and democratic decision-making (Shucksmith et al., 1995). Stepfathers, in particular, find it relatively easy and satisfying to assume a parental role (MacDonald & DeMaris, 1996; Fine, Ganong, & Coleman, 1997; Marsiglio, 1992), but it is not known how pleased stepchildren and mothers are with this arrangement.

As we noted earlier, defining the nature of the step-relationship is not a unilateral activity done by stepparents. Stepchildren, residential parents, nonresidential parents, and even siblings and stepsiblings of stepchildren all contribute to defining step-relationships. For example, in an attempt to understand discrepant findings on stepfathers' parenting style and stepfather-stepchild relationship quality, MacDonald and DeMaris broadened their research lens to include nonresidential fathers. They attempted to reconcile Marsiglio's (1992) finding that the greater the stepfather demanded conformity from the stepchild, the better the relationship, with clinicians' assertions that stepfathers should not try to demand that stepchildren conform to their rules (e.g., Visher & Visher, 1996). Using social capital theory as a framework, MacDonald and DeMaris proposed and tested a model that illustrated that the effects of a stepfather's demands for conformity on relationship quality are related to the nonresidential father's input and amount of influence. Thus, stepparents may not re-create parent-child relationships because stepchildren, particularly adolescents, do not readily accept the stepparent as a parent (Visher & Visher, 1996) or because nonresidential parents disrupt and compete with the stepparents' efforts (Clingempeel & Brand, 1985). Although stepparents are often encouraged to function as substitute parents by their partners (Papernow, 1993), parents and stepparents do not always agree about co-parenting responsibilities, which becomes a source of marital conflict (Keshet, 1990) that may cause stepparents to back away from parenting. There is some evidence that adults in stepfamilies are happier with their relationships when the stepfather is not expected to be a father to the stepchildren (Bray & Berger, 1993).

Stepfathers as Friends

Clinicians argue that the best model for step-relationships is probably friendship (Visher & Visher, 1996). Developing a friendship is less likely to elicit opposition from anyone who otherwise might feel threatened (e.g., nonresidential parents, grandparents, stepsiblings) (Ganong et al., 1999). Several researchers have found that stepparents who initially engage in supportive relationships, rather than disciplinary relationships, have more positive bonds with stepchildren (Bray & Berger, 1993; Crosbie-Burnett & Giles-Sims, 1994; Hetherington & Clingempeel, 1992). Moreover, it is better if stepparents go slowly in approaching stepchildren, letting children take the lead in how fast the relationship develops (Bray & Berger, 1993; Ganong et al., 1999).

It is not clear how many stepparents try to build friendships with their stepchildren and then maintain the relationship as a friendship. We do not know of studies that have examined the extent to which stepfathers attempt to interact as friends with stepchildren. This is likely to be more frequently a choice for older stepfathers who remarry a woman with adult children or for nonresidential stepfathers. Maintaining a cross-generation friendship with a child may be nearly impossible for residential stepfathers—for one thing, friendships between adult men and children are relatively rare. In addition, it may be hard to hold more power in the household, as a stepfather would, and still be just friends (i.e., one friend does not make another friend take out the trash or make the bed).

Some stepfathers may not think that being a friend to stepchildren is an appropriate role, choosing instead to relate to the stepchildren as a father or as an authority figure of some kind. In our study, men who were not fathers before remarriage were somewhat more likely than other men to work continuously at building and maintaining a friendship with their stepchildren (Ganong et al., 1999). Perhaps they felt less comfortable acting like fathers to their stepchildren, and so were more willing to try other ways of relating. They also were younger, and perhaps they could relate to their stepchildren as friends more easily for that reason.

Stepfathers as Quasi-kin

A few stepfathers attempt to create the step-relationship as a quasi-kin relationship. That is, some stepfathers define their role as being something between a father and a friend (Ganong et al., 1999). Other stepparents may act like aunts or uncles to stepchildren, showing interest and warmth but less emotional involvement than a parent. Quasi-kin stepparents may assume some, but not all, of the functions of parents, and they defer to the parents to make final decisions about children (Erera-Weatherly, 1996; Fine et al., 1997).

Some studies support the notion that this quasi-kin stance is effective in developing good relationships. For instance, the most effective parenting style for stepparents to adopt is one in which they demonstrate high warmth toward their stepchild (e.g., having fun together, helping them with problems, listening) while providing structure (e.g., monitoring whom they are with, clearly communicating expectations) (Crosbie-Burnett & Giles-Sims, 1994). Thus, if supportive stepparents engage in some dimensions of control (monitoring, helping the parent enforce the parent's rules for children), but not all (disciplining, establishing new rules for behavior), stepchildren tend to fare better in a number of ways, including how they perceive their relationships with their stepparents. The quasi-kin model may be optimal for enhancing stepparent-stepchild relationships.

Stepfathers assume quasi-kin stances more often with older stepchildren and stepchildren who do not reside with them, an approach that probably reflects the ambiguity of their roles and responsibilities. Successfully managing the balancing act required of quasi-kin is tricky—for instance, stepparents must balance engaging in daily parenting activities such as getting children ready for school, giving allowances, and supervising household chores, while taking a more distant, interested-friend stance when the stepchildren's parents are making major decisions about the children. Stepparents as quasi-kin must constantly be aware of the boundaries between themselves and their stepchildren's parents. The ambiguity of being a quasi-parent can make maintenance of step-relationships harder because adults and children may struggle with deciding on appropriate boundaries.

We hypothesize that a key to being an effective stepparent is to be able to function like a parent and still recognize that you are NOT the parent. That is, a good stepparent may have to be able to *think both like a parent and like quasi-kin*, moving in and out of the parent role as appropriate. For example, one stepfather we interviewed in our affinity study indicated throughout the interview that most of the time he thought of his stepdaughter as his daughter. He treated her the same as he did a son who was born from the remarriage union, but he let her mother lead in making household rules and disciplining his stepdaughter. This stepfather was highly conscious about not intruding into issues that were the purview of his stepdaughter's father and mother, such as making holiday arrangements for the child and talking to her teacher about her school performance. This stepfather realized that he must make sure that his stepdaughter did her household chores and her homework, remind her of upcoming school events, make sure she shared crayons with her (half)brother, do everything that a good father should do when she was in his household (which was most of the time). Yet he also realized that he must take a secondary role at other times. This seemed to be working for this stepfamily—the stepdaughter, whom we interviewed separately, loved both her stepfather and her father, and after a brief adjustment period following her mother's remarriage she had felt very comfortable with her two stepfamily households.

It is likely that what Burgoyne and Clark (1984) called *progressive stepfamilies* are those in which the stepfather functions as a quasi-kin to the stepchild, with support in this role from mothers and stepchildren. However, hypotheses related to stepfathers (and stepmothers) as quasi-kin and ambiguity and ambivalence in step-relationships have yet to be tested. We think investigations of these relationships in the future are likely to yield important information about relational maintenance between stepparents and stepchildren.

Stepfathers as Intimate Strangers

Some stepfathers and stepchildren relate to each other as if they were distant acquaintances—emotionally remote, relatively uninvolved in each other's lives. Compared to fathers, stepfathers show less affect toward stepchildren, are less involved with them, engage in less supervision and control, and exhibit more neglectful and problematic parenting styles (Cooksey & Fondell, 1996; Erera-Weatherly, 1996; Hetherington & Clingempeel, 1992; Shucksmith et al., 1995).

There are many reasons why stepparents and stepchildren may relate as distant acquaintances. First, cultural expectations are that stepparents are not emotionally engaged with stepchildren (Ganong & Coleman, 1997). In addition, the role of stepparent may not be an important identity for many stepparents so they may not invest much into being successful in the role, particularly if stepchildren resist their efforts at developing a warm relationship (Thoits, 1992). Finally, evolutionary scholars have postulated that stepparents invest less of themselves in their stepchildren because they are not genetically related (Daly & Wilson, 1996; Flinn, 1992). We discuss these arguments at length later in this chapter when we review the effects of stepfamily living on stepchildren.

NONRESIDENTIAL STEPFATHERS

These men are the partners of nonresidential mothers. As such, they have been studied even less than their partners. This is a gap in the professional literature that should be addressed, given the fluid nature of post-divorce physical custody and the proclivity of court awards of shared custody arrangements (Bauserman, 2002).

STEPMOTHERS

There are slightly more than one million stepmothers who live with their stepchildren (Fields, 1996). Although there is no way to know for sure how many nonresidential stepmothers there are, most scholars estimate that the majority of stepmothers do not live with their stepchildren most of the time (Nielsen, 1999), because mothers usually have physical custody of the children. Overall, there are about four or five times more residential stepfathers than there are stepmothers (Fields, 1996).

One caution is in order before we explore stepmother-stepchild relationships. Nonresidential and residential stepmothers are often not distinguished in studies. Early researchers did not make that distinction, and it still is common for stepmother samples to be a mix of residential and nonresidential stepmothers (e.g., Ceglian & Gardner, 2000; Guisinger et al., 1989; Morrison & Thompson-Guppy, 1985; Orchard & Solberg, 1999; Whitsett & Land, 1992).

Stepmothers and the Motherhood Mandate

If mothers in stepfather family households have difficulty coping with the idealized images of mothers, the stepmother may be even more hapless. The *motherhood mandate* may contribute to making stepmothers' roles and relationships especially challenging. Stepmothers are in a difficult situation in light of cultural values and ideals attached to women in families. Although they are *not* the mothers of their stepchildren, in order to be a good woman, they are asked to be responsible for the quality of family relationships and for the well-being of all family members (Hays, 1996; Walzer, 2004). The motherhood mandate is a formidable task for mothers, but stepmothers must figure out how to achieve some semblance of these responsibilities without triggering a backlash from their stepchildren's mothers.

Just as mothers in stepfamilies may feel caught between the competing demands of their roles as mothers and spouses, stepmothers may feel trapped as well, but in different ways. Stepmothers feel caught between their partners and their partners' children, between the reality of their lives and the myth of motherhood, and between the cultural norm of the ideal mother (i.e., nurturing, caring) and the negative stereotype of the wicked stepmother (Ganong & Coleman, 1995). Unlike mothers in stepfamilies, however, most stepmothers identify more strongly with their spousal/partner role functions than with their parenting functions (Church, 1999). As long as women focus on their spousal/partner roles, they can avoid dealing with the issue of motherhood and stacking up against nearly impossible expectations. However, if her spouse attempts to promote the assumption of a parenting role, the stepmother is likely to experience role overload when the stepchildren visit.

Clinicians asserted long ago that women have a more difficult time in stepfamilies than men do (Bernstein, 1989; Visher & Visher, 1979). Some researchers (MacDonald & DeMaris, 1996), but not all (Sturgess, Dunn, & Davies, 2001), have reported that stepmothers have a more difficult time relating to stepchildren than stepfathers do. This may be due to societal expectations that women should be more closely involved than men are with the daily care of children. The role of father has been less idealized than the mother role (Chodorow & Contratto, 1992), so stepmothers must emulate a more unrealistic model than stepfathers in their attempts to be like a parent to their stepchildren (Bernstein, 1994; Nielsen, 1999). Enacting a parent role may also be more difficult for women because mothers tend to be more active in their children's lives and their daily care than fathers (Furstenberg & Nord, 1985).

Developing and maintaining positive relationships with stepchildren may be difficult for residential stepmothers if they are involved in the day-to-day care of the children and the control of the household (Ambert, 1986). Because residential stepmothers may spend more time with the children than their fathers, they may be responsible for or perceive that they should engage in discipline and setting of rules, behaviors that interfere with building warm, close relationships (Ganong et al., 1999). Nonresidential stepmothers, given the combination of their part-time involvement and ambiguous roles, may have a more stressful time in deciding how to interact with stepchildren than residential stepmothers do. However, these women generally know what they do *not* want to be—*wicked stepmothers* (Church, 1999; Quick, McKenry, & Newman, 1994).

Researchers investigating a stepfamily telephone counseling service in Great Britain found that approximately half of the calls they received came from stepmothers. Another quarter of the calls were from mothers, stepfathers made 14% of the calls, 4% were attributed to fathers, and the rest came from a mix of stepchildren, children, grandparents, and "other" (Batchelder, 1994). Many of the stepmothers' calls were related to feelings either of being dumped on or excluded. Not surprisingly, mothers' calls were mostly about feelings of being caught—"piggy in the middle" as the British authors labeled it.

In a second study of women in stepfamilies conducted by Weaver and Coleman (in review), 11 nonresidential stepmothers were interviewed in depth, multiple times over a period of years. Eight of these women were also mothers of children either from previous relationships or they had a child with their current partner.

To the casual observer the roles these nonresidential stepmothers played when the children visited would be difficult to distinguish from those of a mother. For example, stepmothers described engaging in behaviors for their stepchildren such as cooking and doing their laundry, cleaning up after them, taking care of them, attending school and extracurricular events, helping them with homework, and arranging their social activities. Some even mentioned financially providing for the stepchildren. Nonetheless, the stepmothers all stressed the importance of not usurping the mother's role. In their minds the role functions of mother and stepmother should be quite distinct. Examples they gave to describe their role function included that of being a friend, a responsible and caring adult, a provider of emotional support, and a mentor.

The stepmothers were both ambiguous and ambivalent about their place in their stepchildren's lives. The ambiguity was obvious in one stepmother's description of her role function—"a mothering kind of role, but not a mother." These women were careful to let us know they did not want to either replace or displace the mother. However, in our experience, it is fathers and not mothers who are concerned about being replaced in their children's affections and loyalty. This is not surprising, considering Kranichfeld's (1987) conclusion that it is mothers who have the power within families. For example, they invest far more in vertical bonds (parent/child) than do men. "... when it comes to securing the kind of power that exists in the family realm, nothing—not superior physical strength, nor greater economic resources, nor culturally ascribed authority—can substitute for investment, attention, connection, and care" (p. 53). Because men have little family power, they may be more concerned than are mothers about losing what little they do have.

Some stepmothers who were also mothers were ambivalent about developing close relationships with visiting stepchildren because they were afraid it might strain the bonds they had with their own children. If they invested in their stepchildren would this reduce their power and influence with their children? They also expressed ambivalence and frustration at perceiving themselves to be in a situation that required them to provide emotional and physical care to their stepchildren yet they had no power or authority to do so. They did not perceive that there would be a payoff for their investment in the stepchildren, even in added good will and appreciation from their husbands. In essence they fulfilled the role function of mother when the children were with them, but it was "black market mothering"—they had no authority, legal or otherwise, to do it. It was their socialized obligation to care for others that appeared to dictate their behaviors with their stepchildren.

Women who experienced role conflicts but perceived their spousal role as distinct from and more personally relevant than their stepparenting role often resolved any stress this caused them by reducing their investment in the stepparenting role. Rather than the *mothering but not a mother* role function that some stepmothers described, these women expressed their role function in a manner that we labeled *other focused*, a role function was manifested in two ways. Women who were other focused described serving as the liaison between their husband and their stepchildren's mother or as a facilitator, attempting to improve relationships between their spouse and his children or between their spouse and his ex-wife. Vinick (1998) made similar observations about stepmothers who were considerably older than those we interviewed. She described stepmothers as often serving as family carpenters who made efforts to help build relationships between their husband and his children. In both Vinick's study and ours, the stepmother role sometimes became an extension of their spousal role, it was performed to reduce stress and take pressure off of their husbands rather than to provide service to the stepchildren. Because of hostile relationships between husbands and ex-spouses, stepmothers would sometimes serve as chauffeurs to transport the stepchildren from house to house, or they would make the arrangements for child visits. They also made recommendations to their husbands about parenting; they would talk to the stepchildren in attempts to explain their father's behavior to them ("Give him time, he's just now learning how to be a dad to girls. Give him some time to learn how"), and they would tell the children how much their father loved them.

A third role function we labeled *the outsider*. This role function was manifested in two ways. Women were either involved outsiders or they had no direct function with the stepchildren at all. Involved outsiders were present but did not participate in family activities when the stepchildren visited. They were available to fix snacks, do laundry and other household chores, but they were bystanders who stayed out of the way of their husband's and his children's activities.

The most distant of the nonresidential stepmothers were those who described their responsibilities as *role by relation*. They had no problems with role conflict because they did not believe they had a role function with the stepchildren, and they did not see stepchildren as being important in their lives. They perceived themselves to be the wives of the children's fathers, and that was it. This stance was often difficult to maintain—about half of the women experienced a residential shift of the children at some point during their marriage. Nearly all of the shifts occurred when the stepchildren were adolescents, and the stepmothers had neither voice nor choice in the matter.

The idealized image of motherhood influenced both mothers in stepfamilies and nonresidential stepmothers. The mothers felt as if they must always put their children first, that they are blamed if their children don't turn out well, and that they are rarely praised if they do. The stepmothers worried about being seen as "wicked," and they also felt that they must engage in saint-like behavior by overlooking the incidents in which they felt they were being taken for granted, ignored, underappreciated, rejected, and treated rudely in general. They also worried about crossing boundaries and competing with the mother although many of them thought that they would do a better job than the mothers if they were allowed to fulfill a mother function with the children. All complained about poor parenting practices on the part of the "real" mothers.

Because researchers have typically assumed that family power is acquired by gaining resources (i.e., money, status) outside the family, there has been little understanding of the power that women have within families (Kranichfeld, 1987). Nonresidential stepmothers in our study made frequent reference to their lack of both personal and interpersonal control or power in their families. Their concerns centered on value differences they had with mothers regarding child rearing, differences that negated stepmothers' abilities to enforce rules and regulations within their own homes, and with decisions about child support, child residence, and visitation schedules that were either made before they entered the picture or without their input. No matter how much they invested in the stepchildren or how much attention and care they provided them, these nonresidential stepmothers felt that they were completely powerless to influence the stepchildren. If the marriage to the children's father ended, they would no longer even have the right to see the children. Compared to most women in families, the position of these women was quite perilous.

Nonresidential stepmothers responded to feeling powerless in several ways. Probably the most common way for them to gain power within their family was to have a child of their own. A great deal of the childbearing in the United States occurs within remarriage (Stewart, 2002). A second commonly mentioned approach was to encourage their husbands to attempt to gain custody of their children. Gaining more access to the children may have been seen as a means of diluting the influence of the mother and imposing the stepmother's values on the children in order to shape them as a "good mother" would want to do. The third way of dealing with the lack of control was to encourage their husbands to pay less child support.

None of these nonresidential stepmothers' solutions to their lack of family power has been investigated to any extent, especially in regards to consequences of these behaviors for stepchildren, remarriages, or stepfamilies. It might be in the best interest of the children if mothers shared their mothering role to a limited extent with nonresidential stepmothers. Broadening women's power beyond the boundaries of the family (i.e., better jobs, better pay, more shared household responsibilities) might also lessen the struggles stepmothers perceived they endured trying to gain a modicum of family power as it related to mothering functions, at least in their own household.

Stepchildren's Gender

Although we have organized this chapter primarily around the gender of the parent and stepparent (and their residence) we have said relatively little about (step)children's gender. This is not because researchers have ignored the gender of children in their investigations—the general conclusion is that boys relate to stepparents better than girls do, and boys are less at risk for negative outcomes than girls are. However, gender differences are not universally reported in studies; often there are no gender differences and occasionally girls fare better than boys do. Moreover, interactions of stepparent gender and stepchild gender are similarly convoluted and precarious to generalize about. Stepmothers and stepdaughters may have the hardest challenge developing positive relationships, stepfathers and stepsons the easiest, but there are so many conditions that qualify or limit these generalizations that we hesitate to make them. As we have repeatedly noted, contexts are important in understanding stepfamily relationships. For instance, step-relationships are contingent on the age of the stepchild when the relationship began, the amount of contact and involvement of the nonresidential parent, the level of inter-household and intra-household conflicts, how stepfamily members define their roles and relationships, what functions the residential parent fulfills in terms of the stepparent-stepchild bonding process, ethnicity, socioeconomic status, the residential parent's ability to raise children, individuals' personality characteristics and temperaments, the interactions among stepfamily members personality characteristics and temperaments, individuals' expectations, and the list could continue. The main point is that researchers need to know much more about the specific conditions under which boys and girls relate to stepparents and experience stepfamily living.

ADULT STEPCHILDREN AND OLDER PARENTS AND STEPPARENTS

Research on the development of relationships between adult stepchildren and older stepparents when the remarriage occurs after the adult stepchild has left home is limited. In recent years researchers have begun to consider later life stepfamilies and their relationships, but we are not aware of researchers who have examined the process of adult step-relationship development. This is another issue that should be investigated, given the aging of Western societies and the likelihood of increases of later life remarriage.

Most research on relationships between remarried parents and their adult children or between older stepparents and their adult stepchildren has examined the amount of contact between them, global relationship quality, and the intergenerational transfer of resources (e.g., Hao, 1996; Pezzin & Schone, 1999). Most of this work has focused on post-divorce families, so little is known about relationships following parental death. The relationships among adult children and older cohabiting parents and stepparents, either heterosexual or gay and lesbian, have not been studied.

Closeness to Parents and Stepparents

Compared to married parents and their children, relationship quality and contact between parents and adult children are lower in families where there has been a divorce, whether the divorce occurred when children were young or when they were adults (Aquilino, 1994; Cooney & Uhlenberg, 1990; Lye, Klepinger, Hyle, & Nelson, 1995). Moreover, fewer resources are exchanged between generations following divorce than are exchanged between married parents and their children. Following divorce, father-child bonds are less close than are mother-child relationships.

Remarriage further affects parent-child relationships—there is growing evidence that parents who remarry when children are minors have less contact with their adult children than non-divorced parents do (Aquilino, 1994; Bulcroft & Bulcroft, 1991; Lawton, Silverstein, & Bengston, 1994), but more than divorced parents who do not remarry (Lye et al., 1995; White, 1992). Additionally, remarried mothers have more frequent contact and better relationships with children than remarried fathers do (Amato, Rezac, & Booth, 1995).

Aquilino (1994) found that remarriage of a parent who had raised the adult child was related to small reductions in the quality and contact of adult children with both of their parents. Cooney et al. (1995) reported that parental remarriage was associated with sons' but not daughters', intimacy with parents. Maternal remarriage limited intimacy with both parents, but paternal remarriage contributed to mother-son intimacy.

Less is known about parent-adult child relationships when remarriages occur after the offspring are grown. White and Wang (1999) reported that adult children's relationships with newly remarried mothers grew closer, but relationships with fathers became more distant after remarriage. In part, this was related to the fact that the adult children got along better with mothers than fathers before the remarriage, and in part it was due to closer ties with stepfathers than with stepmothers (Vinick, 1998; White & Wang, 1999). Evidence regarding parent-adult child relationships for older widowed persons is hampered by the small samples of most of these studies, but in general it appears as if the relationships become less close after the older parent remarries (Lopata, 1996).

Support and Resource Exchange

Remarriage increases the amount of aid mothers give to adult children, but decreases the help adult children give to mothers and stepfathers (Amato, Rezac, & Booth, 1995). Remarried mothers give as much as married mothers do to their children, but receive less, perhaps because there is greater emotional and geographic distance between remarried mothers and adult children. Remarried fathers give and receive less than married fathers do, and about the same as divorced single fathers. Remarried parents (White, 1992) and stepparents (Amato et al., 1995; Pezzin & Schone, 1999; Spitze & Logan, 1992) in general provide less support to adult (step)children than do parents in first marriages, but remarried mothers give some types of support as much as married mothers do (Amato et al., 1995; Marks, 1995; Spitze & Logan, 1992). However, when help given to or received from *both* parents are combined for adult children of divorced and remarried parents, there are no significant family structure differences in exchanges between parents and adult children.

Most of the rationale for intergenerational transfers of resources (e.g., money, assistance, emotional support) are based on the assumption that parents take care of and nurture children when the children are young and helpless, behaviors that later elicit aid from the younger generation when they become adults and the older generation is relatively more dependent. For instance, several reasons have been proposed to explain why people engage in intergenerational assistance:

- A *norm of family obligation* suggests that intergenerational transfers are culturally-prescribed duties that must be performed because individuals are related (Piercy, 1998).
- *Altruism based on kinship* ties is a proposition from evolutionary theory that there is a genetic predisposition to care for those with whom one is genetically related (Cheal, 1988).
- A *norm of reciprocity* is the belief that children owe debts to their parents that should be repaid (Brakman, 1995).
- A *norm of gratitude* is the belief that offspring want to help parents because they are grateful for parents' help and sacrifices (Brakman, 1995).
- Helping across generations is seen as a *moral duty* that must be performed if one is to fulfill religious beliefs or to meet personal standards of what a good person does (Finch, 1989), regardless of whether or not the recipient is deserving.
- Help is provided to kin with whom there are close *emotional attachments* (Cicirelli, 1991).
- Helping is a *function of intergenerational solidarity*. In one model of intergenerational solidarity, intergenerational transfers are based on familistic

norms, affection, an opportunity structure that facilitates interactions between generations, and perceptions that intergenerational exchanges have been reciprocal (Bengtson & Roberts, 1991). Another model of intergenerational solidarity proposes that intergenerational aid is based on frequent association, positive sentiments, agreement on values and beliefs, commitment to meeting family obligations, and the opportunity structure for interaction (Rossi & Rossi, 1990).

Most of these explanations (i.e., *reciprocity, altruism* based on kinship ties, *gratitude, intergenerational solidarity*) are explicit in asserting that intergenerational transfers of adult children are based on repaying debts to parents for past help. This repayment assumption is more implicit in the *emotional attachment* explanations for intergenerational transfers. For example, attachments to parents are stronger when children's needs are met by parents throughout the life course. An adult child who is securely attached to a parent who has been a supportive and loving caretaker is more likely to help that parent than a less securely attached adult will be to help an unsupportive parent. Only in the *normative family obligations, altruism,* and *moral duty* arguments is the assumption of reciprocity absent. Recently, criticism has been directed toward the solidarity and normative family obligations models for not recognizing inherent ambivalences in intergenerational relationships (Luescher & Pillemer, 1998). The critique also applies to the other explanations. Familial responsibilities become more ambiguous following marital transitions; divorces and remarriages cause family members to rethink whether certain individuals continue to be relatives or not. For example, after divorce, parents may lose contact with their children, and remarriage potentially adds members to the pool of kin (new partners, their children, and extended family; Furstenberg, 1981). Step-kin acquired through remarriage may be seen as replacements for relatives lost via divorce (with family-based obligations transferred from old kin to new step-kin), as additional family members, or they may not be seen as kin (thus no obligations to allocate resources across generations are added). For some individuals, family members are only people who share genetic (Daly et al., 1997) or legal ties (Schneider, 1980).

Divorce, and the relationships between children and parents that subsequently evolve, may have the effect of giving adult offspring fewer reasons to help parents, especially parents who did not live with them when they were children. Reduced contact over time may lead to decisions not to allocate resources to help parents when children reach adulthood and parents reach old age (Cooney, 1994). Children may be seen as having a lesser debt to repay than they would have had if parents had maintained contact with the child and continued to provide financial, tangible, and emotional support to them. Moreover, the decision to help or not may be dissolved completely if definitions of kinship are altered when parents divorce and remarry.

Decisions about helping and transferring resources between stepparents and stepchildren may not involve the same factors as decisions regarding resource allocations between children and parents. Stepparent-stepchild bonds are ambiguous, and there are few legally mandated responsibilities between stepchildren and stepparents. The emotional bonds between stepparents and stepchildren tend to be less cohesive than parent-child bonds, and these weaker emotional bonds may contribute to structurally weaker social networks than in first marriage families (White, 1994b), resulting in lower family solidarity and fewer felt obligations between stepfamily members. Even when stepparents develop close relationships with stepchildren the fact that most stepparents are additional adults in the lives of adult children rather than substitutes for deceased or absent divorced parents may mean that stepparents are perceived as having less claim for assistance from adult stepchildren. Rossi and Rossi (1990) found that people perceived greater family obligations to parents than to stepparents. Consequently, in some families resources may not be adequate to include stepparents. If stepparents are seen as having less right to aid than parents do, then stepparents may have to seek help from non-family sources.

However, *norms of reciprocity, gratitude,* and *emotional attachments* could be the bases for making intergenerational transfers between stepchildren and stepparents. In several studies that we have conducted about intergenerational responsibilities following divorce and remarriage, we found that perceived obligations to assist stepparents or stepchildren were similar to obligations in parent-child relationships when stepparent-stepchild relationships are emotionally close, when the stepparent and stepchild have spent years together in the relationship, and when stepparents have served as the functional equivalents of parents (Ganong & Coleman, 1999). The more step-relationships deviate from parent-child ties, then the less likely it is that similar decisions about intergenerational transfers between stepchildren and stepparents will be made.

SUMMARY

In order to understand the dynamics of stepfamilies one must examine the relationships among parents and stepparents with both residential and nonresidential children from prior relationships. Moreover, the direct and indirect influences of the children's other parent are relevant. These parents may affect the intergenerational ties in stepfamilies even if they have minimal or no contact with children. The context of parenting and stepparenting relationships includes more than other stepfamily members—cultural beliefs about mothering and fathering are critical, as are individual family members' role expectations and role performance. Given this complexity, it is not surprising that researchers have uncovered a diverse array of parenting and stepparenting relationship dynamics. As researchers continue to investigate these relational processes we anticipate that a better comprehension will be gained regarding the outcomes for children and adults of these various styles or patterns of relating.

Finally, given the aging of Western societies and the changes in family structure—fewer children, longer life spans, more complex family arrangements—the nature of older stepparent-adult stepchild relationships and parent-adult child relationships should become the focus of greater attention by researchers, practitioners, and policymakers. Parenting and stepparenting continue and are important across the life course.

Chapter **8**

Effects of Stepfamily Living on Children

The single most widely studied issue involving stepfamilies has been the effect on stepchildren of living in a stepparent household (Coleman et al., 2000). Some researchers frame this issue as the *effects of parental remarriage* on children or the *effects of having a stepparent* on stepchildren. Sometimes researchers examine how specific phenomena in the step-household, such as parental conflict, are related to children's outcomes. We will refer to research in this area as studies of the *effects of stepfamily living*. Interest in stepchildren's well-being is global—in recent years there have been studies conducted on this subject in North America, Europe, Asia, Australia, Israel, and New Zealand.

Researchers concerned about young and adolescent stepchildren have focused primarily on four general areas: (1) *academic achievement* (e.g., grades, school completion, achievement test scores), (2) psychological adjustment and emotional well-being, which are also known as *internalizing behaviors*, (3) behavior problems, known sometimes as *externalizing behaviors*, and (4) *interpersonal relationships*. In recent years, there have been a handful of studies of stepchildren's *physiological development* as well, such as cardiovascular reactivity (Torres, Evans, Pathak, & Vancil, 2001) and the onset of menarche (Comings, Muhleman, Johnson, & MacMurray, 2002; Ellis & Garber, 2000), but physiological development barely has been investigated in comparison to the four areas listed above. In investigations of the effects of stepfamily living on stepchildren researchers typically compare stepchildren to children living with both parents on various outcome measures. Another common comparison group is children living with one parent, usually the mother, and there are occasionally other comparison groups as well, such as adopted children or children living with neither parent. Many of these studies are based on large, sometimes national data sets (e.g., National Study of

Families and Households and Panel Study of Income Dynamics in the United States, National Child Development Study in the United Kingdom, Christchurch Health and Development Study in New Zealand) that allow researchers to analyze models that include demographic characteristics of stepchildren and their families and an assortment of variables that potentially mediate or moderate the effects of living in a stepfamily.

In virtually every area of assessment, stepchildren are found to fare more poorly, on average, than children living with both of their parents. Stepchildren are generally similar on outcome measures to children living with single parents, who are usually single mothers. Sometimes, but not always, these mean differences disappear when social class, time living in the stepfamily, and other variables are added to statistical models. The overall conclusion is that stepchildren generally are at greater risk for problems than are children living with both of their parents, and they are comparable to children living with mothers only.

Stepchildren and children with single parents on average do not achieve as well as children living with both parents in grades earned in school (e.g., Bogenschneider, 1997), grades completed (e.g., Teachman et al., 1996), scores on achievement tests (e.g., Pong, 1997), dropout rates (e.g., Pong & Ju, 2000), and school attendance (e.g., Upchurch, 1993). Stepchildren also leave home to establish independent households at younger ages than children living with both parents (e.g., Aquilino, 1991b; Kiernan, 1992), which may also be related to their higher rates of dropping out of school. The academic performance of stepchildren in cohabiting-parent stepfamilies is roughly the same as that of stepchildren in married stepfamilies (Clark & Nelson, 2000; Morrison, 2000) or slightly worse (Hanson et al., 1997; Thomson et al., 1994).

On average, stepchildren have been found to exhibit more internalizing behavior problems, such as depression (e.g., Zill et al., 1993), and to be more at risk for having emotional problems than children in first marriage families (e.g., Hanson, McLanahan, & Thomson, 1996). It is not clear whether stepsons or stepdaughters have more difficulties. Earlier studies tended to report that girls had more problems than boys (e.g., Needle, Su, & Doherty, 1990), but more recently other researchers have reported that boys have more problems than girls (e.g., Coley, 1998; Dunn et al., 1998). Research findings also have been mixed on whether stepdaughters fare better when living with stepfathers or stepmothers—some researchers found that girls had more adjustment problems than boys only when living with stepfathers (e.g., Lee, Burkam, Zimiles, & Ladewski, 1994), and others found more problems for girls living with stepmothers (e.g., Suh, Schutz, & Johanson, 1996).

Adolescent stepchildren generally exhibit more externalizing behavioral problems than children living with both parents, such as using drugs and alcohol (e.g., Hoffman, 2002), engaging in sexual intercourse (e.g., Upchurch, Aneshense, Sucoff, & Levy-Storms, 1999), nonmarital childbearing (e.g., Astone & Washington, 1994), engaging in aggressive behavior (Kowelski-Jones,

2000), and being arrested (e.g., Coughlin &Vuchinich, 1996). Relative to children living with both parents, the risks or benefits of having stepfathers for African American children are unclear. Some researchers find African American children benefit from having a stepfather (e.g., Salem et al., 1998), some find stepdaughters to be more at risk for early sexual activity (e.g., Wu & Thomson, 2001), and some report no differences (e.g., Davis & Friel, 2001). Few researchers have compared stepchildren in cohabiting-parent stepfamilies and married-parent stepfamilies on behavior problems, and findings from those studies are somewhat inconsistent. Overall, there do not appear to be differences between them (Clark & Nelson, 2000; Morrison, 2000).

Stepchildren have more peer problems and prosocial behavior problems than children living with both of their parents (Dunn et al., 1998). Sibling negativity is also greater in stepfamilies. However, when psychosocial status of the mother, quality of the mother-child relationship, and various social risk factors are taken into account, these differences in family structure are not significant (Dunn et al., 1998). Additional externalizing behaviors are gender related. That is, stepdaughters are more likely to cohabit (e.g., Goldscheider & Goldscheider, 1998) and to marry early than are women from first marriage families (Aquilino, 1991b) or from other family forms (Thornton, 1991).

It should be noted that not all studies find differences between stepchildren and children from other family forms, including children in first marriage families. However, when differences are found they are in the directions mentioned above. The inevitable conclusion from this large body of over 300 published studies would seem to be that children are harmed by living with stepparents, a conclusion that has been drawn many times by researchers and those reviewing the literature. If we stopped our discussion right here, then conservative pundits who would like to ban remarriage would have a good case. However, this is only part of the story.

The rest of the story is that most researchers find that the differences between stepchildren and children in first marriage families are quite small. In a meta-analytic review, Paul Amato (1994) calculated that effect sizes for differences between stepchildren and children living with both of their parents ranged from −.07 for academic achievement and −.14 for social relationships to −.32 for conduct/behavior problems and −.37 for psychological adjustment. According to commonly used standards for interpreting effect sizes, effect sizes of .20, .50, and .80 are considered small, moderate, and large, respectively (Cohen, 1969). This means that the differences in academic achievement and social relationships from the 21 studies Amato reviewed are negligible, and the differences in internalizing and externalizing behavior problems are small. In Amato's review, the mean effect size for all outcomes was −.17—this translates into the conclusion that yes, on average, stepchildren exhibit more negative behaviors, *but 43% of all stepchildren scored better on these outcomes than the average child living with two parents.* More recently, in their British study, Dunn and colleagues found effect sizes for externalizing, internalizing, and peer problem behaviors to be between .22 and .46 (Dunn et al., 1998). In another meta-analytic review of research done between 1990 and 1999 on the effects of divorce on children, effect sizes for externalizing behavior averaged −.28, internalizing behavior averaged −.18, self-concept was −.12, social adjustment was −.16, and school achievement was −.16 (Reifman, Villa, Amans, Rethinam, & Telesac, 2001). All of these effect sizes were small (Cohen, 1969). So, it is extremely important to note that *most stepchildren do well in school* (e.g., Pong, 1997) and *do not have emotional, social, or behavioral problems* (e.g., Lansford, Ceballo, Abbey, & Stewart, 2001; Lissau & Sorenson, 1994). Hetherington and Kelly (2002) have asserted that, on most outcome measures, 75–80% of stepchildren are doing fine.

In the last few years, family researchers have calculated and reported effect sizes as they attempted to make sense of their data. This is quite useful information because effect size calculations combined with tests of significance present a more complete picture—that is, stepchildren are more at risk for a variety of problems, and, on average, they perform more poorly on outcome measures than children living with both parents. Nonetheless, most stepchildren function quite well and are not at risk for problems. Our conclusion in examining these data is that stepfamily living effects on stepchildren are somewhat complicated to understand, but they are not universally negative as they are typically portrayed. Unfortunately, there appears to be a strong tendency to generalize without limits from studies finding negligible to small differences between stepchildren and other children. The result is that the data are interpreted to mean that *all* stepchildren have problems.

LONG-TERM EFFECTS ON STEPCHILDREN

In addition to the plethora of cross-sectional studies focusing on children and adolescents, a substantial number of researchers have investigated the long-term effects of having a stepparent. The availability of several large, longitudinal data sets that extended data collection from birth or early childhood into adulthood or that followed adolescents into adulthood have allowed researchers to examine effects over time.

Although the negative effects of having a stepparent are often reported to be long-lasting (e.g., Biblarz, Raftery, & Bucur, 1997; Kiernan, 1992), parental remarriage during childhood was found not to be related to emotional problems during early (e.g., Chase-Lansdale, Cherlin, & Kiernan, 1995; Rodgers, Power, & Hope, 1997) and middle adulthood (Rodgers, 1994) in a British longitudinal study. In a New Zealand longitudinal study differences in adjustment between adult stepchildren and adults who grew up with both parents were related to "confounding social, contextual, and individual factors that were present prior to the formation of the stepfamily" (Nicholson, Fergusson, & Horwood, 1999, p. 405).

Studies of small, local samples also reported no relation between parental remarriage and stepchildren's adjustment in early adulthood (e.g., Lissau & Sorenson, 1994). Long-term effects may be related to age at parental remarriage (Zill et al., 1993).

THEORETICAL EXPLANATIONS FOR STEPPARENT EFFECTS ON STEPCHILDREN

Although views vary in the scholarly community regarding the effects of stepfamily living on children (e.g., see Booth & Dunn, 1994), most researchers have sought to explain why, on average, living with a stepparent is more harmful to children and adolescents than is living with both parents. Many explanations have been proposed, but most can be categorized as variations of one of four frameworks: (1) stress models, (2) models of (step)parent involvement, (3) (step)parent style models, and (4) selection hypothesis.

Stress Models

One major tenet of scholars who take a stress approach to understanding stepfamily effects on children is that a parent's remarriage increases the stress in the lives of both children and adults (e.g., Henry & Lovelace, 1995). When a custodial parent remarries or cohabits with a new partner, many changes ensue—moving to a new residence, adapting to new household members, learning new household routines and activities. For school age children and adolescents, a new residence after parental remarriages may mean that they have to change schools and leave behind familiar neighborhoods and old friends. As we have noted in earlier chapters, the amount of contact with the nonresidential parent often changes when either the residential parent or the nonresidential parent remarries. New household routines and activities imply new rules for children. These accumulated changes are thought to increase stress for children, which, in turn, leads to poorer performances in school and more internalizing and externalizing behavior problems (e.g., Menaghan, Kowalski-Jones, & Mott, 1997).

The *cumulative effects hypothesis* proposes that it is multiple marital and relational disruptions that increase the chances that the children will exhibit internalizing and externalizing problems as a result of having to cope with all the transitions (e.g., Capaldi & Patterson, 1991; Martinez & Forgatch, 2002; Wu & Thomson, 2001). Considering that a stepchild whose parent is in a second marriage or long-term relationship has probably experienced at least two parental relationship transitions (e.g., marriage-divorce-remarriage, marriage-death-remarriage), the cumulative effects hypothesis would suggest that stepchildren whose parents are in their third or higher relationship should fare worse because each transition accumulates stress. Support for this hypothesis has been found. Children whose custodial parent had lived with several partners over time had more problems than children who lived with a parent who had re-partnered only once (e.g., Capaldi & Patterson, 1991; Dunn et al., 1998; Martinez & Forgatch, 2002).

Another stress model proposes that *parental competencies are compromised* when entering new marital/partner relationships (e.g., Hoffman & Johnson, 1998). According to this perspective, parents who have new partners are so overwhelmed adapting to changes related to their new relationship status that their parenting skills are diminished. This model proposes that stepchildren's problems are due to diminished or poor-quality parenting from stressed-out parents who lack the personal resources to monitor their children's behavior, participate in school activities, or interact with their children at the same levels that they did prior to remarriage or cohabiting (e.g., Yeung, Linver, & Brooks-Gunn, 2002).

On the other hand, a variation of the compromised parent hypothesis suggests that the stepparent, as an added adult, reduces familial stress related to economic burdens and the monitoring of children (e.g., Bulcroft et al., 1998). This *added adult hypothesis* has received only partial support from researchers. These models are difficult to study because stepparents generally do bring resources to the step-household that have the potential to reduce stress for parents and children, but they also bring demands for resources (e.g., time, space) from parents and children. Over time, the benefits may or may not outweigh the costs, but it is hard for researchers, particularly in cross-sectional studies, to sort this out. For instance, it is likely that stepchildren welcome and appreciate some of the resources a stepparent brings to the household, but they will not necessarily welcome all of the resources all of the time.

Conflicts between divorced co-parents and between stepfamily members also have been hypothesized as stress-related explanations for stepchildren generally faring worse on behavioral and psychological outcomes than children living with both parents (e.g., Downey, 1995; Hanson et al., 1996; Kurdek & Fine, 1993a). Researchers have attributed higher rates of early home leaving (e.g., Kiernan, 1992) and lower rates of co-residence of adult children in stepfamilies (e.g., Aquilino, 1991a) to the stressful atmosphere in step-households. Conflicts in stepfamilies often are related to adolescents' externalizing and internalizing behaviors (Doyle, Wolchik, & Dawson-McClure, 2002), and researchers speculate that stepchildren may move out or withdraw from others in the household as a way to keep peace in the family and to try to maintain their own well-being (Hanson et al., 1996). However, not all researchers have found that stepfamilies have more conflicts than do first marriage families (Barber, 1994; Salem et al., 1998), and researchers do not always find that intra- and inter-household conflicts are related to stepchildren's outcomes (e.g., Hanson et al., 1996). In fact, it may be that stepchildren are less affected by spousal conflict than are children in first marriages because stepchildren are less invested in the stability and quality of the remarriage than children are with their parents' marriage. Stepchildren may be affected, however, when they are involved in a conflictual relationship with stepparents and parents. In an excellent review of the effects of marital conflict on children, Cummings and Davies (2002) emphasized the importance of process models in understanding the relationship between marital conflict and child outcomes. "Processes of change are complex and multidimensional and are also dynamic and subject to change. Nonetheless, this level of analysis, while admittedly daunting, is at the heart of understanding of causality and etiology" (p. 39). Although Cummings and Davies were referring to marital conflict in first marriage families, they also have concluded that children react to interparental and interadult conflict with fear, distress, and anger. Children in stepfamilies may have been and continue to be exposed to their parents' conflicts, and they may experience conflict in the stepfamily as well. The accumulation of the results of continued parental conflict over time is likely to have negative effects on children, but these process studies have not yet been done.

The amount of conflict in stepfamilies is greater when stepchildren are adolescents than when they are younger. This may be because adolescents resist directions and discipline from a stepparent more than younger stepchildren do. Regardless of the reason, adolescent stepchildren often report more conflict with stepparents than do adolescents in first-marriage families (e.g., Barber & Lyons, 1994; Kurdek & Fine, 1993b). Vuchinich, Hetherington, Vuchinich, and Clingempeel (1991) found that adolescent girls had more difficulty than boys interacting with stepfathers. They also had more extended conflicts with, and were more likely to withdraw from, stepfathers and treat them like outsiders.

Another stress-related explanation for the greater risk of problems for stepchildren is the *economic deprivation hypothesis*. According to this hypothesis, stepchildren are at a disadvantage compared to children living with both parents because they have experienced financial hardships related to parental relationship transitions. In addition, the associated conditions that accompany poverty, such as inadequate schools, dangerous neighborhoods, and parents working long hours, also place stepchildren at risk for problems (e.g., Pong, 1997). Although parental remarriage generally brings the household income close to first marriage household incomes, stepchildren likely have experienced some financial problems due to having spent time in a single parent household. Evidence to support the economic deprivation hypothesis has been mixed; when researchers control for differences in household income or socioeconomic status, stepfamily effects are sometimes attenuated (e.g., Pong, 1997), but not always (e.g., Hoffman & Johnson, 1998; Pong & Lu, 2001).

A few researchers propose that *social stigma* creates stress for adolescents and their parents and stepparents (Doyle et al., 2002; Lansford et al., 2001). Although few have investigated the effects of social stigma on stepchildren, there is some evidence to support this proposition. Because of adolescents' stage of development, they may be particularly sensitive to stigma related to stepfamilies. Adolescents want to "fit in" with others. However, it is during this stage of development that adolescents tend to feel that other people are as interested in what they do and think as they are interested in themselves, a phenomenon known as the imaginary audience (Elkind, 1967). Further, adolescents are also likely to engage in the creation of personal fables. They presume that they and their own personal problems are unique and singularly important, that no one else could possibly understand what they are experiencing (Elkind, 1967). Given the stigma associated with being a stepchild, these common developmental issues of adolescents could indicate that adolescent stepchildren experience stress related to their stepfamily status.

Stepparent and Parent Involvement Models

Another set of explanations centers on the amount of involvement that either parents or stepparents have in the stepchildren's lives. In general, stepparent households are hypothesized to lack social capital; that is time and energy to engage in positive interactions with children. Parents' abilities to competently raise their children are reduced, according to this perspective, because they are investing their time and energy in building relationships with new partners rather than in childrearing (e.g., Downey, 1995; Pong, 1997). Stepparents do not invest as much social capital in stepchildren because they also are expending resources on the adult relationship or on their children from prior unions (e.g., Bogenscheider, 1997; Teachman, Paasch, & Carver, 1996). Consequently, children in stepparent households have more problems than other children do because they are thought to be receiving inadequate parenting and adult support. Researchers who employed the *social capital model* to investigate stepparent effects on stepchildren's academic achievement generally reported that stepparents and remarried parents spent less time working with stepchildren on schoolwork and being involved with school related activities than did parents in first marriage families (e.g., Leung, 1995; Pong, 1997). Also, support for the social capital model was found in studies of behavior problems (e.g., Kim, Hetherington, & Reiss, 1999). However, other researchers have found that cooperation between the parent and stepparent in raising stepchildren may be as important as the amount of stepparents' involvement with the stepchildren (Bronstein et al., 1994; Skopin, Newman, & McKenry, 1993).

In general, stepparents interact less often with stepchildren than parents do (e.g., Doyle et al., 2002; Hofferth & Anderson, 2003). The social capital model is but one explanation—a number of other interpretations have been investigated. For instance, stepfathers may find it hard to break into tightly knit mother-child systems because both mothers and children work to keep them at a distance (Bray & Kelly, 2000; Hetherington & Clingempeel, 1992). Some mothers want partners but not co-parents (Giles-Sims, 1984), and so they may discourage active involvement by stepfathers. Nonresidential parents may also discourage active involvement by stepparents out of jealousy and fears that the stepparent might replace them in their children's lives. Cultural beliefs and societal expectations also may play a role—people generally expect stepparents to be less supportive and less close to stepchildren than parents (e.g., Ganong & Coleman, 1995), so stepparents may not try to be more involved. Moreover, the stepparent role has low salience for the personal identities of many stepparents, so they may find more satisfaction in work, marriage, or raising their own children than they do in relating to their stepchildren (Thoits, 1992).

Evolutionary scholars postulate that stepparents invest little in their stepchildren because they are not genetically related to them (Daly & Wilson, 1996). This theory proposes that stepparents who also are parents discriminate in favor of their genetic children and that stepfathers interact with stepchildren to impress their new partners rather than to foster stepchildren's growth and well-being. The *parental investment/parental discrimination proposition* has been supported in some studies (e.g., Flinn, 1999; Mekos, Hetherington, & Reiss, 1996), but not in all (e.g., Bulcroft et al., 1998; Menaghan et al., 1997). For example, men who lived with their children and stepchildren spent as much time with their stepchildren as did men who did not live with their children (Cooksey & Fondell, 1996).

Stepparental and Parental Styles

The parenting styles of stepparents and parents have been hypothesized as placing children at risk for problems (e.g., Fine & Kurdek, 1992; Salem et al., 1998). Unfortunately, making comparisons across studies is difficult because most researchers have developed their own measures of stepparenting styles.

Consistent with the research on stepparents' involvement with stepchildren, on average, stepfathers showed less affection toward stepchildren and engaged in less supervision of them (e.g., Hetherington & Clingempeel, 1992; Kurdek & Fine, 1995). Similar findings were reported for stepmothers (Kurdek & Fine, 1993b).

However, not all investigators found differences in parenting style between stepparent households and first marriage-parent households. For example, stepfather households containing adolescents did not differ from nuclear families in permissiveness and in democratic decision-making (Barber & Lyons, 1994); in support and monitoring of adolescents (Salem et al., 1998); or in permissive, authoritarian, or authoritative parenting styles (Shucksmith, Hendry, & Glendinning, 1995). Also, no major differences were found in adolescent independence giving (i.e., staying home alone, household rules, and weekend curfews) between nuclear, single parent, and stepparent households (Bulcroft et al., 1998).

Researchers generally found that authoritative parenting (high warmth and high control) was positively related and authoritarian parenting (low warmth and high control) was negatively related to adolescent well-being, suggesting that the same family processes that influence adolescent well-being in first-marriage families are also associated with well-being in stepfamilies (e.g., Hetherington & Clingempeel, 1992; Fine & Kurdek, 1992). Stepparent support was a better predictor of adolescent stepchildren's adjustment than stepparents' monitoring behaviors (Crosbie-Burnett & Giles-Sims, 1994).

Although several studies identified sex differences in stepchildren's perceptions of stepparents' warmth and control, consistent patterns are difficult to discern (e.g., Kurdek & Fine, 1993a, 1993b). There are indications that residential stepmothers have a harder time raising stepchildren than residential stepfathers do (MacDonald & DeMaris, 1996). Additionally, Thomson, McLanahan, and Curtin (1992) found that parenting was less gendered in father-stepmother families than in mother-stepfather or first-marriage families, although the differences were considered to be "relatively small" (p. 376).

Selection Hypothesis

The *selection hypothesis* is that differences between stepchildren and children living with both parents are due to factors that predated parental remarriage or cohabitation (see Amato, 2000). Because correlational data do not allow researchers to make causal inferences, some researchers employ the selection hypothesis to question whether differences between stepchildren and other children are due to pre-existing factors, such as parental psychopathology or poverty, that influence either family transitions or children's problems, or both (Capaldi & Patterson, 1991). In general, findings regarding selection factors indicate that children's behavior problems predate parental remarriage (e.g., Nicholson et al., 1999; Sun, 2001; Sun & Li, 2002), although some have found that girls show negative effects before parental separation but boys show more negative effects after separation (Doherty & Needle, 1991). Longitudinal data from a study done by Furstenberg and Kiernan (2001) suggest that the effects of parental divorce (and perhaps later transitions such as parental remarriage) are due to a complex blend of selection and socialization factors.

CHILD ABUSE IN STEPFAMILIES

Among the most serious children's outcomes that have been studied in stepfamilies is sexual and physical abuse. Researchers have explored child abuse in stepfamilies in a number of ways. Some researchers use data drawn from surveys of the general population, others have used court records or legal documents as data bases, and still others have sampled women and children who use social services designed for victims of family violence. All of these approaches have limitations, of course, some of which may inflate the rates of abuse in stepfamilies and some which may lead to underreporting (Giles-Sims, 1997).

In general, although not all studies have reported that stepchildren are more likely to be abused by stepparents than children are by their parents (Gelles & Harrop, 1991; Malkin & Lamb, 1994; Sullivan, Juras, Bybee, Nguyen, & Allen, 2000), the preponderance of research indicates that children are more at risk for abuse if they live in a household with an adult who is not their genetic parent (Giles-Sims, 1997). Most researchers report that children in households with non-natal adults, particularly stepfathers, mothers' boyfriends, and other non-natal males, are at greater risk for sexual abuse (Margolin, 1992) and physical abuse (Daly & Wilson, 1996) than are children in households with both parents. The overall conclusion is that stepchildren are at greater risk for abuse than are children living with both parents.

However, the magnitude of this risk is open to debate (Giles-Sims, 1997). In other words, to what extent are stepchildren at greater risk for being abused by a stepparent? One problem in answering this question is that nobody knows for sure how many stepchildren there are—one approach to determining their risk for abuse is to examine the rates of abuse for stepchildren and compare that rate to the *estimated* proportion of all children who are stepchildren. Most estimates have underreported stepchildren because demographers have defined households by adults' marital status or the number of adults in residence (Bumpass & Raley, 1995). The question of the magnitude of risk for stepchildren is related to how many stepchildren there are estimated to be—9%, 10%, 17% of all children, or, more? Most researchers have used the smaller estimates; which result in larger estimates of risk (Daly & Wilson, 1999).

Another issue in determining the degree of risk is related to problems in determining if the perpetrator of child abuse is a stepparent or another adult. For example, mothers' boyfriends and remarried stepfathers are often categorized together as one group. Sometimes other men such as uncles, grandfathers, and "father figures" are included with stepfathers. Because of the sensitive nature of the information, nearly all child abuse data are somewhat suspect. Abuse victims and other family members may be more reluctant to report sexual abuse by a father than by a stepfather or other male, especially when the family is financially dependent on the father. It is also likely that medical personnel may be more inclined to attribute and report stepchildren's injuries to abuse than those of children in first marriage families. Of course, nobody knows for sure the direction of errors in the reporting of abuse, but it seems likely, given the general confusion about what a stepfamily is and how to define a step-relationship, that some misreporting occurs that inflates stepparent perpetrators.

Theories of Child Abuse in Stepfamilies

Although empirical studies offer conflicting information about the prevalence of child abuse in stepfamilies, theories about child abuse in stepfamilies abound. Kalmuss and Seltzer (1989) proposed a framework that suggested three reasons why family violence is more likely in stepfamilies than in first-marriage families. First, at least some individuals in stepfamilies are more likely to have been socialized to patterns of family conflict and violence in their previous family units (Giles-Sims & Finkelhor, 1984). Second, characteristics of post-divorce step-households (e.g., complexity, lack of institutional support, role ambiguity) may increase the likelihood of conflict and violence. Lastly, at least some members of step-households have experienced the cumulative stress of multiple family transitions that is often related to family conflict and violence. This *family socialization* model, loosely based on social learning theory, predicts that characteristics of families containing divorced, cohabiting, and remarried individuals make conflict more probable, but certainly not inevitable.

Greater stress in stepfamilies, combined with less ability to cope with stress, also has been proposed as a reason why stepparents would be more physically abusive (Giles-Sims, 1997). The *selection hypothesis* proposes that stepfamilies contain a greater proportion of individuals with characterological problems and who are violence prone. *Normative theory* attributes the higher rates of sexual abuse by stepfathers to the fact that non-kin relatives are less subject to taboos against incest. However, normative theory does not explain why British married and cohabiting stepfathers were more likely to abuse stepchildren but less likely than fathers to subject victims to intercourse (Gordon & Creighton, 1988). *Resource theory* predicts that the more resources a person has (e.g., money, power, education, or parenting skills), the less likely it is that he or she will have to resort to physical force to get their way. This theory suggests stepfathers with fewer resources would be more prone to violence. This may interact with the type of stepfamily; because cohabiting stepfamilies on average have fewer resources, children living with a cohabiting parent and non-natal adult may be more at risk than those living with a remarried parent and stepparent.

None of these theories have received the attention that *evolutionary theory* has in recent years (Giles-Sims, 1997). Evolutionary theory predicts that physical abuse and neglect of stepchildren is likely to occur because stepparents have a lesser investment in children who do not carry their genes. The principle of *natural selection* inclines males and females to invest in their own offspring and to "avoid squandering valuable reproductive effort on someone else's offspring" (Daly & Wilson, 1980, p. 279). The evolutionary perspective argues that stepchildren are at risk because parents protect their own reproductive efforts and not those of others. Just as animals attack and kill the offspring of others so that their offspring might have a better chance of survival, so stepparents abuse those who are not the product of their reproductive efforts. Moreover, evolutionary theory posits that because inbreeding reduces fitness, sexual relations with offspring are taboo. Stepchildren are at risk for sexual abuse by their stepparents because the incest taboo does not apply to them. Wilson and Daly (1987) argue that "children's extreme dislike of discord between their natural parents and their alarm at the prospect of parental remarriage reflect a remarkably astute assessment of their own best interests, and may even be adaptive emotional responses that have been specifically favored in our natural selective history" (p. 227). Evolutionary theorists and researchers point to studies that show lower investment of time and financial support in stepchildren than in genetic children and to studies conducted on non-human species as evidence for genetically based differences in parental solicitude that lead, in some situations, to abuse of stepchildren.

Critics of evolutionary theory note that the theory does not explain the often-reported physical and sexual abuse of children by their genetic parents (Giles-Sims, 1997), and as noted earlier in this chapter, not all studies find less involvement and investment in stepchildren by stepparents. Critics also point out that most stepparents are not abusive or neglectful, and some even engage in substantial sacrifices to aid their stepchildren (Mason, 2003). Non-natal adult nurturance of dependent young is not limited to humans; there are cross species examples of various animals, from birds to primates, in which there are nurturing stepparents (Mason, 2003).

However, evolutionary theorists counter that stepfathers' (and presumably stepmothers') investments in stepchildren fit with the theory as well. By being nice to their stepchildren and investing resources in them to ensure their survival, step-fathers enhance the likelihood that the mothers of their stepchildren will reproduce with them (Anderson, 2000). In short, stepfathers' investments are best understood as an investment in the children's mother. Although the evolutionary arguments seem to have some difficulties explaining the disconfirming evidence, for the last few years this is the most prevalent theory being employed to explain child abuse and neglect.

Physical abuse and sexual abuse of children are important topics of research that should receive further study. Despite the methodological problems that impede the advancement of knowledge in this important area (i.e., lack of comparability across research designs, inaccurate reporting of data, and the private nature of family interaction in households), researchers will no doubt continue to investigate these outcomes. We discuss this research further in the final chapter.

Chapter 9

Siblings, Half-Siblings, and Stepsiblings

Although the bulk of stepfamily research focuses on children, only minimal attention has been paid to the potential changes that can occur as a result of adding stepsiblings and half-siblings to children's family constellations. Many researchers identify a target child when collecting and analyzing stepfamily data so little is known regarding how siblings may be differentially affected by remarriage. In this chapter we present sibling definitions, a brief summary of the research on siblings in stepfamilies, and suggestions for future research.

Underlying much of the research on the effects of living in a stepfamily on children are several assumptions that involve the influence of adults and/or adults' relationships on children's adjustment: (a) parents' marital transitions affect children's well-being because transitions add stress to children's lives (Martinez & Forgatch, 2002), (b) children's' emotional and behavioral adjustment to stepfamily living is a function of marital conflict (Hanson et al., 1996), and (c) children's adjustment is a consequence of the stepparent-stepchild relationship (Salem et al., 1998). Rosenberg and Hajfal (1985) argued that these assumptions imply a *dripolator effect*, in which influences from the top of the stepfamily system filter down to the bottom. They suggest there also may be *percolator effects* in stepfamilies, where influences from relationships at the bottom bubble to the top, resulting in either negative or positive effects on the family. A major source of these percolator effects is the relationships between children in stepfamilies.

In stepfamilies, children may acquire stepsiblings, and eventually, half-siblings, in addition to the brothers and sisters they may have had prior to parental remarriages. To further add to the complexity, children may reside either full-time or part-time with any combination of siblings, stepsiblings, and half-siblings, or they may not live with them at all. In stepfamilies formed after children are grown, stepsiblings may not even meet each other, or may have only limited encounters. When there is a big age difference for remarried parents the age range of stepsiblings can be greater than the age range of siblings.

As with other stepfamily relationships, data on the prevalence of step- and half-siblings are difficult to acquire. The best estimations are that approximately 75% of the children who reside with a remarried parent have at least one sibling, and nearly one-third of stepchildren living in stepparent households have a half-sibling (Bumpass, 1984), usually acquired within the first few years after stepfamily formation (Wineberg, 1990, 1992). The number of children who have stepsiblings is not known, but in approximately 1 out of 15 stepfamily households both adults have children from prior relationships living in the household (Sweet, 1991), meaning that they contain stepsiblings. However, this underestimates the number of stepsiblings, because it does not count nonresidential stepsiblings. Bumpass (1984) estimated that two-thirds of the children in stepfamilies have either a stepsibling or a half-sibling.

Before we discuss what is known about the relationships between children in stepfamilies, we want to define what we mean by siblings, half-siblings, and stepsiblings (see Figure 9.1). We use the term *siblings* to refer to children who are biologically related to the same mother and father. In Figure 9.1 you can see that there are two sets of full siblings connected to the stepfamily. One set of full siblings is the product of their remarried mother and her former spouse/partner, and these siblings live in the stepfamily household with their mother and stepfather. They are labeled *resident outsiders* because, although they share the stepfamily residence, they are not part of the nuclear family in the residence (i.e., the stepfamily adults and their mutual child). These genetically related brothers and sisters are sometimes called *full-siblings* or *biological siblings*. Sibling relationships also exist when the same two parents have adopted children.

The distinction between half-siblings and (full) siblings is not clear to many people. A *half-sibling relationship* is when two or more children share a biological (or adoptive) connection to one parent, but not both. In Figure 9.1, you can see that the mutual child of the stepfamily couple is labeled a *resident insider*. This is because the mutual child is part of the nuclear family inside the stepfamily household. The mutual child shares a mother and a household residence with the *resident outsiders* and shares a father but not a household residence with the *visiting outsiders*. However, both the resident outsiders and the visiting outsiders are half-siblings to the mutual child. For example, former President Bill Clinton and Roger Clinton are half-brothers because they have the same mother, but different fathers (Roger's father was Bill's stepfather; Bill's father was his mother's first husband). Bill Clinton allegedly may have another half-brother, a man from California, who claims to have been fathered by Clinton's father. It is possible, as in this example, for a person to have half-siblings who are not related to each other (i.e., Roger Clinton is unrelated to the man from California).

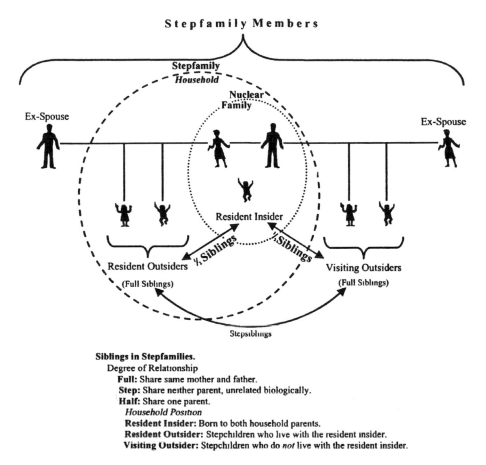

Figure 9.1. Full, Step- and Half-Sibling Relationships.

Stepsiblings are not biologically or legally related to each other (see Figure 9.1). In Figure 9.1, the two sets of full siblings are stepsiblings and they share neither a parent nor a household, although they could share the household and probably do, from time to time. These siblings have no genetic or legal ties to each other yet they are members of this stepfamily. The only genetic tie the stepsiblings have in common is with their half-sibling. Both sets of stepsiblings are half-siblings of the resident insider. For example, when a man and woman marry and they each have children from a previous relationship, the new husband's children become stepsiblings to the new wife's children. Stepsiblings are always part of *complex stepfamilies* because there are two stepparents in the family. The households in which they live, however, may contain only the father's children or only the mother's children.

We try to be careful in defining what these different types of sibling relationships mean. In the past, researchers sometimes have not distinguished between full, half-, and stepsiblings (e.g., Amato, 1987; Ferri, 1984), making it impossible to assess the unique dynamics of each type of relationship. For example, in the first wave of the National Survey of Families and Households (NSFH), the interview protocol included stepsiblings and half-siblings in the same question—apparently the researchers who wrote this item did not think it was necessary to differentiate between these two types of children's sibling bonds, leaving researchers with little choice but to assess them as one group (White, 1992). On a side note, but one that is related to the issue of defining sibling relationships, White (1998), in examining changes between the first two waves of the NSFH data sets, found that approximately 15% of the respondents added or subtracted children in their families, even though there had not been births or deaths in the ensuing 4 years. Instead of assuming that these discrepancies simply were reporting errors, White probed further, and considered the influence of changes in how items were worded, the complexity of family structures, changes in family structures between waves, such as remarriages that added stepsiblings, and what she called low sibling salience, or the fact that stepsiblings (and other siblings) might not be consistently counted as kin if they lived elsewhere, changed residences periodically, or had minimal or erratic contact with respondents. White cautioned researchers about defining their terms more clearly so that study participants might more clearly understand researchers' meanings that might differ from their own, and consequently answer questions in a way that matches researchers' assumptions. This is good practice, but we think researchers should also be aware that family members construct their own realities of family life that are independent of scholarly conceptualizations, and there are limits to what clear research definitions will be able to accomplish in the face of a family member's cognitive constructions of their family. For instance, we know of people who refer to stepsiblings as their siblings and to stepfathers as their fathers, and no amount of researcher definition would change how these individuals would respond to questions about their families. We think there is little doubt that step-relationships of all kinds are underreported in studies because of this phenomenon. In the next few sections we discuss what is known about siblings, half-siblings and step-siblings.

SIBLINGS

In general, relationships between siblings have received less attention from scholars than other important family bonds. Although research on siblings has increased in recent years (Dunn & Davies, 2001), little of this interest has been extended to research about siblings in stepfamilies.

In two studies in which sibling relationships in stepfamilies were examined it was found that siblings were less close than was true in other family types (Anderson & Rice, 1992; Dunn et al., 1998). As part of the Virginia Longitudinal Study of Divorce and Remarriage, Anderson and Rice (1992) assessed changes in the quality and functioning of sibling relationships over a 2.5 year period in newly remarried stepfamilies, divorced maternal custody families, and nondivorced families. In addition to asking mothers, fathers, and target children (ages 9–13 at the beginning of the study) about sibling relationships, sibling interactions were observed in a play situation, a family problem-solving situation, and at the dinner table. All family members agreed that boys in stepfamilies were less supportive and more negative to siblings than were boys and girls from other families. However, girls in stepfamilies did not significantly differ from other girls, and even offered more support to siblings during the first year of parental remarriage. Observations indicated that sibling interactions in divorced families were more negative than in stepfamilies or married families, but sibling relationships in stepfamilies became more negative over time. Although children from all three family types increasingly disengaged from their siblings as they entered adolescence, parental remarriage seemed to have accelerated this normative process (Anderson & Rice, 1992). Rather than bonding together in the face of parental remarriage, siblings disengaged from each other.

Results from the Avon Longitudinal Study of Pregnancy and Childhood (ALSPAC), a large-scale study of families in England, suggest that siblings in stepfamilies may start out being more negative towards each other than children living with both of their parents. Dunn and her colleagues (1998) found that, compared to siblings in nonstepfamilies, there was more negativity in sibling relationships for 4-year-olds and their older siblings (mean age = 7.3 years) in stepfamilies. Sibling negativity and disengagement in stepfamilies may carry over into adulthood; White and Reidmann (1992), using data collected in the National Survey of Families and Households, found that siblings who were part of a stepfamily prior to age 18 had slightly less contact as adults than siblings whose parents remained married during their childhood years. They attributed the difference to "stepfamily dynamics" (p. 206), presumably related to stressful interactions. Anderson and Rice speculated that children in stepfamilies had more negative and less positive interactions with siblings as a result of stresses they were experiencing due to their parent's relatively recent remarriage.

However, sibling relationships in stepfamilies have not consistently been found to be more hostile and/or distant. Data from a longitudinal study of adolescent sibling pairs indicated that sibling relationships in stepfamilies were just as positive as sibling relationships in nonstepfamilies (Anderson, 1999). Given that these findings contrasted sharply with data from an earlier investigation in which he took part, Anderson speculated that these differences were due to adolescents in the second project being older and having been in a stepfamily longer than the adolescent sibling pairs in the earlier study (Anderson & Rice, 1992). Over time, adolescent siblings may gradually pull together and help each other following parental remarriage.

White (1994) found that parental remarriage (and divorce) was not related to sibling solidarity for either adult males or adult females. White concluded that positive or negative effects of parents' marital changes on sibling relationships do not outlive childhood.

Sibling relationships can be extremely important to an individual's psychological and behavioral development (Anderson, 1999; Dunn & Davies, 2001; Dunn et al., 1998). It is believed that siblings perform several important functions for each other, among them: identity formation, protection from parents and others, mutual regulation of behavior, socialization, support, and the exchange of direct services, such as loaning money or giving rides (Bank & Kahn, 1997). If siblings disengage from each other following remarriage, do they continue to perform these functions for each other? How and why do sibling relationships in stepfamilies change over time? If increased stress within the stepfamily affects siblings, what are the mechanisms by which greater stress changes sibling dynamics? These and other questions remain to be answered.

HALF-SIBLINGS

How well do half-siblings get along? Bernstein (1989), in a qualitative study of stepfamilies who had reproduced, found that relationships were better when there were larger age differences between half-sibs, when the stepfamily had been together longer, when half-siblings lived together, and when children were similar in temperament.

Half-siblings who live together all of the time or most of the time generally think of each other simply as siblings (Anderson, 1999; Bernstein, 1989; Ganong & Coleman, 1988). The "half" is a meaningless abstraction to these siblings, and they do not refer to each other as half-brothers or half-sisters. However, when children have little contact, distinctions between half- and full-siblings are more common; in these situations, the "sibling" part of the label half-sibling is the meaningless abstraction (Bernstein, 1989). More research is needed on nonresidential half-sibling relationships, but the few studies that have been done lead to the conclusion that residential half-siblings function similarly to siblings. Ahrons' (in press) longitudinal study of post-divorce families found that over 90% of those who had half-siblings think of them as brothers or sisters. Even though the average age discrepancy in Ahrons' study was large (10 years), and at the time of the half-sibling's birth the older half-siblings in her sample thought it was weird to have a new baby in the family, these sibling relationships developed to be positive ones. Ahrons reported that the amount of time spent together did not affect their perceptions of half-sibling relationships as adults, and the gender of the shared parent also did not seem to matter.

Some interest has been shown on the *percolator effects* of half-sibling relationships on other family relationships. The rationale is that because a child born to the stepfamily couple is biologically related to everyone else in the household, this shared genetic connection will help to facilitate integration as a family unit and will draw the marital dyad and step-relationships (e.g., stepparent-stepchild, stepsiblings) closer (Ganong & Coleman, 1988). As we mentioned in chapter 4, our study of *concrete babies*, inspired partly by self-help books that indicated having a child together would help *cement* family bonds, did not support this assertion (Ganong & Coleman, 1988), although parents in Bernstein's (1989) study felt that having a mutual child helped them as a couple. This finding may be due to cognitive dissonance ("we did this so of course it was a good thing") or social desirability.

Research findings on the effects of mutual children on other family relationships are generally mixed. For example, investigators found that the presence of a half-sibling negatively affected the stepmother-stepchild relationship (Ambert, 1986; Santrock & Sitterle, 1987), positively affected the stepfather-child relationship (Ambert, 1986; Hobart, 1988), was not related to stepmother-stepchild ties (Ahrons & Wallisch, 1987; Ganong & Coleman, 1988; Hobart, 1988), had little effect on stepfamily relations (Ahrons & Wallisch, 1987; Booth, Brinkerhoff, & White, 1984; Ganong & Coleman, 1988), had a negative influence on older children's behavior (Zill, 1988), and reduced the amount of time mothers had to spend with their children from prior marriages (Ahrons & Wallisch, 1987). Some of these discrepant results may be explained by differences in the timing of the assessment; half-sibling relationships may be more stressful when children are younger than when they are older (Bernstein, 1989; Ganong & Coleman, 1988). Also, the amount of time since the half-sibling was born may make a difference, if children are still adjusting to the birth. Researchers generally have not examined potential moderator variables that could influence the effects of half-siblings on other family relationships (e.g., age differences, gender combinations, amount of contact, and other variables related to family structure). In addition to these structural variables, unexamined intrapersonal variables such as temperament, expectations, and reasons for reproducing in remarriage potentially are factors in determining the quality of half-sibling relationships, as well as the effect the mutual child has on other relationships. Most of the studies simply investigated the presence/absence of a half-sibling in a family as the sole predictor for other outcome variables.

Information about half-siblings could have important implications, especially for those stepfamilies most likely to reproduce: younger, post-divorce stepfamilies in which one of the adults has not been married before or has not had children prior to the marriage (Bernstein, 1989; Ganong & Coleman, 1988). Despite inconclusive evidence regarding the *concrete baby effect*, adults in stepfamilies continue to have children partly in order to strengthen stepfamily bonds.

STEPSIBLINGS

The existence of stepsiblings suggests that both adults may have been married or in a serious cohabiting relationship at least once before. Consequently, there may be at least two living parents for each child, at least two sets of extended kin, and children in the stepfamily may reside periodically in other households. Plus, there are at least two stepparents in the family, because each adult partner is a stepparent as well as a parent.

If two sets of children live together all or most of the time, stepfamilies may have to move into housing large enough to accommodate both sets of children. Accompanying such moves may be shifts into new schools, loss of friends and the familiarity of the old neighborhoods, and a host of other stressors to be added to the transition into stepfamily life. If one set of children, or some children from both sets, live most of the time elsewhere (with their other parent, for instance), then efforts still have to be made to accommodate/incorporate the nonresidential children into the stepfamily household for visits or extended stays.

When there are stepsibling relationships, there are also many financial, interpersonal, and residential challenges. When two parents combine their offspring, lifestyle changes for children are highly probable. As we have seen with other dimensions of stepfamily life, researchers and clinicians have generally associated increased complexity with increased problems, and stepsibling relationships in complex stepfamilies are no exception. Clinicians have identified a number of potential difficulties when there are stepsibling relationships: sibling rivalry; competition over scarce resources, such as parental attention and space; sexual attraction; having little in common; changes in family size; and changes in the child's position in the family (Rosenberg & Hajfal, 1985; Walsh, 1992). Few researchers have examined these clinically identified issues.

In one study that did, however, the researchers found some support for the notion that stepsiblings create more complex family dynamics (Mekos, Hetherington, & Reiss, 1996). In stepfamilies where adolescent children were stepsiblings, compared to nonstepfamilies and stepfamilies in which all children were full or half-siblings, there were greater differences in parenting of the children and more problem behaviors (i.e., alcohol and marijuana use). Differences in parenting and sibling adjustment in nonstepfamilies and in stepfamilies in which siblings share a parent were negligible. However, the relation between differential parenting and problem behavior in stepfamilies with full or half-siblings more closely resembled the relation between differential parenting and problem behavior in stepfamilies with stepsiblings than in nonstepfamilies. The researchers speculated that adults and children in stepfamilies, regardless of sibling constellation, were more "sensitive to differential treatment of children by adults, so that even small differences in parental negativity make a difference in children's adjustment" (p. 2161). Parents' differential treatment of children in the household has to reach a certain threshold of variation to be noticed by family members—in stepfamilies people may be more attuned to noticing differences of whatever magnitude. Siblings in two-parent families develop specializations (Kowal & Kramer, 2003)—"I am the pretty one, and my sister is the smart one". There is less time for that level of specialization and differentiation to happen in stepfamilies. There is also the possibility that siblings' identities from the prior household will lead to conflicts when specializations overlap; a child who was "the pretty one" may be threatened if a stepsibling is much prettier, and who also was "the pretty one" in her prior family unit.

Differential treatment in stepfamilies may be due to adults showing preferential treatment to their own genetic children (cf. Trivers, 1972), stepparents backing off discipline and rule-setting for stepchildren compared to their own children (Bray, 1988), and adults responding differently to genetic differences in children (e.g., favoring children who have more genetic similarity to themselves). Although Mekos and colleagues did not use the term *percolator effects*, these findings are an example of such effects. That is, the sibling constellation appeared to stimulate differential patterns of parental reactions, which in turn led to diverse reactions from and outcomes for children in the household.

Although only a few researchers have examined the relationship between stepsiblings (Anderson, 1999; Beer, 1991; Duberman, 1975; Ganong & Coleman, 1987; Mekos et al., 1996; White & Reidmann, 1992), what is known about stepsiblings and siblings in stepfamilies is growing due to two large studies, one done in the United States (Hetherington, Henderson, & Reiss, 1999) and one in the United Kingdom (Dunn et al., 1998, 1999). The U.S. study specifically focused on adolescent sibling pairs in different types of families, and has produced rich insights about siblings and stepsiblings (Hetherington et al., 1999). The British study is longitudinal, has a large number of families from one geographical area, and the overall project has yielded many valuable papers on various aspects of family structure and family relationships, including siblings (e.g., Dunn et al., 1998, 1999).

In the eyes of parents and stepparents, stepsiblings get along well with each other (Duberman, 1975; Ganong & Coleman, 1993), although many stepfamily adults recognize periodic conflicts. In an in-depth study that we did of 52 complex stepfamilies, 39% of the adults perceived normal sibling rivalry between stepsiblings, 33% saw jealousy, 12% reported that sharing space was a problem, 12% felt that their children had nothing in common with their stepsiblings, and 4% identified competition as a source of trouble in stepsibling relationships (Ganong & Coleman, 1993).

Although some studies find few differences between stepsiblings and siblings in other family structures (Anderson, 1999), in general, stepsibling relationships are not as close as sibling relationships, both during childhood (Ganong & Coleman, 1993) and as adults (White & Reidmann, 1992). This is not to suggest that stepsibling relationships are negative and hostile; on the contrary, stepsibling relationships were reported to be characterized by generally positive affect (Anderson, 1999; Ganong & Coleman, 1993) and substantial contact is maintained in adulthood (White & Reidmann, 1992). In general, stepsiblings do not think of each other as brothers or sisters (Ahrons, in press). Those who have a sibling relationship likely shared a residence together over an extended period of time.

Ihinger-Tallman (1987) outlined several propositions concerning how and why sibling (and stepsibling) bonds develop or fail to develop in post-divorce stepfamilies. She speculated that there are normative pressures on stepsiblings to hold affectionate feelings for each other. She hypothesized that stepsiblings were more likely to bond if:

- they have frequent contact;
- they share experiences;
- there are conditions that foster intimacy (i.e., freedom to express emotions and a lack of competition for resources) and interdependency (i.e., exchanges of rewards between stepsiblings);
- they are similar in age, gender, experiences, and values;
- there are few perceived costs and more perceived benefits to associating together; and
- there is perceived equality in giving up aspects of their pre-remarriage lifestyle.

To date, these speculations have not triggered much interest by researchers.

In summary, a number of questions remain to be answered or have yet to be answered fully about the relationships between children in stepfamilies. For example:

- What is the nature of stepsibling and nonresidential half-sibling bonds?
- Are stepsiblings considered to be "real" kin?
- What effects do stepsiblings have on each other?
- Do stepsiblings provide stress-buffering effects or do they increase stress related to parental remarriage?
- Under what conditions do half-siblings strengthen emotional ties in the stepfamily?
- Are there sex differences in adaptation to stepsiblings?
- How are half-sibling and stepsibling relationships related to developmental changes in children?

- How do stepsibling relationships change over time?
- What kinds of relationships do adult stepsiblings have with each other?

The notion of percolator effects in stepfamilies holds intuitive appeal. The relationships between children in stepfamilies, and the effects of these relationships on other family relationships, should be fruitful areas of inquiry in the future. Researchers interested in the relationships between children in stepfamilies should examine the growing literature on sibling relationships in nonstepfamilies for conceptual and methodological ideas. However, researchers should be cautious about assuming that processes that affect siblings in first-marriage families also affect stepsiblings in stepfamilies (Dunn & Davies, 2001).

Chapter **10**

Grandparents and Stepgrandparents

GRANDPARENTS

Estimates are that 95% of children today will still have at least one grandparent when they are 20 years old (U. S. Bureau of the Census, 1998). A steadily increasing number also will have stepgrandparents. In this chapter we present a very brief overview of the literature on grandparents in general (see Hayslip & Goldberg-Glen, 2000; Szinovacz, 1998, for comprehensive reviews of grandparent research), introduce the three types of stepgrandparents, and discuss our work on intergenerational obligations.

Grandparents often are important characters in their grandchildren's lives (Kornhaber, 1996). Grandparent-grandchild relationships are embedded within larger family systems, and they often are contingent upon the relationship between the grandparent and the parents of the grandchild (Mueller & Elder, 2003). The relationship can be broken by either side. Thus, the grandparent role is voluntary and ambiguous, and family transitions (i.e., divorce, remarriage) often make the grandparent-adult child bond more fragile, which in turn likely affects the grandparent-grandchild relationship. Because of the importance of grandparents to grandchildren, it is important that more attention be paid to those ties and how they are affected by family transitions.

Grandparents and grandchildren can play important roles in each other's lives. This intergenerational phenomenon is shaped by demographic factors such as: the total number of grandchildren a grandparent has; the grandparent's income, educational level, proximity, and age; the gender of grandparent, adult child, and grandchild; individual traits of the grandchild; and frequency of contact (Mueller & Elder, 2003). It is not demographic factors alone, however, that shape grandparent-grandchild relationships nor do demographic factors determine the importance of those relationships, and there is little doubt but that they are important. In one study, grandparent-grandchild bonds were second in emotional importance only to parent-child ties (Kornhaber, 1996). Young adult grandchildren have reported that they feel emotionally close to their grandparents, know them well, and are strongly influenced by them (Kennedy, 1992). Given the increased life span of people in the industrialized world, it is likely that current and future adults will spend more years as grandparents and great-grandparents than ever before in human history (Mills, Wakeman, & Fea, 2001).

The position of grandparent is one of the most revered of all family positions. In fact, even the terms *grandmother* or *grandfather* evoke positive feelings (Ganong & Coleman, 1983). Cultural stereotypes portray grandparents as warm, caring individuals who are full of wisdom and love for their grandchildren. In this idealized view, grandchildren can turn to grandparents when they need love, understanding, and kindly, helpful advice. Grandparents are seen as potential sources of support for grandchildren who experience stress related to changes in their parents' marital status, such as divorce, bereavement, and remarriage. Although not all grandparents are kind and warmly supportive of grandchildren, grandparents are a major source of support for grandchildren during times of stress (Johnson, 1988; Kennedy & Kennedy, 1993; Lussier, Deater-Deckard, Dunn, & Davies, 2002) and an increasing number of grandparents are raising their grandchildren (King, Elder, & Conger, 2000; Tomlin, 1998).

Divorce and Grandparents

The position of grandparent when an adult child divorces is similar to that of children when their parents divorce. Both grandparents and grandchildren generally have little control over whether or not the divorce occurs, they may be caught by surprise when the couple separates or announces their plans to split up, and their contacts with each other are mediated by adults in the middle generation.

The role of grandparent, always somewhat ambiguous, becomes even more so when a child divorces. Following divorce, grandparents become *quasi-kin* to their former daughter- or son-in-law (Bohannan, 1970). Normative expectations and prescriptions for quasi-kin interactions are evolving, but most people still are unsure about how they should feel and act towards former in-laws (Duran-Aydintug, 1993). For example, if an adult child and her/his former partner hate each other, what is the former parent-in-law supposed to do—cut off ties? Also hate the former partner? Continue to maintain a relationship for the sake of grandchildren? Or what? Grandparents may be in a quandary about these choices and the ramifications of any choice they might make.

For a lot of people good relationships between former in-laws are hard to maintain in any form after divorce because (1) the interactions become cold and impersonal, (2) they feel ill-at-ease with each other, or (3) they engage in hostile behavior (e.g., yelling, accusing) (Ambert, 1988). In fact, deterioration of these quasi-kin relationships often occurs very quickly. When this happens, some grandparents reject not only their ex-in-law but their grandchildren as well, particularly if they have other grandchildren (Ambert, 1988).

Most grandparents probably want to continue to maintain ties with their grandchildren after their children divorce, but the ambiguities of quasi-kin relationships with former in-laws introduce uncertainties regarding how relationships should be conducted between grandparents and their grandchildren. Moreover, the grandparents do not freely choose their roles, even in families in which there have not been divorces. Instead, grandparents' roles are negotiated with adult children and their partners, and they are contextual rather than universally applied. For example, health and age of grandparents (Johnson, 1992), geographical distance, quality of relationships between grandparents and grandchildren (Uhlenberg & Hammill, 1998), and grandparent-parent relationship quality (Whitbeck, Hoyt, & Huck, 1993) are factors that are related to frequency of contact for grandparents in general. Among the other contextual factors that influence grandparent-grandchild relationships after divorce are physical custody of grandchildren and the gender of grandparents and their child (Lussier et al., 2002).

Custody

After divorce, the parent with physical custody of the children typically regulates grandparents' access to them. Because mothers most often have physical custody, maternal grandparents are more likely to be involved with grandchildren than are paternal grandparents (Johnson, 1992). Mothers often determine the post-divorce roles of the grandparents, which means that the roles of the paternal grandparents, whose son is usually the nonresidential parent, are gradually limited and contact diminishes over time. Even when the involvement of maternal and paternal grandparents immediately following divorce is similar, over time paternal grandparents have significantly less contact with grandchildren, and they provide less social and emotional support to their children and grandchildren (Johnson, 1992). Paternal grandparents may only see their grandchildren when the children are visiting their son. Paternal grandmothers who realize that the mother of her grandchild is the key to maintaining ties may actively court her ex-daughter-in-law in order to preserve her relationship with her grandchild.

In recent years, some grandparents in the United Kingdom and United States have reacted to their lack of control over whether or not they see their grandchildren by pushing for grandparent visitation laws. These are laws designed to give grandparents some legal rights in being able to see their grandchildren after divorce, sometimes even when the parents object (Drew & Smith, 1999). In general, given the control that custodial parents have over access, it is likely that such laws do not work as well for families in which the parents and grandparents are in disagreement, and may, in fact, serve to add additional strain to parent-grandparent relationships (Johnson, 1999), which may ultimately harm grandparent-grandchild ties as well (Lussier et al., 2002).

Gender

The gender of the adult child is not the only gender difference affecting grandparent-grandchild contacts following divorce. For example, few grandfathers seem to remain actively involved with their divorced children and grandchildren independently of their wives. Johnson (1992) attributed this to the fact that women usually are the *kinkeepers* in families, the ones who decide about establishing and continuing relationships following family changes. This is another reason why maternal grandparents usually have more contact with grandchildren and are involved in more aspects of their lives than are paternal grandparents.

Several scholars have speculated that, at least in some families, intergenerational family ties are latent when families function well, but emerge as important relationships when families experience stress; maternal grandparents have been likened to *volunteer firefighters* (Cherlin & Furstenberg, 1986) and *watchdogs* (Troll, 1983) who come to the rescue when the family is disrupted, but otherwise they remain in the background. Clingempeel, Colyar, and Hetherington (1992) labeled this tendency the *latent function hypothesis* and speculated that the stress of divorce would activate grandparents to become more involved in the lives of their divorcing child and grandchildren. They found partial support for the latent function hypothesis in a longitudinal study of families and maternal grandparents; the relationship between grandparents and their divorced daughter's children was of higher quality (i.e., more frequent contact and greater perceived closeness) than the relationship between grandparents and grandchildren in either first-marriage families or stepfather families. These results were corroborated over time by the perceptions of all three generations. Similarly, the large majority of grandparents in Johnson's (1988) study provided help such as financial assistance and some services to their children and grandchildren after divorce. It becomes normatively more appropriate for grandparents to intrude in what they believe to be helpful ways into their divorced offspring's life, and the boundaries between households become more flexible. As noted above, this is particularly so when daughters are divorced and have custody of the grandchildren.

Not all studies have found gender differences in closeness to grandparents (e.g., Lussier et al., 2002), although maternal grandmothers often are reported to be the closest to grandchildren, especially granddaughters (e.g., Mills et al., 2001). It is likely that other factors besides gender are important as well, such as shared interests between grandparents and grandchildren, personality attributes of both, and geographic proximity.

Grandparents' Divorce

A substantial and increasing number of grandparents have experienced divorce (Uhlenberg & Kirby, 1998) so it is not always the divorce of the adult child that challenges intergenerational ties. Before we leave the topic of divorce and grandparent-grandchild relationships, we should briefly examine the effects of grandparents' divorces on these relationships. Although gender differences are relevant here as well, with divorced grandfathers having less contact with grandchildren than divorced grandmothers do, both grandfathers and grandmothers who are divorced have less contact than married and widowed grandparents do (Uhlenberg & Hammill, 1998). For men, this is partially attributed to the fact that they do not have a wife to maintain kin ties, and for both men and women, reduced contact is likely a consequence of poorer relationships with their children. Additionally, Iowa Youth and Families Project researchers found that divorced grandfathers lived twice as far from their grandchildren as divorced grandmothers do (King, 2003), although all of the divorced grandparents lived relatively close. Proximity, therefore, appeared to play an important role in grandfather-grandchild contact.

Child or Child-in-law Death and Grandparents

The ambiguities related to grandparents' roles and their relationships with grandchildren are less stressful and easier to resolve following bereavement. Although the quality of relationships between family members of different generations is relevant, there are fewer issues around redefining relationships than there are after offspring divorce, and with the *latent function norm* and other cultural norms in play, grandparents generally feel freer to offer assistance and maintain, if not increase, their contact with and support of grandchildren after bereavement. Mutual comfort and solace in their joint loss of a loved one may even strengthen grandparent-grandchild relationships.

We speculate that grandparenting after bereavement is partly a function of which middle-generation adult dies, the elders' child or a son- or daughter-in-law. Distance, gender of the remaining parent, and the ages of grandchildren also may be factors in post-bereavement involvement. It is probable when the grandparents' child is widowed, involvement with grandchildren will be greater than when a widowed in-law is the one who is mediating the grandparent-grandchild relationship. Gender differences likely come into play here as well, so that parents of widows are likely to be involved more than parents of widowers. Physical distance, of course, is also a factor in how much involvement with and assistance to grandchildren are generated by grandparents.

Younger grandchildren may receive more support and tangible assistance than adolescent and adult grandchildren, and contact may also be greater when grandchildren are young. Parents often need more help taking care of younger children, who require more supervision. Parents with younger children generally are younger than parents with adolescents and adult offspring, and so they may have fewer resources themselves. Additionally, grandparents also are likely to be younger, with more energy available to lend childcare assistance after bereavement.

Remarriage and Grandparents

Bridges or Walls?

Grandparents can be either helpful or harmful to remarried children's attempts at developing and maintaining a satisfying stepfamily life. In the words of John and Emily Visher, grandparents can build bridges or they can build walls (Visher & Visher, 1996). They can build bridges by accepting the remarriage and warmly welcoming stepgrandchildren into their lives. They can offer assistance, deliver it when requested, and otherwise allow the next generations to develop in their own ways.

On the other hand, they can build walls by criticizing a new stepparent's attempts to help raise their grandchildren, by taking sides when former spouses argue over finances or childrearing, by actively trying to break up a child's new marriage (or the remarriage of a former son- or daughter-in-law), by refusing to accept into their family new stepgrandchildren or a new son- or daughter-in law, by using money and inheritance as weapons to punish or to divide younger generations, and by clearly favoring genetic grandchildren, particularly *concrete babies* (children born into the remarriage), over stepgrandchildren (Kalish & Visher, 1982). Not all of these walls are purposively built to disrupt stepfamily unity or create stress for the remarriage of a child or a former child-in-law, but some are. Grandparents usually have little or no control when a child or former child-in-law divorces and remarries, so some try to exert control in ways that are destructive to the remarriage or to the establishment of a functional stepfamily.

As with post-divorce families, relationships between grandparents and grandchildren after remarriage are related to where children reside. It is logical to expect that the remarriage of a former son- or daughter-in-law would reduce grandparents' contacts with grandchildren, if the former in-law is the residential parent of the grandchildren. However, it appears that remarriage of either the residential or non-residential parent reduces grandparents' involvement with grandchildren—in two studies researchers found that the amount of contact and support between grandchildren and paternal grandparents (Bray & Berger, 1990) and maternal grandparents (Clingempeel et al., 1992) were reduced after remarriage. Nonetheless, grandparents are perceived by grandchildren to be important sources of emotional support for them after a parental remarriage (Kennedy & Kennedy, 1993), and the reduction in contact and support after remarriage may be due to the increased support grandparents provide their children during the adult child's separation and divorce. In other words, the reduction in time and support may actually be a relief and a return to normal (Clingempeel et al., 1992).

Clingempeel and colleagues had speculated that the stress of a new remarriage might cause grandparents to remain involved with their child and grandchildren, at least temporarily. However, their data did not support this hypothesis for maternal grandparents following their daughter's remarriage (Clingempeel et al., 1992). Cherlin and Furstenberg (1986) found that the remarriage of daughters did not alter the amount of contact between maternal grandparents and grandchildren, although the amount of financial assistance they provided was reduced when the daughter remarried.

Little research on relationships between grandparents and grandchildren in stepfamilies has been conducted. Clearly, much more research is needed. Given the potential source of support grandparents represent, it is imperative that more research be done to help us understand the nature of these relationships.

Stepgrandparents

A person can become a stepgrandparent in three ways: (1) by marrying someone who is a grandparent, (2) when an adult child marries a person with children from a prior relationship, and (3) when an adult stepchild gives birth to or adopts children (Ganong & Coleman, 1999). When a person marries a grandparent, he or she becomes an instant stepgrandparent by inheriting the grandchildren of the new partner (see Figure 10.1a). The second way of becoming a stepgrandparent may be thought of as a twist on the old bromide offered to a parent whose child is about to be married, "You are not losing a daughter, you are gaining a son"—in this case, a person becoming a stepgrandparent is gaining not only a new child-in-law, but his/her children (see Figure 10.1b). The third way of becoming a stepgrandparent parallels the process by which genetic and adoptive parents acquire their grandparent status (see Figure 10.1c). These three pathways to stepgrandparenthood may be distinguished based on who is remarrying—in the first way, an individual remarries a grandparent—obviously, the (step)grandchild was born prior to the remarriage. In the second way, the (step)grandchild also was born prior to the remarriage, but here it is the adult child who is marrying someone who has children—the adult child's parent becomes a stepgrandparent. Finally, in the third pathway, the remarriage of the parent and stepparent occurs years before stepgrandchildren are born; in fact, the future parents of the stepgrandchildren are likely to be children themselves. Figures 10.1a, 10.1b, and 10.1c represent three different stepgrandmothers, each of whom has a stepgranddaughter named Sue. The year of Ann's marriage and year of the birth of her stepgranddaughter are represented on each genogram. It is likely that these different pathways to stepgrandparenthood lead to quite different relationships between generations. However, researchers have yet to differentiate between these three types of step-relationships in their studies.

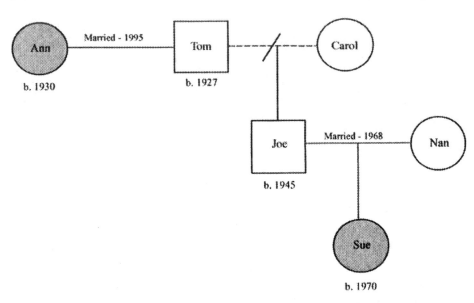

Figure 10.1a. Later Life Remarried Stepgrandparent[1].

Regardless of how the role is acquired, the number of stepgrandparents is increasing. Overall, 39% of American families have a stepgrandparent (Szinovacz, 1998). Over half (55%) of African American families and about 40% of Hispanic families have stepgrandparents. Despite the prevalence, stepgrandparent-stepgrandchild relationships have seldom been studied, and the functions expected of stepgrandparents are largely unexplored and unknown (Ganong & Coleman, 1999). Normative expectations for relationships between stepgrandparents and stepchildren are unclear. In fact, expectations for this relationship are so vague that some families do not even recognize the possibility of a relationship existing between the stepparents' parents and the stepparents' stepchildren.

Later-Life Remarried Stepgrandparenthood

Marrying someone who has adult children and grandchildren creates a situation somewhat similar to that of a nonresidential stepparent. That is, the stepgrandparent is a relative stranger to most of the family members (except the spouse, and, occasionally, other step-kin whom they might have known before). As with a nonresidential stepparent, the instant stepgrandparent likely comes in contact with stepgrandchildren episodically, and these contacts may be quite rare if there is great distance between residences. For example, in Figure 10.1a, Sue was 25

---

[1]Sue was 25 when Ann married Tom and became Sue's stepgrandmother.

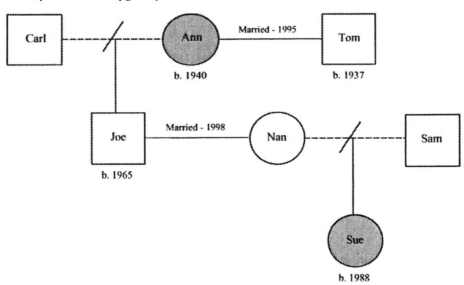

Figure 10.1b. Inherited Stepgrandparent[2].

when she acquired a stepgrandmother. She may seldom see her grandfather and stepgrandmother.

In our conversations with people who were adults when a parent remarried, they almost never identify themselves as a stepchild, nor do they think of the parent's spouse as a stepmother or stepfather. Instead, they refer to their *mother's husband* or their *father's wife*. From what we have been able to determine, these adult stepchildren have no desire to identify themselves as members of a stepfamily. Their language seems to us to be a way to distance themselves from thinking of themselves as being in a step-relationship. We hypothesize that this way of thinking about a stepparent acquired in adulthood is common, and it is not necessarily a reflection of the relationship quality between the stepparent and stepchild. We mention this here because it seems to us unlikely that *later-life remarried stepgrandparents* would be defined and labeled as such. We hypothesize that references to these new spouses of Grandpa or Grandma would be referred to as my *grandfather's new wife* or *Grannie's new husband*. Such folks probably would be seen more as a family friend than as a full-fledged member of the family or kin network, at least for a few years, if not longer. It is also likely that these *later-life remarried stepgrandparents* would not see themselves as fulfilling a grandparent role. It is even less likely, we believe, that cohabiting elders achieve family-member

---

[2]Ann and Tom had been married 3 years when Joe married Nan and became Sue's stepfather. Sue was 10 when Ann became her stepgrandmother.

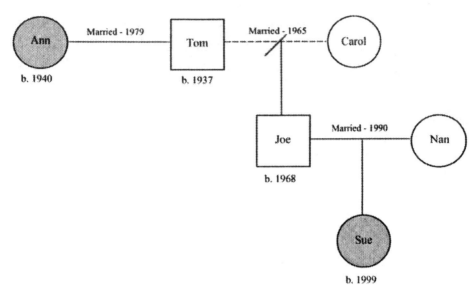

Figure 10.1c. Long-Term Remarried Stepgrandparent[3].

status, or that they will develop close relationships with "instant" stepgrand-children.

Inherited Stepgrandparenthood

In the second pathway to stepgrandparenthood, an older individual could be married, remarried, or single (i.e., widowed, divorced, separated, or never-married), and "inherit" stepgrandchildren when a grown son or daughter becomes a stepparent by marrying someone with children from a prior relationship. In some ways, this is like grandparenthood in that the older adult does nothing himself or herself to acquire this new status. Instead, the roles are gained by virtue of a child's actions. This, too, is a form of instant acquisition into a stepgrandparent role, but to distinguish it from the first path to this role, we will call it *inherited stepgrandparenthood*.

We mention the marital status of inherited stepgrandparents because this could affect how individuals define themselves. For instance, some inherited stepgrand-parents are in their first (and only) marriages, and the marriage of their child to

---

[3]Ann and Tom had been married 20 years when Sue was born, making Ann a step grandmother. Joe had lived with Tom since he was 3, and he had lived with Ann since she joined the household when he was 11.

someone with children may be the first time in the recent histories of their family that there are step-relationships (*all* families have step-relationships in their pasts; shorter life spans in previous generations and the need for household/farm workers led to remarriages being a common occurrence in the past). How inherited stepgrandparents think about the acquisition of stepgrandchildren is likely to vary, depending on their own marital history and on how the remarried offspring think about their new stepchildren. Giles-Sims (2003) found in her case studies that relationships with stepgrandchildren varied depending on whether or not the stepgrandparent had genetic grandchildren. One stepgrandmother with no genetic grandchildren readily adopted a grandparent role, while another who had genetic grandchildren tried to treat the children the same (same presents and privileges) and felt guilty for not feeling as close to the stepgrandchildren. Our observations have been similar to Giles-Sims—inherited stepgrandparents often have ambivalent feelings regarding their stepgrandchildren and feel guilty about their ambivalence.

Henry, Ceglian, and Ostrander (1993) have created a 4-stage developmental model that focuses on the transition to what we call *inherited stepgrandparenthood*. Henry et al. proposed that grandparents who become stepgrandparents must: (1) accept the losses that accompany a child's divorce, (2) accept the adult child's status as a single person, (3) accept the adult child's entrance into a new romantic relationship, and (4) establish new stepfamily relationships. In the first stage of this developmental process, grandparents must adjust their hopes for their child's marriage, deal with fears about changes in their relationships with grandchildren, and cope with their own feelings about divorce and the presumed causes of their child's divorce. In the second stage, grandparents have to adapt to changes in their child's family reorganization, they have to adjust to changes in how often they see their grandchildren, they have to redefine their relationship with former in-laws, and they have to renegotiate boundaries between generations, among other tasks. The tasks of the third stage, accepting the child's entrance into a new romantic relationship, seems a little vague to us (e.g., preparing to accept the potential of new family members), or as simply extensions of earlier tasks (e.g., adapting to redefinition of the adult child's family boundaries). It is likely, unless the adult child is living with or near the grandparents, that most of the tasks of this third stage will not be accomplished. If they are separated by long distances, it is more probable that the tasks of stage 3 and stage 4, establishing relationships with new stepfamily members, will occur at the same time. Although their model was designed to be useful to stepgrandparents seeking guidelines regarding how to proceed in establishing a relationship with their stepgrandchildren, it could also serve as a stimulus for further research on this relationship. Given the paucity of research, it is not known how stepgrandparents are similar to grandparents.

Long-Term Remarried Stepgrandparents

In the final pathway to stepgrandparenthood, an older stepparent becomes a stepgrandparent when an adult stepchild reproduces or adopts. The factors that seem potentially important in this stepgrandparent-stepgrandchild relationship are length of time the stepparent-stepchild relationship has existed, quality of the step-relationship, as well as other variables that influence grandparent involvement in general, such as distance, and gender of the stepchild and stepparent.

For instance, in a long-term stepparent-stepchild relationship, particularly one that began when the stepchild was younger than 18 and he or she lived with the stepparent, it is probable that stepgrandparent-stepgrandchild relationships will resemble grandparent-grandchild relationships in most, if not in all, ways. This is especially likely, we think, when stepparent-stepchild relationships are generally positive, or even when they are affectively neutral. In fact, there is evidence that close and loving relationships between stepgrandparents and their stepgrandchildren can help facilitate the development of emotionally closer relationships between stepgrandparents and their adult stepchildren, even years into the relationship (Clawson & Ganong, 2002). In a small, in-depth study of adult stepchild-older stepparent relationships, Clawson and Ganong reported that adult stepchildren reconsidered the nature of their judgments about and relationships with their older stepparents when they saw how close their children felt towards these older adults, their stepgrandparents.

The cultural norm of having multiple family members in the family position of *grandparent* is one reason why *long-term remarried stepgrandparents'* relationships are likely to be similar to genetic grandparent-grandchild ties. In Western culture people expect children to have multiple grandparents—typically, at least two grandmothers and two grandfathers are the norm. Given the increase in the life span, many children now have great-grandparents as well. In most families, all of these grandparents are given unique names to identify them and to distinguish them from the other grandparents. So, children may have a Grandpa and Grandma, a Nanna and Poppa, a Big Grandma and Big Grandpa, all of whom are potentially loved and recognized as grandparents who have legitimate claims to the grandchildren's affections. It is relatively easy for *long-term remarried stepgrandparents* to be named and recognized as one of the cast of grandparents a child might have.

Stepparents face a cultural norm that says a child cannot have more than two parents—this normative barrier is absent for *long-term remarried stepgrandparents* (and potentially for other types of stepgrandparents as well). Normatively, grandparents are not subjected to a zero-sum game of love (e.g., "Timmy, you can't love Grandpa Jones because Grandad Smith will be hurt" is not a common message) in the same way that stepparents and parents are. Stepgrandchildren are therefore less likely to experience loyalty conflicts between grandparents and stepgrandparents, are less confused about why they have multiple grandparents, and are able to more readily accept that they can relate to multiple adults in the grandparent roles. This is especially true for stepgrandchildren who have always known their stepgrandparents. Many are unaware that Poppa is a stepgrandparent rather than a grandparent with genetic ties to them. Only if their parents made the step-relationship an issue are stepgrandchildren likely to be aware that their stepgrandparents are different from their grandparents.

Of course, jealous genetic grandparents can interfere, or hostile relationships between adult stepchildren and their stepparents can hinder the development of stepparent-stepgrandchild relationships, despite the presence of helpful cultural norms. There are other factors that influence those relationships as well (e.g., distance). However, it is worth noting that cultural beliefs about grandparents may function to help stepgrandparents in much the same way that cultural beliefs function to make stepparenting harder.

Research on Stepgrandparents and Stepgrandchildren

There are a number of factors that affect the relationship between stepgrand-parents and stepgrandchildren. For example, Cherlin and Furstenberg (1986) found that the older grandchildren were when parents remarried, the less likely they were to regard stepgrandparents as important as genetic grandparents (this applies only to instant and inherited stepgrandparenthood). Whether or not the step-grandchild lives with the offspring of the stepgrandparent also may affect the relationship. For example, parents of residential stepparents may be more likely to have contact with their stepgrandchildren than parents of nonresidential step-parents (Lussier et al., 2002). Nonresidential stepparents may themselves have minimal interaction with their stepchildren (e.g., weekends only or maybe short summer visits and holidays, if they don't live nearby), so the opportunity for a stepgrandparent to form a relationship with their stepgrandchildren may be quite limited.

Given the gender differences in stepparent-stepchild relationships, and the fact that the middle-generation adults mediate the relationships between members of the adjacent generations, it is likely that stepchildren's relationships with stepgrandparents differ depending on whether the older adults are step-maternal or step-paternal grandparents. This has not been studied, however, so we can only speculate that relationships with step-paternal grandparents may be closer than relationships with step-maternal grandparents. In one study, grandchildren had less contact with the parents of their nonresidential stepparents than with the parents of their residential stepparents (Lussier et al., 2002), but this was true regardless of the gender of the stepparents or stepchildren.

Another factor influencing the relationship is the acceptance of the remarriage by the stepgrandparents and stepgrandchildren (Sanders & Trygstad, 1989).

If either the stepgrandparents or the stepgrandchildren are upset about or don't support the remarriage, it is less likely that a good relationship will develop between them.

However, stepgrandparents can potentially play an important part in the lives of their stepgrandchildren. Although relationships between later-life remarriage and inherited stepgrandchildren and stepgrandparents are typically less involved than grandparent-grandchildren ties, many stepgrandchildren think of their stepgrandparents as valuable resources and see stepgrandparent relationships as important (Henry, Ceglian, & Matthews, 1992; Sanders & Trygstad, 1989). Although Sanders and Trygstad found that children rated their grandparent as more involved than their stepgrandparent, 48% of stepgrandchildren viewed the stepgrandparent relationship as either important or extremely important, and 63% wanted more contact with their stepgrandparent.

The functions expected of stepgrandparents are largely unexplored and unknown (Coleman, Ganong, & Cable, 1997; Schneider, 1980). In fact, stepgrandparenthood is perhaps even a more voluntary status than grandparenthood. Stepgrandparents and stepgrandchildren have no legal ties, they are not genetically related, and, in some families, they may not know each other well or at all. Therefore, they do not fit any of the standard criteria used in Western culture to define family relationships. As a result, the obligations that stepgrandparents are perceived to have to stepgrandchildren, and whether or not stepgrandparents assume similar roles and responsibilities as grandparents, are not known. The status of their relationships and their functions may depend in part on attitudes about them. Therefore, we embarked on a pair of studies to investigate perceived financial obligations of grandparents and stepgrandparents.

In both of these studies we examined the perceived obligations of *inherited stepgrandparents* and their stepgrandchildren. We presented respondents with stories about hypothetical families facing a variety of dilemmas. In these stories we systematically varied conditions, as in experimental designs, so that we could assess the effects of a variety of family contexts on obligation beliefs (Ganong & Coleman, 1999). We gathered both quantitative data about obligations as well as open-ended responses about why people believed as they did.

In one study, we asked a randomly selected sample of several hundred adults about grandparents' and stepgrandparents' obligations to financially support the education of a talented (step)granddaughter. Paying for tuition was seen as more of a choice for stepgrandparents than for grandparents, and stepgrandparents' financial help was perceived to be dependent on the quality of the stepgrandparent-stepgranddaughter relationship. In contrast, grandparents were more likely seen as having an obligation based on kinship ties, regardless of the quality of those bonds. Divorce in the middle generation increased grandparents' obligations, but it effectively eliminated or reduced the obligations of former stepgrandparents because most people saw stepgrandparent-stepgrandchild relationships existing only as long as the middle-generation remarriage lasted. However, a few people perceived that ongoing financial support was a family-based obligation for former stepgrandparents *if* relationships were close—close ties seemed to justify, for some people, a family-like responsibility for the former stepgrandparents. A subsequent remarriage of the middle-generation parent only slightly lowered grandparents' obligations to grandchildren, but this essentially ended former stepgrandparents' perceived responsibility to help. For former stepgrandparents, ongoing emotional closeness between step-kin provided justification for stepgrandparents to help, but this was seen as their choice, not a duty. Throughout this study, concerns were expressed that the two adult generations needed to be in agreement about whether or not the older generation should assist. Evidence to support a norm of noninterference was expressed, but only when the middle generation was remarried or married, not when they were single. Middle-generation marital transitions shifted the degree to which people were concerned about the older generation meddling in the affairs of the younger adults. In this study, concerns were expressed about the elders not interfering with the perceived responsibilities of middle-generation men (either fathers or stepfathers) to financially provide for the youngest generation. The fact that middle generation women were rarely mentioned in the context of financially providing for their children reflected a stereotypically gendered view of men as the providers for their family's financial needs. In spite of changing family patterns and numerous transitions (e.g., divorce, remarriage), traditional notions of family and gender roles were salient factors in the thinking about family obligations for a substantial minority of people.

In the other study, we asked another randomly selected sample of several hundred adults about inheritance issues. Very few people suggested that inherited stepgrandchildren should inherit from a stepgrandfather. Many respondents believed that there was no need for family members to inherit other than the elder's child (in this study, it was a son). This belief weakened somewhat as the adult child's family moved through transitions because of divorce and remarriage. As the number of the adult children's relationship transitions increased, concern rose for the grandchildren. This may have been due to a concern about keeping the estate within the genetic kinship boundaries—some people thought the son might ignore his children in favor of spending the inheritance on his new wife and stepchild. Although most people limited who they thought should inherit to genetic kin only, a substantial minority of respondents thought that maintaining close relationships was enough for some non-genetic kin (such as a daughter-in-law) to be included as family, although this did not replace the importance of blood ties. The design of this study was rather simple in that the father had only one son. It would be interesting to know how people would have responded if the father had only a daughter, had more than one child, or had several children or stepchildren. What would happen, for example, if the stepgrandchildren who appeared in this story had not been inherited but had been the children of a stepchild whom the older adult had raised from infancy? Would the stepgrandchild be viewed as an "outsider"?

What do these two studies tell us about older family members' financial obligations to younger generations? Kinship counts when making judgments about financial obligations between older and younger generations, at least if kinship is defined rather narrowly as genetic, or "blood" ties. Grandparents clearly are thought to be obligated to remember children and grandchildren in their wills. This obligation is not easily broken and is not much affected by the divorce and remarriage of their offspring. However, grandparents are not necessarily thought to be obligated to help pay for a grandchild's tuition expenses (although nearly half of our sample thought they should), but once they agree to help, that agreement is seen as an enduring commitment. Once this voluntary assistance becomes an obligation, it is not easily broken; divorce and remarriage does not diminish this responsibility. If anything, divorce and remarriage in the middle generation strengthens the perceived financial responsibility of grandparents for their grandchildren. The youngest generation is seen as blameless observers, if not victims, of their parents' divorce and remarriage, and there is strong sentiment that children should not be punished for their parents' transgressions. In general, steprelationships are perceived to be family ties until divorce. After that, most people redefine those relationships as non-familial ones, and as such they are not seen to be operating under the same edicts of intergenerational responsibility as are family bonds. For some people, if former step-kin acted like family members who kept in contact and cared about each other, then they were perceived to be family members to each other. Otherwise, they were out of the kin network. Generally, remarriage after divorce further removes former step-kin from being bound by family-based obligations.

Researchers should examine the aftermath of divorce in stepfamilies on individuals and their relationships. Ahrons (2003), in her longitudinal investigation of families formed after second marriages, found that remarriages of short duration severed extended step-kin ties, but this was less often the case in longer-lasting remarriages. When the extended step-kin ties ended when the remarriage ended, some stepgrandchildren perceived this to be a loss of their grandparents—"We had a really good relationship with my stepdad's parents until my mom and stepdad divorced. Now we don't hear from them. They were our grandparents. We called them grandma and grandpa."

SUMMARY

The relationships of grandparents and stepgrandparents with (step)grandchildren are perhaps the least studied relationships in stepfamilies. Like many other relationships we discuss in this book, expectations for relationships between stepgrandparents and stepchildren are unclear. In fact, expectations for this relationship are so ambiguous that some families may not even recognize the possibility of a relationship between the parents of a stepparent and the stepparent's stepchildren.

However, given the importance of grandparents for grandchildren, especially when grandchildren are under stress, the lack of research focus seems to us to be an oversight that must be addressed soon. Clinicians have long argued that grandparents "can be instrumental in the success or failure of the child's single parenting, post-divorce life, and eventual remarriage" (Kalish & Visher, 1982, p. 135). Knowing more about the processes by which success or failure is facilitated by grandparents would be helpful not only to stepfamily members, but to practitioners who work with stepfamilies.

Researchers who study stepgrandparents need to distinguish in their studies between the three types of stepgrandparents outlined in this chapter. Evidence from the early studies, although researchers seldom differentiate between these varied pathways, suggests that the experiences and the relationships formed by these different types of stepgrandparents are qualitatively dissimilar from each other.

Finally, we think researchers should be aware that there are three perspectives to consider—that of the (step)grandparent, the adult (step)child, and the (step)grandchild (Lussier et al., 2002). A complete picture of the relationships between three generations, or of the relationships between any two generations, needs to have all of these perspectives (Whitbeck et al., 1993).

Chapter **11**

Clinical Perspectives on Stepfamily Dynamics

In Chapter 1 we referred to the historical impact of clinical writers on the development of the study of stepfamilies. Before researchers expressed much interest in stepfamilies, clinicians had written prodigiously about stepfamily relationships and the dynamics of stepfamilies (e.g., Crohn et al., 1981; Goldstein, 1974; Visher & Visher, 1979). The influence of clinicians is not just historical, however; they continue to significantly contribute to existing knowledge about stepfamilies. We define *clinician* broadly to include any helping professional who works with stepfamilies in applied settings (e.g., family life educators, family therapists, social workers, counselors, psychologists, psychiatrists).

Nearly 2 decades ago, we published an integrative literature review that compared the clinical and empirical literature on stepchildren (Ganong & Coleman, 1987). We concluded that researchers and clinicians, like the proverbial blind men and the elephant, were discovering truths separately about stepfamilies with little evidence of communication between them. We bemoaned these findings because researchers and clinicians have much to offer each other, and the limited exchange of information between the two groups slowed the expansion of knowledge about stepfamily relationships. As a result of this schism, the picture of stepfamily relationships drawn by either group of family professionals was fragmented.

In the years following our review, the gap between stepfamily researchers and clinicians narrowed substantially. In fact, the plethora of research in the last decade of the 20th century was partially due to researchers' attention to issues that clinicians had long identified as important (see Table 11.1). This change was facilitated by three trends that enhanced social science researchers' abilities to examine critical issues identified by clinicians. First, new statistical analysis procedures (e.g., Lisrel, structural equation models, hierarchical linear modeling) allowed

Table 11.1. Issues and Problems Found in Clinical Works on Stepchildren

Family Dynamics

Loyalty	Boundary issues
Coparental conflicts	Triangulation
Biological parent-child bonds	Rejection by stepparents
Jealousy	Extreme intimacy
Custody	Discipline
Sibling relationships	Competition and rivalry
Couple relations	Grandparents
Idealization of absent parent	Stepchild expelled
Pseudomutuality	Subgroups within family
Scapegoating	Rejection of stepparent
Child born of remarried parents	Low cohesion
Sexually charged atmosphere	Poor communication
Push for cohesion	Scapegoating noncustodial parent
Surnames	Stepmothers who lack experience
Turf or space issues	Stepsibling relations
Two households	

Transitional Adjustments

Adjustment to change	Age at parental remarriage
Conflict in merging	Lifestyle difference
Myth of instant love	Holidays
No shared rules	Birth order changes
Lack of shared rituals	Lack of privacy
Child not told prior to marriage	Increased activity
No shared history	Time between marriages

Incomplete Institution

Role confusion	How much to parent
No legal ties	No model for stepparent-child relations
No societal rituals	How much affection to show
Family identity confusion	How to show affection
Kinship terms	Money issues

Emotional Responses

Guilt	Stress, emotions, or greater vulnerability
Loss, mourning	Identity confusion
Feeling unwanted	Fear of being misunderstood
Reuniting fantasies	Anger
Ambivalence	Fear of family breakup
Feeling responsible for parent's loneliness	Rebellion

Stepfamily Expectations

Negative image	Stepparent as rescuer
Love conquers all	Higher expectations
Step same as nuclear	

researchers to more easily analyze data from multiple stepfamily members over time. Second, the increased acceptance of qualitative research led to interpretive, in-depth studies of individuals and stepfamilies using grounded theory, ethnographic methods, and other holistic approaches to studying relationship dynamics. The third trend was an increase in the number of individuals involved in stepfamily scholarship who were committed to both research and practice. A growing number of these scholars have contributed to practitioners' understanding of stepfamilies by linking research and application in ways that furthered both (e.g., Constance Ahrons, Gill Gorell Barnes, James Bray, Glenn Clingempeel, Marilyn Coleman, Margaret Crosbie-Burnett, Pauline Erera, Mark Fine, Lawrence Ganong, Jean Giles-Sims, Mavis Hetherington, Lawrence Kurdek, Kay Pasley, Mary Whiteside). As a result of these trends, both the quality and the quantity of what is known about stepfamily relationships have been enhanced.

We have attempted throughout this volume to comingle clinical and empirical knowledge. However, in this chapter, we primarily examine clinicians' perspectives on stepfamily relationships, and we review current clinical interventions with stepfamilies.

CLINICAL PERSPECTIVES

Prior to the latter part of the 1970s, clinicians working with remarried couples and stepfamilies grounded their work in family therapy models that were based primarily on conceptualizations of how first marriage families should function. The goal of most clinicians was to help stepfamilies function as much like nuclear families as possible. For instance, 25 years ago a family therapist who was enrolled in our graduate course on remarriage and stepfamilies blurted out that he thought he owed many of his former stepfamily clients an apology. He specifically recalled telling a stepmother who told him that no matter how hard she tried, she just did not love her 3-year-old stepdaughter, that she *had* to love her—she was her *mother*! It is little wonder that stepfamilies we interviewed in that same era indicated that they did not find therapy helpful (Ganong & Coleman, 1989).

An evolution in clinicians' thinking about stepfamilies started when several outstanding practitioner-scholars (e.g., Goldner, 1980; Messinger, 1976; Sager et al., 1983; Visher & Visher, 1979) began focusing on the unique dynamics of stepfamilies. These first generation stepfamily clinicians argued that therapists should think about stepfamilies in new ways—as reconfigured families with distinctive characteristics rather than as reconstituted nuclear family units. These pioneers laid a solid foundation for later clinicians to build upon—by our estimates, about 75% of what current practitioners write about stepfamilies are restatements of the work of these early clinicians. Given their seminal insights, we have decided to cite first generation stepfamily clinical authors in this chapter as well as more recent ones.

The second generation of stepfamily clinicians also moved practitioners towards new interventions and new modes of thinking about stepfamilies. For example, several of these clinical scholars proposed developmental models that broadened practitioners' views beyond the original family development/family life cycle models that had privileged first marriage families (e.g., McGoldrick & Carter, 1999; Mills, 1984; Papernow, 1993). The new developmental models focused on stepfamily dynamics and responsibilities. Other second generation clinicians turned practitioners' attentions to gender issues in stepfamily functioning, particularly in couple dynamics, parenting, and stepparenting issues (e.g., Bernstein, 1997; Carter, 1988). These clinicians brought to practitioners' awareness how gendered scripts for family roles and relationships contributed to stepfamily dilemmas in childrearing and marital decision-making. For instance, inflexibility in gendered expectations makes it harder for couples in stepfamilies to creatively address childrearing issues and to generate innovative solutions (e.g., stepmothers are forced into most of the child care because child care is women's responsibility).

More recently, clinical writers have turned their energies toward new therapeutic approaches (e.g., brief therapy techniques, behavioral family intervention, stress inoculation training) for clinicians to employ with stepfamilies (Burt & Burt, 1996; Nicholson & Sanders, 1999). For example, Browning (1994) has suggested creative ways in which clinicians can complete the epistemological shift away from traditional family systems therapies when dealing with remarriages and stepfamilies. Using basic tenets of systemic thought, Browning offers alternative suggestions for clinical practice that are grounded in the realities of stepfamily dynamics. For instance, the need to see all family members in therapeutic sessions may not work as well clinically for stepfamilies, and Browning offers suggestions for how clinicians could work with subsystems toward a goal of stepfamily integration. Similarly, the assumption based on first marriage families that all child-focused problems are indicators of marital problems is less often true in stepfamilies, particularly those blending two sets of children. Insisting that family members must agree on the presenting problem also may be counterproductive with stepfamilies because there may be multiple views of problems (i.e., parents in a complex household may see the discipline issues quite distinctly, as might their children). Browning argues for clinicians to work flexibly with stepfamilies, respecting their unique histories and dynamics.

STEPFAMILY CHARACTERISTICS

Most clinicians contend that understanding differences between stepfamilies and first marriage families is fundamental to understanding and working effectively with stepfamilies in practice (cf. Burt & Burt, 1996; Papernow, 1995; Robinson, 1991; Sager et al., 1983; Visher & Visher, 1996). What follows are 11 tenets (see

Table 11.2. Stepfamily Characteristics

---

1. Stepfamilies are more structurally complex than other family forms.
2. Children often are members of two households.
3. Children's parent is elsewhere in actuality or in memory.
4. Stepfamily members have different family histories.
5. Parent-child bonds are older than adult partner (spousal) bonds.
6. Individual, marital, and family life cycles are more likely to be incongruent
7. Stepfamilies begin after many losses and changes.
8. Children and adults come with expectations from previous families.
9. Stepfamilies often have unrealistic expectations.
10. Stepfamilies are not supported by society.
11. Legal relationships between stepparent and stepchild are ambiguous or nonexistent.

Table 11.2) regarding stepfamily characteristics—not all clinicians would agree with all of these points, but most would agree with most of them.

Stepfamilies Are More Structurally Complex than Other Family Forms

Stepfamilies are more complex units than first marriage families because they tend to have more people, roles, and relationships. Unlike most first marriage families, which typically begin with only the married couple, stepfamilies are most often multi-generational units from the beginning—the couple, one or more children, and at least one former partner (either living or deceased).

More people means more relationships. For instance, a first marriage family with three people has three dyadic relationships: Husband-wife, mother-child, and father-child. If a divorced woman with physical custody of her child remarries a divorced man with physical custody of his child, there are *10* relationships—the remarried couple, stepfather-stepchild, stepmother-stepchild, mother-child, father-child, stepsibling-stepsibling, another mother-child relationship (nonresidential parent), another father-child relationship (nonresidential parent), and two former husband-wife co-parenting dyads. This example could be even more complicated if there were additional children, perhaps from additional prior unions.

Remarriages following divorce often result in four adults in parental positions—a mother, a stepfather, a father, and a stepmother. Between the two households there may be several sets of *his* and *hers* children, as well as the possibility of *ours* children if the couple reproduces together. Although both first marriage families and stepfamilies have extended kin, stepfamilies often have more of them (e.g., stepgrandparents in addition to grandparents, whole complements of step-aunts, -uncles, and -cousins). In order for adults and children to get their needs met in a newly formed stepfamily, clinicians argue that stepfamilies have to integrate all of these relationships into some kind of workable whole (Visher & Visher, 1996), or create what Goldner (1982) called a new *family culture*.

The multiplicity of people and relationships demands clear communication between stepfamily members if the system is to function smoothly. Therefore, by virtue of their complexity stepfamilies place great demands on their members' problem-solving and communication skills (Nelson & Levant, 1991). It should be noted, however, that complexity does not equal problems, distress, or dysfunction. Some people like the challenges, stimulation, and excitement of more people and relationships, and they may welcome the additional complexity of stepfamilies. Others may find the complexity a minor inconvenience, and still others may equate complexity with chaos and their stress levels reach crisis proportions.

Clinicians postulate several reasons why complexity is an important contributor to the greater stress experienced by some stepfamily members. For example, some people (e.g., individuals with substance abuse problems, clinical depression, or certain personality characteristics such as low frustration tolerance) may be predisposed in general to difficulties in establishing and maintaining satisfying relationships and they do not have the necessary skills to solve problems in complicated interpersonal environments (Clingempeel, Brand, & Segal, 1987; Fishman & Hamel, 1981; Ganong, Coleman, & Weaver, 2001).

Other individuals are not cognitively or emotionally comfortable dealing with ambiguity, and complexity creates ambiguity. Ambiguities in stepfamily relationships are legion, ranging from what stepparents should be called to how to celebrate holidays and what time and when to eat dinner (Berger, 1998; Wald, 1981; Whiteside, 1982). A major source of ambiguity in stepfamilies concerns internal and external boundaries (Crosbie-Burnett, 1989; McGoldrick & Carter, 1998; Pasley, 1987). Internal boundaries refer to rules about task performance and membership in specific subsystems within the stepfamily, and external boundaries refer to rules about who is and is not a member of the stepfamily. In new stepfamilies, the internal boundaries that establish a hierarchy are sometimes challenged; a stepparent may assume that he or she will be the head of the household (or will share these duties), but children may resist the authority of the stepparent and may resent what they see as a demotion in rank for themselves. Stepfamily members may also have different rules about personal space and privacy, and these boundaries must be created anew when stepfamilies form (Browning, 1994).

Individuals who are exceptionally impatient or who have little tolerance for ambiguity may attempt to reduce the complexity by pushing for relationships to develop quickly. For instance, individuals with low tolerance for uncertainty may rush stepparent adoption in the belief that legally transforming step-relationships will resolve ambiguous feelings and clarify how individuals should interact with each other (Ganong et al., 1999), thus making family life seem more manageable.

The structural complexity of stepfamilies also contributes to *stepfamily systems being emotionally different from first marriage families*. In the early months and years of stepfamily life, feelings among family members may be extremely

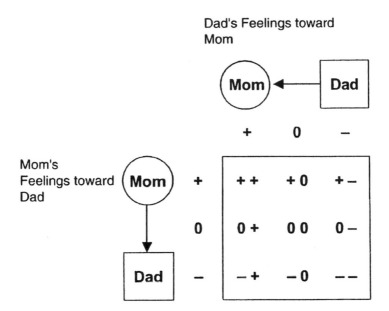

Figure 11.1. Batchelder's Combinational Model: Matrix of Individuals' Relationship Orientations

varied. The structural complexity of stepfamilies intersects with relationship quality to create a staggering array of emotional environments. For example, Batchelder (1995) identified what she called a *relationship orientation*, which is a *directional attitude* toward another person in a relationship (i.e., positive, negative, or neutral). Each individual has an orientation toward the other person in a dyadic relationship—for example, a husband can feel positive (+), neutral (0), or negative (−) toward his wife, who may feel positive (+), neutral (0), or negative (−) toward him. When these individual orientations are taken together (e.g., they can both feel positive about each other, both negative, one neutral and the other positive, etc.), for any given dyadic relationship there are 9 potential relationship orientations that can be portrayed on a matrix (see Figure 11.1). Consequently, as more people and more relationships are added, the numbers of relationship orientations increase dramatically. For example, Batchelder calculates 27 relationship orientations in a family of three members (9 times 3), a number that swells to 89 after post-divorce remarriage. According to Batchelder, post-divorce families with four children have 251 possible relationship orientation combinations following a parent's remarriage. This actually underestimates the potential emotional complexity in stepfamilies because it does not reflect ambivalent feelings in relationships or the fact that individual relationship orientations can change. Although Batchelder's *combinatorial model* is not strictly about stepfamilies, it underscores the potential for emotional complexity among stepfamily members, particularly when families are first forming. That is, at any point in time some stepfamily relationships are emotionally close (e.g., between mother and child, between spouses), while others may be experienced as hostile or neutral. Given the emotional complexity, it is not surprising that stepfamily members in general report that their relationships are less close than do members of first marriage families (Anderson & White, 1986; Peek, Bell, Waldron, & Sorell, 1988).

Children Often Are Members of Two Households

Another characteristic of stepfamilies is that stepchildren may hold membership in two households. Of course, many children have virtually no contact with their nonresidential father (Hofferth, Pleck, Stueve, Bianchi, & Sayer, 2002), but the increased prevalence of joint legal and physical custody in recent years has resulted in more stepchildren being part-time members of two households (Bauserman, 2002). Joint custody arrangements can range from almost full-time residence in one parent's household with rare visits to the other parent's household to half-time residence in each. Most stepchildren probably fall in between these two extremes, residing mostly with one parent but spending time periodically with the other parent.

When children are members of two households, these households gain and lose children from time to time. For example, Jack and Jill, a remarried couple, raise Jill's child, Mary, from a prior marriage during the week (see Figure 11.2). On Saturdays, they add Jack's three children from a prior relationship, but Mary goes to stay with her dad, her stepmother, and her half-brother. On Sundays, Mary returns from her father's household and spends the day with her three stepsiblings, her mother, and her stepfather, Jack.

This *accordion effect* creates logistical and emotional complications for adults and children. Children who go back and forth may have difficulty adjusting to different sets of rules and expectations (Visher & Visher, 1982), and standards for behavior may differ markedly between the two households. Although children can usually adjust to differing expectations, differing rules for children can also be a rallying point for conflict between former partners.

Communication with the former spouse becomes a necessity when decision-making about children and time with children are shared, and this may be a difficult and challenging task for former partners who are still angry with each other over their breakup (Gerlach, 2001). Discipline issues, in particular, may be accentuated when children belong to two households (Pill, 1981; Visher & Visher, 1978). For example, stepparents may have a hard time deciding how they expect children to behave who are only in the household part of the time—should part-time residents be held to the same rules and expectations for behavior as children who are full-time residents of the household?

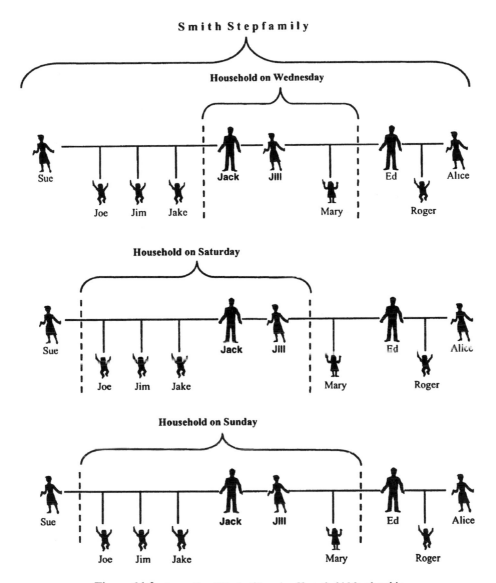

Figure 11.2. Accordion Effects: Changing Household Membership

Adults must make adjustments when children are part of two households. The diagram in Figure 11.2 showing the accordion effect or permeable boundaries of the Smith family reveals that Jack and Jill Smith are never without children. Unlike the Smiths, some couples are able to "tune their accordion" to have some weekends when the couple can be alone.

Sharing children often interjects issues related to control and power. In first marriage families, parents have sole responsibility for financial decisions regarding children, they have all legal rights and responsibilities for their children, they can make strong claims on their children's love and affection, and they have the sole authority to make decisions related to child rearing. Although parents in first marriage families do not always agree with each other on parenting, they have much common ground. In contrast, stepfamilies in which children belong to two households must share to some degree the financial, legal, emotional, and child rearing rights and responsibilities for the children (Gerlach, 2001). Given the preference for joint legal custody in many jurisdictions, co-parents *must* develop and follow a court approved parenting plan. This sharing could be positive; when child-rearing responsibilities are shared, fewer demands are put upon any one person or household. However, parents and stepparents often feel uncomfortable without sole control and therefore some resist following the parenting plan (Hetherington & Kelly, 2002). There is a danger that stepfamilies may try to close boundaries around their household (i.e., exclude the other household) as a way to gain control (Coale Lewis, 1985). Attempts to exclude the other household lead to greater conflict between former spouses and loyalty conflicts for children, who feel forced to choose one parent over the other. Loyalty conflicts are believed to be extremely common, even among stepchildren who have good relationships with all of their parents and stepparents (Berger, 1998; Gerlach, 2001).

Sometimes a parent will try to enlist her or his children in campaigns to punish the other parent (e.g., divorce revenge). In some cases the goal is to gain control over the household by solidifying the family boundaries (i.e., excluding the child's other parent). Paradoxically, this strategy may damage the targeted relationship, but it also can hinder the development of satisfying relationships with all adults in the stepfamily. Putting children in the position of taking sides with a parent increases their power in the stepfamily, sometimes beyond that of the parents or stepparents. For example, a child with warring parents who does not get his or her way can threaten to go live with the other parent. They can, in essence, peddle their affection and their presence to the highest bidder. This power is overwhelming for most children, and although they may have sought it, they often are relieved when their control over the important adults in their lives is removed. Such power and control in the hands of children is more rare in first marriage families.

Children's Parent Is Elsewhere in Actuality or in Memory

The nonresidential parent is an important factor in stepfamily relationships (Visher & Visher, 1988). This is true whether children physically go back and forth between households or don't. Even if the child and nonresidential parent have no contact with each other or even if the parent is no longer living, if children are old enough to remember life with their deceased or absent parent, then that parent probably is a significant figure to them. Children who were too young to remember living with the absent parent have probably had stories told to them by grandparents, older siblings, the remaining parent, other family members, and friends, that help create memories of the absent parent. In the absence of memories or stories, children with active imaginations might hallucinate what the absent parent would be like if they lived with them.

In fact, parents with whom children have had minimal contact sometimes take on a larger-than-life status. Children imagine a perfect parent, one who never punishes them and who is always supportive. With no conflicting real-life evidence to the contrary, children can cling tenaciously to the belief that their lives would be better if they lived with their nonresidential parent instead of with their "flawed" parent and stepparent. Stepparents and parents who have daily interactions with a child cannot compete with an idealized absent parent, which contributes to feelings of frustration and hopelessness on the part of some stepparents and parents (Visher & Visher, 1988).

The stepparent and residential parent often end up competing with the nonresidential parent over the child, which is stressful for children. In these situations, children are made to feel that they must choose one parent over the other. If they do not choose they remain torn between conflicting loyalties. For example, children who have strong loyalties to a nonresidential parent may avoid forming close relationships with a stepparent for fear of hurting the feelings of their nonresidential parent (Bray, 1995).

Stepfamily Members Have Different Family Histories

Another unique characteristic of stepfamilies is that the members have differing family histories. Adults in first marriage families enter marriage with individual family-of-origin histories, but they go on to develop a mutual family culture, with its own rituals and shared history. Children raised in first marriage families are socialized into that common family culture, and they share the history. Consequently, in first marriage families there is a collective past and expectations for a common future that contributes to a sense of family bonds and the creation of a family identity that feels normal and natural (Goldner, 1982).

Stepfamilies not only have to figure out new patterns of interacting, but they must do so while struggling to develop a common sense of family, a mutual identity as a unit (Ahrons & Perlmutter, 1982; Goldner, 1982). The absence of family rituals and shared rules for conduct, two dimensions of family life that are taken for granted and frequently go unnoticed in first marriage families, results in feelings of artificiality for stepfamilies (Imber-Black & Roberts, 1993; Whiteside, 1998). In stepfamilies, the parent and child(ren) have mutual experiences and collective recollections of a family life that does not include the stepparent (and any children he or she may have). This is important, not only because some stepfamily members are excluded from "remember when . . ." stories, but because different relationship histories can result in patterns of living and relating that seem odd to those who were not involved in developing those patterns (Baxter, Braithwaite, & Nicholson, 1999; Wald, 1981). This merging of different family cultures can create misunderstandings and confusion, and, if not resolved, may result in a chronic sense that family interactions feel awkward or unnatural in the stepfamily (Goldner, 1982). Unless expectations are clearly communicated and individuals are willing to be flexible, misunderstandings and mistaken assumptions will likely occur.

Parent-Child Bonds Are Older Than Adult Partner (Spousal) Bonds

Another major characteristic that distinguishes stepfamilies from first marriage families is that the parent-child bond is formed prior to the marital or adult couple bond. Fishman and Hamel (1981) called this an "anomalous family life course pattern" (p. 186), because parent-child relationships are well-established bonds with histories as long as the child has lived, while the marital (or couple) relationship is at a stage of development of still learning about each other. This may mean that the primary emotional tie for newly partnered parents is with their children rather than with their new partners. Unlike first-time marriages, couples in stepfamilies must simultaneously develop a cohesive marital/couple unit, maintain parent-child relationships, and begin stepparent-stepchild ties. As a result, couple bonds may be somewhat tenuous and fragile.

Achieving these tasks simultaneously is challenging for many stepfamilies, and because stepfamilies find themselves with subsystems that have competing needs (Papernow, 1993; Visher & Visher, 1991), not every member may be working to help meet all of these goals. For example, a child and a new partner may compete with each other for the time and attention of the person who is both the child's parent and the new partner's lover.

Setting aside time for the parent and child to be alone together can help them maintain strong ties. Time alone with a parent is reassuring to a child who may have had the parent's undivided attention prior to remarriage. Clinicians suggest that children may need help in assertively asking parents for what they want and need from them, rather than sabotaging the time parents spend with new partners or threatening to leave. Rituals or routine daily activities that hold special meaning for the parent and child should be continued if possible and new routines and rituals could also be established. This seemingly simple directive is difficult for parents to remember, perhaps because ordinary behaviors are not considered as either rituals or strategies to enhance relationships. Consequently, children and adults probably need to be given specific strategies and scripts for asking for the renewal or instigation of ordinary and special opportunities to maintain the parent-child relationship (Papernow, 1993; Visher & Visher,

1996). Parents who are focused on creating a sense of family often underestimate the importance of spending time alone with, and paying attention to, their children (Visher & Visher, 1996). Clinicians advise remarried couples to strengthen their bond by creating relationship boundaries that exclude children, former partners, and other third parties (Browning, 1994). One way to do this is to periodically spend time together relaxing, having fun, or talking (Visher & Visher, 1996). Spending time enhancing specific relationships helps promote overall family ties and functioning. Ideas for developing and strengthening dyadic relationships in stepfamilies can be found in several sources (e.g., Burt, 1989; Gerlach, 2001; Lutz, 2000).

Individual, Marital, and Family Life Cycles Are More Likely to Be Incongruent

That parent-child relationships predate the marital relationship is but one example of incongruence in stepfamily life cycles. Another common discrepancy is a greater age difference between partners in stepfamilies than in first marriage couples. Stepfamily couples who differ in age may each have children whose ages vastly differ as well, creating several developmental disparities. For example, if Ward, a 55-year-old man whose children are 29 and 33, remarries June, a woman in her mid-30s whose children are preschoolers, Ward, June, and their respective children are simultaneously experiencing different parts of the family life course (Goldner, 1982; McGoldrick & Carter, 1999). Ward and June are in the beginning (newlywed) stage, but June is a parent to young children, and Ward is, or rather was, experiencing the empty nest stage. Ward and June may be at quite different places in their life courses as well. Ward may be feeling the need to relax, slow down, take time to enjoy the fruits of his earlier labors, and plan for retirement. June may feel the need to focus more on her career and work harder so that she can solidify her standing with her employer. Ward, who may have thought his PTA days were long past, can now contemplate over a decade more of back-to-school nights. June, who may not have thought much about grandmotherhood, could instantly become a stepgrandmother to children the age of her preschoolers. One of the wackiest examples of developmental disparities in stepfamilies is the case of Rolling Stones' guitarist Bill Wyman's son. This young man married the mother of his father's ex-wife (young Wyman's former stepmother), making Bill Wyman's former mother-in-law his new daughter-in-law, and young Wyman's former stepmother became his new stepdaughter!

Other, far less exotic, disparities occur fairly frequently. For instance, a newly remarried couple may try to foster family closeness by planning family outings and home activities at the same time that an adolescent stepchild is striving for individuation and personal independence. This is an example of marital/family development needs being at odds with the developmental needs of individuals in the family. Adults who have little knowledge of normal adolescent development may feel rejected by the stepchild who refuses to participate in these family plans, the parent may worry that the remarriage is harming her or his relationship with the child; the stepparent may think the stepchild is being a disrespectful jerk. The stepchild is merely trying to grow up! Basic child development knowledge could be quite helpful for some stepfamily adults (Ganong et al., 2000).

Stepfamilies Begin after Many Losses and Changes

As we discussed in Chapter 3, stepfamilies generally are formed following several family transitions or changes. Some of these changes entail losses—adults have lost a romantic partner, children may have lost some or all contact with a parent living elsewhere, and families may have moved, with resulting changes in neighborhoods, living arrangements, schools, friendship and support networks, employment, and lifestyles. There are lost opportunities, lost dreams, losses in relationships, losses in experiences. There are also changes in role expectations, self-identity, and family identity, all of which entail some degree of loss. Not recognizing and not dealing with losses and the lingering emotional attachments interfere with the formation of stepfamily relationships (Visher & Visher, 1996).

If losses from prior family situations are not mourned before stepfamilies are formed, and if successful adaptations to previous changes have not been made, then "the stepfamily inherits trouble" (Coale Lewis, 1985, p. 16). The view of many clinicians is that energies cannot be focused on stepfamily relationships until earlier issues and developmental tasks are resolved (Sager et al., 1981; Visher & Visher, 1996). Unresolved feelings related to losses may serve as barriers to engaging wholeheartedly in developing and nourishing stepfamily relationships; incomplete mourning of losses prevents people from moving ahead (Papernow, 1995).

Although adults in stepfamilies have typically endured prior losses, they usually perceive remarriage or re-partnering as a gain. They have gained or regained whatever they perceive as the benefits of being involved with a new partner—it might be companionship, a sex partner, someone to love them, a financial partner. From our experiences in interviewing stepchildren, we think they see the stepfamily as a gain only if it results in enhanced stability in their lives and if they gain resources, such as money, love, and emotional support. We also think that the stepfamily represents additional losses from children's perspectives if they have less contact with the nonresidential parent, spend less time with their residential parent, lose power and status in the household, and lose resources (e.g., sharing space, time, and other resources with stepsiblings and the stepparent). This disparity in perceptions—the parent and stepparent viewing the remarriage as a gain that partly offsets past losses and the stepchild tallying more losses than gains—may obscure from adults the need to be supportive of children as they adjust to their new surroundings. The adults and children are looking at the same events with different perspectives, and they may need help in understanding each other's views.

Not surprisingly, it is common for some family members to at least appear to adapt to changes and to resolve feelings of loss more quickly than others. However, adults often mourn the end of their marriage and their dream of living happily-ever-after *before* the divorce takes place, sometimes long before. Children typically begin this mourning process *after* their parents separate or *after* the divorce. Therefore, single parents who initiate new romantic relationships may be more ready for change than are their children. Parents, happy because they found a new partner, may be oblivious to their children's negative reactions to this new relationship.

Children and Adults Come with Expectations from Previous Families

Expectations from previous family life experiences are not inherently good or bad, but they do influence how people interact in stepfamilies. In first marriage families, the couple brings expectations to marriage that are based partly on observations and experiences in their families of origin and partly on cultural expectations about marriage. Later, as they become parents, they again draw upon personal experiences they had while growing up and on cultural expectations to guide their parenting behaviors. In stepfamilies, adults bring cultural beliefs regarding remarriages and stepparenting, personal expectations based on their family of origin and adult experiences in prior marital/parental/family situations. Stepchildren also bring expectations from their prior family experiences, as do former partners and extended kin. These competing sets of expectations or "world-views" in stepfamilies often can create many misunderstandings (Leslie & Epstein, 1988; Visher & Visher, 1991).

For example, years ago a colleague who married a younger woman with two school age children shared with us that he was irritated beyond all reason with how inconsiderate and sloppy his stepchildren were in putting things in the refrigerator. Constant harping about this perceived misconduct did not change the stepchildren's behavior and greatly irritated his new wife, who thought he was picking on her children. It finally dawned on him that he was inappropriately expecting his stepchildren to apply his previous families' refrigerator-storage rules. He had taught his seven children, when they were growing up, to carefully put food in assigned spots in the refrigerator, necessary behavior for a household of nine people sharing one refrigerator. But in his new household of four, refrigerator-storage rules were not so necessary—there was room for everything. By sharing with his stepchildren his reasons for harping about things needing to go in assigned spots our colleague let his stepchildren know a little about his history. He also let them know he would try hard to be more understanding of their "world-view." Another friend, also a new stepfather, thought his stepchildren were both lazy and rude because at meals they asked their mother to get them more milk from the refrigerator rather than excusing themselves from the table and getting it themselves. His wife thought his children were being rude because when they wanted more milk they would get up from the table and rummage around in "her" refrigerator. Family members were mildly irritated with each other for months around shared mealtimes until the adults realized that their respective expectations were clashing. In his world-view children helped themselves, and in her world-view children asked politely to be served. Once they figured this out, they talked about their implicit expectations and what felt right for their household and family.

Given the diversity of prior experiences, it should not be surprising that stepfamily members enter their new family with variable expectations for what the nature of their relationships will be. For example, an adolescent stepchild's expectations may be that the stepparent joined the family to be the parent's companion, not to become their new parent or friend. The stepparent, on the other hand, may expect to forge a close, warm relationship and become an important person in the stepchild's life. If these conflicting expectations are not addressed and compromises reached, then stepparents' attempts to get close to the stepchild will be rebuffed because the stepchild perceives such behaviors to be unnecessary and unwelcome. Rebuffs may be in the form of overt rejection of friendly overtures by the stepparent ("Leave me alone") or ignoring such overtures, what we call the *end table phenomenon* (i.e., treating the stepparent as if he or she was a not very important piece of furniture, to be used occasionally, but mostly ignored). Children are not passive participants in the step-relationship formation process, and they often respond to stepparents in ways that create distance between them and the stepparent (Russell & Searcy, 1997).

Stepfamilies Often Have Unrealistic Expectations

Couples entering their first marriages also may have unrealistic expectations; some observers argue that the high divorce rate is a testament to impossibly high expectations not being met adequately (Hackstaff, 1999). However, couples in first marriages often have time to work through their unrealistic expectations before they have children.

Nobody knows if stepfamily members have more unrealistic beliefs than members of first marriage families do, but clinicians argue that stepfamilies are prone to belief systems that include unrealistic expectations. Cultural beliefs about how families *should* be are based on nuclear families and do not provide stepfamilies much assistance in anticipating problems and figuring out workable solutions to existing ones (Coale Lewis, 1985; Visher & Visher, 1988). Cultural beliefs about stepfamilies are either negative (stepparents are mean and uncaring) or incredibly unrealistic (e.g., stepparents will love their stepchildren as much as they do their own children) (Coale Lewis, 1985; Ganong et al., 1990; Leslie & Epstein, 1988;

Visher & Visher, 1985). These negative and/or unrealistic beliefs may adversely affect stepfamily members' expectations. For example, if stepchildren expect their stepmother to be mean and uncaring, they may be blind to her attempts to be nice because nice behaviors do not fit stepmother stereotypes. Therefore, nice behaviors are either ignored or are interpreted by stepchildren in negative ways (i.e., as manipulation, bribery, or attempts to usurp emotional bonds between the children and the nonresidential parent).

Clinicians have identified several unrealistic expectations that contribute to problematic interactions in stepfamilies (Burt & Burt, 1996; Kaplan & Hennon, 1992; McGoldrick & Carter, 1999; Pill, 1990). For instance, some adults expect that relationships in stepfamilies will be good with little effort. This expectation has been labeled the *myth of instant love* (Visher & Visher, 1996); stepparents are expected and expect to instantly feel love and affection for their stepchildren. According to clinicians this myth causes guilt in stepparents who do not experience instantaneous love feelings. To assuage their guilt they may deny their ambivalent feelings, and push too hard for a parental relationship with the stepchild rather than letting bonds develop at the child's pace (Gerlach, 2001).

A second unrealistic belief is that stepchildren will unquestionably accept discipline from the stepparent (Berger, 1998; Whiteside, 1982). Stepparents often move quickly into parental roles that focus their energies on discipline, new rules, and other parental responsibilities and do not realize the necessity of first developing strong bonds with stepchildren that are based on affection and friendship (Ganong et al., 2000; Gerlach, 2001; Papernow, 2001; Visher & Visher, 1996). These stepparents usually encounter resistance from stepchildren and their spouses (Weaver & Coleman, in review), often leaving the stepparent confused and anxious, and eventually dissatisfied (Burt & Burt, 1996).

Adults who re-partner following a previous relationship that was unhappy may hold expectations that are not unrealistically high, but are impractical in other ways. For example, expectations that one should not bring up problems but should instead focus on positive aspects of the relationship tend to discourage open communication and promote the denial of problems, which leads to what family therapists call *pseudomutuality* (i.e., the tendency to deny history, ambivalence, and conflict) (McGoldrick & Carter, 1999; Sager et al., 1983). Rather than confront and challenge each other when things are not going smoothly, stepfamily members who worry that conflict will lead to re-divorce "walk on eggs" around each other. Consequently, problems go unresolved, which leads to feelings of alienation and powerlessness and the deterioration of the relationship (Sager et al., 1983).

Stepfamilies Are Not Supported by Society

Stepfamilies receive little formal or informal social support from non-family members and social systems (see Chapter 2). They also seldom seek or receive support from friends and extended family members—potential sources of informal social support. The reasons are subtle, but a lot of the underlying rationale has to do with how stepfamilies are thought about in Western culture. For instance, stepmothers are not likely to disclose feelings or experiences to co-workers if they think the co-workers may either misunderstand what they are saying or attach negative attributions to what they hear. The phrase, "My 10-year-old child is driving me nuts," has different connotations than the statement, "My 10-year-old stepchild is driving me nuts," to someone whose only exposure to stepparent-stepchild relationships is from fairy tales, slasher films, and cultural stereotypes. Consequently, stepparents often are careful about what images they project and about what they say. By not talking openly with friends about family concerns stepparents do not get much social support, which creates feelings of isolation and makes them more likely to think their experiences and feelings are unusual (Gerlach, 2001).

Legal Relationships between Stepparent and Stepchild Are Ambiguous or Nonexistent

Clinicians contend that the absence of a legal relationship serves as a barrier to the development of emotionally close stepparent-stepchild bonds. Unlike biological parents, whose obligations to their children are dictated in state and federal statutes, stepparents' obligations to stepchildren are based on whatever family members want them to be. Although this flexibility could be seen as an advantage, it is likely that for many stepparents the absence of legal ties further adds to the ambiguity and lack of control they feel (Ganong et al., 1998). Stepparents have shared with us their pique at being legally allowed to add stepchildren to their medical insurance but not being legally allowed to make decisions about their medical care or even be allowed to sign emergency room paperwork enabling injured or sick children to receive treatment. Stepparents may be cautious about emotionally investing in children they would have no legal right to visit if they divorce the stepchildren's parent or if the parent dies.

In the United States, the only way to resolve legal ambiguities of the stepparent's role is through adoption (Duran-Aydintug & Ihinger-Tallman, 1995; Ganong et al., 1998; Mahoney, 1997; Mason, 1998). More than half of the 130,000 adoptions in the United States each year involve stepchildren being adopted by their stepparents (Mahoney, 1999). A dilemma associated with U.S. stepparent adoption, however, is that children cannot have more than two legal parents. This means that before the stepparent can adopt, the non-residential parent must have his or her parental rights terminated either by voluntary consent or by court order. Only a few states allow incomplete or open adoptions, which means that nonresidential parents (or other kin) can seek enforceable visitation rights post-adoption, and these are granted only under extraordinary circumstances (Mahoney, 1999). The need to terminate the nonresidential parent's rights in order for the stepparent to adopt has the potential to exacerbate loyalty struggles in children, to create conflicts between co-parents, and to fuel animosity between extended kin of nonresidential parents and the adults in the stepparent household. Indeed, anticipation of such hostile interactions function as barriers to adoption for some families (Ganong et al., 1998). In England, the Children Act of 1989 allowed for stepparents to acquire limited legal rights and responsibilities as *social parents* without the necessity of terminating the biological parents' rights (De'Ath, 1997). The idea behind this law was to provide stepparents some form of legal status without disempowering the nonresidential parent. It is not yet clear how effective this law has been in helping stepparents feel more connected with stepchildren and in helping stepfamilies function more efficiently (Edwards et al., 1999).

OTHER PROBLEMS IN STEPFAMILY RELATIONSHIPS

In Table 11.1 is a list of issues and problems found in clinical works on stepchildren and their relationships. We first generated this list nearly 2 decades ago, but it remains as relevant today as it was then. All of these issues or problems are either directly or indirectly related to the stepfamily characteristics just presented.

Note that *none* of these issues and problems are related to personal pathologies (i.e., manic-depression, borderline personality disorders) or to addictions such as alcoholism and drug abuse. However, it is likely that many members of stepfamilies experience these personal pathologies and addictions, which in the context of stepfamilies become relationship problems. In fact, as we noted in Chapter 3, the higher re-divorce rate for remarriages may be due to the greater incidence of addictions and other personality problems (Brody et al., 1989). We have noticed when conducting interviews that it is not unusual for individuals in stepfamilies to spontaneously mention that at least one stepfamily member has drinking or psychological problems. This anecdotal evidence of the prevalence of behavioral or psychological obstacles points out that some stepfamilies probably function as they do because of problems that are not related to divorce, bereavement, or other structural characteristics of their stepfamilies but are the consequence of individuals' psychopathology.

Unfortunately, a thorough examination of each of the stepfamily concerns in Table 11.1 is beyond the scope and purpose of this book. However, one general concern should be emphasized because it is the basis for many of the problems listed in Table 11.1—the inappropriate use of a first marriage family model to guide the thinking and interactions of stepfamilies. Several times in this book we have mentioned the first marriage family model, also known as the nuclear family ideology. In the next section we discuss briefly how clinicians see this as problematic.

Nuclear Family Ideology and Stepfamily Functioning

A constant refrain heard from clinicians is that the nuclear family model is generally inappropriate for stepfamilies (Berger, 2000; Bernstein, 1999; Bray, 1995; Browning, 1994; Goldner, 1982; Papernow, 1994; Visher & Visher, 1996). Stepfamilies use this model when the expectation is that they will function as if they were a first marriage family unit. That is, the residential stepparent is expected to replace the absent biological parent completely—emotionally, psychologically, financially, and behaviorally (e.g., disciplining children, making household rules). Children are to call the stepparent "mom" or "dad," and step-relationships are expected to function as if they were genetic relationships. Because in first marriage families household membership and family membership are the same, stepfamilies using the nuclear family model try to establish boundaries around their household that exclude the nonresidential parent and his/her kin. This means that efforts are made to discourage or even to prohibit contact between children and their nonresidential parents and grandparents (i.e., the parents of the absent parent). In some stepfather families stepchildren use their stepfather's last name so that they will be seen by others to be a nuclear family. Adoption is initiated by some stepfamilies in efforts to legally complete the ideological and behavioral metamorphosis from stepfamily into nuclear family (Ganong et al., 1999).

If the first marriage, nuclear family model worked for the *Brady Bunch* family and, presumably, for a number of real-life stepfamilies, why do clinicians consider this particular response to complexity to be a problem for most stepfamilies? To begin with, in order to assume the identity of a first marriage family, stepfamilies must engage in massive denial and distortions of reality (Goldner, 1982). These denials and distortions take enormous emotional energy and have considerable costs psychologically and interpersonally because they force stepfamily members to forget about prior relationships, and live as if nothing that went on before the remarriage or cohabitation happened. Secondly, nonresidential parents and their families must be cut off from children, resulting in emotional losses for adults and children alike. Feelings of abandonment, anger, guilt, resentment, and unresolved feelings of loss are likely when ties between nonresidential parents and children are severed. Rather than emotionally replace a parent with a stepparent, these children may never accept the stepparent, who in their view has robbed them of knowing their biological parent.

This suggests a third reason clinicians think the first marriage family model and ideology are inappropriate for most stepfamilies. For a stepfamily to effectively re-create themselves as a first marriage family every member of the stepfamily, including nonresidential parents and their extended kin, has to be on board. It is highly unlikely that this will happen, and interactions with dissenters can be stressful. For example, if a nonresidential parent refuses to be replaced by the stepparent, then he or she may institute a legal custody battle over the children, or if a child refuses to accept a stepparent as a parent, then the stepparent may feel hurt and withdraw emotionally from the child. Children also may be excluded from the households of their nonresidential remarried parents if the adults in that household have decided to re-create the nuclear family.

Not only is it unrealistic to expect everyone to agree to replicate a first marriage family, it is unrealistic to expect relationships to be similar to the relationships found in first marriage families (Kelley, 1996; Mills, 1984; Papernow, 1994; Visher & Visher, 1978). Leslie and Epstein (1988) pointed out that expecting the new stepfamily couple to co-parent smoothly is expecting them "to work like a team even though they have had no practice" (p. 154), an analogy that could be applied to other relationships in stepfamilies as well.

Goldner (1982) called the use of the first marriage nuclear family model "the retreat from complexity" (p. 205). Stepfamilies, lacking established rituals and rules for behaving, try to re-create the first marriage family because it is what they know. One reason why families in general run into difficulties is because people do not think creatively about different ways to be a family (Minuchin, 1993). If this is true for families in general, then the inability to act and think flexibly about family life may be especially problematic for stepfamilies (Fishman & Hamel, 1981).

Despite the prevailing clinical perspective on this issue, it is possible, albeit unlikely, that acting like and thinking of themselves as a first marriage family unit may work for some stepfamilies (Coleman et al., in press). In a few small-scale studies, researchers have acknowledged that some stepfamilies function as if they were a first marriage family without encountering problems that would require a clinician's help (e.g., Berger, 1995; Braithwaite et al., 2001; Bray & Kelly, 1998; Burgoyne & Clark, 1984; Erera-Weatherly, 1996). We hypothesize that stepfamilies can function as first marriage families when: (a) the nonresidential parent and their kin have no contact with children in the stepfamily household, (b) the children are young at the time of the creation of the stepfamily household and remember little about prior family life, and (c) *all* stepfamily members want to re-create the first marriage family and agree, implicitly or explicitly, to do so. These hypotheses have yet to be tested systematically. The key element to making the first marriage model work is the cooperation of stepchildren in *the retreat from complexity*. From our observations, this happens when a stepchild feels abandoned by the absent parent, wants the stepparent to function as a mother or father, and has an emotionally close relationship with the stepparent. We hypothesize that *all* of these conditions must be present for the nuclear family model to work; the stepfamily may function adequately without all three in place, but the child likely will have unresolved feelings regarding the nonresidential parent and the stepfamily if that is the case. Longitudinal research is needed to examine the long-term effects of stepfamilies assuming a first marriage family identity.

An Example: How the Nuclear Family Model Affects Financial
Support of Children

In the idealized nuclear family, the father is the head of the household and
the primary breadwinner in the household. Note that this ideal exists even when
women contribute substantially more than men to household finances through
wages and investments (McGraw & Walker, 2004). What role is left for the father
after divorce? After his former wife remarries? Some fathers reject the continued
responsibility of financially supporting their children after divorce because they do
not associate paying child support with their bread winning role and because they
no longer see a family role for themselves—to them the family has ended (Mandell,
2002). In essence, these fathers argue that they are no longer obligated to fulfill
father-role responsibilities because their families are dissolved. Ironically, they will
support stepchildren and new children born to them in subsequent relationships
and with whom they share a residence (Manning & Smock, 2000). For such men,
the family and the household are the same.

The nuclear family ideology fosters further confusion about financial responsibility for children after mothers remarry. Are stepfathers obligated to financially
support their stepchildren and relieve fathers of this duty? If not, how much should
nonresidential fathers pay to financially support their children, given that they
no longer enjoy the same access and control over economic decisions in their
children's households? For some stepfamilies, using the nuclear family model re-
solves these dilemmas—the issue of who is financially responsible for the child
ceases to be a problem because the answer is clear—the residential parent and
stepparent are responsible. However, difficulties arise when the absolute nature
of the arrangement is qualified, such as when the nonresidential parent wants to
stay involved with the children or the stepparent has to pay child support for his
children living elsewhere and cannot afford to assume all financial obligations for
his stepchildren. For these families, questions about who is financially responsible
for the child continue.

CLINICAL MODELS OF STEPFAMILY DEVELOPMENT:
THE STEPFAMILY CYCLE

Over the years, several clinical writers have proposed models of stepfamily
development (e.g., McGoldrick & Carter, 1999; Mills, 1984; Papernow, 1993;
Ransom et al., 1979). Most of these models were adaptations of the family
development/family life cycle models that were based on first marriage families;
these clinical variations were attempts to broaden the traditional family development framework to include tasks that post-divorce families and stepfamilies might

encounter (McGoldrick & Carter, 1999; Mills, 1984; Ransom et al., 1979). Although clinicians now rarely use these early developmental models, they helped extend clinicians' views about stepfamilies. However, one model, Patricia Papernow's (1984, 1993, 1995) stepfamily life cycle, continues to be widely cited and is one that we think has utility for researchers as well as clinicians.

Papernow's model, drawn from Gestalt psychology and family systems theories, identifies seven stages of stepfamily development: (1) Fantasy, (2) Immersion, (3) Awareness, (4) Mobilization, (5) Action, (6) Contact, and (7) Resolution (Papernow, 1993). This model, based on Papernow's experiences as a clinician and a qualitative study of both clinical and nonclinical stepfamilies, blends individual and family dynamics to describe developmental processes of stepfamilies.

The first three stages, Fantasy, Immersion, and Awareness are considered to be the Early Stages. The developmental tasks of the early stages include giving up comforting fantasies, working through confusion and disappointment when fantasies are not met, and identifying and communicating about divergent experiences related to different positions in the stepfamily. There is wide variation in the amount of time it takes a stepfamily to complete the Early Stages. Middle Stages include Mobilization and Action. In these stages the stepfamily gets to work at becoming a unit; conflict is aired during Mobilization and resolved during the Action stage. In the two Later Stages, Contact and Resolution, the family functions without conscious awareness of unique stepfamily issues.

Fantasy

Stepfamily members bring a host of fantasies, wishes, and unrealistic expectations to the beginning of the stepfamily. Some of these are based on previous family experiences, some are due to a lack of information about stepfamilies, and some are based on cultural ideals, but the goals seem to be to ease the pain of prior losses. Adults often wish for the warm, loving perfect family life that escaped them in prior marriages/partnerships and perhaps in their families of origin. They fantasize about stepparents easily and quickly replacing absent parents (i.e., instant love), about re-creating the nuclear family, and about finding a partner who will share the financial responsibility and household workloads and bring them emotional security and love. Children often have different fantasies, wishing that their parents were still together, or that they did not have to share their parent with the new stepparent. Some children may welcome a stepparent, and may expect the stepparent to rescue them from poverty or loneliness. The task for stepfamilies is to bring to awareness unrealistic hopes and expectations, to articulate them, and then to give them up.

Immersion

At this stage the reality of stepfamily relationships hits home. When fantasies are not matched by experience, stepfamily members become confused, and they develop negative or ambivalent feelings about other family members. There may be a sense that things are not going as they should, things don't feel right, something is wrong. The stepparent is often the first family member to be aware of these feelings, and he or she may blame himself or herself. It is in this stage that differing realities/experiences are first manifested between stepparents and parents, between adults and children, and between "insiders" and "outsiders." The task for stepfamilies in this stage is to keep struggling through this period until family members can figure out what is wrong and communicate with each other about their feelings and experiences.

Awareness

Papernow considers this to be the most important stage. The tasks of this stage are to identify one's own feelings and needs and to try to understand the feelings and needs of others. Fantasies of how stepfamily relationships ought to be are replaced by more realistic perceptions of how these relationships may be different from those of first marriage families. Some stepfamilies begin the Stepfamily Cycle at this stage, or spend little time in Immersion before entering Awareness.

Mobilization

The task in this stage is to actively confront differences between family members and to constructively influence each other to make changes. This period may seem chaotic and full of stressful interactions over seemingly trivial issues, such as our earlier example about where the milk should be placed in the refrigerator or which adult's rules about table manners for children will prevail. These struggles are not trivial; they are conflicts over fundamental changes in the way the stepfamily, or relationships within it, will function in the future. Conflicts over the placement of milk in the refrigerator or table manners may really be conflicts over the stepparent's role and relationship vis-á-vis the children, or over which subsystems' household rules will be the rules for the stepfamily household.

Action

Papernow subtitled this stage, "going into business together" (p. 384), and that is what happens for stepfamilies who reach this stage without dissolving. The developmental task is to generate new rituals, customs, and codes of conduct for relationships. New boundaries are drawn around step-relationships, and family members begin to figure out how to retain interaction patterns from previous families while developing new, more comfortable stepfamily relationships.

Contact

After the major changes in family interaction patterns of the Middle Stages, stepfamily relationships can begin to develop deeper intimacy and attachment. Tasks are to enjoy this period and to further solidify the stepparent role, which Papernow asserts begins to emerge clearly during this stage.

Resolution

Stepfamily norms have been established, there is a growing family history, and individual members have a sense of what their roles and relationships are. Step issues continue to arise, and during stressful periods there may be a recycling of stepfamily patterns from earlier stages, but relationships are secure enough that they are not threatened by conflicts or stressful encounters. The developmental task is to continue to work through grief and loss associated with earlier family changes/losses and loyalty conflicts.

The Stepfamily Cycle has received considerable favorable attention from clinicians since it was initially presented (Papernow, 1984). The model has intuitive appeal to clinicians, perhaps because it is a useful framework for conceptualizing individual and stepfamily developmental changes, and perhaps because it also contains intervention suggestions appropriate for individuals and families.

Stepfamily Tasks

In addition to the developmental models just described, the Vishers identified eight tasks that must be addressed before stepfamilies can establish their own family identity (Visher & Visher, 1988). A team of clinicians designed a self-help program around these tasks for The Stepfamily Association of America called *Stepfamilies Stepping Ahead* (Burt, 1989). The tasks are: dealing with losses and changes; negotiating different developmental needs for different family members; establishing new traditions; developing a solid couple bond; forming new relationships, particularly stepparent-stepchild bonds; creating a parent coalition with former spouses; accepting continual shifts in household composition; and risking involvement despite little support from society.

These tasks are not simple nor are they easily or quickly completed. Some stepfamilies never successfully master any of them. Other stepfamilies may accomplish some tasks and fail miserably at others. It has been our experience that stepfamilies continue to work towards mastery of some of these tasks long after the children have left the household. Unlike first marriage families, little is taken for granted in stepfamilies, and efforts to develop and maintain close relationships are ongoing. Hard earned successes can be unusually satisfying.

Visher and Visher (1990) asserted that stepfamilies are successful to the degree they can master challenges in shifting from previous family cultures to a joint stepfamily culture. They identified six characteristics of successful stepfamilies: (a) losses have been mourned, (b) expectations are realistic, (c) there is a unified couple, (d) constructive rituals are established, (e) satisfactory step-relationships have formed, and (f) the separate households cooperate.

SUMMARY OF CLINICIANS' PERSPECTIVES

In clinicians' extensive writing about stepfamily relationships and stepfamily dynamics, they have focused on what they perceive to be the unique dimensions of stepfamily processes, emphasizing characteristics that distinguish stepfamilies from other family forms, particularly first marriage families. Their interests have centered mainly on stepfamilies with children in the home—stepfamilies with adult children and later-life stepfamilies have received minimal attention from clinicians thus far. Clinicians also have focused on the formative period of stepfamily development, in part because this is when problems first appear and in part because they view many of the problems as preventable at that stage. Consequently, stepfamilies at later stages of development have not received much attention.

WORKING WITH STEPFAMILIES

In this section we examine ways in which practitioners work with stepfamilies. As we noted in Chapter 4, remarrying adults seldom seek counseling, education, or legal consultation prior to creating a stepfamily household. Regardless of the reason for this lack of preparation, the evidence suggests that avoiding preparation is generally problematic. Of course, many stepfamilies figure out how to function well on their own, either through trial and error learning or by communicating clearly and often with each other. But many others do not. This means that stepfamilies and stepfamily members frequently seek counseling after problems occur. The irony is that stepfamily members, who avert seeking help to *prevent* problems are over-represented in family therapy case loads as they attempt to rectify unhappy situations that could have been diminished or avoided altogether with some advance preparation.

Many, if not most, stepfamilies need education rather than therapy (Visher & Visher, 1980), and it is important that those who require therapy also have an educational component incorporated into the therapeutic process (Browning, 1994). Communication skill building and education regarding stepfamily functioning are generic approaches that clinicians use to address the general problems that confront stepfamilies (Ganong et al., 2000).

HELPING STEPFAMILY MEMBERS WHO LACK SKILLS OR KNOWLEDGE

First, clinicians need to assess whether or not an individual stepfamily member lacks specific interpersonal skills, and, if so, why. If personal problems or unusual personality characteristics prevent an individual from engaging in satisfying relationships, then individual therapy may be necessary before relational therapy or skills training is effective. Referrals to 12-step programs for substance abusers, and individual or group psychotherapy focusing on specific problems may be necessary. If the individual's problems warrant intensive therapy and the stepfamily has not yet started to live together, then the clinician may want to encourage them to delay moving ahead until these problems are resolved.

When a person has interpersonal skills but lacks knowledge about topics that would help him or her relate better to other stepfamily members, clinicians may assign reading or refer them to adult education courses or University Extension programs designed to address the information gap. For instance, stepparents who have not raised children or been around them much may know little about children's emotional, social, cognitive, and physical development, and consequently may not know what to expect from or how to relate to children at different ages. Clinicians could suggest that they read child development books written for lay audiences or that they could attend parenting workshops or short courses.

Communication Skills

Relationship development and maintenance in stepfamilies are facilitated by conflict resolution skills, the ability to negotiate, and competencies in constructively voicing feelings and opinions (Ganong et al., 2000). Even normally adept communicators sometimes find themselves in need of skill-building training when confronted with new and changing relationships. For example, stepparents and stepchildren may be unsure about how to talk to each other, former spouses may not know how to effectively communicate as co-parents, and nonresidential parents may be clueless about ways to interact and maintain relationships with their children. Stepfamily members may need to develop both general communication skills and explicit ways of successfully communicating with various family members.

Numerous family life education programs have been developed that include communications skills training (see Hughes & Schroeder, 1997, for a review). These programs range from leaderless, self-guided curricula (e.g., Duncan & Brown, 1992) to programs that require a fairly high degree of clinical skills to lead effectively (e.g., Bielenberg, 1991). The children's programs Hughes and Schroeder reviewed were for children in single-parent-headed and re-partnered parents' households, and focused on feelings as well as some communication skill building. Most of the adult and family programs promoted skill-building activities, usually involving communication skills.

In stepfamilies, negotiation is a necessary communication skill for developing, maintaining, and enhancing relationships (Visher & Visher, 1996). This is especially true in the early months and years when new stepfamilies are attempting to merge two family cultures. For example, a stepparent may believe that children should earn their spending money; the parent thinks that they should receive an allowance. Whose "culture" should prevail? It is important for clinicians and educators to facilitate methods of interacting that allow everyone to state their needs and preferences, to recognize and acknowledge when these differ from those of others, and to create acceptable solutions. Given the often tenuous nature of new stepfamily relationships, the indiscriminate expression of thoughts and opinions may be damaging, and should not be encouraged (Papernow, 1995). Instead, stepfamilies who encounter disagreements may need to be coached on how to be assertive, but constructive, in stating what they see as problems or what they would like to see changed.

Papernow (2001) calls this "conducting difficult conversations wisely" (p. 4) and in ways that have "the best chance of being able to be heard and . . . that will be most likely to build and strengthen relationships rather than damage them" (p. 1). She proposed 10 tools for conducting difficult conversations in stepfamilies. Some of these are basic communication skills (e.g., sending 'I' versus 'you' messages, empathizing, taking turns), and others are tailored to stepfamily situations. Among the latter are what Papernow calls, "In my world. . ." (p. 4). This is a tool to aid stepfamily members in expressing what they believe are the ways in which families should normally function. Papernow calls these their "no brainers"— behaviors and household practices that are obviously "correct" for some stepfamily members. However, they may be foreign concepts to new step-kin with different family histories. Our examples about getting milk and stocking the refrigerator illustrate these "cultural clashes." Papernow thinks that constructive communication that builds relationships creates what she calls *middle ground*. According to Papernow (1993) middle ground is the area of shared values and experiences that makes being together easier; it is that "no brainer" area where everyone agrees. No one has to think about milk and refrigerator space because there is no disagreement about it.

Shared middle ground brings stability to stepfamilies, but it is not always easy to acquire. Stepfamilies tend to lack middle ground; even minor issues have to be thought about and negotiated when they are starting out. Therefore, a goal for those working with stepfamilies is to thicken the middle ground—to communicate, and negotiate if necessary, until there are more and more areas of agreement. Beginning with small disagreements and solving them satisfactorily can create confidence in stepfamily members that they can slowly thicken their middle ground to a level that is comfortable without being stultifying.

Stepfamilies who communicate early in the relationship formation process and share realistic assumptions about the tasks that must be accomplished develop middle ground much sooner than those that do not. As newly formed stepfamilies communicate about rules (e.g., mealtimes, curfews) and rituals (e.g., holiday celebrations, birthdays), they build middle ground that reduces the intensity of effort it takes to accomplish understanding and stability. However, as family transitions occur (e.g., babies born, children moving in and out of the household), stepfamilies who do not communicate with renewed vigor may get stuck, the development of middle ground stalls, which decreases satisfaction and stifles positive and nurturing interaction.

Some stepfamilies have told us that family meetings have worked well for them and have helped create middle ground. Adults who hold family meetings need to be careful to maintain meetings as problem-solving sessions rather as than gripe sessions or thinly disguised attempts by adults to control the children. However, if everyone has a chance to talk about what they think and feel and family members are heard with respect, then family meetings can help stepfamilies collaboratively build a shared culture.

Affinity Strategies

Communication scholars define *affinity-seeking* strategies as active processes that are intentionally performed by people in efforts to get others to like them and to feel positive toward them (Daly & Kreiser, 1994). In developed, stable relationships, *affinity-maintaining* strategies may be employed by people to enhance the probability that liking will continue. Affinity-seeking and -maintaining strategies are used by nearly everyone, in multiple settings, including families, social settings, businesses, and schools.

Stepparents and stepchildren are advised by clinicians to develop their relationship just as they would develop any friendship, by spending time getting acquainted and by having fun together (Visher & Visher, 1979). Stepparents are especially encouraged to focus initially on nurturing their stepchildren and developing feelings of affection in the relationship before attempting to discipline stepchildren (Mills, 1984; Visher & Visher, 1996). According to clinicians, many stepparents do not make efforts to build friendships with stepchildren before they move into disciplinary roles, thereby creating resistance and negative reactions from stepchildren and often from their parents (Mills, 1984; Visher & Visher, 1996). In particular, clinicians assert that spending one-on-one time in relationships builds affinity and is especially helpful in the early stages of stepfamily development (Papernow, 1995).

Even though affinity-building and -maintaining strategies are ubiquitous, and they seem like common sense, a surprising number of stepparents either engage in none of these behaviors or stop using them once they share a residence with their stepchildren (Ganong et al., 1999). Clearly, the importance of affinity strategies is not obvious. Therefore, practitioners teach stepparents, and sometimes stepchildren, the importance of engaging in such behaviors. Stepparents can be taught to look for things that they can do with a stepchild as a pair (without the parent or other children), noting that keys to success are letting stepchildren choose the pace at which the friendship develops and engaging in activities that the stepchild likes to do. Parents can be taught to facilitate such encounters by allowing the step-relationships time to bond and by giving the stepparent ideas of activities that would appeal to the child. Stepchildren can be taught to be aware of stepparents' efforts to build affinity with them and how to reciprocate in ways that will appeal to their self-interests but will also improve relationships.

Increasing Reciprocity toward Affinity Behaviors

Teaching strategies for forming close relationships may not be enough. Clinicians may also find it necessary to work with stepfamily members, especially stepchildren, to increase their odds of reciprocating relationship building and maintaining behaviors.

When individuals' attempts to maintain or enhance a relationship are rejected, the consequences can be extremely damaging for the rejected individuals, the relationship, and the entire stepfamily. Rebuffed individuals feel badly about themselves and the other person, they eventually quit making attempts if continual efforts fail, and the indirect fallout from unhappy individuals and distant, distressed relationships taints other stepfamily relationships. For example, if an ignored or rebuffed stepparent becomes upset and angry towards the stepchild, a parent who observes this may feel guilty for exposing their loved ones to each other with such negative results. If such interactions continue unabated, then all stepfamily relationships become strained. Consequently, clinical interventions focus on helping rejected individuals cope, teaching alternative strategies for maintaining and enhancing relationships, and working with individuals to increase their incentives to reciprocate others' attempts to improve relationships.

Dyadic relationships develop at the pace of the person who is least ready, least interested, and least motivated, so it does little good for the other person to push for intimacy at a more rapid pace (e.g., Papernow, 2001). Sometimes by not trying so hard, stepparents find that their efforts to build good relationships are more successful. Stepfamily members who want to be closer to others are advised to not give up their efforts but to continue them in a low-key manner. This advice is difficult to follow for individuals with high needs for control. Therefore, clinicians assist stepfamily members gain a realistic sense of control by helping them differentiate between aspects of stepfamily life they can control and those they cannot. Often, making stepfamily members aware of how complex their families are and how much they differ from first marriage families is enough to reduce inappropriate and insensitive efforts to control.

If stepchildren are using distancing techniques because of loyalty conflicts, clinicians can assure them that it is possible to be close to both a stepfather and a father, or a mother and stepmother. Stepchildren also can be helped to think of each adult's specialties. A stepfather might specialize in math homework while the father remains the social studies homework expert. Parents also should be helped to accept the notion that affection is not a zero sum game; loyalty conflicts are not likely to occur when parents specifically give children permission to like their new stepparents. Papernow (2001) encourages adults to help stepchildren avoid loyalty conflicts by not criticizing the other parent, not asking children to take sides, and by discussing differences in households in neutral, nonjudgmental tones. Parents can also tell children that love is not a zero sum game—that they do not have to choose to love either one person or the other, but that they can love both, perhaps in the same way or in different ways.

Clinicians may have to teach stepfamily members how to act in ways that are different from how they feel (Visher & Visher, 1996). Suggesting that stepchildren respond politely, even enthusiastically, to stepparents' attempts to bond with them even when they don't feel like it helps change the tenor of interactions and reduces conflicts and bad feelings. This usually takes less energy than rejecting the stepparent. Moreover, behaving towards a person as if a closer, more positive relationship exists can help bring about a cognitive shift; by acting as if they feel closer than they do, feelings and thoughts often become more positive. Although stepchildren (and others) may initially see this as hypocritical, by appealing to their self-interests, stepchildren often can be persuaded to try this strategy. Teaching adolescents the concept of *quid pro quo* (i.e., something for something) provides them with a frame of reference for cooperatively interacting with stepparents and parents in ways that maximize their gains (e.g., "If I am polite to my stepfather when he asks me how my day was, I can avoid a big fight about my attitude and will not get grounded for talking back").

Another way to increase reciprocity to another person such as a stepparent or stepsibling is to appeal to individuals' obligations to third parties. For instance, stepchildren can be invited to "be nice to your stepfather, it will make your mother happy."

TEACHING STEPFAMILY DYNAMICS

Educating stepfamily members about the unique dynamics of stepfamilies is extremely important. Stepfamily adults who had been in therapy identified learning about stepfamily dynamics as one of the most positive aspects of intervention (Visher et al., 1997). Consequently, one goal for practitioners is to help individuals understand normative experiences of stepfamily development.

Losses and Gains

To facilitate acknowledgement of losses by clients, the Vishers (1996) suggest helping stepfamily members examine the changes they have experienced prior to and following the formation of the stepfamily. Family members may be only vaguely aware of the magnitude of changes they have experienced (e.g., moves, children going back and forth between two households; loss of daily routines). Once aware of these changes, they can be helped to identify their losses and gains. For instance, household finances may have improved, and individuals may have gained skills and knowledge from new stepfamily members. Clinicians can help stepfamily members move through the processes of mourning losses and celebrating gains (as well as noting those changes that have mixed or variable effects for family members). Once losses have been faced, individuals are more able to cope with new challenges.

Complexity

Sometimes stepfamily members do not anticipate how complicated, sometimes overwhelmingly so, their family lives will be (Goldner, 1982). For adults, challenges include maintaining ties with children from previous relationships, continuing to co-parent with a former spouse or partner, and developing and maintaining relationships with new partners and perhaps stepchildren. Stepchildren are faced with maintaining ties with nonresidential parents, and perhaps nonresidential siblings, while developing and maintaining relationships with one or more stepparents and stepsiblings.

Using genograms has been recommended as a way to help stepfamilies understand better the complexity of their family structure (Visher & Visher, 1996). Genograms are "family trees," graphic representations of family histories (usually three generations are portrayed) that also include family relationships, multi-generational and cross-household patterns of interaction, and information about family structure and changes in structure over time. Genograms provide people with a clear visual image of how complex their families are (read McGoldrick, Gerson, and Schellenberger, 1998 or Visher and Visher, 1996 for suggestions on how to use genograms for assessment and intervention). After completing the genogram on a large piece of paper we have asked individual family members to show us who they consider to be in their family (by drawing a circle around their family members, or in other ways). Invariably, each family member selects slightly different groups of people as members of their family. For example, a residential stepfather usually does not include the nonresidential father and his wife as members of his family, whereas stepchildren often do so (Funder, 1991; Gross, 1987). This usually is a surprise to the adults, and it can lead to a discussion about boundaries and varying perceptions and expectations.

Expectations

Clinicians try to help stepfamily members become aware of their expectations, with the goal of assisting them in creating more realistic and attainable expectations. For example, teaching stepparents that love between stepparents and stepchildren is not likely to happen immediately and may *never* happen can help dispel the guilt that many stepparents experience at their inability to feel love towards their stepchild and allows them to develop more realistic expectations.

Helping adults see that children may be less motivated than they are to build new step-relationships and that family members may want differing levels of closeness gives them a perspective with which to plan strategies for improving the quality of family relationships. This also helps reduce their sense of urgency to integrate the family as rapidly as possible.

Stepchildren often have definite expectations regarding stepparents, and they should be encouraged by clinicians to identify what it is they want and need from their stepparents. The poorer the match between the stepchildren's and stepparents' wants and expectations, the harder it will be to build good relationships. Even young children should be asked about their expectations for the new stepparent. Until expectations and desires are clarified, it is often recommended that parents retain responsibility for most of the parenting, especially discipline (Bernstein, 1994; Kelley, 1992; Papernow, 2001). Clinicians can then facilitate the development of strategies that maintain discipline as a responsibility of the parent, particularly during the early years in a stepfamily.

Some clinicians have suggested that stepfamily members write *contracts* with each other as a method to help them become aware of their expectations for themselves and their partners in these relationships (Kaslow, 1999; Sager, 1981).

Although such contracts are not intended to be legal documents, by using the analogy of a legal agreement, clinicians can facilitate stepfamily members' understanding of what they expect to receive and what they are willing to do in return. Similar to divorce mediation agreements in which divorcing parents identify the content of each person's responsibilities to each other and to their children as well as the limits of their responsibilities, stepfamily agreements could help individuals increase awareness of their expectations and negotiate mutual obligations. Although this would be a more valuable activity prior to beginning to share a stepfamily household (Kaslow, 1999), it could be helpful at any time.

HELPING INDIVIDUALS COPE

In addition to teaching about stepfamily dynamics and about ways to build and maintain positive relationships, clinicians focus on helping individuals cope with specific family problems. For individuals or stepfamilies experiencing a crisis, clinicians focus on the presenting issues, help the clients make practical plans toward resolutions, and provide emotional support and validation for those in distress (Visher & Visher, 1996).

For example, sometimes stepparents' attempts to establish or enhance relationships are openly rejected or ignored. In order to encourage stepfamily members who may feel discouraged to try again to strengthen relationships, it is important for clinicians to (a) validate feelings that arise, (b) work to reduce feelings of helplessness, and (c) reframe the situation.

Validating Feelings

Knowing that it is normal and acceptable to feel frustrated and upset lessens negative self-perceptions by normalizing emotional reactions to stressful relationships. Validating feelings is particularly important for women in stepfamilies (Visher, Visher, & Pasley, 1997), because women often feel responsible for family functioning (Wood, 1994). Mothers may feel especially torn when trying to balance and maintain relationships with their new partner and their children (Weaver & Coleman, in review). Support groups or group therapy may assist with this.

It may be particularly important for clinicians to help clients become aware that ambivalent feelings are common when relationships are strained. For example, although stepparents may feel affection for their stepchildren, they also may feel relieved when they leave the household to spend time with their other parent. Ambivalent feelings are not unique to stepfamilies, but stepfamily members tend to be acutely aware of them, which results in guilt and confusion. Clinicians should assist stepfamily members in accepting the normality of their feelings.

Reducing Feelings of Helplessness

Rejected individuals commonly feel powerless to change the situation. For instance, stepparents often encounter the paradoxical scenario in which the warmer and friendlier they act, the more rejecting the stepchildren are. The children are reacting is to feeling torn loyalty between the stepparent and nonresidential parent. However, stepparents are seldom aware of the cause, they are only aware of their own feelings of frustration and helplessness. These feelings are important to address because they eventually lead to withdrawal from the child.

Helping stepfamily members understand the dynamics that may be underlying rejections may lower feelings of impotence by helping them understand that their efforts may not be doomed forever (Bernstein, 1994). By helping them to realize that their experiences are not unusual, self-esteem is enhanced, and their sense of incompetence is reduced (Visher & Visher, 1996).

Reframing the Situation

Intervention strategies that help individuals change the way in which they think about a situation, such as failed attempts at strengthening a relationship, make the situation more manageable. *Reframing* teaches individuals to redefine a situation or experience in a more positive and manageable way (Pasley & Dollahite, 1995; Visher & Visher, 1996), which can help both adults and children (Quick, McKenry, & Newman, 1994). For example, adolescent stepchildren can be encouraged to think of their stepparents' questions about their activities, not as intrusive and nosy, but in other ways: (1) "My stepmom asks questions because she cares about me"; (2) "My stepfather asks what I do for fun because he wants to know more about me"; or (3) "If I tell him what he wants to know, he will like me better and will be more likely to do things for me when I ask."

Increasing Awareness through Bibliotherapy or Biblioeducation

One way that clinicians can aid stepfamily members in becoming more aware of stepfamily dynamics and individuals' responses to them is via bibliotherapy or biblioeducation. Bibliotherapy is an educational, preventive set of methods that revolve around assigned readings, which may include novels, short stories, or non-fictional self-help materials (Coleman & Ganong, 1988, 1990). Practitioners who use bibliotherapy have several goals—sharing information and new ways of thinking about a situation, promoting self-understanding, and stimulating discussion. For instance, having adults read novels about stepfamilies written for children and adolescents that feature stepchild protagonists can help make the adults aware of how the stepfamily is experienced from the stepchildren's perspective (Coleman & Ganong). Bibliotherapy may be used with children and adults in stepfamilies and also with helping professionals who work with stepfamilies. Guidelines for the use of bibliotherapy with stepfamilies can be found in Coleman and Ganong (1988).

Self-help books can be used in the practice of bibliotherapy, but they also can be used independently by stepfamily members. These books can be especially helpful to people in small communities or rural areas where therapists trained to work with stepfamilies and educational or self-help groups are not available. Self-help books can also be useful for people who need repetition—they have a constant reference guide to which they can turn. Those who believe stigma is attached to persons seeking therapy also might benefit from self-help books.

In addition to general stepfamily self-help books, there are several good offerings specifically for stepmothers or stepfathers. We would recommend avoiding many of the religious offerings that tend to either promote the nuclear family model for stepfamilies and gloss over potential problems or are based primarily on personal experiences rather than clinical principles. A few of our favorite self-help books are by Visher and Visher (1991), Lutz, (2001), Pickhardt (1997), and Gerlach (2001). A religiously oriented book by Frydenger and Frydenger (1984) is also recommended.

Self-help Groups

Self-help groups can also be useful in providing support and information to stepfamily members. The most noteworthy self-help group in the United States, with a sister organization in Great Britain, is the Stepfamily Association of America, founded about 30 years ago by John and Emily Visher as an educational organization designed to help stepfamily members help themselves. This organization serves as a clearinghouse for books, articles, games, and other products for stepfamilies. The organization also publishes *Your Stepfamilies: Embrace the Journey*, a magazine for stepfamily members, supports training workshops for professionals, holds conferences for stepfamilies, and serves as an advocacy group for stepfamily public policy issues. The British version of SAA also has run a hot line for stepfamily members, staffed by volunteer clinicians (Batchelder et al., 1994).

There are other self-help groups for stepfamilies, sometimes for specific family members (e.g., second wives) and sometimes for the entire family. None of these have the national presence that SAA does, but it is likely that some of these groups are successful locally. In our experience, adults in stepfamilies are reluctant to attend self-help programs unless and until they are having major problems. If they are functioning well as a family unit, then many adults probably reason that they do not need to attend a self-help group like SAA. If there are problems, feelings may be tender enough that people are reluctant to share the difficulties they are having with the children of their partner. Too, some people seem superstitious and wary of talking about potential problems lest they jinx themselves and cause the problems to bloom. (We have even seen this when recruiting research participants.)

Consequently, local stepfamily self-help groups tend to be short-lived except in rare settings in which there are committed, determined leaders. In our experience, people join such groups soon after they have remarried and drop out after a few months or a couple of years. Some people and their families need more help than support groups and educational interventions can offer, and some individuals and families function better, feel better about themselves and other family members, and leave because they see no continuing needs to be met.

Stepfamily Life Education Programs

A decade ago, stepfamily members who wanted to attend family life education programs or workshops would have had a difficult time finding them. This is less true now, at least in urban areas. Stepfamily and remarriage education programs are offered by colleges and universities (e.g., through Cooperative Extension Services), through public and private social service agencies, and from religious organizations (e.g., churches, synagogues). Several institutions have developed "canned" programs that can be offered by leaders with minimal training (e.g., Duncan & Brown's RENEW program). There does not appear to be a shortage of materials and educational programs.

However, few of these programs have been evaluated (Hughes & Schroeder, 1997), so wary consumers should raise questions about program quality and effectiveness. The *validity* of the information presented should be questioned unless the instructional material is from a recognized, reliable source. For instance, land grant University Cooperative Extension programs are often based on current research and clinical thought. Other programs grounded in trustworthy scholarship, whether produced by university and college personnel or not, are also available (e.g., Kaplan & Hennon, 1992; Larson, Anderson, & Morgan, 1984), but it is hard, if not impossible, for lay people to distinguish good information from more questionable offerings.

World Wide Web

For many post-modern individuals and families, the Internet serves as their self-help organization (Hughes & Hans, 2004). For a growing number of Americans, turning to the Internet for information, emotional support, and advice is an everyday occurrence. Although the Web can be an invaluable resource, we are uneasy about the naive and uncritical approach with which many educated adults and young people make use of resources they find on the Web. There is no quality control with Web pages, so consumers must use caution when seeking valid information or help on the Web.

In fact, what we found in our forays into the often poorly charted territory of the Internet for resources and Web sites about remarriage and stepfamilies, more often than not makes us cringe. Besides misinformation, misinterpretation, and biased points of view about research findings, there are many sites that contain what we consider to be potentially damaging advice—advice that, if believed or followed, would lead to more serious problems for stepfamilies. Of course, many professional journals now are available on the Web, and there are many reputable organizations that have Web sites that may contain sound information on stepfamilies, including most University Cooperative Extension services.

Chapter 12

Epilogue

In this final chapter we want to accomplish two goals. First, we summarize what we think has been learned about stepfamily relationships in the last decade or so. Given the plethora of studies, we do not intend to catalog all of the new information that has been generated in that time period. Instead, we mention what we see as the highlights, general conclusions, and contributions that have led or likely will lead to even more growth in knowledge. Our second goal is to do what researchers are usually reluctant to do—make predictions about the future. Most scholars are so thoroughly trained in the necessity of making measured generalizations about phenomena, and of postulating only the most well-tempered conclusions, that students and other consumers of scholarly products (e.g., journalists) are often irked by the lack of a "sound bite" or simple message (e.g., "Are stepparents mean and wicked or not?" "Are stepfamilies harmful environments for children?"). Although we do not intend to abandon the judicious use of conditional statements in this chapter, we speculate about what researchers, clinicians, and stepfamilies will be doing in a decade hence.

WHAT WE HAVE LEARNED

What has the field of family scholarship learned about stepfamilies in the past few years? With apologies to David Letterman and his fans, we offer our top 10 list of general conclusions.

1. In remarriages, women seek more power and control than they had in their first marriages.

Consequently, remarried couples are somewhat more egalitarian in their decision-making processes than first married couples are. This may be true for cohabiting heterosexual and homosexual stepfamily partnerships as well.

2. The nature and quality of the stepparent-stepchild relationship are contingent on several factors.

How much the stepparent invests in the relationship. This factor is mediated by whether or not the stepparent has children of his or her own, the expectations of stepfamily members, and a host of other conditions (see Chapter 7 for these).

The stepchild's willingness to have a good relationship with the stepparent. Stepchildren have more power than children living with both parents, especially when they can claim membership in more than one household because: (1) they can leave the household or threaten to leave if they are unhappy (with a reasonable expectation that the other household would take them); (2) they can create problems by complaining to their nonresidential parent or others (e.g., legal authorities); and (3) unless they are infants or very young children, they often are in the position of being "courted" or "befriended" by a stepparent who wants to fit into the stepfamily. These three sources of power give children a lot of control in that they can negotiate rules and discipline, they can accept the stepparent's overtures or refuse to acknowledge him or her, and they can negotiate how the step-relationship will be defined and lived. Several researchers have reported that stepchildren play key roles in determining how well stepfamilies function and how well stepparents get along with them (e.g., Ganong et al., 1999; Golish, 2000; Golish & Caughlin, 2002; O'Connor, Hetherington, & Clingempeel, 1997; Russell & Searcy, 1997). As more researchers focus their attention on bi-directional influences in stepfamilies, a more complete picture of stepfamily dynamics is beginning to emerge.

The nonresidential and residential parents' relationships with the child. Stepparents are as involved as their partners and their stepchildren's other parent want them to be. We need to learn more about how this is communicated and negotiated in stepfamilies, and we need to think in terms of *at least* triads, rather than focusing only on stepparent-stepchild dyads. Some researchers have begun to do this (e.g., Amato & Rezac, 1994; MacDonald & DeMaris, 2002). More studies in which both step-households and the entire stepfamily system are included are needed if we are to fully grasp the ways that nonresidential and residential stepparents' relationships with their stepchildren evolve after remarriage. The importance of triads and systems thinking is evident in studies of parent-child relationships—in one study partners' experiences were better predictors of parent-child relationships than were parents' own life course experiences (Dunn, Davies, O'Connor, & Sturgess, 2000), illustrating the importance of assessing data from multiple adults, and of taking a systemic perspective.

Time. Step-relationships change over time, and they change in many ways. Research is needed that explores the conditions under which stepparent-stepchild relationships become better or worse. There is evidence that in some stepfamilies stepparents relate to stepchildren somewhat like parents do (Hetherington et al., 1999; Vuchinich et al., 1991; Weaver & Coleman, in review), and there are other patterns as well (Erera-Weatherly, 1996). The key element is that relationships are not static, and stepparent-stepchild bonds are no exceptions to this.

3. Stepchildren generally are at greater risk for problems than are children living with both of their parents, but most stepchildren do well in school and do not have emotional, social, or behavioral problems.

This is not a new conclusion, but we include it because this information often is lost, misinterpreted, or only partially communicated. We could add to this that differences between stepchildren and children living with both parents are usually small. When we present the results of stepfamily research to students and adult lay audiences, they are seldom surprised by the existence of differences (parents and children have special relationships, after all), but they are shocked at how small these differences are. The culture of stepfamily stigma is well ingrained in North American society. For example, we are believed when we say that stepparents are over-represented as abusers of stepchildren, but questioned when we discuss why the degree of risk may not be as high as is often claimed.

4. Parents love their children more than other people do; children love their parents more than they love other adults.

We think these are obvious points, and yet worthy of restating. Most people agree with them; they expect parents and children to demonstrate this truth and are shocked and upset when they do not. These two statements are generally accepted as evident facts, the kind of conclusions that comedians and critics make fun of when questioning the value of social science research. We mention these statements in our general conclusions about stepfamilies because the special relationship between parents and children is at the heart of understanding stepfamily relationships. Yet, researchers often interpret stepparents being less emotionally close to stepchildren than they are to their own children or stepparents being less involved with helping stepchildren do homework than parents are in helping their children as examples of problems, as indicators of risk, and as rationale for preventing or reducing remarriages of people with children (Popenoe, 1994). To us, however, it is a giant leap of logic to move from a position that children and parents love each other more than they love others to a position assuming that harm comes from exposing children to other adults (i.e., stepparents) who will likely come to, if not love, at least like the children.

Although some people have taken issue in public and in print with our efforts to study the potential benefits for children of living in a stepfamily household, in our defense, we think it is at least as useful to investigate non-evident phenomena, such as potential stepfamily benefits, as it is to study widely held cultural truths, such as parents love their children and are more invested in them than anyone else. Focusing all of our efforts on the children who do not thrive in stepfamilies seems ill advised, especially when we lack surety regarding how well the children would have thrived had they remained in conflicted first marriage families.

That parents and children have special bonds is important to understand for stepfamily members, for clinicians, for researchers, and for policymakers. That these special bonds are genetically coded in the human gene structure is a logical explanation, and one that we can accept. However, such an argument must be accompanied by a recognition of the effects of environmental factors on parents and children to be able to explain most of the variance in parent-child interactions. We think awareness of this special parent-child bond helps new stepparents approach the task of developing a relationship with stepchildren. It also helps parents understand how their partner might interpret their child's behavior in a way that is different from their own benign, well-informed view, and it helps clinicians working with stepfamilies to develop more realistic goals than re-creating a nuclear family. Additionally, it helps researchers think about study designs that move beyond describing structural differences in family types. Finally, this knowledge can even help policy makers design more appropriate laws and social policies.

To us, here is what the phrase, *parents love their children more than other people do*, does not mean—it does not mean that stepparents automatically pose a risk for stepchildren's well-being. It does not mean that stepfamilies should be discouraged as a family form. It does not mean that stepparent adoption will change feelings and relational quality. It does not mean that researchers should stop doing comparative studies of stepfamilies and other families. It does not mean that negative cultural stereotypes are okay to promote just because some stepparents are abusive. It also does not mean that stepparents and stepchildren cannot have positive relationships with each other. It does not mean that remarriages are doomed to fail. It does not mean that evolutionary or genetic theories are irrelevant. And it does not mean that stepparents should not invest more of themselves into stepchildren.

5. Stepfamilies function successfully in several different ways.

By success we mean that individuals' needs and the family's needs as a group are met most of the time. It is our observation that most stepfamilies base their interactions and their model of family life on the first marriage family, despite decades of clinical advice against this model. However, we also see encouraging signs that more stepfamilies than in the past are attempting to use a different model (e.g., Berger, 1995; Erera-Weatherly, 1996). Some of this is probably out of necessity. Given the rapid increase in shared legal and physical custody of children after divorce, couples with children who re-partner or remarry are finding it harder to emulate a nuclear family. We are not sure, but it seems likely that these shared custody families are the ones that are building a new set of norms related to step-households, norms that are not merely watered down versions of nuclear family norms.

6. Stepfamilies define themselves—they construct their identities and relationships.

All families do this, of course. We have written a great deal in this book about Cherlin's (1978) incomplete institutionalization hypothesis. We would be remiss if we did not point out that this hypothesis seems to apply mostly to white middle-class stepfamilies of European heritage. Black stepfamilies seem to struggle less than white stepfamilies do in defining external family boundaries, creating new roles and relationships, and generally improvising solutions to the blending of families. African American scholars have long pointed out that "African Americans, located at the social, economic, and political margins of American life, have created ways of living that support survival and challenge dominant cultural narratives about marriage, childbearing, and the ideal social organization of families" (Hunter, 2002, p. 44). Crosbie-Burnett and Lewis (1993) have argued that stepfamilies in general could learn relational strategies from African American families. For instance, African American communities do not vest the sole responsibility for raising children in the hands of mothers and fathers; the community shares responsibility for childcare and child rearing. Children have *bloodmothers* and they have *othermothers*, women who assist mothers by sharing mothering duties (Crosbie-Burnett & Lewis). This is a very child-focused perspective, and one that does not perceive children as the property of their parents only. The African American community also recognizes social fathers as important to the development of children (Jayakody & Kalil, 2002), particularly when there are no men in the household. Other notions from African American families, such as *fictive kinship* and the benefits of permeable household boundaries, are lessons that could benefit stepfamilies of every color. Similarly, gay and lesbian stepfamilies intentionally choose kin and redefine themselves and their relationships in purposive strategies to survive and thrive in non-supportive communities (Oswald, 2002)—such behaviors and mind-sets could serve all stepfamilies well.

In some ways, this shift towards constructing stepfamily identities and relationships has already started; that is, European American and Hispanic stepfamilies and heterosexual stepfamilies of any ethnicity that function well have often devised ways to allow their children to find emotional and psychological places for their parents and stepparents to dwell without placing them in hurtful loyalty binds. Role models for this kind of stepfamily dynamic appear to be increasing. For instance, as we were writing this chapter *USA Today* newspaper pictured actor Bruce Willis, his former wife, Demi Moore, their three daughters, and Ashton Kutcher, Ms. Moore's boyfriend, as they attended a movie premiere together. Although the adults' facial expressions were somewhat oblique, the three children were smiling broadly. We would never recommend emulating movie stars as role models, but media portrayal is useful when it illustrates that stepfamily members can get along and that children benefit when they do so.

7. Norms are being established for stepfamilies.

Clinicians, authors of popular media publications, and self-help books emulating, Dr. Phil, Stepfamily Associations in the United States, United Kingdom, and elsewhere, educators and researchers—all have contributed to the development of flexible guidelines for stepfamilies to follow. For instance, researchers are finding that remarried spouses are in general concordance that stepfathers are expected to be friendly towards stepchildren, supportive of the mother, provide some financial support to children, but not to act as if they were the primary disciplinarian (e.g., Hofferth & Anderson, 2003). Of course, this description permits a great deal of latitude in how these behaviors are performed, and the studies on which the findings are based are seldom informed by stepchildren's perceptions. They do, however, imply that remarried couples, at least those in stepfather households, have some idea about how they expect stepparents to relate to stepchildren, a set of ideas that not coincidentally roughly concurs with suggestions that clinicians have been making for decades (e.g., Visher & Visher, 1982).

8. Western societies still stigmatize stepfamilies,

One of our predictions is that, paradoxical as it may seem, stepfamilies will continue to be stigmatized, even as they continue to increase in number and as more of them figure out ways to function well. Those who fear the demise of the traditional family are threatened by the emergence of other family forms. Signs that stepfamilies can potentially successfully provide positive environments for varied children are doubly threatening to these people.

9. Stepfamilies are more complex than we knew.

Clinicians have long written about structural diversity among stepfamilies, but researchers are just beginning to uncover exactly how complex stepfamilies are. For instance, rarely were stepgrandparents mentioned in the professional literature a decade ago; it was as if they did not exist. Once "discovered", a few studies were done that examined what adolescents thought of the quality of their relationships with their stepgrandparents. These studies did not differentiate the origin of these intergenerational relationships, because professionals had not yet realized the diverse types of stepgrandparent-stepgrandchild relationships (see Chapter 10 for discussion of the three pathways to stepgrandparenthood). Now that we have identified them, we expect that there will be studies in the next few years that will illuminate the dynamics of how these relationships develop and are maintained.

10. Researchers have broadened their approaches.

One of the biggest changes in the last decade is that the ways in which researchers think about stepfamilies have become more complex. Over time, we have seen a clear progression of how researchers have conceptualized stepfamilies, a progression that reflects more awareness of stepfamily diversity and greater caution in drawing widespread generalizations about stepfamilies. This evolution is not complete by any means, and most research does not yet reflect the best practices approach we describe here. However, as increasing numbers of scholars point out the necessity to think about stepfamilies and stepfamily relationships in more complex ways than in the past, it becomes harder for other researchers to ignore this necessity.

Early studies of stepfamilies treated them as if they were a monolithic, homogeneous group. Sometimes data were gathered from children, parents, and stepparents of both sexes and analyzed together as if there were no differences between these family positions. In many early studies, stepfamilies were compared to first marriage families and single-parent households, and these family forms also were conceptualized as if they were monolithic, uniform groupings. Remarriages generally were assumed to be second marriages, distinctions were not made between households and families, which meant that nonresidential stepfamily members were ignored, and data were often gathered from one household member only.

Gradually, researchers began to add covariates to their comparative studies—sometimes these were demographic variables that reflected the growing recognition that stepfamilies were not a uniform group, and sometimes the covariates were process variables. The inclusion of process variables reflected researchers' understandings that family structure alone was not enough to explain outcomes regarding individuals' well-being. Attempts were made to assess interactions between structure and process, and some researchers tried to determine whether process or structure variables were the best set of predictors of individuals' well-being. Sometimes variables were added to analytic models as controls or to remove extraneous variables.

The increased awareness of diversity has led to more fine-grained comparisons and clearer statements about individuals, relationships, and stepfamilies. A growing number of researchers are no longer willing to lump all stepfamilies in their data sets together. For instance, some researchers now are examining cohabiting stepfamilies, blended step-households, and other sub-groupings of stepfamilies in their studies. Consequently, a clearer picture is emerging of the dynamics of different types of stepfamily households.

This better picture goes beyond examinations of stepparents' gender and stepchildren's gender as classification markers for comparing types of stepfamilies. Researchers are determining that stepfamilies are not only diverse structurally, but that they vary in other ways—including process and how stepfamily members interact with each other. As a result, researchers approach their work more disparately than in the past. For instance, family scholars have known for decades that socialization of children is a bi-directional process. That is, children influence the behavior and development of adults who interact with them at the same time that adults are influencing them. However, most studies of children in stepfamilies have employed theories, proposed hypotheses, and used data analytic strategies that implicitly and/or explicitly assume that stepparent or stepfamily living effects on stepchildren are unidirectional. This has begun to change.

Some of the most important recent contributions have been from researchers using mixed methods designs. These researchers typically gather immense amounts of data from large enough groups of stepfamilies to be able to simultaneously conduct statistical tests of significance, while exploring relational dynamics in depth, often using qualitative approaches. These mixed methods studies usually employ multiple data collection techniques, and include more than one family member in the sample. Although expensive and difficult to do, these studies have yielded much useful process information, and we anticipate that there will be more of these studies in the future. Hetherington's longitudinal studies and Bray's longitudinal study are prime examples of mixed methods designs used to examine triads and entire stepfamilies.

For years we have called for more innovative methods to assess the effects of family structure on children (Coleman & Ganong, 1990; Coleman et al., 2000; Ganong & Coleman, 1994). Recently, other qualitative and quantitative researchers have made similar suggestions (e.g., Cherlin, 1999; MacDonald & DeMaris, 2002). Demographer Wendy Manning, for instance, has called for a shift from a variable oriented approach to a *person- centered approach* (Manning, 2002). "Family structure alone does not guarantee extreme negative or positive outcomes, but instead has to be considered in the context of the life of the child . . . to understand family structure researchers need to do more than simply report significant differences" (Manning, p. 143). Increasingly, researchers reflect an understanding that there can be significant differences among children's outcomes in stepfamilies and other family structures. Dropping out of school is an example. Significantly more stepchildren than children living with both parents drop out of school, but that does not mean it is a common occurrence for stepchildren. Also, researchers increasingly understand that there may not be significant differences at the aggregate level and yet family structure may interact with specific child characteristics to predict problems for certain types of stepchildren.

The qualitative, interpretive research paradigm is designed for person-centered approaches to research. In the past decade all of family social science has experienced a rapid rise in holistic, in-depth studies of individuals and families. The area of stepfamily relationships research is not an exception to this trend. These holistic methods are inductive approaches, grounded in data obtained directly from the members of stepfamilies. The increased use of qualitative designs has contributed to the recent volume of process research on stepfamilies, and because qualitative scholars are more able than quantitative researchers to examine more directly some of the clinicians' assumptions and assertions, these studies have helped bridge the division between clinicians and researchers. Qualitative researchers also have helped focus other scholars' attention on processes as critical phenomena to understand when studying the development, maintenance, and even dissolution of relationships.

We would be remiss to imply, however, that the increased focus over the last few years on relational processes and the dynamics of stepfamilies has been limited to qualitative investigators. Quantitative researchers, whether using large national data sets or smaller samples, have focused their energies on understanding stepfamily dynamics.

Prediction of more longitudinal studies is a safe one because there are a larger number of longitudinal data sets for researchers to access than ever before. Although not the main focus of the studies, many longitudinal data sets contain information about stepfamilies. These data sets, coupled with statistical innovations that allow researchers to analyze data from multiple family members, have already contributed greatly to our understanding of stepfamily relationships.

Nature/Nurture and Stepfamilies

In most areas of social science research, the old dichotomy of nature versus nurture has given way to interactional explanations that employ both genetic and environmental factors in explaining human behavior and interpersonal relationships. Stepfamily relationships would seem to be an ideal natural laboratory to investigate the intersections of genetics and culture, and, indeed, some researchers have developed studies that allow them to examine these intersections (e.g., Mekos et al., 1996). We anticipate more research programs in the future like the NEAD study led by David Reiss and Mavis Hetherington, who focused on siblings, half-siblings, and stepsiblings to examine the relative influences of shared environments and shared genes in children's development.

Model-building

Earlier, we remonstrated that consumers of scholarship want simple one-variable explanations for stepfamily phenomena that are often incredibly complicated. Instead, the trend may be shifting towards the development and testing of more complex models. For example, Cummings and Davies (2002) have proposed a promising process-oriented approach to the study of the effects of marital conflict on children. Their model encompasses individual, interpersonal (parent-child, marital, other family subsystems), external family influences, and changes over time. We think that models such as this one represent the next wave of research on stepfamilies.

We have been greatly encouraged for stepfamilies as we have delved into the rising volume of stepfamily research. There are far fewer of the "one-variable explanation" studies that filled the academic journals not long ago. Although many research questions remain to be asked and answered, the field of stepfamily scholarship is on the right track. Fifteen years ago we thought that researchers could learn a lot from clinicians about what to study and what questions to ask. There are many signs that this has taken place, On the other hand, clinical work on stepfamilies has changed very little in the last 15 years. It appears now that clinicians could benefit by paying more attention to what can be gleaned from recent research—so again, we encourage researchers and clinicians to mutually inform each other as they develop the next generation of stepfamily knowledge. Ultimately, stepfamilies are the ones who will benefit.

References

Ahrons, C. R. (2003). Personal Communication.

Ahrons, C. R. (1980). Divorce: A crisis of family transition and change. *Family Relations, 29*, 533–540.

Ahrons, C. R. (1981). Redefining the divorced family: A conceptual framework, *Social Work, 25*, 437–442.

Ahrons, C. R. (1983). Predictors of parental involvement postdivorce: mothers' and fathers' perceptions. *Journal of Divorce, 6*, 55–69.

Ahrons, C. R. (1994). *The good divorce*. New York: HarperCollins.

Ahrons, C. R., & Perlmutter, M. S. (1982). The relationship between former spouses: A fundamental subsystem in the remarriage family. In L. Messinger (Ed.), *Therapy with remarried families* (pp. 31–46). Rockville, MD: Aspen Systems Corp.

Ahrons, C. R., & Wallisch, K. (1987). Parenting in the binuclear family: Relationships between biological and stepparents. In K. Pasley & M. Ihinger-Tallman (Eds.), *Remarriage and stepparenting: Current research and theory* (pp. 225–256). New York: Guilford.

Ahrons, C. R., & Wallisch, L. S. (1987). The relationship between former spouses. In S. Duck (Ed.), *Dissolving Personal Relationships* (pp. 269–296). Beverly Hills: Sage.

Albrecht, S. L. (1979). Correlates of marital happiness among the remarried. *Journal of Marriage and the Family, 41*, 857–867.

Allan, G., Hawker, S., & Crow, G. (2004). Britain's changing families. In M. Coleman & L. Ganong (Eds.), *Handbook of contemporary families: Considering the past, contemplating the future* (pp. 302–316). Thousand Oaks, CA: Sage.

Allen, E. S., Baucom, D. H., Burnett, C. K., Epstein, N., & Rankin-Esquer, L. A. (2001). Decision-making power, autonomy, and communication in remarried spouses compared with first-married spouses. *Family Relations, 50*, 326–334.

Amato, P. R. (1987). Family processes in one-parent, stepparent, and intact families: The child's point of view. *Journal of Marriage and the Family, 49*, 327–337.

Amato, P. R. (1994). The implications of research findings on children in stepfamilies. In A. Booth & J. Dunn (Eds.), *Stepfamilies: Who benefits? Who does not?* (pp. 81–87). Hillsdale, NJ: Erlbaum.

Amato, P. R. (1996). Explaining the intergenerational transfer of divorce. *Journal of Marriage and the Family, 58*, 628–640.

Amato, P. R. (2000). The consequences of divorce for adults and children. *Journal of Marriage and the Family, 62*, 1269–1287.

Amato, P. R (2004) To have and have not: Marriage and divorce in the United States. In M. Coleman & L. Ganong (Eds.), *Handbook of contemporary families: Considering the past, contemplating the future* (pp. 265–281). Thousand Oaks, CA: Sage.

Amato, P. R., & Booth, A. (1996). A prospective study of parental divorce and parent-child relationships. *Journal of Marriage and the Family, 58,* 356–365.

Amato, P. R., & Booth, A. (1997). *A generation at risk.* Cambridge, MA: Harvard University Press

Amato, P., & Keith, B. (1991). Parental divorce and adult well-being: A meta-analysis. *Journal of Marriage and the Family, 53,* 43–58.

Amato, P. R., & Rogers, S. J. (1997). A longitudinal study of marital problems and subsequent divorce. *Journal of Marriage and the Family, 59,* 612–624.

Ambert, A. M. (1983). Separated women and remarriage behavior: A comparison of financially secure women and financially insecure women. *Journal of Divorce, 6,* 43–54.

Ambert, A. M. (1986). Being a stepparent. Live-in and visiting stepchildren *Journal of Marriage and the Family, 48,* 795–804.

Ambert, A. M. (1988). Relationships with former in-laws after divorce: A research note. *Journal of Marriage and the Family, 50,* 679–686.

Ambert, A. M. (1989). *Ex-spouses and new spouses: A study of relationships.* Greenwich, CN: JAI Press.

Anderson, E. A. (1999). Sibling, half-sibling, and stepsibling relationships in remarried families. In E. M. Hetherington, S. H. Henderson, & D. Reiss, in collaboration with E. R. Anderson, M. Bridges, R. W. Chan, G. M. Insabella, K. M. Jodl, J. E. Kim, A. S. Mitchell, T. G. O'Connor, M. J. Skaggs, & L. C. Taylor. *Adolescent siblings in stepfamilies: Family functioning and adolescent adjustment* (pp. 101–126). *Monographs of the Society for Research in Child Development, 64,* Malden, MA: Blackwell.

Anderson, E. R., Lindner, M. S., & Bennion, L. D. (1992). The effect of family relationships on adolescent development during family reorganization. In E. M. Hetherington & W. G. Clingempeel *Coping with marital transitions. Monographs of the Society for Research in Child Development, 57,* 178–199.

Anderson, E. R., & Rice, A. M. (1992). Sibling relationships during remarriage. *Monographs of the Society for Research in Child Development, 57,* 149–177.

Anderson, J., & White, G. (1986). An empirical investigation of interactive and relationship patterns in functional and dysfunctional nuclear families and stepfamilies. *Family Process, 25,* 407–422.

Anderson, K. (2000). The life histories of American stepfathers in evolutionary perspective. *Human Nature, 11,* 307–333.

Aquilino, W. S. (1991a). Predicting parents' experiences with coresident adult children. *Journal of Family Issues, 12,* 323–342.

Aquilino, W. S. (1991b). Family structure and home-leaving: A further specification of the relationship. *Journal of Marriage & the Family, 53,* 999–1010.

Aquilino, W. S. (1994). Impact of childhood family disruption on young adults' relationships with parents. *Journal of Marriage and the Family, 56,* 295–313.

Arditti, J. A. (1991). Child support noncompliance and divorced fathers: Rethinking the role of paternal involvement. *Journal of Divorce and Remarriage, 14,* 107–119.

Arditti, J. A. (1992). Factors related to custody, visitation, and child support for divorced fathers: An exploratory analysis. *Journal of Divorce and Remarriage, 17,* 23–41.

Arditti, J. A., & Allen, K. R. (1993). Understanding distressed fathers' perceptions of legal and relational inequities postdivorce. *Family and Conciliation Courts Review, 31,* 461–476.

Arditti, J. A., & Bickley, P. (1996). Fathers' involvement and mothers' parenting stress postdivorce. *Journal of Divorce & Remarriage, 26,* 1–23.

Arditti, J. A., & Keith, T. (1993). Visitation frequency, child support payment, and the father-child relationship postdivorce. *Journal of Marriage and the Family, 55,* 699–712.

Arditti, J. A., & Kelly, M. (1994) Fathers perspectives of their co-parental relationships postdivorce. *Family Relations, 43*, 61–67.

Arendell, T. (1992). After divorce: Investigations into father absence. *Gender & Society, 6*, 562–586.

Arendell, T. (1995). Fathers and divorce. Thousand Oaks, CA: Sage.

Astone, N. M., & Washington, M L (1994). The association between grandparental coresidence and adolescent childbearing. *Journal of Family Issues, 15*, 574–589.

Axinn, W. G., & Thornton, A. (1993). Mothers, children, and cohabitation: The intergenerational effects of attitudes and behavior. *American Sociological Review, 58*, 233–246.

Axinn, W. G., & Thornton, A. (1996). The influence of parents' marital dissolutions on children's attitudes toward family formation. *Demography, 33*, 66–81.

Bank, S. P., & Kahn, M. D. (1997). *The sibling bond* New York· Basic Books

Banker, B. S., & Gaertner, S. L. (1996). Achieving stepfamily harmony: An intergroup-relations approach. *Journal of Family Psychology, 12*, 310–325.

Barber, B. (1994). Cultural, family, and personal contexts of parent-adolescent conflict. *Journal of Marriage and the Family, 56*, 375–386.

Barber, B. L., & Lyons, J. M. (1994). Family processes and adolescent adjustment in intact and remarried families. *Journal of Youth and Adolescence, 23*, 421–436.

Batchelder, J., Dimmock, B, & Smith, D. (1994). *Understanding stepfamilies: What can be learned from callers to the stepfamily telephone counseling service.* London: Stepfamily Publications.

Batchelder, M. L. (1995). Adolescents' adaptation to structural changes in family relationships with parental divorce: A combinatorial model. In T. Kindermann & J. Valsiner (Eds.), *Development of person-context relations* (pp. 165–203) Hillsdale, NJ: Erlbaum.

Bateson, M. C. (1990). *Composing a life.* New York: Plume.

Baucom, D., & Epstein, N. (1990). *Cognitive-behavioral marital therapy.* New York: Brunner/ Mazel.

Bauserman, R. (2002). Child adjustment in joint-custody versus sole-custody arrangements: A meta-analytic review, *Journal of Family Psychology, 16*, 91–102.

Baxter, L. A., Braithwaite, D. O., & Nicholson, J. (1999). Turning points in the development of blended families. *Journal of Social and Personal Relationships, 16*, 291–313.

Becker, G. S., Landes, E. M., & Michael, R. T. (1977). An economic analysis of marital instability. *Journal of Political Economy, 85*, 1141–1187.

Beer, W. (1988). *Relative strangers: Studies of stepfamily processes.* Totowa, NJ: Littlefield, Adams, & Co.

Beer, W. (1991). *American stepfamilies.* New Brunswick, NJ: Transaction Publishers.

Bengtson, V. L., & Roberts, R. E. L. (1991). Intergenerational solidarity in aging families: An example of formal theory construction. *Journal of Marriage and the Family, 53*, 856–870.

Berger, R. (1995). Three types of stepfamilies. *Journal of Divorce and Remarriage, 24*, 35–50.

Berger, R. (1998). The experience and issues of gay stepfamilies. *Journal of Divorce and Remarriage, 29*, 93–102.

Berger, R. (2000). Stepfamilies in cultural context. *Journal of Divorce and Remarriage, 33*, 111–130.

Bernard, J. (1956). *Remarriage: A study of marriage.* New York: Russel & Russel.

Bernard, J. (1972). *The future of marriage.* New York: Bantam.

Bernard, J. (1981). The divorce myth. *Personnel and Guidance Journal, 60*, 67–71.

Bernhardt, E. M., & Goldscheider, F. K. (2001). Men, resources, and family living: The determinants of union and parental status in the United States and Sweden. *Journal of Marriage and Family, 63*, 793–803.

Bernstein, A. (1989). *Yours, mine and ours.* New York: Scribner's.

Bernstein, A. (1994). Women in stepfamilies: The fairy godmother, the wicked witch, and Cinderella reconstructed. In M. Mirkin (Ed.), *Women in context: Toward a feminist reconstruction of psychotherapy* (pp. 188–213). New York: Guilford.

Bernstein, A. (1997). Stepfamilies from siblings' perspectives In I. Levin & M. Sussman (Eds.), *Stepfamilies: History, research, and policy* (pp. 153–176). New York: Haworth.

Bernstein, A. (1999). Reconstructing the Brothers Grimm: New tales of stepfamily life. *Family Process, 38,* 415–429.

Biblarz, T. J., Raftery, A. E., & Bucur, A. (1997) Family structure and social mobility. *Social Forces, 75,* 1319–1339.

Bielenberg, L. T. (1991). A task-centered preventive group approach to create cohesion in the new stepfamily: A preliminary evaluation. *Research on Social Work Practice, 1,* 416–433.

Black, L. E., Eastwood, M. M., Sprenkle, D. H , & Smith, E. (1991). An exploratory analysis of the construct of Leavers versus left as it relates to Levinger's social exchange theory of attractions, barriers, and alternative attractions. *Journal of Divorce, 15.* 127–139

Blumstein, P., & Schwartz, P. (1983). *American couples: Money, work, sex.* New York· Morrow.

Bogenscheider, K. (1997). Parental involvement in adolescent schooling A proximal process with transcontextual validity. *Journal of Marriage and the Family, 59,* 718–733.

Bograd, R., & Spilka, B. (1996). Self-disclosure and marital satisfaction in mid-life and late-life remarriages. *International Journal of Aging & Human Development, 42,* 161–172.

Bohannan, P. (1970). Divorce chains, households of remarriage, and multiple divorcers. In P. Bohannan (Ed.), *Divorce and after.* (pp. 347–362). New York: Doubleday & Co.

Bohannan, P. (1984). Stepparenthood: A new and old experience. In R. S. Cohen, B. J. Cohler, & S. H. Weissman (Eds.), *Parenthood: A psychodynamic interpretation* (pp. 204–219). New York: Guilford.

Booth, A., & Dunn, J. (Eds.). (1994). *Stepfamilies: Who benefits? Who does not?* Hillsdale, NJ: Erlbaum.

Booth, A., & Edwards, J. N. (1992). Starting over: Why remarriages are more unstable. *Journal of Family Issues, 13,* 179–194.

Booth, A., Brinkerhoff, D., & White, L. (1984). The impact of parental divorce on courtship. *Journal of Marriage and the Family, 46,* 85–94.

Boss, P. (1980). Normative family stress: Family boundary changes across the life-span. *Family Relations, 29,* 445–450.

Bowerman, C. E., & Irish, D. (1962). Some relationships of stepchildren to their parents. *Marriage and Family Living, 24,* 113–121.

Bowman, M. E., & Ahrons, C. R. (1985). Impact of legal custody status on fathers' parenting post-divorce. *Journal of Marriage and the Family 47,* 481–488.

Bozett, F. W. (Ed.). (1987). *Gay and lesbian parents.* NY: Praeger.

Bradbury, T. N., Fincham, F. D., & Beach, S. (2000). Research on the nature and determinants of marital satisfaction: A decade in review. *Journal of Marriage and the Family, 62,* 964–980.

Braithwaite, D., Olson, L. N., Golish, T. D., Soukop, C., & Turman, P. (2001). "Becoming a family": Developmental processes represented in blended family discourse. *Journal of Applied Communication Research, 29,* 221–247.

Brakman, S. V. (1995). Filial responsibility and decision-making. In L. B. McCullough, & N. L. Wilson (Eds.), *Long-term care decisions: Ethical and conceptual dimensions* (pp. 181–196). Baltimore: Johns Hopkins University Press.

Bramlett, M. D., & Mosher, W. D. (2001). *First marriage dissolution, divorce, and remarriage*: United States. Center for Disease Control, Advance Data No. 323. Department of Health and Human Services. Hyattsville, MD: National Center for Health Statistics.

Braver, S. L., & Griffin, W. A. (2000). Engaging fathers in the post-divorce family. *Marriage and Family Review, 29,* 247–267.

Braver, S. L., Wolchik, S. A., Sandler, I. N., & Sheets, V. L. (1993). A social exchange model of nonresidential parent involvement. In C. E. Depner & J. H. Bray (Eds.), *Nonresidential parenting: New vistas in family living* (pp. 87–108). Newbury Park, CA: Sage.

Braverman, L (1988). Beyond the myth of motherhood. In M. McGoldrick & C. Anderson (Eds.). *Women in families: A framework for family therapy* (pp. 227–243). New York: W. W. Norton.

Bray, J. (1988). Children's development during early remarriage. In E. M. Hetherington & J. Arasteh (Eds.), *Impact of divorce, single-parenting and stepparenting on children* (pp. 279–298). Hilldale, NJ: Erlbaum.

Bray, J. H. (1992). Family relationships and children's adjustment in clinical and nonclinical stepfather families. *Journal of Family Psychology, 6*, 60–68.

Bray, J. (1995). Family oriented treatment of stepfamilies. In R. Mikesell, D. D. Lusterman, & S. McDaniel (Eds.), *Integrating family therapy* (pp. 125–140). Washington, DC: American Psychological Association.

Bray, J H (1999) From marriage to remarriage and beyond Findings from the Developmental Issues in Stepfamilies Research Project. In E. M. Hetherington (Ed.), *Coping with divorce, single parenting and remarriage. A risk and resiliency approach* (pp. 253–271). Mahwah, NJ: Erlbaum.

Bray, J., & Berger, S. (1990). Noncustodial father and paternal grandparent relationships in stepfamilies *Family Relations, 39*, 414–419.

Bray, J. H., & Berger, S. H. (1993). Developmental issues in stepfamilies research project. Family relationships and parent-child interactions. *Journal of Family Psychology, 7*, 76–90.

Bray, J., Berger, S. H., Silverblatt, A. H., & Hollier, A. (1987). Family process and organization during early remarriage: A preliminary analysis. In J. P. Vincent (Ed.), *Advances in family intervention, assessment, and theory* (pp. 253–279). Greenwich, CT: JAI Press.

Bray, J., & Kelly, J. (1998). *Stepfamilies: Love, marriage, and parenting in the first decade.* New York: Broadway.

Brody, G. H., Neubaum, E., & Forehand, R.(1988). Serial marriage: A heuristic analysis of an emerging family form. Psychological Bulletin, 103, 211–222.

Bronstein, P., Stoll, M. F., Clauson, J., Abrams, C. L., & Briones, M. (1994). Fathering after separation or divorce: Factors predicting children's adjustment. *Family Relations, 43*, 469–479.

Brown, A. C., Green, R.-J., & Druckman, J. (1990). A comparison of stepfamilies with and without child-focused problems. *American Journal of Orthopsychiatry, 60*, 556–566.

Brown, S., & Booth, A. (1996). Cohabitation versus marriage: A comparison of relationship quality. *Journal of Marriage and the Family, 58*, 668–678.

Browning, S. W. (1994). Treating stepfamilies: Alternatives to traditional family therapy. In K. Pasley & M. Ihinger-Tallman (Eds.), *Stepparenting: Issues in theory, research, and practice* (pp. 175–198). Westport, CT: Greenwood.

Bryan, H., Ganong, L., Coleman, M., & Bryan, L. (1985). Counselors' perceptions of stepparents and stepchildren. *Journal of Counseling Psychology, 32*, 279–282.

Bryan, L., Coleman, M., Ganong, L., & Bryan, S. H. (1986). Person perception: Family structure as a cue for stereotyping. *Journal of Marriage and the Family, 48*, 169–174.

Bryant, A. S., & Demian. (1994). Relationship characteristics of gay and lesbian couples: Findings from a national survey. *Journal of Gay and Lesbian Social Services, 1*, 101–117.

Buchanan, C. M., Maccoby, E. E., & Dornbusch, S. M. (1996). *Adolescents after divorce.* Cambridge, MA: Harvard University Press.

Buckle, L., Gallup, G. G., & Rodd, Z. A. (1996). Marriage as a reproductive contract: Patterns of marriage, divorce, and remarriage. *Ethology and Sociobiology, 17*, 363–377.

Buehler, C. (1987). Initiator status and the divorce transition. *Family Relations, 36*, 82–86.

Bulcroft, K. A., Bulcroft, R. A. (1991). The timing of divorce: effects on parent-child relationships in later life. *Research on Aging, 13*, 226–243.

Bulcroft, K., Bulcroft, R., Hatch, L., & Borgatta, E. (1989). Antecedents and consequences of remarriage in later life. *Research on Aging, 11*, 82–106.

Bulcroft, R., Carmody, D., & Bulcroft, K. (1998). Family structure and patterns of independence giving to adolescents. *Journal of Family Issues, 19*, 404–435.

Bumpass, L. (1984) Some characteristics of children's second families. *American Journal of Sociology, 90*, 608–623

Bumpass, L., & Sweet, J. (1989). *National estimates of cohabitation: Cohort levels and union stability.* NSFH Working Paper No. 2, Center for Demography and Ecology, University of Wisconsin, Madison.

Bumpass, L., & Raley, R K. (1995). Redefining single-parent families: Cohabitation and changing family realities. *Demography, 32*, 97–109.

Bumpass, L., Raley, R K , & Sweet, J. (1995). The changing character of stepfamilies: Implications of cohabitation and nonmarital childbearing. *Demography, 32*, 425–436.

Bumpass, L. L., & Lu, H. (2000). Trends in cohabitation and implications for children's family contexts in the United States. *Population Studies, 54*, 19–41

Bumpass, L. L., Sweet, J A , & Cherlin, A (1991) The role of cohabitation in declining rates of marriage. *Journal of Marriage & the Family, 53*, 913–927.

Bumpass, L., Sweet, J., & Castro Martin, T. (1990). Changing patterns of remarriage. *Journal of Marriage and the Family, 52*, 747–756.

Burgoyne, J., & Clark, D. (1984). *Making a go of it: A study of stepfamilies in Sheffield.* Boston: Routledge & Kegan

Burgoyne, C. B., & Morison, V. (1997). Money in remarriage: Keeping things simple and separate. *Sociological Review, 45*, 363–395.

Burks, V. K., Lund, D. A., Gregg, C. H., & Bluhm, H. P. (1988) Bereavement and remarriage for older adults. *Death Studies, 12*, 51–60.

Burt, M. (Ed.). (1989). *Stepfamilies stepping ahead.* Lincoln, NE: Stepfamily Association of America.

Burt, M., & Burt, R. (1996). *Stepfamilies: The step by step model of brief therapy.* New York: Brunner/Mazel.

Byrd, A., & Smith, R. (1988). A qualitative analysis of the decision to remarry using Gilligan's ethic of care. *Journal of Divorce, 11*, 87–102.

Capaldi, D. M., & Patterson, G. R. (1991). Relation of parental transitions to boys' adjustment problems: I. A linear hypothesis. II. Mothers at risk for transitions and unskilled parenting. *Developmental Psychology, 27*, 489–504.

Carter, B., & McGoldrick, M. (Eds.). (1998). *The expanded family life cycle: Individual, family and social perspectives*, (3rd ed.), Boston: Allyn & Bacon.

Carter, E. A. (1988). Counseling stepfamilies effectively. *Behavior Today, 19*, 1–2.

Cartwright, C. (2003). Therapists' perceptions of bioparent-child relationships in stepfamilies: What hurt? What helps? *Journal of Divorce & Remarriage, 38(3/4)*, 147–166.

Casper, L. M., & Bianchi, S. M. (2002). *Continuity and change in the American family.* Thousand Oaks, CA: Sage.

Castro Martin, T., & Bumpass, L. (1989). Recent trends in marital disruption. *Demography, 26*, 37–51.

Cate, R. M., & Lloyd, S. A. (1992). *Courtship.* Newbury Park: Sage.

Ceglian, C. P., & Gardner, S. (1999). Attachment style: A risk for multiple marriages. *Journal of Divorce and Remarriage, 31*, 125–139.

Ceglian, C. P., & Gardner, S. (2000). Attachment style and the "wicked stepmother" spiral. *Journal of Divorce & Remarriage, 34*, 111–129.

Chandler, J. (1991). *Women without husbands: An exploration of the margins of marriage.* New York: St. Martin's.

Chase-Lansdale, P. L., Cherlin, A. J., & Kiernan, K. E. (1995). The long-term effects of parental divorce on the mental health of young adults: A developmental perspective. *Child Development, 66*, 1614–1634.

Cheal, D. J. (1988). Theories of serial flow in intergenerational transfers. *International Journal of Aging and Human Development, 26*, 261–273.

Cherlin, A. J., & Furstenberg, F. F. (1994) Stepfamilies in the United States: A reconsideration. *Annual Review of Sociology, 20*, 359–381.

Cherlin, A. (1978). Remarriage as an incomplete institution. *American Journal of Sociology, 84*, 634–650.

Cherlin, A. J. (1999). *Going to extremes: Family structure, children's well-being, and social science.* Demography 36, 421–428.

Cherlin, A., & Furstenberg, F. F. (1986). Grandparents and family crisis. *American Society on Aging, 10*, 26–28.

Chevan, A. (1996). As cheaply as one: Cohabitation in the older population. *Journal of Marriage and the Family, 58*, 656–667.

Chipperfield, J. G., & Havens, B. (2001) Gender differences in the relationship between marital status transitions and life satisfaction in later life *Journal of Gerontology: Psychological Sciences, 56B*, 176–186.

Church, E. (1999). Who are the people in your family? Stepmothers' diverse notions of kinship. *Journal of Divorce and Remarriage, 31*, 83–105.

Cicirelli, V. (1991). Attachment theory in old age. Protection of the attached figure. In K. Pillemer & K. McCartney (Eds.), *Parent-child relations throughout life* (pp. 25–42). Hillsdale, NJ: Erlbaum.

Cissna, K. N., Cox, D. E., & Bochner, A. P. (1990). The dialectic of marital and parental relationships within the stepfamily. *Communication Monographs, 57*, 44–61.

Clark, R. & Nelson, S. (2000, March). *Beyond the two-parent family.* Paper presented at the annual meeting of the Population Association of America, Los Angeles, CA.

Clarke, S. C. (1995). Advance report of final marriage statistics, 1989 and 1990. *Monthly Vital Statistics Report, 43*(12), supple. Hyattsville, Maryland: National Center for Health Statistics.

Clawson, J., & Ganong, L. (2002). Adult stepchildren's obligations to older stepparents. *Journal of Family Nursing, 8*, 50–73.

Claxton-Oldfield, S. (2000). Deconstructing the myth of the wicked stepparent. *Marriage and Family Review, 30*, 51–58.

Claxton-Oldfield, S., Goodyear, C., Parsons, T., & Claxton-Oldfield, J. (2002). Some possible implications of negative stepfather stereotypes. *Journal of Divorce and Remarriage, 36*, 77–88.

Claxton-Oldfield, S., & Kavanagh, P. (1999). The effect of stepfamily status on impressions of children's report card information. Journal of *Divorce and Remarriage, 32*, 145–153.

Claxton-Oldfield, S., & Voyer, S. (2001). Young adults' perceptions of stepchildren. *Journal of Divorce & Remarriage, 35*, 107–114.

Cleveland, W. P., & Gianturco, D. T. (1976). Remarriage probability after widowhood: A retrospective method. *Journal of Gerontology, 31*, 99–103.

Clingempeel, W. G. (1981). Quasi-kin relationships and marital quality. *Journal of Personality and Social Psychology, 41*, 890–901.

Clingempeel, W. G., & Brand, E. (1985). Quasi-kin relationships, structural complexity, and marital quality in stepfamilies: A replication, extension, and clinical implications. *Family Relations, 34*, 401–409.

Clingempeel, W. G., & Brand-Clingempeel, U. (2004). Pathogenic conflict families and children: What we know, what we need to know. In M. Coleman & L. Ganong (Eds.), *Handbook of contemporary families: Considering the past, contemplating the future* (pp. 244–262). Thousand Oaks, CA: Sage.

Clingempeel, W. G., Brand, E., & Segal, S. (1987). A multilevel-multivariable-developmental perspective for future research on stepfamilies. In K. Pasley & M. Ihinger-Tallman (Eds.), *Remarriage and stepparenting today: Research and theory.* (pp. 65–93). New York: Guilford Press.

Clingempeel, W. G., Colyar, J. J., Brand, E., & Hetherington. E. M. (1992) Children's relationships with maternal grandparents: A longitudinal study of family structure and pubertal status effects. *Child Development, 63*, 1404–1422.

Clingempeel, W. G., Flesher, M., & Brand, E. (1988). Research on stepfamilies: Paradigmatic constraints and alternative proposals. In J. P. Vincent (Ed.), *Advances in family intervention: Assessment and theory.* Greenwich, CT: JAI Press.

Clingempeel, W. G., & Segal, S. (1986). Stepparent-stepchild relationships and the psychological adjustment of children in stepmother and stepfather families *Child Development, 57*, 474–484.

Clunis, D. M., & Green, G. D. (1993). *Lesbian couples.* Seattle, WA: Seattle Press.

Coale Lewis, H. C. (1985). Family therapy with stepfamilies. *Journal of Strategic and Systemic Therapies, 4*, 13–23.

Cohen J. (1969). *Statistical power analysis for behavioral sciences.* New York Academic Press

Coleman, M., Fine, M., Ganong, L., Downs, K , & Pauk, N. (2001). When you're not the Brady Bunch: Identifying perceived conflicts and resolution strategies in stepfamilies. *Personal Relationships, 8*, 55–73.

Coleman, M., & Ganong, L. (1984). Effect of family structure on family attitudes and expectations. *Family Relations, 33*, 425–432.

Coleman, M., & Ganong, L. (1985). Remarriage myths: Implications for the helping professions. *Journal of Counseling & Development, 64*, 116–120.

Coleman, M., & Ganong, L. (1987). Marital conflict in stepfamilies: Effects on children. *Youth and Society, 19*, 151–172.

Coleman, M., & Ganong, L. (1988). *Bibliotherapy with stepchildren.* Springfield, IL: Thomas.

Coleman, M., & Ganong, L. (1989). Financial management in stepfamilies. *Lifestyles: Family and Economic Issues, 10*, 217–232.

Coleman, M., & Ganong, L. (1990a). Remarriage and stepfamily research in the '80s: New interest in an old family form. *Journal of Marriage and the Family, 52*, 925–940.

Coleman, M. & Ganong, L. (1990b). Using literature in working with adolescents and children in stepfamilies. *Journal of Counseling and Development, 68*, 327–331.

Coleman, M., & Ganong, L. (1995). Insiders' and outsiders' beliefs about stepfamilies: Assessment and implications for practice. In D. Huntley (Ed.), *Understanding stepfamilies: Implications for assessment and treatment* (pp. 101–112). Alexandria, VA: American Counseling Association Press.

Coleman, M., & Ganong, L. (1997). Stepfamilies from the stepfamily's perspective. *Marriage and Family Review, 26*,107–122.

Coleman, M., & Ganong, L. (1998). Attitudes toward men's intergenerational financial obligations to older and younger male family members following divorce. *Personal Relationships, 5*, 293–309.

Coleman, M., & Ganong, L. (2000). Changing families, changing responsibilities? *National Forum, 60*, 34–37.

Coleman, M., Ganong, L., & Cable, S. (1997).Perceptions of stepparents: An examination of the incomplete institutionalization and social stigma hypotheses. *Journal of Divorce and Remarriage, 26*, 25–48.

Coleman, M., Ganong, L., & Fine, M. (2000). Reinvestigating remarriage: Another decade of progress. *Journal of Marriage and the Family, 62*, 1288–1307.

Coleman, M., Ganong, L., & Fine, M. (in press). Communication in stepfamilies. In A. Vangilisti (Ed.), *Handbook of family communication.* Mahwah, NJ: Erlbaum.

Coleman, M., Ganong, L., & Gingrich, R. (1985). Stepfamily strengths: A review of popular literature. *Family Relations, 34*, 583–589.

Coleman, M., Ganong, L., & Goodwin, C. (1994). The presentation of stepfamilies in marriage and family textbooks: A reexamination. *Family Relations, 43*, 289–297.

Coleman, M., Ganong, L., & Henry, J. (1984). What teachers should know about stepfamilies *Childhood Education, 60*, 306–309.

Coleman, M., Ganong, L., & Weaver, S. (2001). Maintenance and enhancement in remarried families. In J. Harvey & A. Wenzel (Eds.), *Close romantic relationships: Maintenance and enhancement* (pp. 255–276). Hillsdale, NJ: Erlbaum.

Coley, R. L. (1998). Children's socialization experiences and functioning in single-mother households: The importance of fathers and other men. *Child Development, 69*, 219–230.

Collins, S. (1995). Ideological assumptions in the lives of stepchildren. In J. Brannen & M. O'Brien (Eds.), *Childhood and parenthood* (pp. 79–92). London, UK: University of London.

Coltrane, S. (2004). Fathering: Paradoxes, contradictions, and dilemmas. In M. Coleman & L Ganong (Eds.), *Handbook of contemporary families: Considering the past, contemplating the future* (pp. 224–243). Thousand Oaks, CA. Sage.

Comings, D. E., Muhleman, D., Johnson, J. P, & MacMurray, J. P (2002). Parent-daughter transmission of the androgen receptor gene as an explanation of the effect of father absence on age of menarche. *Child Development, 73*, 1046–1051.

Cooksey, E. C., & Craig, P. H. (1998). Parenting from a distance: The effects of paternal characteristics on contact between nonresidential fathers and their children. *Demography, 35*, 187–200

Cooksey, E. C., & Fondell, M. M. (1996). Spending time with his kids: Effects of family structure on fathers' and children' lives. *Journal of Marriage and the Family, 58*, 693–707.

Cooney, T. M. (1994). Young adults' relations with parents: The influence of recent parental divorce. *Journal of Marriage and the Family, 56*, 45–56.

Cooney, T. M., Hutchinson, M. K., & Leather, D. M. (1995). Surviving the breakup? Predictors of parent-adult child relations after parental divorce. *Family Relations, 44*, 153–161.

Cooney, T. M., & Uhlenberg, P. (1990). The role of divorce in men's relations with their adult children after mid-life. *Journal of Marriage and the Family, 52*, 677–688.

Coontz, S. (1997). *The way we really are: Coming to terms with America's changing families.* New York: Basic.

Cornman, J. M., & Kingson, E. R. (1996). Trends, issues, perspectives, and values for the aging of the baby boom cohorts. *The Gerontologis, 36*, 15–26.

Coughlin, C. & Vuchinich, S. (1996). Family experience in preadolescence and the development of male delinquency. *Journal of Marriage and the Family, 58*, 491–501.

Counts, R. M. (1992). Second and third divorces: The flood to come. *Journal of Divorce and Remarriage, 17*, 193–200.

Crane, D. (1972). *Invisible colleges.* Chicago: University of Chicago .

Crohn, H., Sager, C. J., Rodstein, E., Brown, H. S., Walker, L., & Beir, J. (1981). Understanding and treating the child in the remarried family. In I. R. Stuart & L. E. Abt (Eds.), *Children of separation and divorce: Management and treatment* (pp. 293–317). New York: Van Nostrand Reinhold Co.

Crosbie-Burnett, M. (1984). The centrality of the step relationship: A challenge to family theory and practice. *Family Relations, 33*, 459–464.

Crosbie-Burnett, M. (1988). Impact of joint versus maternal legal custody, sex and age of adolescent, and family structure complexity on adolescent in remarried families. *Conciliation Courts Review, 26*, 47–52.

Crosbie-Burnett, M. (1989). Impact of custody arrangement and family structure on remarriage. *Journal of Divorce, 13*, 1–16.

Crosbie-Burnett, M. (1994). The interface between stepparent families and schools: Research, theory, policy, and practice. In K. Pasley & M. Ihinger-Tallman (Eds.), *Stepfamilies: Current issues in theory, research, and practice* (pp. 199–216). Westport, CT: Greenwood.

Crosbie-Burnett, M., & Giles-Sims, J. (1991). Marital power in stepfather families: A test of normative-resource theory. *Journal of Family Psychology, 4*, 484–496.

Crosbie-Burnett. M., & Giles-Sims. J. (1994). Adolescent adjustment and stepparenting styles *Family Relations, 43*, 394–399.

Crosbie-Burnett, M., & Helmbrecht, L. (1993). A descriptive empirical study of gay male stepfamilies. *Family Relations, 42*, 256–262.

Cuber, J F., & Harroff, P. B. (1965). *The significant Americans: A study of sexual behavior among the affluent* New York: Appleton-Century-Crofts.

Cummings, E. M., & Davies, P. (1994). *Child and marital conflict: The impact of family dispute and resolution.* New York: Guilford.

Dainton, M (1993). The myths and misconceptions of the stepmother identity: Descriptions and prescriptions for identity management. *Family Relations, 42*, 93–98.

Dalton, S E., & Bielby, D.D (2000). That's our kind of constellation: Lesbian mothers negotiate institutionalized understandings of gender within the family *Gender & Society, 14*, 36–61.

Bell, R., & Daly, J. (1996). The affinity-seeking function of communication. *Communication Monographs, 51*, 91–115.

Daly, J. A., & Kreiser, P. O. (1994). Affinity seeking. In J. A. Daly & J. M. Wiemann (Eds.), *Strategic interpersonal communication* (pp. 109–134). Hillsdale, NJ: Lawrence Erlbaum.

Daly, M., & Wilson, M. (1980). Discriminative parental solicitude: A biological perspective. *Journal of Marriage and the Family, 42*, 277–288.

Daly, M., & Wilson, M. (1996). Violence against stepchildren. *Current Directions in Psychological Science, 5*, 77–80.

Daly, M., & Wilson, M. (1998), *The truth about Cinderella: A Darwinian view.* New Haven, CT: Yale.

Daly, M., & Wilson, M. (2001). An assessment of some proposed exceptions to the phenomena of nepotistic discrimination against stepchildren. *Annales Zoologici Fennici, 38*, 287–296.

Daly, M., Salmon, C., & Wilson, M. (1997). Kinship: The conceptual hole in psychological studies of social cognition and close relationships (pp. 265–296). In J. A. Simpson & D. T. Kenrick (Eds.), *Evolutionary social psychology.* Mahweh, NJ: Erlbaum.

Daly, M., & Wilson, M. (1987). Risk of maltreatment of children living with stepparents, R. J. Gelles & J. B. Lancaster, *Child abuse and neglect: Biosocial dimensions* (pp. 215–232). New York: Aldine de Gruyter.

Davis, E. C., & Friel, L. V. (2001). Adolescent sexuality: Disentangling the effects of family structure and family context. *Journal of Marriage and the Family, 63*, 669–681.

Day, R. D., & Bahr, S. J. (1986). Income changes following divorce and remarriage. *Journal of Divorce, 9*, 75–88.

Deal, J. E., Stanley Hagan, M., & Anderson, J. C. (1992). The marital relationships in remarried families. In E. M. Hetherington & W. G. Clingempeel, *Coping with Marital transitions* (pp. 73–93). *Monographs of the Society for Research in Child Development, 57*, 73–93.

Dean, G., & Gurak, D. T. (1978). Marital homogamy the second time around. *Journal of Marriage and the Family, 40*, 559–570.

De'Ath, E. (1997). Stepfamily policy from the perspective of a stepfamily organization. In I. Levin & M. Sussman (Eds.), *Stepfamilies: History, research, and policy* (pp. 265–280). New York: Haworth.

DeLuccie, M. (1995). Mothers as gatekeepers: A model of maternal mediators of father involvement. *Journal of Genetic Psychology, 156*, 115–131.

Demo, D. H., & Acock, A. C. (1993). Family diversity and the division of domestic labor: How much have things really changed? *Family Relations, 42*, 323–331.

Doherty, W., Kouneski, E. F., & Erickson, M. (1998). Responsible fathering: An overview and conceptual framework. *Journal of Marriage and the Family, 60*, 277–292.

Doherty, W., & Needle, R. (1991). Psychological adjustment and substance use among adolescents before and after a parental divorce. *Child Development, 62*, 328–337.

Dornbusch, S. M., Ritter, P. L., Leiderman, P. H., Roberts, D. F., & Fraleigh, M. J. (1987). The relation of parenting style to adolescent school performance. *Child Development, 58*, 1244–1257.

Downey, D. B. (1995). Understanding academic achievement among children in stephouseholds: The role of parental resources, sex of stepparent, and sex of child. *Social Forces, 73*, 875–894.

Doyle, K. W., Wolchik, S. A., & Dawson-McClure, S. (2002). Development of the stepfamily events profile. *Journal of Family Psychology, 16*, 128–143.

Drew, L. A., & Smith, P. K. (1999). The impact of parental separation divorce on grandparent-grandchild relationships. *International Journal of Aging & Human Development, 48*, 191–216.

Duberman, L. (1975). *The reconstituted family.* Chicago: Nelson-Hall.

Dudley, J. R. (1991). Increasing our understanding of divorced fathers who have infrequent contact with their children. *Family Relations, 4*, 279–285.

Dudley, J. R. (1996). Noncustodial fathers speak about their parental role. *Family and Conciliation Courts Review, 34*, 410–426

Duncan, S. F., & Brown, G. (1992) RENEW· A program for building remarried family strengths *Families in Society, 14*, 149–158.

Dunn, J., Davies, L. C., O'Connor, T. G., & Sturgess, W. (2000). Parents' and partners' life course and family experiences: Links with parent-child relationships in different family settings. *Journal of Child Psychology and Psychiatry, 41*, 955–968.

Dunn, J., Davies, L. C., O'Connor, T G., & Sturgess, W. (2001). Family lives and friendships: The perspectives of children in step-, single-parent, and nonstep families. *Journal of Family Psychology, 15*, 272–287.

Dunn, J., Deater-Deckard, K., Pickering, K I., O'Connor, T., Golding, J., & the ALSPAC Study Team. (1998). Children's adjustment and pro-social behaviour in step-single and non-step family settings: Findings from a community study, *Journal of Child Psychology and Psychiatry, 39*, 1083–1095.

Dunn, J., Deater-Deckard, K., Pickering, KI. Beveridge, M. & the ALSPAC Study Team. (1999). Siblings, parents and partners: Family relationships within a longitudinal community study. *Journal of Child Psychology and Psychiatry, 40*, 1025–1037.

Duran-Aydintug, C., & Ihinger-Tallman, M. (1995). Law and stepfamilies. *Marriage & Family Review, 21*, 169–192.

Duran-Aydintug, C. (1993). Relationships with former in-laws: Normative guidelines and actual behavior. *Journal of Divorce and Remarriage, 19*, 69–81.

Edwards, R., Gillies, V., & McCarthy, J. R. (1999). Biological parents and social families: Legal discourses and everyday understandings of the position of step-parents. *International Journal of Law, Policy & the Family, 13*, 78–105.

Elkind, D. (1967). Egocentrism in adolescence. *Child Development, 38*, 1025–1034.

Ellis, B. J., & Garber, J. (2000). Psychosocial antecedents of variation in girls' pubertal timing: Maternal depression, stepfather presence, and marital and family stress. *Child Development, 71*, 485–501.

Emery, R. E. (1999). *Marriage, divorce, and children's adjustment* (2nd ed.). Beverly Hills, CA: Sage.

Erera, P. I., & Fredriksen, K. (1999). Lesbian stepfamilies: A unique family structure. *Families in Society, 80*, 263–270.

Erera-Weatherly, P. I. (1996). On becoming a stepparent: Factors associated with the adoption of alternative stepparenting styles. *Journal of Divorce and Remarriage, 25*, 155–174.

Erickson, R. J. (1993). Reconceptualizing family work: The effect of emotion work on perceptions of marital quality. *Journal of Marriage and the Family, 55*, 888–900.

Espinoza, R., & Newman, Y. (1979). *Stepparenting.* (DHEW Publication #48–579). Rockville, MD: U. S. Department of Health, Education, & Welfare.

Esses, L., & Campbell, R. (1984). Challenges in researching the remarried. *Family Relations, 33*, 415–424.

Falkner, A., & Garber, J. (2002). *2001 gay/lesbian consumer online census.* Syracuse, NY: Syracuse University, OpusComm Group, and GSociety.

Farrell, J., & Markman, H. (1986). Individual and interpersonal factors in the etiology of marital distress: The example of remarital couples. In R. Gilmour & S. Duck (Eds.), *The emerging field of personal relationships* (pp. 251–263). Hillsdale, N.J.: Lawrence Erlbaum.

Farrington, K., & Chertok, E. (1993). Social conflict theories of the family In P. G. Boss, W. J. Doherty, R. LaRossa, W. R. Schumm, & S. K. Steinmetz (Eds.), *Sourcebook of family theories and methods: A contextual approach* (pp. 357–381). New York: Plenum.

Ferri, E. (1984). *Stepchildren: A national study.* Atlantic Highlands: Humanities.

Fields, J.(1996). *Living arrangements of children: Household economic studies* U.S. Census Bureau. Current Population Reports.

Fields, P. (2001). *Living arrangements of children 1996.* Current Population Reports, P70–74. Washington DC: U.S. Census Bureau.

Filinson, R. (1986). Relationships in stepfamilies—an examination of alliances. *Journal of Comparative Family Studies, 17,* 43–62.

Finch, J. (1989). *Family obligations and social change* Oxford: Polity Press.

Fine, M (1997). Stepfamilies from a policy perspective: Guidance from the empirical literature. *Marriage and Family Review, 26,* 249–264.

Fine, M. A., Coleman, M., & Ganong, L. (1998). Consistency in perceptions of the stepparent role among stepparents, parents, and stepchildren. *Journal of Social and Personal Relationships, 15,* 810–828.

Fine, M. A., Coleman, M., & Ganong, L. H. (1999). A social constructionist multi-method approach to understanding the stepparent role. In E. M. Hetherington (Ed.), *Coping with divorce, single parenting and remarriage: A risk and resiliency approach* (pp. 273–294). Mahwah, NJ: Erlbaum.

Fine, M., Ganong, L., & Coleman, M. (1997). The relation between role constructions and adjustment among stepparents. *Journal of Family Issues, 18,* 503–525.

Fine, M., & Kurdek, L. (1992). The adjustment of adolescents in stepfather and stepmother families. *Journal of Marriage and the Family, 54,* 725–736.

Fine, M., & Kurdek, L. (1994). A multidimensional cognitive-developmental of stepfamily adjustment. In K. Pasley & M. Ihinger-Tallman (Ed.), *Stepparenting: Issues in theory, research, and practice* (pp. 15–32). Westport, CT: Greenwood.

Fine, M. A., & Schwebel, A. I. (1991). Stepparent stress: A cognitive perspective. *Journal of Divorce and Remarriage, 17,* 1–15.

Fisher, H. E. (1989). Evolution of human serial pairbonding. *American Journal of Physical Anthropology, 78,* 331–354.

Fisher, P. A., Leve, L. D., O'Leary, C. C., & Leve, C. (2003). Parental monitoring of children's behavior: Variation across stepmother, stepfather, and two-parent biological families. *Family Relation, 52,* 45–22.

Fishman, B. (1983). The economic behavior of stepfamilies. *Family Relations, 32,* 359–366.

Fishman, B., & Hamel, B. (1981). From nuclear to stepfamily ideology: A stressful change. *Alternative Lifestyles, 4,* 181–204.

Flinn, M. (1988). Step- and genetic parent/offspring relationships in a Caribbean village. *Ethology and Sociobiology, 9,* 335–369.

Flinn, M. (1992). Paternal care in a Caribbean village. In B. S. Hewlett (Ed.), *Father-child relations: Cultural and biosocial contexts* (pp. 57–84). New York: Aldine deGruyter.

Flinn, M. V. (1999). Family environment, stress, and health during childhood. In C. Panter-Brick & C. Worthman (Eds.), *Hormones, health, and behavior* (pp. 105–138). Cambridge: Cambridge University Press.

Folk, K. F., Graham, J. W., & Beller, A. H. (1992). Child support and remarriage: Implications for the economic well-being of children. *Journal of Family Issues, 13,* 142–157.

Fox, G. L., & Inazu, J. K. (1982). The influence of mother's marital history on the mother-daughter relationship in black and white households. *Journal of Marriage and the Family, 44,* 143–153.

Frydenger, T. & Frydenger, A. (1984). *The blended family.* Grand Rapids, MI: Baker.

Funder, K. (1991). Children's constructions of their post-divorce families: A family sculpture approach. In K. Funder (Ed.), *Images of Australian families* (pp. 73–101). Melbourne: Longman Cheshire.

Furstenberg, F F., Jr. (1979). Recycling the family: Perspectives for a neglected family form *Marriage and Family Review, 2,* 1, 12–22.

Furstenberg, F. F., Jr. (1981). Remarriage and intergenerational relations. In R. W. Fogel, E. Hatfield, S. B Kiesler, & E. Shanas (Eds.), *Aging: Stability and change in the family* (pp. 115–142). New York: Academic Press.

Furstenberg, F. F. (1988). Child care after divorce and remarriage. In E. M. Hetherington & J D. Arasteh (Eds.), *Impact of divorce, single parenting, and stepparenting* (pp. 245–261). New York: Lawrence Erlbaum.

Furstenberg, F. F., Jr., & Cherlin, A. J. (1991). *Divided families: What happens to children when parents part.* Cambridge, MA: Harvard University Press.

Furstenberg, F F., & Harris, K. M. (1992). The disappearing American father? Divorce and the waning significance of biological parenthood. In S South & S Tolnay (Eds), *The changing American family: Sociological and demographic perspectives* (pp. 197–223) Boulder, CO. Westview.

Furstenberg, F F., & Kiernan, K. E. (2001). Delayed parental divorce: How much do children benefit? *Journal of Marriage and the Family, 63,* 446–457.

Furstenberg, F. F., Jr., & Nord, C. W. (1985). Parenting apart: Patterns of childrearing after marital disruption. *Journal of Marriage and the Family, 47,* 893–904.

Furstenberg, F. F., Nord, C. W., Peterson, J. L., & Zill, N. (1983). The life course of children of divorce: Marital disruption and parental conflict. *American Sociological Review, 48,* 656–668.

Furstenberg, F., & Spanier, G. (1984). *Recycling the family: Remarriage after divorce.* Beverly Hills: Sage.

Gamache, S. J. (1997). Confronting nuclear family bias in stepfamily research. In I. Levin & M. B. Sussman (Eds.), *Stepfamilies: History, research, and policy* (pp. 41–70) New York: Haworth.

Ganong, L. (1993). Family diversity in a youth organization: Involvement of single-parents families and stepfamilies in 4-H. *Family Relations, 42,* 286–292.

Ganong, L., & Coleman, M. (1983). Stepparent: A pejorative term? *Psychological Reports, 52,* 919–922.

Ganong, L., & Coleman, M. (1984). Effects of remarriage on children: A review of the empirical literature. *Family Relations, 33,* 389–406.

Ganong, L., & Coleman, M. (1986). A comparison of clinical and empirical literature on children in stepfamilies. *Journal of Marriage and the Family, 48,* 309–318.

Ganong, L., & Coleman, M. (1987). Effects of stepfamilies on children: A comparison of two literatures. In K. Pasley & M. Ihinger-Tallman (Eds.), *Remarriage and stepparenting: Current research and theory* (pp. 94–140). New York: Guilford.

Ganong, L., & Coleman, M. (1988). Do mutual children cement bonds in stepfamilies? *Journal of Marriage and the Family, 50,* 687–698.

Ganong, L., & Coleman, M. (1989). Preparing for remarriage: Anticipating the issues, seeking solutions. *Family Relations, 38,* 28–33.

Ganong, L., & Coleman, M. (1993a). An exploratory study of stepsibling relationships. *Journal of Divorce and Remarriage, 19,* 125–141.

Ganong, L., & Coleman, M. (1993b). A meta-analytic comparison of the self-esteem and behavior problems of stepchildren to children in other family structures. *Journal of Divorce and Remarriage, 19,* 143–163.

Ganong, L., & Coleman, M. (1994). *Remarried family relationships.* Thousand Oaks, CA: Sage.

Ganong, L., & Coleman, M. (1995). The content of mother stereotypes. *Sex Roles, 32,* 495–512.

Ganong, L., & Coleman, M. (1997a). Effects of patient's marital status and parental status on nurses' cognitions and behaviors. *Journal of Family Nursing, 3,* 15–35.

Ganong, L., & Coleman, M. (1997b). Family structure information on nurses' impression formation. *Research in Nursing & Health, 20,* 139–151.

Ganong, L.. & Coleman, M (1997c) How society views stepfamilies. *Marriage and Family Review,* 26, 85–106

Ganong, L, & Coleman, M. (1998a). An exploratory study of grandparents' and stepgrandparents' perceived financial obligations to grandchildren and stepgrandchildren. *Journal of Social and Personal Relationships, 15,* 39–58.

Ganong, L., & Coleman, M. (1998b). Attitudes regarding filial responsibilities to help elderly divorced parents and stepparents. *Journal of Aging Studies, 12,* 271–290.

Ganong, L., & Coleman, M. (1999). *New families, new responsibilities: Intergenerational obligations following divorce and remarriage.* Hillsdale, NJ: Erlbaum.

Ganong, L., & Coleman, M. (2000). Close relationships in remarried families. In C. Hendrick & S. Hendrick (Eds), *Handbook on close relationships* (pp. 155–168). Newbury Park, CA. Sage

Ganong, L , Coleman, M , Fine, M A , & McDaniel, A K (1998) Issues considered in stepparent adoption. *Family Relations, 47,* 63–72.

Ganong, L., Coleman, M., Fine, M., & Martin, P. (1999). Stepparents' affinity-seeking and affinity-maintaining strategies with stepchildren. *Journal of Family Issues, 20,* 299–327.

Ganong, L., Coleman, M., & Kennedy, G. (1990). The effects of using alternate labels in denoting stepparent or stepfamily status. *Journal of Social Behavior and Personality, 5,* 453–463.

Ganong, L., Coleman, M., & Mapes, D. (1990). A meta-analytic review of family structure stereotypes. *Journal of Marriage and the Family, 52,* 287–298.

Ganong, L., Coleman, M., & Mistina, D. (1995). Home is where they have to let you in: Normative beliefs regarding physical custody changes of children following divorce. *Journal of Family Issues, 16,* 466–487.

Ganong, L., Coleman, M., & Weaver, S. (2001). Maintenance and enhancement in remarried families: Clinical applications. In J. Harvey & A. Wenzel (Eds.), *A clinicians guide to maintaining and enhancing close relationships* (pp. 105–129). Hillsdale, NJ: Erlbaum.

Ganong, L., Coleman, M., Fine, M. A., & McDaniel, A. K. (1998). Issues considered in stepparent adoption. *Family Relations, 47,* 63–72.

Ganong, L., Coleman, M., Fine, M., & Martin, P. (1999). Stepparents' affinity-seeking and affinity-maintaining strategies with stepchildren. *Journal of Family Issues, 20,* 299–327.

Gartrell, N., Hamilton, J., Banks, A., Mosbacher, D., Reed, N., Sparks, C. H., & Bishop, H. (1996). The National Lesbian Family Study: I. Interviews with prospective mothers. *American Journal of Orthopsychiatry, 66,* 272–281.

Gelles, R. J. (1980). Violence in the family: A review of research in the seventies. *Journal of Marriage and the Family, 42,* 873–885.

Gelles, R. J., & Harrop, J. W. (1991). The risk of abusive violence among children with nongenetic caretakers. *Family Relations, 40,* 78–83.

Gentry, M., & Schulman, A. (1988). Remarriage as a coping response for widowhood. *Psychology and Aging, 3,* 191–196.

Gergen, K. J. (1985). The social constructionist movement in modern psychology. *American Psychologist, 40,* 266–275.

Gerlach, P. (2001). *Building a high-nurturance stepfamily.* Philadelphia: Hibris Corporation.

Gersick, K. (1979). Fathers by choice: Divorced men who receive custody of their children. In A. Levinger & O.C. Moles (Eds.), *Divorce and separation* (pp. 374–397). New York: Basic Books.

Giles-Sims, J., & Crosbie-Burnett, M. (1989). Adolescent power in stepfather families: A test of normative resource theory. *Journal of Marriage and the Family, 51,* 1065–1078.

Giles-Sims, J., & Finkelhor, D. (1984). Child abuse in stepfamilies. *Family Relations, 33,* 407–414.

Giles-Sims, J. (2003). Personal Communication.

Giles-Sims, J. (1997). Current knowledge about child abuse in stepfamilies. In I. Levin & M. Sussman (Eds.), *Stepfamilies: History, research, and policy* (pp. 215–230). New York, NY: Haworth.

Giles-Sims, J. (1984). The stepparent role: Expectations, behavior, sanctions. *Journal of Family Issues, 5,* 116–130.

Giles-Sims, J. (1987) Social exchange in remarried families. In K. Pasley & M. Ihinger-Tallman (Eds.), *Remarriage and stepparenting today: Research and theory* (pp. 141–163). New York: Guilford.

Glenn, N. D. (1997). A critique of twenty family and marriage and family textbooks. *Family Relations, 46,* 197–208.

Goetting, A. (1982). The six stations of remarriage. Developmental tasks of remarriage after divorce. *Family Relations, 31,* 213–222.

Goldner, V. (1982). Remarriage family: Structure, system, future. In J. C. Hansen & L. Messenger (Eds.), *Therapy with remarried families* (pp. 187–206). Rockville, MD: Aspen.

Goldscheider, F., & Goldscheider, C. (1998). The effects of childhood family structure on leaving and returning home. *Journal of Marriage and the Family, 60,* 745–756.

Goldsmith, J (1981). Relationship between former spouses Descriptive findings. *Journal of Divorce, 4,* 1–20.

Goldstein, H. S. (1974). Reconstituted families The second marriage and its children. *Psychiatric Quarterly, 48,* 433–440.

Gordon, M., & Creighton, S. (1988). Natal and nonnatal fathers as sexual abusers in the United Kingdom: A comparative analysis. *Journal of Marriage and the Family, 50,* 99–105.

Greif, G. L., & Kristall, J. (1993). Common themes in a group for noncustodial parents. *Families in Society, 74,* 240–245.

Griffith, J. D., Koo, H. P., & Suchindran, C. M. (1984). Childlessness and marital stability in remarriages. *Journal of Marriage and the Family, 46,* 577–585.

Grizzle, G. (1996). Remarriage as an incomplete institution: Cherlin's (1978) views and why we should be cautious about accepting them. *Journal of Divorce and Remarriage, 26,* 191–201.

Grizzle, G. (1999). Institutionalization and family unity: An exploratory study of Cherlin's (1978) views. *Journal of Divorce and Remarriage, 30,* 125–141.

Gross, P. E. (1987). Defining post-divorce remarriage families: A typology based on the subjective perceptions of children. *Journal of Divorce, 10,* 205–217.

Guisinger, S., Cowan, P., & Schuldberg, D. (1989). Changing parent and spouse relations in the first years of remarriage of divorced fathers. *Journal of Marriage and the Family, 51,* 445–456.

Hackstaff, K. B. (1999). *Marriage in a culture of divorce.* Philadelphia: Temple University Press.

Hall, K. J., & Kitson, G. C. (2000). Lesbian stepfamilies: An even more "incomplete institution." *Journal of Lesbian Studies, 4,* 31–47.

Halliday, T. (1980). Remarriage: The more compleat institution. *American Journal of Sociology, 86,* 630–635.

Hanna, S. L., & Knaub, P. K. (1984). Cohabitation before remarriage: Its relationship to family strengths. *Alternative Lifestyles, 4,* 507–522.

Hanson, T. L., McLanahan, S. S., & Thomson, E. (1996). Double jeopardy: Parental conflict and stepfamily outcomes for children. *Journal of Marriage and the Family, 58,* 141–154.

Hanson, T. L., McLanahan, S., & Thomson, E. (1997). Economic resources, parental practices, and children's well being. In G. Duncan & J. Brooks-Gunn (Eds.), *Consequences of growing up poor* (pp. 190–238). New York: Russell Sage Foundation.

Hare, J. (1994). Concerns and issues faced by families headed by a lesbian couple. *Families in Society, 75,* 27–35.

Hare, J., & Richards, L. (1993). Children raised by lesbian couples: Does context of birth affect father and partner involvement? *Family Relations, 42,* 249–255.

Hare-Mustin, R. T., & Marecek, J. (1988). The meaning of difference: Gender theory, postmodernism, and psychology. *American Psychologist, 43,* 455–464.

Hawkins, A. J., & Eggebeen, D. J. (1991). Are fathers fungible? Patterns of coresident adult men in maritally disrupted families and young children's well-being. *Journal of Marriage and the Family, 53,* 958–72.

Hays, S. (1996). *The cultural contradictions of motherhood.* New Haven. CT Yale.

Henderson, S. H., & Taylor, L. C. (1999). Parent-adolescent relationships in nonstep-, simple step-, and complex stepfamilies. In Hetherington, E. M., Henderson, S. H., & Reiss, D., in collaboration with Anderson, E. R., Bridges, M., Chan, R. W., Insabella, G. M., Jodl, K. M., Kim, J. E., Mitchell, A. S., O'Connor, T. G., Skaggs, M. J., & Taylor, L C. *Adolescent siblings in stepfamilies: Family functioning and adolescent adjustment* (pp. 79–101). *Monographs of the Society for Research in Child Development, 64* (4, Serial No. 259). Malden, MA: Blackwell.

Hendrick, S., & Hendrick, C. (1992). *Liking, loving, and relating.* Pacific Grove, CA: Brooks/Cole.

Henry, C. S. (1994). Family system characteristics, parental behaviors, and adolescent family life satisfaction. *Family Relations, 43,* 447–455.

Henry, C. S., Ceghan, C. P., & Matthews, D. W. (1992) The role behaviors, role meanings, and grand-mothering styles of grandmothers and stepgrandmothers. Perceptions of the middle generation *Journal of Divorce and Remarriage, 17,* 1–22.

Henry, C. S., Ceghan, C. P., & Ostrander, D L. (1993). The transition to stepgrandparenthood. *Journal of Divorce and Remarriage, 19,* 25–44.

Henry, C. S., & Lovelace, S. G. (1995). Family resources and adolescent family life satisfaction in remarried family households. *Journal of Family Issues, 16,* 765–786.

Hequembourg, A. (in press). Unscripted motherhood: Lesbian mothers negotiating incompletely institutionalized family relationships. *Journal of Social and Personal Relationships.*

Hequembourg, A., & Farrell, M. (1999). Lesbian motherhood: Negotiating marginal-mainstream identities. *Gender & Society, 13,* 540–557.

Hetherington, E. M., & Camara, K. A. (1984). Families in transition: The processes of dissolution and reconstitution. In R. D. Parke (Ed.), *Review of child development research Vol. 7: The family.* (pp. 398–431). Chicago: University of Chicago Press.

Hetherington, E. M., & Clingempeel, W. G. (1992). Coping with marital transitions: A family systems perspective. *Monographs of the Society for Research in Child Development, 57*(2–3, Serial No. 227).

Hetherington, E. M., Cox, M., & Cox, R. (1982). Effects of divorce on parents and children. In M. Lamb (Ed.), *Nontraditional families* (pp. 233–285). Hillsdale, NJ: Erlbaum.

Hetherington, E. M., & Henderson, S. H. (1997). Fathers in stepfamilies. In M. Lamb (Ed.), *The role of fathers in child development* (3rd ed.) (pp. 212–226). Erlbaum.

Hetherington, E. M., & Kelly, J. (2002). *For better or for worse: Divorce reconsidered.* New York: Norton.

Hetherington, E. M., Henderson, S. H., & Reiss, D., in collaboration with E. R. Anderson, M. Bridges, R. W. Chan, G. M. Insabella, K. M. Jodl, J. E. Kim, A. S. Mitchell, T. G. O'Connor, M. J. Skaggs, & L. C. Taylor (1999). Adolescent siblings in stepfamilies: Family functioning and adolescent adjustment. *Monographs of the Society for Research in Child Development, 64* (4, Serial No. 259). Malden, MA: Blackwell.

Hetherington, E. M., & Jodl, K. M. (1994). Stepfamilies as settings for child development. In A. Booth & J. Dunn (Eds.), *Stepfamilies: Who benefits? Who does not?* (pp. 55–79). Hillsdale, NJ: Erlbaum.

Hetherington E. M. (Ed.). (1983). *Socialization, personality, and social development.* New York.

Hetherington, E. M. (1988). Parents, children, and siblings six years after divorce. In R. Hinde & J. Stevenson-Hinde (Eds.). *Relationships within families.* (pp. 311–331). New York: Oxford University Press.

Hill, M. S. (1992). The role of economic resources and remarriage in financial assistance for children of divorce. *Journal of Family Issues, 13,* 158–178.

Hill, R. (1986). Life cycle stages for types of single parent families: Of family development theory. *Family Relations, 35,* 19–29.

Hobart, C. W. (1988). Perception of parent-child relationships in first married and remarried families. Family Relations, 37, 175–182.

Hobart, C (1991). Conflict in remarriages. *Journal of Divorce and Remarriage, 15,* 69–86.

Hochschild, A., & Machung, A. (1989). *The second shift.* New York. Avon Books.

Hofferth, S., & Anderson, K. G. (2003). Are all dads equal? Biology versus marriage as basis for paternal investment. *Journal of Marriage and Family 65,* 213–232.

Hofferth, S.. Pleck, J., Stueve, J., Bianchi, S., & Sayer, L. (2002). The Demography of Fathers: What fathers do. In C. Tamis-LeMonda & N. Cabrera (Eds.), *Handbook of Father Involvement* (pp. 63–90). Mahwah, NJ: Erlbaum.

Hoffman, S., & Duncan, G. J. (1988). A comparison of choice-based multinomial and nested logit models: The family structure and welfare use decisions of divorced or separated women *The Journal of Human Resources, 23,* 550–562.

Hoffman, J P. (2002) The community context of family structure and adolescent drug use *Journal of Marriage and Family, 64,* 314–330.

Hoffmann, J. P., & Johnson, R. A. (1998). A national portrait of family structure and adolescent drug use. *Journal of Marriage and the Family, 60,* 633–645.

Holden, K.C., & Kuo, D. (1996). Complex marital histories and economic well-being. The continuing legacy of divorce and widowhood as the HRS cohort approaches retirement. *The Gerontologist, 36,* 383–390.

Holland, D., & Eisenhart, M. (1990). *Educated in romance: Women, achievement, and college culture.* Chicago: University of Chicago Press.

Hughes, R., Jr., & Hans, J. (2004). Understanding the effects of the Internet. In M. Coleman & L. Ganong (Eds.), *Handbook of contemporary families: Considering the past, contemplating the future* (pp. 506–520). Thousand Oaks, CA: Sage.

Hughes, R., & Schroeder, J. D. (1997). Family life education programs for stepfamilies. In I. Levin & M. Sussman (Eds.), *Stepfamilies: History, research, and policy* (pp. 281–300). New York, NY: Haworth.

Hunter, A. G. (2002). (Re)Envisioning cohabitation: A commentary on race, history, and culture. In A. Booth & A. C. Crouter (Eds). *Just living together: Implications of cohabitation on families, children, and social policy* (pp. 41–50). Mahwah, NJ: Erlbaum.

Ihinger-Tallman, M. (1987). Sibling and stepsibling bonding in stepfamilies. In K. Pasley & M. Ihinger-Tallman (Eds.), *Remarriage and stepparenting: Current research and theory* (pp. 164–184). New York: Guilford.

Ihinger-Tallman, M. (1988). Research on stepfamilies. *Annual Reviews of Sociology, 14,* 25–48.

Ihinger-Tallman, M., & Pasley, K. (1986). Remarriage and integration within the community. *Journal of Marriage and the Family, 48,* 395–405.

Ihinger-Tallman, M., & Pasley, K. (1987a). Divorce and remarriage in the American family: An historical overview. In K. Pasley & M. Ihinger-Tallman (Eds.), *Remarriage and stepparenting today: Current research and theory* (pp. 3–18). New York: Guilford.

Ihinger-Tallman, M., & Pasley, K. (1987b). *Remarriage.* Newbury Park, CA: Sage.

Ihinger-Tallman, M. I., Pasley, B. K., & Buehler, C. (1993). Developing a middle-range theory of father involvement postdivorce. *Journal of Family Issues, 14,* 550–571.

Imber-Black, E., & Roberts, J. (1993). *Rituals for our lives.* New York: Harper Perennial.

Ishii-Kuntz, M., & Coltrane, S. (1992). Remarriage, stepparenting, and household labor. *Journal of Family Issues, 13,* 215–233.

Jacobson, D. S. (1987). Family type, visiting, and children's behavior in the stepfamily: A linked family system. In K. Pasley & M. Ihinger-Tallman (Eds.), *Remarriage and stepparenting: Current research and theory* (pp. 257–272). New York: Guilford.

Jacobson, D. (1993). What's fair: Concepts of financial management in stepfamily households. *Journal of Divorce and Remarriage, 19,* 221–238.

Jacobson, D. (1995a). Critical interactive events and child adjustment in the stepfamily: A linked family system. In D. K. Huntley (Ed.), *Understanding stepfamilies: Implications for assessment and treatment* (pp. 73–86). Alexandria, VA: American Counseling Association.

Jacobson, D. (1995b) Incomplete institution or culture shock. Institutional and processual models of stepfamily instability. *Journal of Divorce and Remarriage, 24*, 3–18.

Johnson, C. L. (1988). Postdivorce reorganization of relationships between divorcing children and their parents. *Journal of Marriage and the Family, 50*, 221–231.

Johnson, C. L. (1992). Divorced and reconstituted families: Effects on the older generation. *Generations, 16*, 17–20.

Johnson, C. L (1999) Effects of adult children's divorce on grandparenthood. In M. Szinovacz (Ed.), *Handbook on grandparenthood* (pp. 184–199). Westport, CT: Greenwood.

Johnson, D. R., & Booth, A. (1998). Marital quality: A product of the dyadic environment or individual factors? *Social Forces, 76*, 883–904.

Johnston, J. R (1995) Research update: Children's adjustment in sole custody compared to joint custody families and principles for custody decision making. *Family and Conciliation Courts Review, 33*, 415–425.

Kaar, P., Jokela, J., Merila, J., Helle, T., & Kojola, I. (1998). Sexual conflict and remarriage in preindustrial human populations: Causes and fitness consequences. *Evolution and Human Behavior, 19*, 139–151.

Kaiser Family Foundation (2001, November) *Inside-OUT: A report of the experiences of lesbians, gays and bisexuals in America and the public's views on issues and policies related to sexual orientation.* Retrieved October 27, 2002, from http://www.keff.org/content/2001/3193/LGBChartpack. pdf

Kalish, E., & Visher, E. (1981). Grandparents of divorce and remarriage. *Journal of Divorce, 5*, 127–140.

Kalmuss, D., & Seltzer, J. A. (1986). Continuity of marital behavior in remarriage: The case of spouse abuse. *Journal of Marriage and the Family, 48*, 113–120.

Kalmuss, D., & Seltzer, J. A. (1989). A framework for studying socialization over the life cycle: The case of family violence. *Journal of Family Issues, 10*, 339–358.

Kaplan, L., & Hennon, C. B. (1992). Remarriage education: The personal reflections program. *Family Relations, 41*, 127–134.

Kaslow, F. W. (2000). Prenuptial and postnuptial agreeements: Sunny or stormy bellwethers to marriage or remarriage. In F. W. Kaslow (Ed.), *Handbook of couple and family forensics: A sourcebook for mental health and legal professionals*, (pp. 3–22). New York: John Wiley & Sons.

Keen, S. (1983). *The passionate life: Stages of loving.* New York: Harper & Row.

Kelley, P. (1992). Healthy stepfamily functioning. *Families in Society, 73*, 579–587.

Kelley, P. (1996). Family-centered practice with stepfamilies. *Families in Society, 77*, 535–544.

Kennedy, G. E., & Kennedy, C. E. (1993). Grandparents: A special resource for children. *Journal of Divorce and Remarriage, 19*, 45–68.

Kennedy, G. E. (1991). Grandchildren's reasons for closeness with grandparents. *Journal of Social Behavior & Personality, 6*, 697–712.

Keshet, J. K. (1990). Cognitive remodeling of the family: How remarried people view stepfamilies. *American Journal of Orthopsychiatry, 60*, 196–203.

Kiecolt, K. J., & Acock, A. C. (1988). The long-term effects of family structure on gender-role attitudes. *Journal of Marriage and the Family, 50*, 709–717.

Kiernan, K. E. (1992). The impact of family disruption in childhood on transitions made in young adult life. *Population Studies, 46*, 213–234.

Kim, J. E., Hetherington, E. M., & Reiss, D. (1999). Associations among family relationships, antisocial peers, and adolescents' externalizing behaviors: Gender and family type differences. *Child Development, 70*, 1209–1230.

Kim, H. K., & McKenry, P. C. (2000). Relationship transitions as seen in the National Survey of Families and Household. *Journal of Divorce & Remarriage, 34(1/2)*, 163–167.

King, V. (1994). Nonresident father involvement and child well-being: Can dads make a difference? *Journal of Family Issues, 15*, 78–96.

King, V., & Heard, H. (1999). Nonresident father visitation, parental conflict, and mother's satisfaction: What's best for child well-being? *Journal of Marriage and the Family, 61*, 385–396.

Kinnaird, K. L., & Gerrard, M. (1986). Premarital sexual behavior and attitudes toward marriage and divorce among young women as a function of their mother's marital status. *Journal of Marriage and the Family, 48*, 757–765.

Koepke, L., Hare, J., & Moran, P. B. (1992). Relationship quality in a sample of lesbian couples with children and child-free Lesbian couples. *Family Relations, 41*, 224–229.

Koo, H. P., & Suchindran, C. M. (1980). Effects of children on women remarriage prospects. *Journal of Family Issues*, 497–515.

Koo, H. P., Suchindran, C. M., & Griffith, J. D. (1984). The effects of children on divorce and remarriage: A multivariate analysis of life table probabilities *Population Studies, 38*, 451.

Kornhaber, A. (1996). *Contemporary grandparenting* Thousand Oaks, CA. Sage.

Kowal, A., Kramer, L., Krull, J. L., & Crick, N. R. (2002). Children's perceptions of the fairness of parental preferential treatment and their socioemotional well-being. *Journal of Family Psychology, 16*, 297–306.

Kornhaber, A., & Woodward, K. L. (1981) *Grandparents/grandchildren, the vital connection*. Garden City, NY: Anchor Press/Doubleday.

Kowelski-Jones, L. (2000). Staying out of trouble. Community resources and problem behavior among high-risk adolescents. *Journal of Marriage and the Family, 62*, 449–464.

Kranichfeld, M. L. (1987). Rethinking family power. *Journal of Family Issues, 8*, 42–56.

Kruk, E. (1992). Psychological and structural factors contributing to the disengagement of noncustodial fathers after divorce. *Family and Conciliation Courts Review, 29*, 81–101.

Kurdek, L. A. (1989). Relationship quality for newly married husbands and wives: Marital history, stepchildren, and individual-difference predictors. *Journal of Marriage and the Family, 51*, 1053–1064.

Kurdek, L. A. (1990). Spouse attributes and spousal interactions as dimensions of relationship quality in first-married and remarried newlywed men and women. *Journal of Family Issues, 11*, 91–100.

Kurdek, L. A. (1991). Marital stability and changes in marital quality in newly wed couples: A test of the contextual model. *Journal of Social and Personal Relationships, 8*, 27–48.

Kurdek, L. A. (1999). The nature and predictors of the trajectory of change of marital quality for husbands and wives over the first 10 years of marriage. *Developmental Psychology, 35*, 1283–1296.

Kurdek, L. A. (2000). Attractions and constraints as determinants of relationship commitment: Longitudinal evidence from gay, lesbian, and heterosexual couples. *Personal Relationships, 7*, 245–262.

Kurdek, L. A. (2001). Differences between heterosexual-nonparent couples and gay, lesbian, and heterosexual parent couples. *Journal of Family Issues, 22*, 727–754.

Kurdek, L. (2003). Differences between gay and lesbian cohabiting couples. Journal of Social and Personal Relationships, 20, 411–436.

Kurdek, L. (2004). Gay men and lesbian couples: The family context. In M. Coleman & L. Ganong (Eds.), *Handbook of contemporary families: Considering the past, contemplating the future* (pp. 96–115). Thousand Oaks, CA: Sage.

Kurdek, L., & Fine. M. (1991). Cognitive correlates of satisfaction for mothers and stepfathers in stepfather families. *Journal of Marriage and the Family, 53*, 565–572.

Kurdek, L. A., & Fine, M. A. (1993a). Parent and nonparent residential family members as providers of warmth and supervision to young adolescents. *Journal of Family Psychology, 7*, 245–249.

Kurdek, L. A., & Fine, M. A. (1993b). The relation between family structure and young adolescents' appraisals of family climate and parent behaviors. *Journal of Family Issues, 14*, 279–290.

Kurdek, L. A., & Fine, M. A (1995). Mothers, fathers, stepfathers, and siblings as providers of supervision, acceptance, and autonomy to young adolescents. *Journal of Family Psychology*, *9*, 95–99.

Lampard, R., & Peggs, K (1999). Repartnering: The relevance of parenthood and gender to cohabitation and remarriage among the formerly married. *British Journal of Sociology*, *50*, 443–465.

Landis, P. H. (1950). Sequential marriage. *Journal of Home Economics*, *42*, 625–628.

Lansford, J. E., Ceballo, R., Abbey, A., & Stewart, A J. (2001) Does family structure matter? A comparison of adoptive, two-parent biological, single-mother, stepfather, and stepmother households. *Journal of Marriage and Family*, *63*, 840–851.

Larson, J. H., & Allgood, S. M. (1987). A comparison of intimacy in first-married and remarried couples. *Journal of Family Issues*, *8*, 319–331

Larson, J. H , Anderson, J. O., & Morgan, A (1984) *Effective step-parenting: Participant's manual*. New York: Family Service America.

Lee, V. E., Burkam, D. T, Zimiles, H., & Ladewski, B (1994). Family structure and its effect on behavioral and emotional problems in young adolescents. *Journal of Research on Adolescence*, *4*, 405–437.

Leslie, G. (1976). *The family in social context*. New York. Oxford University Press

Leslie, L. A., & Epstein, N. (1988). Cognitive-behavioral treatment of remarried families In N Epstein, S. E. Schlesinger, & W. Dryden (Eds.), *Cognitive-Behavioral therapy with families* (pp. 151–182). New York: Brunner/Mazel.

Leung, J. J. (1995). Family configurations and students' perceptions of parental support for schoolwork. *Sociological Imagination*, *32*, 185–196.

Levin, I. (1997). Stepfamily as project. In I. Levin & M. Sussman (Eds.), *Stepfamilies: History, research, and policy* (pp. 123–134). New York: Haworth.

Lightcap, J. L., Kurland, J. A., & Burgess, R. L. (1982). Child abuse: A test of some predictions from evolutionary theory. *Ethology and Sociobiology*, *3*, 61–67.

Lissau, I., & Sorensen, T.I.A. (1994). Parental neglect during childhood and increased risk of obesity in young adulthood. *The Lancet*, *343*, 324–327.

Lopata, H. Z. (1979). *Women as widows: Support systems*. New York: Elsevier.

Lown, J. M., & Dolan, E. M. (1988). Financial challenges in remarriage. Lifestyles: *Family and Economic Issues*, *9*, 73–88.

Luescher, K., & Pillemer, K. (1998). Intergenerational ambivalence: A new approach to the study of parent-child relations in later life. *Journal of Marriage and the Family*, *60*, 413–425.

Lussier, G., Deater-Deckard, K., Dunn, J., & Davies, L., (2002). Support across two generations: Children's closeness to grandparents following parental divorce and remarriage. *Journal of Family Psychology*, *16*, 363–376.

Lutz, E. (2001). *The complete idiot's guide to stepparenting*. New York: MacMillan.

Lynch, J. M. (2000). Considerations of family structure and gender composition: The lesbian and gay stepfamily. *Journal of Homosexuality*, *39*, 81–96.

Lynch, J. M., & Murray, K. (2000). For the love of the children: The coming out process for lesbian and gay parents and stepparents. *Journal of Homosexuality*, *39*, 1–24.

MacDonald, W. L., & DeMaris, A. (1995). Remarriage, stepchildren and marital conflict: Challenges to incomplete institutionalization hypothesis. *Journal of Marriage and the Family*, *57*, 387–398.

MacDonald, W. L., & DeMaris, A. (1996). Parenting stepchildren and biological children: The effects of stepparent's gender and new biological children. *Journal of Family Issues*, *17*, 5–25.

Mahoney, M. M. (1994). Reformulating the legal definition of the stepparent-child relationship. In A. Booth & J. Dunn (Eds.), *Stepfamilies: Who benefits? Who does not?* (pp. 191–196). Hillsdale, NJ: Erlbaum.

Mahoney, M. M. (1997). Stepfamilies from a legal perspective. In I. Levin & M. Sussman (Eds.), Stepfamilies: *History, research, and policy* (pp. 231–248). New York, NY: Haworth.

Mahoney, M. M. (1999). Open adoption in context. The wisdom and enforceability of visitation orders for former parents under Uniform Adoption Acts. 4-113. *Florida Law Review, 51*, 89–142.

Malkin, C. M., & Lamb, M. E. (1994). Child maltreatment: A test of sociobiological theory. *Journal of Comparative Family Studies, 25*, 121–133.

Mandell, D (2002). *Deadbeat dads: Subjectivity and social construction.* Toronto: University of Toronto Press.

Manning, W. D (2002). The implications of cohabitation for children's well-being In A Booth & A. C Crouter (Eds.). *Just living together: Implications of cohabitation on families, children, and social policy* (pp. 121–151). Mahwah, NJ: Erlbaum.

Manning, W. D., & Smock, P. J. (2000). "Swapping" families: Serial parenting and economic support for children. *Journal of Marriage and the Family, 62*, 111–122.

Margolin, L. (1992). Child abuse by mothers' boyfriends· Why the overrepresentation? *Child Abuse and Neglect, 16*, 541–551.

Marsiglio, W. (1992). Stepfathers with minor children living at home: Parenting perceptions and relationship quality. *Journal of Family Issues, 13*, 195–214.

Martin, J A., Hamilton, B. E., Ventura, S. J , Menacker, F., Park, M. M., & Sutton, P. D (2002). Births. Final data for 2001. *National Vital Statistics Reports 51*(2), Hyattsville, MD· National Center for Health Statistics.

Martinez, C. R., & Forgatch, M. S., (2002). Adjusting to change: Linking family structure transitions with parenting and boys adjustment. *Journal of Family Psychology, 16*, 107–117.

Mason, M. A. (2003). Was Cinderella right? The new social Darwinism targets stepparents. In M. Coleman & L. Ganong (Eds.), *Points & counterpoints: Controversial relationship and family issues in the 21st century* (pp. 255–262). Los Angeles: Roxbury Publishing.

Mason, M. A. (1998). The modern American stepfamily: Problems and possibilities. In M. Mason & A Skolnick (Eds.), *All our families: New policies for a new century* (pp. 95–116). New York, NY: Oxford University Press.

Mason, M. A., Fine, M. A., & Carnochan, S. (2004). Family law for changing families. In M. Coleman & L. Ganong (Eds.), *Handbook of contemporary families: Considering the past, contemplating the future* (pp. 432–450). Thousand Oaks, CA: Sage.

McCranie, E. W., & Kahan, J. (1986). Personality and multiple divorce: A prospective study. *Journal of Nervous and Mental Disease, 174*, 161–164.

McGoldrick, M., Gerson, R., & Schellenberger, S. (1998). *Genograms in family assessment (2nd ed.).* New York: Norton.

McGraw, L., & Walker, A. (2004). Gendered family relationships: The more things change, the more they stay the same. In M. Coleman & L. Ganong (Eds.), *Handbook of contemporary families: Considering the past, contemplating the future* (pp. 174–191). Thousand Oaks, CA: Sage.

McGue, M., & Lykken, D. T. (1992). Genetic influence on risk of divorce. *Psychological Science, 3*, 368–373.

McKain, W. C. (1972). A new look at older marriages. *The Family Coordinator, 21*, 61–69.

McKenry, P. C., McKelvey, M. W., Leigh, D., & Wark, L. (1996). Nonresidential father involvement: A comparison of divorced, separated, never married, and remarried fathers. *Journal of Divorce and Remarriage, 25*, 1–13.

McKenry, P. C., & Price, S. J. (1991). Alternatives for support: Life after divorce—a literature review. *Journal of Divorce & Remarriage, 15*, 1–19.

McLanahan, S., & Bumpass, L. (1988). Intergenerational consequences of family disruption. *American Journal of Sociology, 94*, 130–152.

McLanahan, S., & Sandefur, G. (1994). *Growing up with a single-parent: What hurts, what helps.* Cambridge, MA: Harvard University Press.

Mead, M. (1970). Anomalies in American post divorce relationships. In P. Bohannan (Ed.), *Divorce and after* (pp. 97–112) New York: Doubleday.

Mekos, D., Hetherington, E. M., & Reiss, D. (1996). Sibling differences in problem behavior and parental treatment in nondivorced and remarried families. *Child Development, 67,* 2148–2165.

Menaghan, E. G., Kowalski-Jones, L., & Mott, F. L. (1997). The intergenerational costs of parental social stressors: Academic and social difficulties in early adolescence for children of young mothers. *Journal of Health and Social Behavior, 38,* 72–86.

Messinger, L. (1976). Remarriage between divorced people with children from previous marriages: A proposal for preparation for remarriage. *Journal of Marriage and Family Counseling, 2,* 193–200.

Messinger, L., Walker, L. N., & Freeman, S. J. J. (1978). Preparation for remarriage following divorce: The use of group techniques. *American Journal of Orthopsychiatry, 48,* 263–272.

Michael, R., & Tuma, N. (1985). Entry into marriage and parenthood by young men and women: The influence of family background. *Demography, 22,* 515–544.

Miller, A. T. (1993). Social science, social policy, and the heritage of African American families In M. B Katz (Ed.), *The underclass debate* (pp. 254–292). Princeton, NJ: Princeton University Press.

Mills, D. (1984). A model for stepfamily development. *Family Relations, 33,* 365–372.

Mills, T., Wakeman, M., & Fea, C. (2001) Adult grandchildren's perceptions of emotional closeness and consensus with their maternal and paternal grandparents *Journal of Family Issues, 22,* 427–455.

Minton, C., & Pasley, K. (1996). Fathers' parenting role identity and father involvement in nondivorce and divorced. *Journal of Family Issues, 17,* 26–45.

Minuchin, S. (1993). *Family healing: Tales of hope and renewal from family therapy.* New York: Free Press.

Montgomery, M. J., Anderson, E. R., Hetherington, E. M., & Clingempeel, W. G. (1992). Patterns of courtship for remarriage: Implications for child adjustment and parent-child relationships. *Journal of Marriage and the Family, 54,* 686–698.

Morris, J. F., Balsam, K. F., & Rothblum, E. D. (2002). Lesbian and bisexual mothers and nonmothers: Demographics and the coming-out process. *Developmental Psychology, 16,* 144–156.

Morrison, D. R. (2000, March). *The costs of economic uncertainty: Child well-being in cohabiting and remarried unions following parental divorce.* Paper presented at the annual meeting of the Population Association of America, Los Angeles, CA.

Morrison, K., & Thompson-Guppy, A. (1985). Cinderella's stepmother syndrome. *Canadian Journal of Psychiatry, 30,* 521–529.

Moss, S. Z., & Moss, M. S. (1980). Remarriage a triadic relationship. *Conciliation Courts Review, 18,* 15–20.

Mott, F. L., & Moore, S. F. (1983). The tempo of remarriage among young American women. *Journal of Marriage and the Family, 45,* 427–435.

National Center for Health Statistics. (1993). *1988 marriages: Number of the marriage by of bride by groom* [Computer program]. Washington, DC:NCHS Computer Center.

Needle, R. H., Su, S. S., & Doherty, W. J. (1990). Divorce, remarriage, and adolescent substance use: A prospective longitudinal study. *Journal of Marriage and the Family, 52,* 157–169.

Nelson, F. (1996). *Lesbian motherhood.* Toronto: University of Toronto Press.

Nelson, W. P., & Levant, R. F. (1991). An evaluation of a skills training program for parents in stepfamilies. *Family Relations, 40,* 291–296.

Nicholson, J., Fergusson, D., & Horwood, L. J. (1999). Effects of later adjustment in a stepfamily during childhood and adolescence. *Journal of Child Psychology and Psychiatry, 40,* 405–416.

Nicholson, J., & Sanders, M. (1999). Randomized controlled trial of behavioral family intervention for the treatment of child behavior problems in stepfamilies. *Journal of Divorce and Remarriage, 30,* 1–23.

Nielsen, L. (1999). Stepmothers: Why so much stress? A review of the literature. *Journal of Divorce and Remarriage, 30,* 115–148.

Nock, S L. (2001). The marriages of equally dependent spouses. *Journal of Family Issues, 22,* 755–775.

Noy, D. (1991). Wicked stepmothers in Roman society and imagination. *Journal of Family History, 16,* 345–361.

O'Connor, T. G., Hetherington, E. M., & Reiss, D. (1998). Family systems and adolescent development: Shared and nonshared risk and protective factors in nondivorced and remarried families. *Development and Psychopathology, 10,* 353–375.

O'Connor, T. G., & Insabella, G. M (1999) Marital satisfaction, relationships, and roles. In Hetherington, E. M., Henderson, S. H., & Reiss, D., in collaboration with Anderson, E. R., Bridges, M., Chan, R. W., Insabella, G. M., Jodl, K. M., Kim, J. E., Mitchell, A. S., O'Connor, T. G., Skaggs, M. J., & Taylor, L. C. Adolescent siblings in stepfamilies: Family functioning and adolescent adjustment (pp. 50–79). *Monographs of the Society for Research in Child Development, 64* (Serial No. 259). Malden, MA: Blackwell

O'Connor, T. G., Pickering, K., Dunn, J., Golding, J., and the ALSPAC Study Team. (1999) Frequency and predictors of relationship dissolution in a community sample in England. *Journal of Family Psychology, 13,* 436–449.

O'Flaherty, K., & Eells, L. (1988). Courtship behavior of the remarried. *Journal of Marriage and the Family, 50,* 499–506.

Oh, S. (1986). Remarried men and remarried women: How are they different? *Journal of Divorce, 9,* 107–113.

Orchard, A. L., & Solberg, K. B. (1999). Expectation of the stepmother's role. *Journal of Divorce and Remarriage, 31,* 107–123.

Oswald, R. F. (2002). Resilience within the family networks of lesbians and gay men: Intentionality and redefinition. *Journal of Marriage and the Family, 64,* 374–394.

Ozawa, M. N., & Yoon, H-S. (2002). The economic benefit of remarriage: Gender and income class. *Journal of Divorce & Remarriage, 36,* 21–39.

Palisi, B. J., Orleans, M., Caddell, D., & Korn, B. (1991). Adjustment to stepfatherhood: The effects of marital history and relations with children. *Journal of Divorce and Remarriage, 14,* 89–106.

Papernow, P. L. (1984). The stepfamily cycle: An experimental model of stepfamily development. *Family Relations, 33,* 355–364.

Papernow, P. L. (1987). Thickening the middle ground: Dilemmas and vulnerabilities of remarried couples. *Psychotherapy, 24,* 630–639.

Papernow, P. (1993). *Becoming a stepfamily.* San Francisco: Jossey-Bass.

Papernow, P. (1994). Therapy with remarried couples. In G. Wheeler & S. Backman (Eds.), *On intimate ground: A Gestalt approach to working with couples* (pp. 128–165). San Francisco: Jossey-Bass.

Papernow, P. (1995). What's going on here? Separating (and weaving together) step and clinical issues in remarried families. In D. K. Huntley (Ed.), *Understanding stepfamilies: Implications for assessment and treatment* (pp. 3–24). Alexandria, VA: American Counseling Association.

Papernow, P. (2001, February). *Working with stepfamilies.* Paper presented at the National Conference on Stepfamilies, New Orleans, LA.

Pasley, K. (1987). Family boundary ambiguity: Perceptions of adult remarried family members. In K. Pasley & M. Ihinger-Tallman (Eds.), *Remarriage and stepparenting: Current research and theory* (pp. 206–224). New York: Guilford.

Pasley, K., & Dollahite, D. C. (1995). The nine Rs of stepparenting adolescents: Research-based recommendations for clinicians. In D. K. Huntley (Ed.), *Understanding stepfamilies: Implications for assessment and treatment* (pp. 87–98). Alexandria, VA: American Counseling Association.

Pasley, K., & Ihinger-Tallman, M. (1982). Remarried family life: Supports and constraints. In G. Rowe (Ed.), *Building family strengths 4* (pp. 367–383). Lincoln: University of Nebraska Press.

Pasley, K., & Ihinger-Tallman, M. (1985). Portraits of stepfamily life in popular literature: 1940–1980. *Family Relations, 34,* 527–534.

Pasley, K., & Ihinger-Tallman, M.(Eds). (1987). *Remarriage and stepparenting. Current research and theory.* New York: Guilford.

Pasley, K., & Ihinger-Tallman, M. (1989). Boundary ambiguity in remarriage: Does ambiguity differentiate degrees of marital adjustment and integration? *Family Relations, 38,* 46–52.

Pasley, K., & Ihinger-Tallman, M. (1990). Remarriage in later adulthood: Correlates of perceptions of family adjustment. *Family Perspectives, 24,* 263–274.

Pasley, K., Koch, M. G., & Ihinger-Tallman, M (1993) Problems in remarriage: An exploratory study of intact and terminated remarriages. *Journal of Divorce and Remarriage, 20,* 63–83.

Pasley, K., Sandras, E., & Edmondson, M. E. (1994). The effects of financial management strategies on the quality of family life in remarriage. *Journal of Family and Economic Issues, 15,* 53–70.

Patterson, C. J. (2000) Family relationships of lesbians and gay men. *Journal of Marriage and the Family, 62,* 1052–1069.

Peek, C., Bell, N., Waldron, T., & Sorell, G. (1988). Patterns of functioning in families of remarried and first-married couples. *Journal of Marriage and the Family, 48,* 767–775.

Peters, A., & Liefbroer, A. C. (1997). Beyond marital status: Partner history and well-being in old age. *Journal of Marriage and the Family, 59,* 687–699.

Peterson, M. (1985) *Mercy flights.* Columbia, MO· University of missouri

Phillips, R. (1997). Stepfamilies from a historical perspective. In I. Levin & M Sussman (Eds), *Stepfamilies: History, research, and policy* (pp. 5–18). New York: Haworth.

Pickhardt, C. E. (1997). *Keys to successful step-fathering.* New York. Barrons.

Piercy, K. (1998). Theorizing about family caregiving. The role of responsibility. *Journal of Marriage and the Family, 60,* 109–118.

Pill, C. J. (1990). Stepfamilies: Redefining the family. *Family Relations, 39,* 186–193.

Pink, J. E., & Wampler, K. S. (1985). Problem areas in stepfamilies: Cohesion, adaptability, and the stepfather- adolescent relationship. *Family Relations, 34,* 327–335.

Pong, S.-L. (1997). Family structure, school context, and eighth grade math and reading achievement. *Journal of Marriage and the Family, 59,* 734–746.

Pong, S. L., & Ju, D-B. (2000). The effects of change in family structure and income on dropping out of middle and high school. *Journal of Family Issues, 21,* 147–169.

Popenoe, D. (1994). The evolution of marriage and the problem of stepfamilies. In A. Booth & J. Dunn (Eds.), *Stepfamilies: Who benefits? Who does not?* (pp. 3–27). Hillsdale, NJ: Erlbaum.

Prado, L. M., & Markman, H. J. (1999). Unearthing the seeds of marital distress: What we have learned from married and unmarried couples. In M. Cox & J. Brooks-Gunn (Eds.), *Conflict and cohesion families: Causes and consequences* (pp. 51–85). Mahwah, NJ: Erlbaum.

Price, S. J., & McKenry, P. C. (1988). *Divorce.* Thousand Oaks, CA: Sage.

Price-Bonham, S., & Balswick, J. O. (1980). The noninstitutions: Divorce, desertion, and remarriage. *Journal of Marriage and the Family, 42,* 959–972.

Pyke, K. D. (1994). Women's employment as a gift or burden? Marital power across marriage, divorce, and remarriage. *Gender and Society, 8,* 73–91.

Pyke, K., & Coltrane, S. (1996). Entitlement, obligation, and gratitude in family work. *Journal of Family Issues, 17,* 60–82.

Quick, D. S., McKenry, P., & Newman, B. (1994). Stepmothers and their adolescent children: Adjustment to new family roles. In K. Pasley & M. Ihinger-Tallman (Eds.), *Stepparenting: Issues in theory, research, and practice* (pp. 105–126). Westport, CT: Greenwood.

Raley, R. K. (2001). Increasing fertility in cohabiting unions. Evidence for a second demographic transition in the United States? *Demography, 38,* 59–66.

Ransom, J.W., Schlesinger, S., & Derdeyn, A. P. (1979). A stepfamily in formation. *American Journal of Orthopsychiatry, 49,* 36–43.

Reimann, R. (1997). Does biology matter? Lesbian couples' transition to parenthood and their division of labor. *Qualitative Sociology, 20,* 153–185.

Roberts, T., & Price, S. (1989). Adjustment in remarriage: Communication, cohesion, marital, and parental roles. *Journal of Divorce, 13*, 17–43.

Robinson, M. (1991). *Family transformation through divorce and remarriage: A systemic approach.* London: Tavistock/Routledge.

Rodgers, B., Power, C., & Hope, S. (1997). Parental divorce and adult psychological distress: Evidence from a national birth cohort: A research note. Journal of Child Psychology and Psychiatry, 38, 867–872.

Rodgers, R. H., & Conrad, L. (1986). Courtship for remarriage: Influences on family reorganization after divorce. *Journal of Marriage and the Family, 48*, 767–775

Rodgers, B. (1994). Pathways between parental divorce and adult depression. *Journal of Child Psychology and Psychiatry, 35*, 1289–1308.

Rogers, S. J. (1996). Marital quality, mothers' parenting and children's outcomes: A comparison of mother/father and mother/stepfather families. *Sociological Focus, 29*, 325–340.

Rogers, S. J. (1999). The nexus of job satisfaction, marital satisfaction and individual well-being: Does marriage order matter? *Research in the sociology of Work, 7*, 141–167.

Rosenberg, E. B., & Hajfal, F. (1985). Stepsibling relationships in remarried families. Social Casework: *The Journal of Contemporary Social Work, 66*, 287–292

Rossi, A. (1995). Wanted: Alternative theory and analysis modes. In V. L. Bengtson, K W Schaie, & L. M. Burton (Eds.), *Adult intergenerational relations. Effects of societal change*, (pp. 264–276). New York: Springer.

Russell, A., & Searcy, E. (1997). The contribution of affective reactions and relationship qualities to adolescents' reported responses to parents. *Journal of Social & Personal Relationships, 14*, 539–548.

Russo, N. (1976). The motherhood mandate. *Journal of Social Issues, 32*, 43–53.

Sager, C. (1981). Generous adult needed to free youngsters to find happiness in "remarried" household. *Today's Child, 30*, 4.

Sager, C. J., Brown, H. S., Crohn, H., Engel, T., Rodstein, E., & Walker, E. (1983). *Treating the remarried family.* New York: Brunner/Mazel.

Sager, C. J., Walker, E., Brown, H. S., Crohn, H., & Rodstein, E. (1981). Improving function of the remarried family system. *Journal of Marital and Family Therapy, 43*, 3–13.

Salem, D., Zimmerman, M., & Notaro, P. (1998). Effects of family structure, family process, and father involvement on psychosocial outcomes among African American adolescents. *Family Relations, 47*, 331–341.

Sanders, G. F., & Trygstad, D. W. (1989). Stepgrandparents and grandparents: The view from young adults. *Family Relations, 38*, 71–75.

Santrock, J. W., & Sitterle, K. (1987). Parent-child relationships in stepmother families. In K. Pasley & M. Ihinger-Tallman (Eds.), *Remarriage and stepparenting: Current research and theory* (pp. 273–299). New York: Guilford.

Scanzoni, J. (2004). Household diversity: The starting point for healthy families in the new century. In M. Coleman & L. Ganong (Eds.), *Handbook of contemporary families: Considering the past, contemplating the future* (pp. 3–22). Thousand Oaks, CA: Sage.

Schmiege, C., Richards, L., & Zvonkovic, A. (2001). Remarriage: For love or money? *Journal of Divorce and Remarriage, 36*, 123–140.

Schneider, D. (1980). *American kinship: A cultural account.* New York: Prentice–Hall.

Schultz, N. C., Schultz, C. L., & Olson, D. H. (1991). Couple strengths and stressors in simple and complex stepfamilies in Australia. *Journal of Marriage and the Family, 53*, 555–564.

Seltzer, J. A. (1991). Relationships between fathers and children who live apart: The father's role after separation. *Journal of Marriage and the Family, 53*, 79–101.

Seltzer, J. A. (1994). Intergenerational ties in adulthood and childhood experience. In A. Booth & J. Dunn (Eds.), *Stepfamilies: Who benefits? Who does not?* (pp. 153–163). Hillsdale, NJ: Erlbaum.

Seltzer, J. (2004). Cohabitation and family change. In M. Coleman & L. Ganong (Eds.), *Handbook of contemporary families: Considering the past, contemplating the future* (pp. 57–78) Thousand Oaks, CA: Sage.

Seltzer, J. A., & Bianchi, S M. (1988). Children's contact with absent parents. *Journal of Marriage and the Family, 50*, 663–677.

Seltzer, J. A., & Brandreth, Y. (1994). What fathers say about involvement with children after separation. *Journal of Family Issues, 15*, 49–77.

Settles, I., & Sellers, R. (2002). One role or two? The function of psychological separation in role conflict. *Journal of Applied Psychology, 87*, 574–582

Shucksmith, J., Hendry, L. B., & Glendinning, A. (1995). Models of parenting: Implications for adolescent well being within different types of family contexts. *Journal of Adolescence, 18*, 253–270.

Simmons, T., & O'Neill, G. (2001). Households and families. 2000. Census 2000 Brief C2KBR/01-8. Washington, DC. U.S. Bureau of the Census Retrieved April 6, 2003, from http://www.census.gov/prod/2001pubs/c2kbr01-8.pdf

Simpson, B. (1994). Bringing the unclear family into focus: Divorce and re-marriage in contemporary Britain. *Man (NS), 29*, 831–851.

Skopin, A R., Newman, B. M., & McKenry, P (1993) Influences on the quality of stepfather-adolescent relationships. View of both family members. *Journal of Divorce and Remarriage, 19*, 181–196.

Smith, D. E. (1993). The Standard North American Family: SNAF as an ideological code. *Journal of Family Issues, 14*, 50–65.

Smith, K. R., Zick, C. D., & Duncan, G. J. (1991). Remarriage patterns among recent widows and widowers. *Demography, 28*, 361–374.

Smith, R. M., Goslen, M. A., Byrd, A. J., & Reece, L. (1991). Self-other orientation and sex-role orientation of men and women who remarry. *Journal of Divorce and Remarriage, 15*, 3–31.

Smith, W. C. (1953). *The stepchild*. Chicago: University of Chicago Press.

Smock, P. J. (1990). Remarriage patterns of black and white women: Reassessing the role of educational attainment. *Demography, 27*, 467–473.

Smock, P. J., & Gupta, S. (2002). Cohabitation in contemporary North America. In A. Booth & A. Crouter (Eds.), *Just living together: Implications for children, families, and public policy* (pp. 53–84). Mahwah, NJ: -Erlbaum.

Smock, P., & Manning, W. D. (2000). Swapping families? Serial parenting and economic support for children. *Journal of Marriage and the Family, 62*, 111–22.

Solomon, C. R. (1995). The importance of mother-child relations in studying stepfamilies. *Journal of Divorce and Remarriage, 24*, 89–98.

South, S. S., & Lloyd, K. M. (1995). Spousal alternative and marital resolution. *American Sociological Review, 60*, 21–35.

Spanier, G. B., & Furstenberg, F. F. (1987). Remarriage and reconstituted families. In M. B. Sussman & S. Steinmetz, *Handbook of marriage and the family* (pp. 419–434). New York: Plenum.

Spanier, G., & Thompson, L. (1987). Parting: *The aftermath of separation and divorce*. Newbury Park, CA: Sage.

Spitze, G., & Logan, J. R. (1992). Helping as a component of parent-adult child relations. *Research on Aging, 14*, 291–312.

Sprey, J. (1979). Conflict theory and the study of marriage and the family. In W.R. Burr, R. Hill, F. I. Nye, & I. L. Reiss (Eds.), *Contemporary theories about the family: Volume II. General theories/theoretical orientations* (pp. 130–159). New York: Free Press.

Stacey, J., & Biblarz, T. J. (2001). (How) does the sexual orientation of parents matter? *American Sociological Review, 66*, 159–183.

Stanley, S. M., Markman, H., & Whitton, S. (2002). Communication, conflict, and commitment: Insights on the foundations of relationship success from a national survey. *Family Process, 41*, 659–675.

Stephen, E. H., Freedman, V A., & Hess. J (1993). Near and far Contact of children with their non-residential fathers. *Journal of Divorce and Remarriage, 20,* 171–191.

Stephens, L. S. (1996). Will Johnny see daddy this week? An empirical test of three theoretical perspectives of postdivorce contact. *Journal of Family Issues, 17,* 466–494.

Stern, P. N. (1982). Affiliating in stepfather families: Teachable strategies leading to stepfather-child friendship. *Western Journal of Nursing Research, 4,* 75–89.

Stewart, S. (1999). Disneyland dads, Disneyland moms? How nonresident parents spend time with absent children. *Journal of Family Issues, 20,* 539–556.

Stewart, S. D. (2002). Contemporary American stepparenthood: Integrating cohabiting and nonresident stepparents. *Population Research & Policy Review, 20,* 345–364.

Stone, G., & McKenry, P. (1998). Nonresidential father involvement: A test of a mid-range theory. *Journal of Genetic Psychology, 159,* 313–316

Sturgess, W., Dunn J., & Davies, L. (2001). Young children's perceptions of their relationships with family members: links with family setting, friendships, and adjustment. *International Journal of Behavioral Development, 25,* 521–529.

Suh, T., Schutz, C. G., & Johanson, C.E. (1996). Family structure and initiating non-medical drug use among adolescents. *Journal of Child & Adolescent Substance Abuse, 5,* 21–36

Sullivan, C M., Juras, J., Bybee, D., Nguyen, H , & Allen, N. (2000). How children's adjustment is affected by their relationships to their mothers' abusers. *Journal of Interpersonal Violence, 15,* 587–602.

Sullivan, O. (1997). The division of housework among 'remarried' couples. *Journal of Family Issues, 18,* 205–226.

Sun, Y., & Li, Y. (2001). Marital disruption, parental investment, and children's academic achievement: A prospective analysis. *Journal of Family Issues, 22,* 27–62.

Sun, Y. (2001). Family environment and adolescents' well-being before and after parents' marital disruption: A longitudinal analysis. *Journal of Marriage and Family, 63,* 697–713.

Sweeney, M. (2002). Remarriage and the nature of divorce. *Journal of Family Issues, 23,* 410–440.

Sweeney, M. (1997). Remarriage of women and men after divorce: The role of socioeconomic prospects. *Journal of Family Issues, 18,* 479–502.

Sweet, J. (1991, November). *The demography of one-parent and stepfamilies changing marriage, remarriage, and reproductive patterns.* Paper presented at the Wingspread Conference on Remarried Families, Denver, CO.

Sweeting, H. (2001). Our family, whose perspective? An investigation of children's family life and health. *Journal of Adolescence, 24,* 229–250.

Szinovacz, M. (1997). Adult children taking parents into their homes: Effects of childhood living arrangements. *Journal of Marriage and the Family, 59,* 700–717.

Szinovacz, M. E. (1998). Grandparents today: A demographic profile. *The Gerontologist, 38,* 37–52.

Szinovacz, M. (Ed.). (1998). *Handbook on grandparenthood.* Westport, CT: Greenwood.

Taanila, A., Laitinen, E., Moilanen, I., & Jarvelin, M. (2002). Effects of family interaction on the child's behavior in single-parent or reconstructed families. *Family Process, 41,* 693–708.

Talbott, M. M. (1998). Older widows' attitudes toward men and remarriage. *Journal of Aging Studies, 12,* 1–16.

Teachman, J. D., Paasch, K., & Carver, K. (1996). Social capital and dropping out of school early. *Journal of Marriage and the Family, 58,* 773–783.

The Advocate sex poll. (2002, August 20). *The Advocate,* pp. 38–43.

Thoits, P. A. (1992). Identity structures and psychological well-being: Gender and marital status comparisons. *Social Psychology Quarterly, 55,* 236–256.

Thompson, L. (1992). Feminist methodology for family studies. *Journal of Marriage and the Family, 54,* 3–18.

Thomson, E., Hanson, T. L., & McLanahan, S S. (1994). Family structure and child well-being: Economic resources vs. parental behaviors. Social Forces, 73, 221–242.

Thomson, E., McLanahan, S. S., & Curtin, R. B. (1992). Family structure, gender, and parental socialization. *Journal of Marriage and the Family, 54*, 368–378.

Thomson, E., Mosley, J., Hanson, T. L., & McLanahan, S. S. (2001). Remarriage, cohabitation, and changes in mothering behavior. *Journal of Marriage and Family, 63*, 370–380.

Thornton, A. (1991). Influence of the marital history of parents on the marital and cohabitational experiences of children. *American Journal of Sociology, 64*, 868–894

Torres, A., Evans, W. D., Pathak, S., & Vancil, C. (2001) Family structure influences cardiovascular reactivity in college students. *Journal of Divorce and Remarriage, 34*, 161–178.

Treas, J., & VanHilst, A. (1976). Marriage and remarriage rates among older Americans The Gerontologist, 16, 132–136.

Trivers, R L (1972) Parental investment and sexual selection In B Campbell (Ed) *Sexual selection and the descent of man* (pp. 136–179). Chicago Aldine Press.

Troll, L. (1983). Grandparents: The family watchdogs. In T. Brubaker (Ed), *Family relationships in later life* (pp. 63–74). Beverly Hills: Sage

Tucker, M. B., Taylor, R. J., & Mitchell-Kernan. C (1993) Marriage and romantic involvement among aged African Americans. Journal of Gerontology Social Sciences, 48, S123–132

Tzeng, J. M., & Mare, R. D. (1995). Labor market and socioeconomic effects on marital stability, *SSR, 24*, 329–351.

U. S. Bureau of the Census. (2000). *Statistical abstract of the United States: 2000* Washington, DC: U.S. Government Printing Office.

U. S. Bureau of the Census. (1995). *Statistical abstract of the United States: 1995*. Washington, DC: U.S. Government Printing Office.

U. S. Bureau of the Census. (1999). *Statistical abstract of the United States: 1999*. Washington, DC: U.S. Government Printing Office.

Uhlenberg, P., & Hammill, B. G. (1998). Frequency of grandparent contact with grandchild sets: Six factors that make a difference. *The Gerontologist, 38*, 276–285.

Uhlenberg, P., & Kirby, J. B. (1998). Grandparenthood over time: Historical and demographic trends. In M. Szinovacz (Ed.), *Handbook on grandparenthood* (pp. 23–39). Westport, CT: Greenwood.

Upchurch, D. M. (1993). Early schooling and childbearing experiences: Implications for postsecondary school attendance. *Journal of Research on Adolescence, 3*, 423–443.

Upchurch, D. M., Aneshensel, C. S., Sucoff, C. A., & Levy-Storms, L. (1999). Neighborhood and family contexts of adolescent sexual activity. *Journal of Marriage and the Family, 61*, 920–933.

Vaughn, D. (1986). *Uncoupling.* New York: Oxford University Press.

Vemer, E., Coleman, M., Ganong, L., & Cooper, H. (1989). Marital satisfaction in remarriage: A meta-analysis. *Journal of Marriage and the Family, 51*, 713–725.

Veum, J. R. (1993). The relationship between child support and visitation: Evidence from longitudinal data. *Social Science Research, 22*, 229–244.

Vinick, B. H. (1978). Remarriage in old age. *The Family Coordinator, 27*, 359–363.

Vinick, B. H. (1998, November). *Is blood thicker than water? Remarried mothers' relationships with grown children from previous marriages.* Paper presented at the Gerontological Society of America Annual Meeting, Philadelphia, PA.

Visher, E. B., & Visher, J. S. (1978). Common problems of stepparents and their spouses. American *Journal of Orthopsychiatry, 48*, 252–262.

Visher, E. B., & Visher, J. S. (1979). *Stepfamilies: A guide to working with stepparents and stepchildren.* New York: Brunner/Mazel.

Visher, E. B., & Visher, J. S. (1980). *Stepfamilies: Myths and realities.* Secus, NC: Citadel Press.

Visher, E. B., & Visher, J. S. (1982). Stepfamilies in the 1980s. *Conciliation Courts Review, 20*, 15–23.

Visher, E B , & Visher, J. S. (1985). Stepfamilies are different. *Journal of Family Therapy, 7,* 9–18.

Visher, E. B., & Visher, J. S., (1988). *Old loyalties, new ties: Therapeutic strategies with stepfamilies.* New York: Brunner/Mazel.

Visher, E. B., & Visher, J. S. (1990). Dynamics of successful stepfamilies. *Journal of Divorce and Remarriage, 14,* 3–12.

Visher, E. B., & Visher, J. S. (1991). *How to win as a step-family (2nd ed.).* Florence, KY: Taylor & Francis

Visher, E. B., & Visher, J. S. (1996). *Therapy with stepfamilies.* New York: Brunner/Mazel.

Visher, E B., Visher, J. S., & Pasley, K. (1997). Stepfamily therapy from the client's perspective *Marriage & Family Review, 26,* 191–213.

Visher, J S , & Visher, E. B (1991). Therapy with stepfamily couples. *Psychiatric Annals, 21,* 462–465

Voydanoff, P (1990) Economic distress and family relations· A review of the Eighties. *Journal of Marriage and the Family, 52,* 1099–1115

Vuchinich, S., Hetherington, E. M., Vuchinich, R. A., & Clingempeel, W. G (1991). Parent-child interaction and gender differences in early adolescents' adaptation to stepfamilies *Developmental Psychology, 27,* 618–626.

Wald, E. (1981). *The remarried family: Challenge and promise.* New York. Family Service Association of America.

Waller, W. (1930). *The old love and the new: Divorce and readjustment.* Philadelphia: Liverright.

Walsh, W. M. (1992). Twenty major issues in remarriage families. *Journal of Counseling and Development, 70,* 709–715.

Walzer, S. (2004). Encountering oppositions: A review of motherhood. In M. Coleman & L. Ganong (Eds.), *Handbook of contemporary families: Considering the past, contemplating the future* (pp. 209–223) Thousand Oaks, CA: Sage.

Weaver, S. E., & Coleman, M. A. (in review). *Caught in the middle. Mothers in stepfamilies.*

Webber, R. (1991). Life in stepfamilies: Conceptions and misconceptions. In K. Funder (Ed.), *Images of Australian families* (pp. 88–101). Melbourne: Longman Cheshire.

Weston, C. A., & Macklin, E. D. (1990). The relationship between former-spousal contact and remarital satisfaction in stepfather families. *Journal of Divorce & Remarriage, 14,* 25–47.

Whitbeck, L., Hoyt, D., & Huck, S. (1993). Family relationship history, contemporary parent-grandparent relationship quality, and the grandparent-grandchild relationship. *Journal of Marriage and the Family, 55,* 1025–1035.

White, L. K. (1992). The effect of parental divorce and remarriage on parental support for adult children. *Journal of Family Issues, 13,* 234–250.

White, L. (1994a). Stepfamilies over the life course: Social support. In A. Booth and J. Dunn (Eds.), *Stepfamilies: Who benefits? Who does not* (pp. 109–138). Hillsdale, NJ: Erlbaum.

White, L. (1994b) Growing up with single parents and stepparents: Long-term effects on family solidarity. *Journal of Marriage and the Family, 56,* 935–948.

White, L. (1998). Who's counting? Quasi-facts and stepfamilies in reports of number of siblings. *Journal of Marriage & the Family, 60,* 725–733.

White, L. K., & Booth, A. (1985). The quality and stability of remarriages: The role of stepchildren. *American Sociological Review, 50,* 689–698.

White, L. K., & Booth, A. (1991). Divorce over the life course. *Journal of Family Issues, 12,* 5–21.

White, L. K., & Gilbreath, J. G. (2001). When children have two fathers: Effects of relationships with stepfathers and noncustodial fathers on adolescent outcomes. *Journal of Marriage and the Family, 63,* 155–167.

White, L. K., & Reidmann, A. (1992). When the Brady Bunch grows up: Step/half-and fullsibling relationships in adulthood. *Journal of Marriage and the Family, 54,* 197–208.

Whiteside, M. F. (1982). Remarriage: A family developmental process. *Journal of Marital and Family Therapy, 4,* 59–68.

Whiteside, M F (1998) The parental alliance following divorce: An overview. *Journal of Marital and Family Therapy, 24,* 3024.

Whitsett, D., & Land, H. (1992). The development of a role strain index for stepparents. Families in Society: *The Journal of Contemporary Human Services, 73,* 14–22.

Williams, J. (2000). Unbending gender. New York: Oxford University Press.

Wilmoth, J., & Koso, G (2002) Does marital history matter? Marital status and wealth outcomes among preretirement adults *Journal of Marriage and the Family, 64,* 254–268.

Wilson, B. F., & Clarke, S. C. (1992). Remarriages: A demographic profile. *Journal of Family Issues, 13,* 123–141.

Wineberg, H. (1990). Childbearing after remarriage. *Journal of Marriage and the Family, 52,* 31–38

Wineberg, H. (1992) Childbearing and dissolution of the second marriage. *Journal of Marriage and the Family, 54,* 879–887

Wineberg, H., & McCarthy, J. (1998). Living arrangements after divorce. cohabitation versus remarriage. *Journal of Divorce and Remarriage, 29,* 131–146.

Winton, C. A., (1995). *Frameworks for studying families* Guilford, CT Dushkin

Wojtkiewicz, R. A. (1994). Parental structure experiences of children Exposure, transitions, and type at birth. *Population Research & Policy Review, 13,* 141–159.

Wood, J. T. (1994). *Who cares? Women, care, and culture* Carbondale, IL: Southern Illinois University Press.

Wu, Z. (1994). Remarriage in Canada: A social exchange perspective. *Journal of Divorce and Remarriage, 21,* 191–224.

Wu, Z., & Penning, M. J. (1997). Marital instability after midlife *Journal of Family Issues, 18,* 459–478.

Wu, Z., & Thomson, E. (2001). Race differences in family experience and early sexual initiation: Dynamic models of family structure and family change. *Journal of Marriage and Family, 63,* 682–696.

Yeung, W. J., Linver, M. R., & Brooks-Gunn, J. (2002). How money matters for young children's development: Investment and family process. *Child Development, 73,* 1861–1879.

Zick, C. D., & Smith, K. R. (1988). Recent widowhood, remarriage, and changes in economic well-being. *Journal of Marriage & the Family, 50,* 233–244.

Zill, N., Morrison, D. R., & Cioro, M. J. (1993). Long-term effects of parental divorce on parent-child relationships, adjustment, and achievement in young adulthood. *Journal of Family Psychology, 7,* 91–103.

Zill, N. (1988). Behavior, achievement, and health problems among children in stepfamilies: Findings from a national survey of child health. In E. M. Hetherington & J. D. Arasteh (Eds.), *Impact of divorce, single parenting, and stepparenting on children* (pp. 325–368). Hillsdale, NJ: Erlbaum.

Index

Printed in the United States
22979LVS00001B/202-204